YALE JUDAICA SERIES

Volume XXIX
Rabbinic Fantasies

222- xfer Hsidi d-phti nwtrb

translations by NORMAN BRONZNICK
            YAAKOV ELMAN
            MICHAL GOVRIN
            ARTHUR GREEN
            MARTHA HIMMELFARB
            IVAN MARCUS
            MARK JAY MIRSKY
            JOEL ROSENBERG
            DAVID RUDERMAN
            RAYMOND P. SCHEINDLIN
            DAVID STERN
            AVI WEINSTEIN

RABBINIC
FANTASIES

IMAGINATIVE NARRATIVES
FROM CLASSICAL
HEBREW LITERATURE

edited by **DAVID STERN**
and **MARK JAY MIRSKY**

YALE UNIVERSITY PRESS
New Haven & London

Published 1990 by the Jewish Publication Society. Reprinted 1998
by Yale University Press.

Illustrations on pages i, 44, 63, 129, 158, 225, and 323 © Mimi Gross
Illustrations on pages 76, 96, 209, and 247 © Inger Johanne Grytting
Illustration on pages 300, 302, 305, 308, and 309 are courtesy of the
Library of the Jewish Theological Seminary of America.

Printed in the United States of America.

Library of Congress Cataloging in Publication
Number 97-61438
ISBN 0-300-07402-6 (pbk.)

A catalogue record for this book is available from the British Library.

The paper in this book meets the guidelines for permanence and
durability of the Committee on Production Guidelines for Book
Longevity of the Council on Library Resources.

10   9   8   7   6   5   4   3   2   1

The editors remember with gratitude the
encouragement they received from the late
novelist and theologian—and friend
  ARTHUR A. COHEN
when the idea for this anthology was first
broached.

CONTENTS

Acknowledgments   ix

INTRODUCTION   3
DAVID STERN

A NOTE ON THE SELECTIONS
AND THE TRANSLATIONS   31

1.   RABBINIC PARABLES   35

2.   TWO NARRATIVES ABOUT GOD   47

3.   JONAH AND THE SAILORS
     from *Pirkei de-Rabbi Eliezer*   59

4.   SEFER ZERUBBABEL   67

5.   MIDRASH ON THE TEN COMMANDMENTS   91

6.   THE TALE OF THE JERUSALEMITE   121

7.   MIDRASH ELEH EZKERAH
     or *The Legend of the Ten Martyrs*   143

8.   THE ALPHABET OF BEN SIRA   167

9.   PARABLES FROM SEFER HA-BAHIR   203

10. NARRATIVE FANTASIES FROM SEFER HASIDIM 215

11. LOVE IN THE AFTERLIFE
A Selection from the *Zohar* 239

X **12.** ASHER IN THE HAREM
by Solomon Ibn Saqbel 253

X **13.** THE MISOGYNIST
by Judah Ibn Shabbetai 269

14. THE SORCERER
from *Meshal Ha-Kadmoni*
by Isaac Ibn Sahula 295

15. JOB'S NOVELLA
from *A Valley of Vision*
by Abraham ben Hananiah Yagel 313

16. THE "DREAM-TALKS" OF NAHMAN OF BRATSLAV 333

IN A TURN OF THE SCROLL:
AN AFTERWORD 349
MARK JAY MIRSKY

ACKNOWLEDGMENTS

This anthology has generated many debts of gratitude along the road to its completion. Eight of the translations in the present collection, along with earlier versions of the Introduction and Afterword, first appeared in *Fiction,* Vol. 7, Nos. 1 and 2, as a special section entitled "Rabbinic Fantasy," edited by David Stern and Mark Mirsky, and in *Fiction,* Vol. 7, No. 3. The editors wish to express their gratitude to *Fiction* for permission to reprint those translations, although several have been revised since their original appearance.

The editors also wish to thank several colleagues and friends who read and criticized translations at different stages: Lynne Rentoul Klein, Christina Brazelton, Daniel Matt, Alan Mintz, Raymond Scheindlin, and Eliezer Slomovic. David Rosenberg was decisive in encouraging us to expand the original anthology into the present volume. Sheila Segal offered invaluable editorial advice and support throughout, and Ilene Cohen provided expert copy editing. Finally, our wives Inger Grytting and Kathryn Hellerstein gave unstintingly of their considerable literary, artistic, and critical gifts.

RABBINIC
FANTASIES

INTRODUCTION

This anthology presents sixteen translations of imaginative narrative from classical Hebrew literature. Spanning a chronological period of nearly seventeen hundred years, from the second century in the Common Era to the nineteenth, the selections in this book reflect the numerous types of narrative found in Hebrew literature from early rabbinic times until the very dawn of the modern age. As the Israeli scholar Joseph Dan has aptly remarked, "There is no generation in Hebrew literature without its original narratives."[1]

Yet despite its constant presence in Jewish culture, narrative—fiction in particular—does not possess an acknowledged existence of its own in classical Hebrew literature. There is nothing in the history of that literature comparable to the discerned narrative tradition in Western or European literature, where it is possible to speak of a continuum passing more or less directly from epic to romance to novel. Classical Jewish narrative, to the extent that it can be said to own a tradition with a history, consists not of one but of several disparate genres having little to do with each other: the retold biblical story, the apocalypse, the exemplum, the rhymed-prose romance. Most fictional narratives in rabbinic and medieval Hebrew literature appeared in their earliest contexts within the framework of other literary forms: the legal code, the commentary, or the sermon. As in the Bible, postbiblical Jewish literature tends anyhow to the encyclopedic, to mingling diverse orders of discourse like law and narrative, and to odd combinations that may seem to us to be generically impure.

It is worth recalling that before the twelfth century the Hebrew language had no word for the imagination.[2] Although the absence of a name surely does not prove that the imagination did not then exist, this fact does suggest just how much the attitudes informing the writing of narrative in those centuries may have differed from our own. For one thing, the authors of most of the narratives in this anthology probably would not have considered their works as being primarily imaginative or fictional. While this anthology excludes narratives that explicitly claim to be true histories, the vast majority of selections do pretend to some kind of historicity, to having actually taken place (a claim that is, of course, unrelated to the separate "historical" question as to whether they really did). No narrative in this book is fictional in the modern sense of being purely subjective.

It would be no less misleading to use contemporary criteria to specify the religious character of the imaginative narratives in this volume. While none of these texts was originally composed to serve as sacred literature or claimed for itself divine inspiration or authorship (although a select few were eventually accorded quasi-canonical status), no narrative in this anthology would ever have been considered by its author to be a secular composition in the sense of being entirely divorced from Jewish concerns. In this regard, the contemporary reader should remember that the line separating the religious from the secular, or the sacred from the profane, is blurred in classical and medieval Judaism. Matters that we would categorize as wholly unreligious—the travails of love or the pleasures of good company—would have been treated by Jews in past centuries as a form of relaxation or entertainment rather than as a separate quarter of existence. Conversely, many of the works in this book were composed expressly to serve a didactic purpose, even though such an explicitly moralistic function would be considered today to be inimical to the free, perhaps transgressive, play of the imagination.

As imaginative fictions, then, the narratives in this anthology do not fall easily into modern categories. Historically, though, the writing of narrative suffered a fate in classical Judaism that was no less problematic. When treated as an activity in its own right, imaginative fiction was most likely to be looked upon with ambivalence if not contempt, and not infrequently by the very authors of works that we would consider to be among the greatest products of the imagination. In a well-known passage from the *Zohar*, Rabbi Simeon ben Yohai, the early talmudic sage and the book's central figure, is quoted (probably fictitiously) as lamenting:

> Woe to that man who asserts that the Torah came to show us mere stories and profane matters. For if this were so, we too could compose a Torah today, one that would deal with profane matters, a Torah worthy of even greater praise![3]

By "mere stories and profane matters," Rabbi Simeon means the narratives in the Bible, the stories of the patriarchs and their descendants, the children of Israel. While the point of his comment, in context, is to posit the supreme importance of an allegorical level of meaning in the Torah, one that contains the secrets of mystical truth, the sheer disparagement of narrative writing is more revealing for our present concerns. In Rabbi Simeon's view, those "mere" narratives and stories in the Torah are profane matters that anybody could write. Even "we" today could write such stories, and perhaps even better ones.

To the contemporary reader, Rabbi Simeon's disdain for fictional narrative, his easy dismissal of its value, may seem bewildering, even discomforting. Yet in the history of Jewish literature before the nineteenth century, a negative attitude toward imaginative writing has been the rule more often than the exception. Although narrative as a literary form pervades Jewish literature, it has generally not been recognized as such, and when it has, its status has typically suffered diminishment. Even though narrative compositions like those included in this book almost always enjoyed a wide popularity among the masses of readers, as the large number of surviving manuscripts and editions attest, these works were officially neglected in favor of the more serious legal and philosophical writings that dominated the higher canon of Jewish literature.

Yet even in the Enlightenment, with the rise of a secular Hebrew literature, the imaginative narrative of the early centuries did not enjoy any happier a fate, in part the result of a newly negative attitude toward all the traditional literature of classical Judaism. The neglect that followed was only reinforced by the fact that the narratives in classical Hebrew literature did not conform to what were by then the conventional norms of fiction. Dismissed as pious curiosities, they were consigned to a new oblivion. At best, a few individual works were rediscovered as folk literature, as the products of what was presumed to be a kind of unlettered, native creativity that had somehow escaped the lethal dryness of rabbinic scholasticism. As imaginative narrative, or as fiction, much of this literature remains to this day almost completely unrecognized, unknown even to some scholars of Jewish literature. Indeed, many people believe that narratives of the sort included in this anthology simply do not exist—indeed never could have—because classical Judaism was, it is asserted, fundamentally inimicable to the narrative imagination. However widespread these beliefs may be, it is a revealing fact that this anthology is the first of its kind ever to be published; even in Hebrew, no comparable book exists.

For various reasons, it is easier for us today to recognize these narratives as imaginative fiction. At the least, we can appreciate that side of them that is fictional without distorting their other aspects or turning them into something they are not. In collecting these works here, under the rubric of "rabbinic fantasy" in classical Jewish literature, our intention has not been to separate them from the rest of classical Jewish literature—within which their status remains problematic indeed. Each one of these texts is exceptional; and viewed as a collective body, they do not constitute a coherent historical tradition of the sort that exists in the realm of poetry, liturgical and secular, in medieval Hebrew literature. Rather, these narratives demonstrate a recurring exceptionality, a spectrum of possibilities and of creative options that the narrative imagination has historically played out within Jewish culture. Although they themselves may not possess their own continuous history, these narratives separately and together hold a significant place in the history of Jewish literature.

THE BIBLE AND MIDRASH

The logical starting point for any discussion of narrative in classical Jewish literature must be the Bible. Yet the most salient feature of postbiblical Hebrew narrative is the fact that it hardly resembles its most famous precursor. The early rabbis, though they doubtless believed themselves to be the sole authentic heirs of the biblical tradition, never attempted to write narrative in the style of the Bible. While others in the ancient world did continue to compose Biblelike books, as can be witnessed in late works preserved in the apocrypha, the pseudepigrapha, and the New Testament Gospels, these efforts only underline the rabbis' decision not to follow in that path.

Precisely what motivated that refusal is not clear. Partly it was their recognition that the period of prophetic inspiration had ended, that the appropriate time for composing narrative in the biblical fashion had passed. Partly it may have been an acknowledgment by the rabbis of their own belatedness, of their feeling that nothing they could write would equal the majesty of biblical narration. Whatever their reason, though, the rabbis' refusal was accompanied by a new conception of the Bible. No longer merely a sacred historical narrative or a divine law code, Scripture now became the blueprint for all existence, the key to all meaning as well as its repository. "Turn it and research it, for everything is in it," remarked the sage Ben Bag Bag about Torah. Yet here also lay the nub of the creative dilemma the rabbis faced in writing their own narratives: If the Torah relates everything that has happened to the Jews in the past; if it intimates everything that will transpire in the future; and if every historical occurrence simply repeats an event already narrated to full effect in Scripture—then what purpose might be served by expending further effort upon narration?

Rather than attempt to write "more" Bible, the Rabbis channeled their imaginative energies into the type of commentary known as midrash— literally "study" but more accurately "interpretation." Contradictions in the scriptural text, discontinuities, lacunae, silences, inexplicable motives, lexical peculiarities, awkward or unusual syntactic constructions— any one of these "irritants" became for the rabbis either an occasion for recounting a narrative of their own invention or a peg upon which to hang an extrabiblical legend or tradition. The biblical narrative thus became for the rabbis a giant screen upon which they projected the story of their own existence. Responding to the most subtle, latent possibilities of meaning in Scripture, these exegetes allowed their narrative imaginations to blossom in the cracks of the biblical text, sometimes literally inside the empty spaces separating words or atop the wavy scribal crowns adorning letters.

The origins of midrash probably go back to the redaction of the Bible in its earliest written form. Scholars have recently pointed to the biblical redactor's tendency to include multiple versions of the same story, such as the two accounts in Genesis of the creation of mankind. Rather than clumsy editing, this tendency may have been the redactor's way of provoking interpretation among his readers, perhaps a method for commenting upon irreconcilable traditions he had received and felt it important to preserve. Yet this exegetical dimension of biblical narrative is utterly different from the combination of narrative and exegesis found in Rabbinic midrash. The Bible presents a more or less unified, consecutive narrative. Midrash rarely does; rather, the unity of its discourse lies in the logic of exegesis, in the connection between the prooftext—the specific scriptural verse or phrase that is under interpretive scrutiny—and its commentary. Even where a midrashic opinion retells a legend or invents a narrative to solve an exegetical problem, it usually presents solely that part of the tale relevant to the interpretation at hand.

As a result, there is nothing in midrash comparable to the biblical narrative history of Israel, a continuous tale that runs from the creation of the universe to the Babylonian exile (which is more or less the sum of the biblical narrative that begins in Genesis and ends in 2 Chronicles). While it is possible to reconstruct a narrative of this sort from the shards and pieces of story interspersed throughout rabbinic literature, as Louis Ginzberg did in his monumental *Legends of the Jews*,[4] such a synoptic reconstruction should not be mistaken for a continuum of midrashic narration. With its condensed allusiveness and fragmentation, the virtual trademarks of its literary character, the midrashic mode of narration is simultaneously a mode of self-expression and interpretation. The genius of midrash is that it exists in a kind of gray area between these separate realms of imaginative literature on the one side, exegetical commentary on the other. Without ever fully crossing over to either side, midrash developed in precisely that hitherto undefined space, drawing upon the resources of both realms, creating narratives in the service of interpretation, and offering imaginative exegeses as if they were laws.

This quality of midrash as a presence at the borders of literature is perhaps what makes its sensibility appear so close to our own. Like Kafka and Borges, our modern exegetes of the imagination, the rabbis seem to have understood that narrative can wear the mask of commentary and that interpretation can be playful as fiction. But the lines of resemblance between ancients and moderns should not be overdrawn. The interplay of exegesis and narrative in contemporary fiction is the play of the imagination reflecting self-consciously upon its own activities. In midrash, the two orders of discourse are joined by their common enlistment in the pursuit of a single divine truth: the meaning of Scripture.

Even so, its "mixed" discourse, the shuttling back and forth in the text between exegesis and story, is the great literary legacy bequeathed by midrash to subsequent Hebrew narrative. Its influence can be seen especially in "late" midrashim such as *Pirkei de-Rabbi Eliezer*. This early medieval composition retells the biblical narrative by weaving the distinct strands of exegetical tradition into more extended tales.

Consider, for example, the retelling of the story of Jonah. The biblical text recounts an errant prophet's futile attempt to escape God and his mission; in the version of *Pirkei de-Rabbi Eliezer* this story is turned into a romance of salvation. While the great unexplained mystery of the original account is the question of why Jonah flees, refusing to deliver God's prophecy of doom to the Ninevites, in *Pirkei de-Rabbi Eliezer* that question is no longer even an issue. Indeed, the midrashic version begins by announcing to the reader Jonah's rationale. He feared that if the Ninevites repented and God then revoked His decree, the gentiles would call him a false prophet. Jonah therefore flees, taking to the sea because he believes that is the only place he might escape God. But Jonah's flight in *Pirkei de-Rabbi Eliezer* is a comedy of mishaps. Embarking on the ship, this Jonah is positively eager to be drowned, but the sailors, righteous gentiles, initially try to spare him from death. When Jonah finally persuades the ship's crew to throw him overboard, the legendary whale swallows him, as in the Bible, but here only to tell Jonah that he has inopportunely been ingested on the very day that the whale is to be eaten by Leviathan, the legendary ruler of the oceans. At this point, the prophet is persuaded to save his host, the whale; in a moment of inspired exhibitionism Jonah shows Leviathan his circumcised member—a display apparently so impressive that the king of fish flees in panic.

Jonah thereupon has the whale take him on a tour of the ocean's depths. Although this tour is nowhere mentioned in the biblical book, the author of the midrash recounts it as though it were, through an exegesis of Jonah's famous prayer to God in chapter 2, each verse of which is now interpreted as referring to a different site in the ocean's depths. At the last of these sites, the base of the Temple Mount, Jonah prays for deliverance, and his prayers are finally answered. But *Pirkei de-Rabbi Eliezer's* version of the prophet's tale does not end with Jonah. From the moment they cast him overboard and throughout Jonah's adventures in the ocean, the gentile sailors, it now appears, have stood as witnesses aboard the ship's deck. When God commands the whale to spit the prophet up, they are so impressed by everything they have seen that they immediately forsake their idolatry. Going up to Jerusalem, the sailors have themselves circumcised and, with their entire households, convert to Judaism in order to worship "the Lord of Jonah." In the hands of the anonymous author of the midrash the biblical character is thus transformed from a rebellious prophet into a servant of Providence who works God's will even when he is unwilling.

THE MASHAL

Retelling the biblical narrative was not the only way the rabbis created fiction. They also legendized history and their own lives, and they even turned law into narrative by injecting story into the discourse of rabbinic law, or halakhah. Many tractates in the Mishnah, the great early law code of classical Judaism, are organized along implicit narrative lines, their legal decisions formulated through specific cases—"If an ox falls into a pit," and so on—rather than conceptually or as abstract rules. Still another kind of narrative impulse informs the Babylonian Talmud, the massive compendium of rabbinic Judaism. It can be seen as an attempt to re-create in writing the world of the sages: the talmudic academy with its cacophonous voices, heated arguments, and lively exchanges, the spirited table talk and intellectual chatter of the rabbis. The whole of talmudic discourse is virtually an imaginative narrative of halakhah, of the development of law.

In all this literature, however, only a single form, the *mashal*, the parable or fable, is consciously acknowledged to be an invention of the imagination. An allusive tale told for an ulterior purpose, the *mashal* typically relates a fictional narrative that parallels a concrete real-life situation confronting the parable's author and his audience—or, as happens most frequently in midrash, a biblical occasion with contemporary relevance. Yet rather than fully explicate the parallels between the fiction and its real-life application or exegetical occasion, the *mashal* tends to imply the parallels, leaving it to the reader to work out the full meaning of the narrative's message. Much of the *mashal*'s rhetorical power stems directly from its planned silence and intentional suggestiveness, the gaps in its narrative that the reader must fill, thereby actively participating in the construction of the *mashal*'s fictional world.

About that fictionality, though, the rabbis were characteristically ambivalent. "Do not treat the parable as a trivial thing," they said (suggesting that there were people who did), "for it is through the parable that one can come to understand the deepest secrets of the Torah" (Song of Songs Rabbah 1:8). According to this statement, the value of the parable lies not in its imaginative power but in its use as a tool for understanding Scripture, as a medium of exegesis. This valuation is reflected in the *mashal*'s conventional form, in which the narrative is nearly always accompanied by an explanation, the *nimshal,* which in turn is tied to a prooftext for which the parable as a whole provides a novel interpretation.

Still, the significance of the parable clearly extends beyond its exegetical application. The parables in midrash are the great examples of the rabbis' anthropomorphic imaginings, of their efforts to portray God in the human image. The most common image that these portraits take in the *mashal* is that of a king, a common metaphor for divinity in ancient Near Eastern culture that was carried over to the Bible as well. The king in the rabbinic parable is not, however, a mere metaphor or a stock character. In the first place, as scholars have long recognized, the figure of the king is modeled specifically upon the Roman emperor (or the emperor's political representatives in Palestine), while the *mashal*'s other characters—the *matrona,* or royal consort, the princes and princesses, the various generals and counselors who serve the king—are also drawn from types who populated the imperial court. But the king's personality, more than being simply historically plausible, is also recognizably, distinctively, human: at times despotic or insecure or vain, at other times unpredictably generous, benevolent, and wise. Yet even when the king's behavior is most negatively exaggerated, even cruel—after all, this was the world of Nero, Caligula, and Heliogabalus—the character never passes beyond credibility as a human actor. If the *mashal* demonstrates the rabbis' imaginative boldness, it shows their restraint as well; in exploiting the human analogy, they accepted its limits.

The self-acknowledged fictionality of the *mashal* serves partly to qualify and delimit the radical anthropomorphism of its narrative; the *nimshal*, simply by its presence in the literary structure, almost reminds the audience that the fiction is solely a likeness, only an analogy. Yet the paradoxical key to the *mashal*, the implicit message of its poetic structure, is its affirmation of the inevitability of the recourse to the human analogy in order to express the complexity of one's feelings about God and His treatment of Israel. Bowing to this recognition, the rabbis resorted to the person of the Roman emperor as the human model most readily available to them, and in doing so, they did not hesitate to use the realia of the world around them as material for their fictions. Some *meshalim* are based upon famous imperial anecdotes that circulated through the ancient world; others derive from the rabbis' own familiarity with the court.

Despite all its borrowings from historical reality, though, the rabbinic *mashal* remains a parabolic rather than a naturalistic narrative. To borrow Eric Auerbach's celebrated description of biblical style, the *mashal*, in its conciseness and sparseness, is "densely fraught with meaning" rather than with realistic details. Yet for all its symbolism, the rabbinic *mashal* is not a secret code to be understood solely by initiates. Only in the later Middle Ages, in medieval Jewish philosophy and mysticism, does the classical parable change into an esoteric allegory, a virtually opaque narrative used to transmit secret doctrines that are all but incomprehensible to anyone who has not already been indoctrinated into the philosophical or mystical mysteries—an ironic fact since it makes the parable essentially superfluous from the outset, a kind of self-destroying artifact.

This change in the *mashal*'s literary function quickly produced its own dialectical form. If the midrashic *mashal* oscillates between the demands of exegesis and the requirements of narrative, the mystical parable shimmers enigmatically with its paradoxical attempts to unite the irreconcilable, to join an expressible outer self with an ineffable meaning within. Such paradoxes can be observed most closely in the early mystical parables recorded in *Sefer ha-Bahir*. One parable, for example, describes a king who carries his throne upon his forehead because it is so beautiful he cannot bear to use it merely as a seat. The throne symbolizes the Shekhinah, which is simultaneously above and below. This inherently inexpressible image is endowed in this mystical narrative with an impressive measure of pathos, which makes its idea sensible, that is, emotionally recognizable if not exactly intellectually graspable.

Not until the thirteenth century, however, with the appearance of the *Zohar*, the masterwork of Spanish Kabbalah, does the allegorical use of narrative reach its full maturity. Composed in an archaic, often neologistic, Jewish Aramaic that partially imitates (and perhaps parodies) the language of the Talmud, the *Zohar* offers what is, in effect, a kabbalistic re-creation of midrash. The academy of the rabbinic sages now becomes an entirely mystical universe, Torah study itself a figure for redemption. Almost Joycean in its imaginative and linguistic ingenuity, the *Zohar* describes a kind of spiritual anagoge—a mystical ascent—in which the blessed sages rise to the heavenly heights to witness the universal redemption fulfilled through the coupling of souls in heaven. The very structure of narrative here is built on the disclosure and concealment of ultimate meaning. To use an image drawn from one of the *Zohar*'s own parables, the quest for mystical enlightenment resembles a pursuit through the endless, winding corridors of the divine palace to glimpse for a second the face of the princess in hiding.

APOCALYPTIC NARRATIVE

Between the midrashic *mashal* and the allegorical parable of the *Zohar*, one traverses nearly the complete arc of medieval Jewish narrative. As we have seen, much of that narrative hints at the longing for redemption that is at the heart of so much Jewish fantasy. Yet even in mystical narrative there is a strange reticence about speaking too directly on this subject. The endless plotting of the end of days and of its thunderous arrival the Rabbis and their successors seem to have preferred to leave to others—

among those others, the sectarian authors of the extensive literature that goes under the name of *apocalyptic*.

A conflated genre, apocalypse is devoted to revealing the secrets of the end of the world. From one perspective, it can be considered a bastardization of classical prophecy, substituting for the latter's social vision and ethical ideals the dubious magic of divination and the prediction of the cataclysmic future at the close of history, when the wicked will be brought to judgment and the righteous—not accidentally, the intended audience of the apocalyptic message—will be saved and rewarded. From another perspective, though, apocalypse is a temperament as much as a literary genre. It grows out of extreme historical despair, a feeling of radical victimization and absolutely helpless neglectedness. With its desperate hopes for a final chance at restoring wholeness and justice to a world gone rotten, apocalypse is literally a state of mind that recurs in history like a bad depression. Apocalypse after apocalypse repeats in numbing tedium the same blighted visions and overripe imagery, much of it crowded with allegorical beasts of dubious pedigree and fourfold kingdoms turning ponderously on the wheel of history.

The Book of Daniel, an early apocalypse and the only example of the genre to be included in the biblical canon, exerted a mighty influence upon subsequent apocalyptic works. Subsequent rabbinic tradition, however, shied away from its powerful longings, perhaps to spare itself the disappointment of witnessing the failure of the apocalypse to arrive. Still, the fascination and force of apocalyptic maintained its hold upon Jewish imagination and eventually joined with popular lore and messianic speculations to create a new apocalyptic literature in medieval Judaism. Of the several works in this emerging tradition, *Sefer Zerubbabel*, the *Book of Zerubbabel* (or the corpus of related texts under that name), is the most significant.

Unlike other apocalypses, *Sefer Zerubbabel* is about more than the chronology of the end time—the series of universal wars that will culminate history with the arrival of the Messiah, the final judgment, and so on. Although it records the usual eschatological timetable, its narrative is actually an account of the circumstances in which the apocalyptic secrets are revealed to its protagonist; it is the story of Zerubbabel's own despair in seeking out revelation from the angels. Indeed, that portrait of despair, with its hinting at character, at the personality of the apocalyptist, is what elevates the work above mere apocalyptic fantasizing.

Sefer Zerubbabel is too scattered a text to work successfully on the level of pure story, but it is remarkable for its energy and its obsessions, which are amazingly this-worldly. For example, instead of journeying to heaven or to hell, as would be expected in a typical apocalypse, the hero Zerubbabel is taken to a symbolic representation of a church (a place that may have seemed more infernal to the book's author), where his horror is focused upon a statue of a female that, as most scholars agree, represents the Virgin Mary. Yet, while the abominable statue has a Jewish counterpart in the character of Hephzibah, the Messiah's mother, who appears in this text for the first and last time in apocalyptic tradition, what remains most memorable about *Sefer Zerubbabel* is its disgust for Christianity. As much as apocalyptic despair, that disgust energizes the narrative, seeming to rush forth from the felt experience of the daily existence in which its author(s) composed the book.

Sefer Zerubbabel, which was probably composed in the seventh century, is a revealing example of the unlikely but powerful influence that a single narrative could exert in medieval Judaism; through it, a mighty stream of messianic imagining flowed back into the discourse of Judaism. It is also one of the last significant original literary works to be composed in the Land of Israel during the classical period of rabbinic creativity.

EARLY MEDIEVAL NARRATIVES

By the eighth century the classical texts of rabbinic literature were either completed or in the final stages of compilation, and the center of Jewish creativity had shifted from Palestine to Babylonia. The subsequent three hundred years in Babylonia and North Africa, roughly from the eighth through the tenth centuries, represent a watershed in medieval Judaism. Known after its scholar-sages, the Babylonian geonim, this period is one of the great ages of transition in Judaism.

While the fresh composition of midrash waned and gradually gave way to new forms of biblical exegesis, other literary and intellectual pursuits— the first codifications of the law, commentaries upon the Talmud, the earliest attempts at systematic philosophy and philology—occupied the intellectual energies of the geonim. During this same period four of the most interesting works of narrative fiction in medieval Hebrew literature were probably composed or edited in their final form; no one knows for certain exactly when or where they were written. Each of these distinctive narratives, translated for this volume, merits a description of its own.

Midrash on the Ten Commandments

Despite its title, there is little that is genuinely exegetical about this work. "Midrash on the Ten Commandments" is a collection of passages, many of them drawn from classical rabbinic literature, that are arranged around the rubric of the Decalogue, as the collection's name suggests. One of several similar collections that appear during this period, "Midrash" reflects a new genre in Jewish literature whose emergence, possibly influenced by an Arabic model, testifies to the Jewish reader's growing interest in narrative.[5] The particular form of narrative that dominates these collections is the *maaseh,* literally an anecdote but, more accurately, an exemplum, that is, a story told in order to illustrate a moral or homiletical lesson (such as one of the Ten Commandments).

In terms of its rhetorical strategies, the exemplum is the virtual opposite to the *mashal.* While the parable builds upon its fictionality, creating a story in order to draw out its audience's imagination, the exemplum lays claim to having actually taken place *precisely* as narrated, to being "true" and "real," not imagined or fictionalized in the least. Moreover, the claim to historical veracity tends to increase in inverse proportion to the plausibility of the narrative. Thus, the less likely the story appears, the more its author insists that it actually happened that way. An analogous inversion characterizes the relationship between story and moral in the exemplum. As Joel Rosenberg notes in his introduction to "Midrash on the Ten Commandments," the most memorable feature of the narratives in that collection may be the incongruity between the homiletical, or legal, lessons they are supposed to teach and the utterly profane human universe they actually portray. One seems to glimpse in these exempla the inevitable tendency of narrative to escape, if not flee, the confines of conventional piety.

Some scholars have used this incongruity to argue that one sees in

"Midrash on the Ten Commandments" (and in similar collections) the beginnings of secular narrative in Jewish literature. According to this argument, these stories are cloaked in the garb of midrashic orthodoxy, perhaps in order to justify their publication, but in reality they are already freed from the fetters of enforced religion. Yet to dismiss the homiletical framework for these exempla would be to misunderstand their meaning completely. If the rabbinic parable is about imagining God, the concern of the exemplum is to convey the force of the law—the ineluctable, inescapable, and impersonal reach of justice. Virtually all the exempla in "Midrash on the Ten Commandments" begin with their main character either transgressing or fulfilling a commandment; which commandment that may be is less significant for the subsequent narrative than the fact of obedience or disobedience and the ultimate reward or punishment that follows.

As in Greek romance, appropriate recompense most often comes only improbably. The plots of these exempla turn on accidental events, unlikely coincidences, fortuitous meetings and mismatches, implausible denouements serving a justice so poetic that it sometimes verges on comedy. Precisely on account of their sheer unlikeliness, these fairy-tale endings point to the hidden hand of a divine Providence that all along has been directing the plot to its fitting end. At the same time, the aspect of the exemplum that resembles the Greek romance also moves these stories in the direction of the novella, toward lengthier narratives that more fully develop the rich possibilities latent in the techniques of improbability and surprise.

The Tale of the Jerusalemite

This movement is seen best in one of the most remarkable narratives in all Hebrew literature, the story known as "The Tale of the Jerusalemite." Though much lengthier than most exempla, the moral at the conclusion of the text—that a son should always obey his father's commands—indicates that "The Tale" was once part of a collection of exempla. And, like other exempla of this sort, "The Tale of the Jerusalemite" begins with the violation of the moral. A son breaks the oath that his father has made him swear—never to go to sea—and is punished by being shipwrecked in the land of demons, where he eventually marries the daughter of Ashma-dai, the king of demons.

Since its modern rediscovery, "The Tale of the Jerusalemite" has been cited by scholars as one of the earliest existing stories documenting the folk motif of the man who marries a demoness. Yet while "The Tale" contains primitive popular elements, it is hardly a folktale. Once the reader accepts the story's premise that a land of demons exists, the rest of the story unfolds with an infallible, though bizarre, logic. But a summary of the plot omits what are, in fact, the tale's most salient features. The first of these is the degree to which the story and its diction are saturated with the world of geonic Judaism, echoing phrases from the Talmud and from halakhic literature even more than those of Scripture. The Jerusalem-ite himself is repeatedly described as a *ben torah*, the traditional designa-tion for a scholar of the law but a term that also carries the special blame attached to a person who should have known better than to have acted as he did and who consequently has brought shame upon the entire Torah as well as on himself. This Jerusalemite, in other words, is straight out of the yeshiva world.

The second feature to be noted about the story is connected to the preceding one as conceit is related to fact. The demons among whom the Jerusalemite finds himself after his shipwreck are more Jewish than the Jews he has left behind in the "human" world. They pray in synagogue every day, they study and quote Talmud flawlessly, their courts of law operate according to principles of halakhah. Indeed, they possess a kind of native piety that makes the Jerusalemite's religious behavior look narrowly legalistic by comparison.

To be sure, these demons are not entirely undemonic. "The Tale of the Jerusalemite," with its story of a Jew who crosses from this world to another, is in fact an extraordinary attempt to imagine Otherness. The irony behind the Jerusalemite's journey is that the other world, which is literally a world of aliens, turns out in practice to be hardly different from the one he has left behind, while the Jerusalemite himself is no different "there" than "here." In both places he is an untrustworthy scoundrel, given to betrayal. Yet this story achieves a kind of empathy for the Other—whether demonic or gentile—that is unparalleled in medieval Judaism. The fact that the reader by design feels more sympathy for the injured demons than he or she does for the Jerusalemite is only one sign of the uniqueness of "The Tale." Despite its strict attention to justice, this narrative raises some strong suspicions about the self-confident righteousness of the world to which the Jerusalemite claims his sole allegiance.

The Legend of the Ten Martyrs

The third great narrative to derive in its present form from the geonic period is *Midrash Eleh Ezkerah*, also known in some versions as "The Legend [*maaseh*] of the Ten Martyrs." The existing text of this most famous medieval Jewish martyrology conflates a number of separate accounts from earlier rabbinic literature into a single narrative about the collective execution of ten rabbis by an unspecified Roman emperor. Although the particular event described in *Eleh Ezkerah* is fictional—ten sages were never collectively executed by a Roman emperor—the author or editor clearly believed in the historicity of his narrative. And however invented his narrative may be, it reflects all too accurately certain historical realities that have recurred with painful frequency in Jewish history—a fact that accounts in part for the legend's persistence in Jewish memory.

Midrash Eleh Ezkerah is not an exemplum; the horrible events it describes do not illustrate a clear-cut moral lesson. Nor is it a parabolic narrative designed to elicit an interpretive response from its audience. Rather, as its alternative title suggests, it is an example of historical mythmaking in which real events are raised to the level of legend and endowed with a transcendental meaning. Thus, the present narrative offers no fewer than three separate justifications for the martyrdoms. The most exceptional of these is the rationale that the Roman emperor himself relates to the sages: that he must execute them in order to fulfill the letter of their own law! The Torah itself, he reminds them, decrees that a person guilty of kidnapping another person must die. And since the sages' ancestors, Jacob's ten sons, were never punished for kidnapping their younger brother Joseph and for selling him into slavery, it is now incumbent upon the sages to atone for that capital transgression with their lives.

When Rabbi Ishmael shortly thereafter ascends to heaven, the sage learns to his astonishment that the emperor's bizarre reasoning has been divinely ordained. A second rationale for the imminent martyrdom is presented by the angel Gabriel, whom Ishmael meets in heaven. The angel tells him that the sages have been selected to die precisely because of their righteousness—they are the first ten Jews in history since the time of the patriarch Jacob who are worthy to serve as surrogates for their ancestors, the fathers of the ten tribes, and to atone for their transgressions. Holiness, not sinfulness, is the cause for their deaths.

At this point in the narrative Ishmael's journey is interrupted by an account of a contest in heaven between God and the wicked angel Samael over the sages' fates. Grimly reminiscent of the sparring between God and Satan in the prologue to the Book of Job, the contest here has nearly the opposite import: God does not yield to Samael's challenge; instead, He proves Himself incapable of saving the sages from the wicked angel. Bound by His own decree, He cannot rescind what is in effect already fated and can merely threaten Samael with Rome's eventual punishment. As the Roman emperor mockingly remarks at a later moment, the God of the sages has been enfeebled by age; He is too old to save His servants. No less remarkably, the sage Ishmael, shortly before descending back to earth, himself beholds a supernal altar in heaven where, he is told, the archangel Michael offers up the souls of the righteous in daily sacrifices.

The divine realm of *Eleh Ezkerah* is far from the image of heaven typically represented in Judaism. Even less conventional is the ambiguously suggestive story that Gabriel tells Ishmael about the sage's conception and birth. Its hint that Gabriel is in fact Ishmael's real father taps the narrative into a truly archaic strata, recalling biblical references (Genesis 6:1–2) to myths about the *benei elohim,* the sons of God, who found the daughters of men so beautiful that they took them for wives. This mix of eroticism and holiness (present as well in the Salome-like story of the sudden desire for Ishmael that seizes the emperor's daughter when she glimpses the handsome sage as he is about to be executed) is not an entirely atypical medieval combination. This is a world in which saintliness is charged with sexual potency; such contradictory erotic moments happen in fact to be quite common in saints' lives as well as in other types of hagiography.

It is revealing that in some later versions of "The Legend of the Ten Martyrs," like the *piyyutim* or liturgical poems recited in the synagogue service on Yom Kippur and on the Fast of Av, both the mythical and the erotic strands have been expurgated. By comparing these other versions with *Midrash Eleh Ezkerah,* one can see that without these seemingly intrusive elements, the martyrology is also much thinner, less incongruous perhaps but also less vivid and potent a narrative. The same result is effected by eliminating or ironing out the contradictory and overdetermined elements in the midrash, for example, the use of three rationalizations for the martyrdom rather than just one. While some modern scholars believe that the account of Ishmael's ascent to heaven may point to the legend's origins among early Jewish mystical circles, *Eleh Ezkerah* is actually a medieval Hebrew narrative with a center that has not held. Its multiple sources have resisted even its editor's brave attempts to unify them.[6]

The Alphabet of Ben Sira

The fourth and final narrative from the early geonic period is "The Alphabet of Ben Sira." This work, which through the centuries has provoked reactions ranging from utter scorn as a thing of blasphemy to pious reverence as a halakhic source, is perhaps the most unusual narrative text in all medieval Hebrew literature. For a just appreciation of the wonderful artistry of this work, I can do no better than refer the reader to Mark Mirsky's Afterword to this anthology, in which he proposes to read "The Alphabet" as a self-aware fiction in its own right. To this I would add only that it may be one of the earliest known parodies in all of Jewish literature. The texts that it parodies include identifiable passages from midrash and Talmud as well as the popular literature of animal tales and sage stories, while the character of Ben Sira is itself a travesty—of the figure of the prophet as well as of the entire literary genre of Wisdom (Ben Sira is the Hebrew name of the author of the apocryphal book Ecclesiasticus, one of the great late examples of the genre).

There is good reason to suppose that "The Alphabet" was not a unique text even if it is the sole lengthy example of its genre from early medieval Jewish literature to survive. Like "The Tale of the Jerusalemite," "The Alphabet" has been taken by some modern scholars for folklore that has been "worked up" into literature, and it has been read by others simply as a gross example of popular entertainment. In fact, the sophistication of both its parodies and its narrative technique suggests that this work is actually as close to an example of "high" literary art as can be found in medieval Jewish literature. More than any other comparable text, "The Alphabet of Ben Sira" demonstrates how imaginative narrative can document and preserve aspects of classical Jewish experience that otherwise would be entirely lost to us.

SACRED BIOGRAPHY

It is characteristic of the unusual position that imaginative narrative occupies in medieval Hebrew literature that "The Tale of the Jerusalemite," *Midrash Eleh Ezkerah,* and "The Alphabet of Ben Sira" are nearly all isolated works, with neither predecessors nor successors. The single form whose literary development can be charted clearly in subsequent medieval Jewish literature is the exemplum, the most prominent example of its later career being the extraordinary and original use to which it is put in *Sefer Hasidim* (The Book of the Pious). This strange and difficult text is a lengthy compendium of the teachings of Judah the Pious, a thirteenth-century sage who lived in Ashkenaz (as the territories of Germany and northern France were called) and whose personal religious ideology inspired an entire movement called pietism, or Hasidut. The focus of this movement was the *Hasid,* "the righteous man," who, utterly alone in this world, distinguished himself less by dint of learning than by his extreme devotion to the law in its absolute rigor.

To convey the ethical philosophy of Hasidut, Judah transformed the traditional genre of the exemplum. Adapting some of his stories from non-Jewish tales and inventing others anew, he used the genre to epitomize the life of the ideal Hasid. The conflict that insistently informs the moral tales in *Sefer Hasidim* derives from the Hasid's desire to efface his individuality in its entirety and his simultaneous need to demonstrate to the world his own religious inadequacy. Yet these narratives are more than ideological documents. They uncannily explore some of the darker regions of the human psyche, especially guilt, often with such precision that one feels that their real subject is not so much religious doctrine as obsession.

Ashkenazic Hasidut arose roughly at the same time as kabbalistic mysticism in Spain. *Sefer Hasidim* was composed shortly before Moses de Leon, living in Castile, first brought the *Zohar* to public notice. The difference between Hasidism and Kabbalism, the two movements represented in these books, can be summed up by comparing their respective conceptions of desire and its effects upon the imagination. The authors of both books are fascinated by the erotic. For Judah the Pious, however, this fascination is torment, a trial; sexuality is a test, an ordeal to overcome or to fail miserably. The major challenge faced by the Hasid is to escape contamination by the feminine. Yet the closer the Hasid comes to such contamination, and the narrower his escape from it, the higher the degree of holiness he attains. This is the central paradox of Hasidut. The pious man is always at risk of being surprised by self-doubt, of awakening to discover himself in the midst of a surreal nightmare of judgment and condemnation.

For the author of the *Zohar*, the powers of sexuality were as formally forbidden as they were for Judah. Yet in the *Zohar* divinity itself is eroticized, and the erotic comes to possess an intrinsic attraction, the fascination of the Other, which is different from the fascination exercised by evil. It is the fascination of the mysterious, of the esoterically forbidden, of that which is off-limits to all but the initiated. Once entered, though, the realm of sexuality is there to be explored, not shunned; only by penetrating to its source can the mystical hero acquire the knowledge of perfection. Revelation thus comes to resemble sexual bliss; the imagination's own appetite for it becomes a cause for delight, not terror.

With *Sefer Hasidim* and the *Zohar* one reaches a kind of crossroads in medieval Hebrew narrative fiction, with subsequent works tending to develop in one of two directions. The first of these was spawned by both Ashkenazic Hasidism and Spanish Kabbalah in the form of biographical legends about founding masters, figures like Judah the Pious himself or the sixteenth-century mystical genius Isaac Luria of Safed. Yet not until Hasidism, the popular ecstatic movement that arose in eastern Europe in the eighteenth century (without, one should add, any direct connection to the earlier Ashkenazic movement), did the tradition of hagiography come fully into its own. *In Praise of the Baal Shem Tov*, about Hasidism's founder, was only the first collection of such sacred biographies to be composed and circulated among the Hasidim.[7] The Baal Shem Tov's successors, the founders of the numerous Hasidic dynasties, enjoyed similar literary homage from their followers.

It was, however, the Baal Shem's great-grandson, Rabbi Nahman of Bratslav, who proved to be the real literary master of Hasidism. Although some of his ideas are anticipated in the *Zohar* and *Sefer Hasidim*, Nahman was the first author in the history of classical Jewish literature to propound an explicit theory of narrative that made fiction a privileged medium for the expression of esoteric truth. The most remarkable feature of Nahman's own narratives is their erasure of the distinction between imaginative fiction and mystical vision. Joining the symbolism of Kabbalah with folk motifs from the surrounding eastern European peasant culture, Nahman created original parablelike tales to give expression to his teachings, particularly those about the anonymous Master, a messianic figure who serves a redemptive function in the world, and about the temptations and the evils that the Master must overcome to accomplish his mission. Nahman was probably writing elliptically about himself. Yet it is a revealing indication of his loyalties that, rather than make himself their explicit subject, he chose to represent his thoughts through the oblique voices of the *mashal* and the exemplum, the paradigmatic modes of classical rabbinic narrative tradition.

With Nahman, one stands upon the threshold of fiction in the modern, or modernist, sense. More than anything else, Nahman's art is a private one. His parabolic tales and "dreamtalks" seem to speak of things that resist speech, which is remarkable if we remind ourselves that Nahman preached these tales in public to his disciples. The symbolism in his tales is sometimes so thick and recondite that the symbols appear to have overtaken the reality of whatever it is they are meant to symbolize (in a way particularly reminiscent of the parables in *Sefer ha-Bahir*).

Despite their modernity, Nahman's narratives continue to inhabit much the same imaginative landscape as narratives like "The Tale of the Jerusalemite" or the exempla in "Midrash on the Ten Commandments" and *Sefer Hasidim*. The same stock characters reappear in them, as do many motifs and narrative lines. Even the world in which these stories take place is less an identifiable geographical locale—one looks in vain for descriptions of nature—than it is the sacred textual universe of Scripture. Little in these stories can be pinned down to the historical here and now, as if their author had retreated from the world around him into another reality that he either knew better (from having studied it) or felt to be more important.

THE MAQAMA

Nearly the opposite stylistic tendencies characterize the second tradition of narrative in later medieval Hebrew literature: the *maqama*, or rhymed-prose narrative. This tradition, the only one in medieval Jewish narrative that might be considered authentically secular, initially grew out of the same soil as the lyric poetry of the Spanish Hebrew Golden Age in the twelfth century. Modeled upon an Arabic genre, Hebrew *maqama* was both ornately rhetorical and highly conventionalized. Thus, the various *maqamat* that together form a collection usually share a common narrator, who, in each episode, describes a character whom he has met on his journeys. The latter character is typically also the common hero of all the *maqamat* in the collection, and his exploits generally include some kind of hoax or deception that he perpetrates upon an innocent victim. While their narratives center upon the illicit but comic machinations of the protagonist, *maqamat* also portray a host of richly imagined characters, including forsaken lovers, village yokels, pretentious philosophers, disreputable poets, corrupt rabbis, unfaithful wives, essentially the array of social types who populate Spanish Jewish culture in all its worldly and unworldly varieties. In the hands of some of its later authors, *maqama* even became a satirical tool for social criticism, directed in particular against the ambitious, aristocratic courtier classes that dominated Spanish Jewry.

The *maqama* was not the first long poetic or quasi-poetic narrative in Hebrew. Classical liturgical poetry had a lengthy tradition of retelling biblical legends as embellished by midrash in more or less epic form. Extended accounts of the Creation story, for example, were often narrated for philosophical and theological purposes. In medieval Hebrew narrative, too, there were antecedents for the mock-heroic narrative of the *maqama*. The Indian fabula of "Kelilah and Dimnah" and "The Tales of Sendebar" (another story collection that originated in the Far East and made its way to Europe, where it became known as "The Seven Sages") both appeared in Hebrew literature in the twelfth and thirteenth centuries.[8] The Alexander Gest and the Arthurian cycle were also retold in Hebrew and

Judaized in the process by the introduction of biblical verses and rabbinic practices into their characters' speeches and actions at crucial moments.[9]

These works were immensely popular among Jews, so much so that the thirteenth-century Jewish writer Abraham Bedersi, desirous of restoring glory to Hebrew literature, wrote that "our anxious longing is for our own works, not for 'Tales of Sendebar' and the like."[10] Yet, unlike these other works, the *maqama* was not a foreign tale translated into Hebrew but a genuinely original Hebrew composition in which language, particularly biblical language, became part of its content, not merely its medium, and an index of "Jewishness" as an identifiable literary feature. Hebrew poets in Spain had early on developed a sophisticated technique of allusion and quotation of biblical words and phrases designed for rhetorical effect. Sometimes the intent of this technique, known as *shibuts* (interweaving), was to extend the connotation of a scriptural phrase to a new and original point; at other times it was to shock the reader into seeing the sacred text in a profoundly profane setting. The effect could be humorous, or scandalous, or even powerfully moving.

In *maqama* the technique of *shibuts* was carried to its extreme by extending the underlying dialectic between outer form and inner content to the orders of style and plot. The tension between the two orders is felt everywhere in *maqama*; not surprisingly, it sometimes inscribes itself in the narratives themselves. To give a single example: a common preoccupation of *maqama* is the relationship between appearance and reality. This is sometimes phrased in terms of phenomenal illusion and metaphysical truth, but it can also be formulated in the persona of an unreliable narrator who contrives to pile up stories within stories so as to complicate the layerings of fictional reality and to confuse the reader into mistaking one narrative illusion for another. Analogously, the hero of each episode in a collection conventionally appears in disguise; when he reveals his identity at the narrative's end, it is usually to the surprise of both narrator and reader.

The corresponding problematic is played out on the level of language as well. Diction—the form of language—is granted a rhetorical appeal far out of proportion to a topic's substantive content or true importance. A narrative's praise may even appear to stand in direct opposition to correct moral sense. Indeed, if there is any standard against which imaginative invention in *maqama* is measured, it is that of the formal requirements of

the medium—the intricate set rhymes of its highly rhetorical prose—
rather than the constraints of morality. While authors of *maqama* collections may have piously claimed that their compositions served the purposes
of moral instruction, their sophisticated morality is usually as qualified as
the rest of reality represented in these clever narratives.

These qualities of the genre were maintained throughout the duration
of its tradition in Spain, through the fifteenth century, and in Italy, where
the form was transplanted by Immanuel of Rome, Dante's contemporary,
in his famous *Mahbeirot* (Compositions) of the late thirteenth century.
Immanuel transformed the *maqama* into the unique idiom of Renaissance
Italian Jewry, complete with sonnets, aesthetic humanism, and bawdy
delights. Yet Immanuel's own style is arguably the most rhetorical in the
entire tradition, so much so that it is virtually untranslatable.

The generic preoccupation of *maqama* with the conflict between reality
and appearance and the troubling implications of that conflict for moral
behavior can be observed as well in later Italian Jewish works like Abraham
Yagel's *A Valley of Vision*. Composed in the sixteenth century, this book
awkwardly joins autobiography, fiction, and homily and is most interesting
precisely for its generic complexity. In recounting the tale of the real
misfortunes that befell him and led to his imprisonment, Yagel relates a
strange narrative of how his dead father appeared to him in a dream at
night and then took him on a tour of heaven. On the tour Yagel meets
the biblical Job, who narrates the tale of a mistreated maidservant whom
Job rushes off to save at the conclusion of his tale. Yet, as modern scholars
have shown and as Yagel's original readers must have known, that tale is
borrowed from a contemporary Italian novella, though David Ruderman
notes that Yagel altered it slightly, making it less happy and morally neat
than its original but also more credible. Once again, in this story's
narrative stratagems, we can recognize a characteristic movement of Jewish
fantasy. The imagination is caught up in the interplay of appearance and
reality but is eventually held to the demands of morality.

TOWARD MODERN LITERATURE

From this point, it is tempting to look slowly forward to the Hebrew
narrative that is born in the eighteenth-century Enlightenment and to

the subsequent tradition of modern storytelling continuing on to our very own time. The sources and precursors of modern Hebrew narrative probably lie more outside than inside Jewish literary tradition. But in the picaresque adventures of the wandering Jew in search of home and identity, the subject of so much modern Jewish fiction, one can hear an echo of the *maqama* and its rhyming quests. And in the "fallen" literature of writers like Kafka, Agnon, and Singer—storytellers wandering in search of the path to wisdom, yet knowing that path was lost to them, their own tradition of wisdom cut off by modernity—perhaps it is possible to glimpse the impress of the classical tradition of exemplary narrative, the tales concerned with law and morality and their incomplete, sometimes failed, realization in the human world.

The "narrative" of classical Jewish narrative that we have told in these pages (despite ourselves, perhaps) thus culminates somewhat inconclusively, its impact and influences upon contemporary Jewish writing partly hidden, and partly lost. A conclusion of this kind is perhaps especially appropriate for a group of narratives that began with midrash and its stories disguised-as-commentaries. If the works represented in this volume do not in the end form a self-contained tradition; if they remain a heterogeneous group, each composed within its own set of conditions, their collective totality nonetheless attests to the persistence of narrative as a modality of the Jewish imagination—indeed, as a radical mode of expression that thrived, formally and thematically, as imaginative literature usually does, upon the paradoxical pleasures of serious play. These narratives attest to their authors' need to speak through the imagination about those things that were most real and important to them. That Jewish concerns figured among those things may make these narratives all the more precious and interesting to us. We need not believe in them fully in order to recover these narratives for ourselves and learn what they can teach us about our past and about an aspect of Jewish creativity that some assert never existed before the breakdown of Jewish tradition in the modern period.

DAVID STERN

NOTES

1. Joseph Dan, *The Hebrew Story in the Middle Ages* (in Hebrew) (Jerusalem: Keter, 1974), 1. Dan's book, the only scholarly monograph to deal with narrative in medieval Hebrew literature, contains invaluable bibliographical information that was indispensable in putting together this anthology.

2. Thus the Hebrew *dimyon* or, more commonly, *koah hamedameh*, the imaginative faculty, as in J. Ibn Tibbon's translation of Maimonides' *The Guide of the Perplexed* 2:36. For an insightful discussion of the Jewish imagination, see Geoffrey Hartman, "Imagination," in *Contemporary Jewish Religious Thought*, ed. Arthur A. Cohen and Paul Mendes-Flohr (New York: Scribner's, 1987), 451–72.

3. *Zohar* 3:152a (Numbers). Ed. R. Margoliot (Jerusalem: Mossad Harav Kook, 1984).

4. Louis Ginzberg, *The Legends of the Jews*, 8 vols. (Philadelphia: JPS, 1913; reprint, 1968). See as well the abridged version entitled *Legends of the Bible* (Philadelphia: JPS, 1968), with the superlative introductory essay by Shalom Spiegel, still the classic essay on this literature. In addition to Ginzberg, other monumental collections of Jewish legend are Chaim Bialik's and H. Ravinetzki's *Sefer ha-Aggadah*, unhappily still unavailable in English translation; and Micha Joseph Bin Gorion's *Mi-Mekor Yisrael*, ed. E. Bin Gorion and trans. I. M. Lask, 3 vols. (Bloomington, Ind.: Indiana University Press, 1976).

5. For another collection from this period, see Nissim of Kairouan, *An Elegant Composition Concerning Relief After Adversity*, trans. from Arabic by W. M. Brinner (New Haven: Yale University Press, 1977). A collection from a later period, *Sefer ha-Maasim*, is also available in English translation by Moses Gaster as *The Exempla of the Rabbis* (1924; reprint, New York: Ktav, 1968). A still later collection, *The Maaseh Book*, containing rabbinic and medieval Jewish tales in Judeo-German, is also available in an English translation by Moses Gaster (Philadelphia: JPS, 1934).

6. A vivid synoptic illustration of the different versions of "The Legend" and their sources is now available in the careful edition with German translation by Gottfried Reeg, *Die Geschichte von den Zehn Martyrern* (Tübingen: J.C.B. Mohr, 1985).

7. *In Praise of the Baal Shem Tov*, trans. Dan Ben-Amos and Jerome R. Mintz (Bloomington, Ind.: Indiana University Press, 1970). Earlier hagiographies are found in Bin Gorion's *Mi-Mekor Yisrael*, while stories of other Hasidic masters are retold in the collections of Martin Buber, though not always in reliable versions.

8. *Tales of Sendebar*, trans. Morris Epstein (Philadelphia: JPS, 1967).

9. For the texts, see *The Book of the Gests of Alexander of Macedon*, ed. and trans. Israel J. Kazis (Cambridge, Mass.: Medieval Academy of America, 1962); and *King Artus: A Hebrew Arthurian Romance of 1279*, ed. Curt Leviant (New York: Ktav, 1969). As examples of Judaization in these texts, consider that the anonymous author of the Alexander romance has his hero quote Micah (4:4): "And you shall sit every man under his vine and under his fig tree" when the young king promises the Indian soldiers freedom if they surrender to him. In the

Hebrew Arthur the knight Lancelot, in the course of a love speech to Queen Zinevra (better known to us as Guinevere), uses the euphemism *Hashem* to refer to God, as any pious Jew would, in order to avoid taking His name in vain.

10. Quoted in Epstein, *The Tales of Sendebar*, 13.

A NOTE ON THE SELECTIONS
AND THE TRANSLATIONS

The sixteen selections in this volume comprise a representative group of the different types of imaginative narrative that exist in Hebrew literature before the modern period. Wherever possible, we have attempted to include texts in their entirety; where that has not been possible because of the lengthiness of the piece, or where it has not been advisable for other reasons, we have tried to choose units that do not misrepresent the character of the work as a whole. In making selections, we have also attempted to reflect the original nonnarrative frameworks or contexts within which many of these narratives were composed.

Most of these narratives are from the Middle Ages, which, in the idiosyncratic terms of Jewish historiography, begin a few centuries earlier and end several centuries later than they do for the rest of the Western world. While many of these texts are anonymous, and though little is known for certain about the specific time and place of their composition, we have tried to order them chronologically.

The first two selections in the volume, the collection of ten parables from classical rabbinic literature and the two rabbinic narratives about God serve as a prologue to the subsequent narratives, beginning with the chapter from *Pirkei de-Rabbi Eliezer* ("Jonah and the Sailors") and *Sefer Zerubbabel,* both of which date from the early medieval period. The next four selections ("Midrash on the Ten Commandments," "The Tale of the Jerusalemite," *Midrash Eleh Ezkerah,* and "The Alphabet of Ben Sira") probably derive from geonic Babylonia between the eighth and the tenth centuries. The following three selections of narrative (from *Sefer ha-Bahir, Sefer Hasidim,* and the *Zohar*) date from the High Middle Ages, as do the

31

subsequent four narratives, the examples of *maqama,* the rhymed-prose narrative composed in Spain and Provence. The last two selections in the book may be taken together to constitute a kind of epilogue to the medieval narratives: "Job's Novella" is selected from an Italian Renaissance work, and Nahman of Bratslav's "Dream-Tales" were composed in the first decade of the nineteenth century.

As discussed in the Introduction, our classification of these texts as fictional imaginative narratives is a complicated formulation whose problematic aspects are as familiar to us as are those features we consider to be its advantages. We wish merely to note here that we have intentionally excluded from this anthology a number of works that might also have fallen under the category of rabbinic fantasy. Some of these, like the mystical visions of Joseph Caro, were excluded because they were not narrative; others, like the Chronicle of Ahimaaz, Josippon, and the Chronicles of Jerahmeel, were not included because they presume to be historiographical compositions rather than imaginative works.

Finally, a word must be said about the special difficulties faced in translating medieval Hebrew narratives. In some cases reliable, critical editions do not exist; in other cases there appears to be a kind of willful disdain for the niceties of style and the finer points of storytelling. As frequently noted in the introductions to the selections, the Hebrew language in many of these narratives is a mélange of biblical allusions and rabbinic references whose unique character is nearly impossible to replicate in translation.

The aim of the translations in this book has been to transmit the flavor of the original Hebrew texts as accurately and directly as possible in contemporary American English. We have tried to avoid archaisms and euphemistic circumlocutions. Wherever the original texts have presented a textual problem or have appeared to be intentionally unusual, we have asked our translators to note the incident and elaborate upon it in their notes. We have also sought to note all quotes from the Bible and rabbinic literature. Where the biblical or rabbinic text is cited in the narrative as a quotation, we have presented the source in the text in parentheses. Where the original text is merely alluded or referred to, we have given the source in the notes. Wherever it is contextually appropriate, the JPS *Tanakh* is the source of biblical translations.

While we have attempted to stay close to the literal surface of the narratives, our general philosophy of translation has been that meaning and nuance—substance, in other words—are more important than sheer word-for-word literalism or external form. Thus, in the case of *maqama*, while we recognize that the rhymes are an intrinsic part of the narrative form in the original Hebrew compositions, we have not tried to duplicate them mechanically in English. Where it was impossible to find an adequate substitute or counterpart for the rhyme, we have placed the emphasis of the translation elsewhere, on double entendre, irony, and allusion. Similarly, where the original text appears to be ambiguous or suggestive, we have tried to preserve the specialness of the moment without flattening the language.

Furthermore, in the belief that not everything that sounds awkward or clumsy to our ears in English translation is necessarily so in Hebrew, we have taken certain liberties in the translations. The dialogue in these narratives in particular tends to sound clumsy, with its repetitious presentation in the standard pattern of "X said . . . , Y said . . . ," and so on, and with the same verb, *amar*, used for every type of utterance and statement. Accordingly, we have translated *amar* with appropriate synonyms: "told," "asked," "responded," "answered," "exclaimed," and so on. Similarly, we have frequently transplaced the "X said" (or its equivalent) from its conventional position in front of the direct quotation either to the middle of the quote or to its end. In a few cases, where the phrase seemed to us unnecessary, we have omitted it altogether. It has sometimes been necessary to supply a phrase or sentence to clarify the narrative; in such cases we have placed the addition in brackets. Finally, because these texts are narratives, we have operated under the assumption that narrative movement is an intrinsic part of the prose; to facilitate that movement, we have occasionally adjusted the language and tightened it to fit the needs of narrative.

Nothing in these translations presumes to be scientific or an adequate substitute for the original text.

DAVID STERN
MARK JAY MIRSKY

1 ◆

RABBINIC PARABLES

The *mashal,* or parable, is the most common narrative form used by rabbis in midrash to interpret the Torah. The literary tradition of the *mashal* is very ancient. Parables are to be found in the Bible, and there almost certainly existed a popular, oral tradition of parabolic literature between the biblical and rabbinic periods. Little of this tradition has survived, however, and it is ironic that our earliest testimony for the types of narratives in rabbinic *meshalim* are those preserved in the parables attributed to Jesus in the three synoptic Gospels. There is little doubt that Jesus' parables are part of the larger tradition for which the rabbinic *meshalim* in midrashic and talmudic literature comprise much later evidence.

Like all parables, the *mashal* is a rhetorical device that works essentially through indirection and obliqueness; it can thus suggest meanings to its audience that are, perhaps, best not spelled out too explicitly. Bizarre deeds, abrupt transitions, unresolved sequences of dialogue and plot, opaqueness in general often take on in the parables suggestive, haunting implications—deliberately exploited by the rabbis for the purpose of interpreting Torah.

As the *mashal* became a popular device in midrash, it also assumed an increasingly conventionalized form, in its language, diction, and theme (evidence that may also suggest the ways in which *meshalim* were spontaneously improvised in the course of oral delivery). The most obvious illustration of this process of conventionalization is the fact that most rabbinic *meshalim* use the device of the king *mashal*. In these parables the protagonist is usually a king, while the other characters in the parable are other members of the royal court, and the kinds of situations portrayed in the narratives are frequently associated with a royal setting.

The *mashal* has two standard parts. The first of these is the narrative, or *mashal* itself. The second part, the *nimshal,* or explanation, usually provides the parable's audience with the context—exegetical or whatever—in which the meaning of the parable is to be understood. The *nimshal* conventionally concludes with the citation of a prooftext, a scriptural verse, that itself is reinterpreted in light of the *nimshal* and the *mashal* preceding it. Sometimes the *mashal* is prefaced by an exegetical opinion that also helps to set the context.

The following ten parables have been chosen for their narrative accomplishment and for the ingenuity of their interpretations. They span the range of midrashic literature, from its earliest compilations in the third or fourth centuries of the Common Era to its last ones, which were probably redacted as late as the seventh or eighth century.

Introduction and translation by
DAVID STERN

I

And Moses held out his arm over the sea (Exodus 14:21). The sea began to oppose Moses. Moses ordered it in the name of God to divide itself, but the sea refused. He showed it his staff, but it still refused.

A parable: What is this like? It is like a king who had two gardens, one inside the other. The king sold the inner garden, but when the man who had bought it came and wished to pass through to the inner garden, the guard would not let him. The man invoked the name of the king, but the guard refused. He showed him the king's ring, but he still refused. Finally, the man brought the king himself. Once the king came, the guard immediately fled. The man who had bought the field called out to him, "All day I have been speaking to you in the name of the king, but you would never yield. So why are you now running away?" The guard replied, "I'm not running away from you. I'm running away from the king!"

So Moses came and stood at the sea. He ordered it in the name of God to divide itself, but the sea refused. He showed it his staff, but it still refused. Finally, the Holy One, blessed be He, revealed Himself in His glory. Once the Holy One, blessed be He, revealed Himself in His might and in His glory, the sea began to flee, as it is said, "The sea saw them and fled" (Psalm 114:3). Moses spoke to the sea, "All day I have been speaking to you in the name of the Holy One, blessed be He, and you refused. Why do you flee now? What alarmed you, O sea, that you fled?" (Psalm 114:5). The sea replied, "I'm not fleeing from you, Moses. No, not from you, son of Amram—but "at the presence of the Lord—tremble, O earth!—at the presence of the God of Jacob, who turned the rock into a pool of water, the flinty rock into a fountain" (Psalm 114:7–8).

—Mekhilta, Beshalah, chap. 5

II

Rabbi Hoshaiah said: When the Holy One, blessed be He, created Adam, the angelic host confused the man with God and wished to recite "Holy, holy, holy" (Isaiah 6:3) before Adam.[1]

What is this like? It is like a king who was with his provincial prefect inside a carriage. The inhabitants of the province wished to hail the king, "O Dominus! Our lord!" but they did not know which one of them was king. What did the king do? He shoved the prefect out of the carriage. *Then* they knew who the king was.

So, too, when the Holy One, blessed be He, created Adam, the angels confused him with God. What did the Holy One, blessed be He, do? He cast sleep upon Adam, and then the angels all knew that Adam was a man. That is what is written: "Oh, cease to glorify man, who has only a breath in his nostrils! For by what does he merit esteem?" (Isaiah 2:22).[2]

—Genesis Rabbah 8:10

III

Rabbi Joshua ben Levi said, What is this like? It is like a king who was on a journey. A princess cried out to him, "Help! Save me from these bandits!" The king heard her and rescued her. Later, he wished to take the princess to be his wife, and he longed for her to speak to him, but she did not wish to. What did the king do? He set bandits against her—so that she would cry out and he would hear her. And as soon as the bandits attacked her, she began to cry out to the king. He said to her, "For this I longed—to hear your voice."

Likewise Israel: When they were enslaved in Egypt, they began to cry out, lifting their eyes to the Holy One, blessed be He, as it is said, "A long time after that, the king of Egypt died. The Israelites were groaning under the bondage and cried out; and their cry for help from the bondage rose up to God" (Exodus 2:23). And immediately, "God looked upon the Israelites, and God took notice of them" (Exodus 2:25). The Holy One, blessed be He, began to take the Israelites out of Egypt with a mighty hand and an outstretched arm. He wished to hear Israel's voice again, but they were not willing. What did He do? He incited Pharaoh to pursue them, as it is said, "As Pharaoh drew near" (Exodus 14:10), and immediately thereafter, "the Israelites cried out to the Lord" (Exodus 14:10). At that moment the Holy One, blessed be He, said, "For this I longed—to hear your voice," as it is said "My dove, in the cranny of the rocks, hidden by the cliff, let me see your face, let me hear your voice (Song of Songs 2:14). The verse does not say "let me hear *a* voice," but "*your* voice"— the same voice that I heard in Egypt. Therefore it is written, "Let me hear your voice." And once the Israelites prayed to God, the Holy One, blessed be He, said to Moses, "What are you doing, standing there and praying! My children's prayers have already reached me—before yours!" As it is said, "Then the Lord said to Moses, Why do you cry out to Me?" (Exodus 14:15).

—Exodus Rabbah 21:5

IV

Rabbi Judah ben Rabbi Simon said: It is like a man who was sitting, making a crown for the king. Another man passed by and asked him, "What are you making?" The first man replied, "A crown for the king." The second man said, "Be sure to embellish it as much as you can. Set emeralds upon it! Set jewels upon it! Set pearls upon it!" For what reason? Because the crown is destined to sit upon the king's head.[3]

So the Holy One, blessed be He, said to Moses, "As much as you can, praise Israel! Exalt them! Glorify them! Why? Because I am destined to be glorified through them." This is what is written, "He said to me, You are my servant, Israel in whom I glory" (Isaiah 49:3).

—Leviticus Rabbah 2:5

V

Rabbi Ishmael taught: It is like the king who owned an orchard with splendid fruit. The king appointed two watchmen to guard the orchard, one a blind man, the other a cripple, and said to them, "Be very careful with this fruit!" Then he left them and went his way. The cripple said to the blind man, "What splendid fruit I see!" The blind man replied, "Then bring them, and let us eat." "Can I walk?" the cripple asked. "Can I see?" the blind man answered. What did they do? The cripple climbed atop the back of the blind man, and so they reached the fruit and ate. Afterward, they returned to their places, each of them sitting alone. Some time later, the king returned. "Where is the fruit?" he asked. "Can I see?" the blind man said to him. "Can I walk?" the cripple asked. The king was wise. What did he do? He made the cripple climb atop the back of the blind man, and then he judged the two of them together, telling them, "This is how you ate."

So the Holy One, in the time to come, will say to the soul, "Why have you sinned before me?" The soul will reply, "Master of the universe! Did I sin before you? The body sinned. From the moment I departed the body, have I ever sinned?" Then He will say to the body, "Why have you sinned?" The body will reply, "The soul has sinned. From the moment it departed me, have I not been cast before you like a piece of earthenware upon a dung heap?" What will the Holy One, blessed be He, do? He will return the soul to the body and judge the two of them together. This is what is written: "He summons the heavens above, and the earth, for the trial of His people" (Psalm 50:4). "He summons the heavens"—to bring the soul. "And the earth"—to bring the body. And afterward, "for the trial of his people": this means "to trial with it."[4]

—Leviticus Rabbah 4:5

VI

"I am the man" (Lamentations 3:1). Rabbi Joshua ben Levi said: The community of Israel said to the Holy One, blessed be He, "I am accustomed to suffer whatever pleases you!"

It is like the king's consort at whom the king became angry and banished from the palace. What did the consort do? She went and hid herself behind a column. When the king passed her, he said, "Must you make trouble?" She responded, "O master, my king! So it is seemly for me to act, and right, and proper. For no other woman would agree to marry you except me!" The king replied, "That is not true. I disqualified all other women for your sake." She answered, "That is not so. *They* were the ones who would not accept you."

So spoke the community of Israel before the Holy One, blessed be He, "Master of the universe! So it is proper for me to act. For no other nation would accept Your Torah save for me." The Holy One, blessed be He, responded, "That is not true. I was the one who disqualified all the nations for your sake." Israel answered, "That is not so. They were the ones who did not accept it. For why did You go to Mount Seir, if not to offer the Torah to the children of Esau? But they did not accept it. Or to the desert of Paran, if not to offer the Torah to the children of Ishmael? But they did not accept it. Why did You go to the Ammonites and the Moabites? Was it not to offer the Torah to the children of Lot? But they did not accept it."

This is what is written: "And he said, the Lord came from Sinai, and rose up from Seir unto them; He shined forth from Mount Paran, and He came with tens of thousands of saints; from His right hand went a fiery law for them" (Deuteronomy 33:2). In the beginning He went to [the children of] Esau at Mount Seir and said to them, "Will you accept the Torah?" They asked, "What is written in it?" He said, "You shall not kill" (Exodus 20:13). They said to Him, "But that is the blessing our father gave us, 'And by your sword shall you live' (Genesis 27:40). We cannot live without it." And so they did not accept the Torah.

He went to the desert of Paran, where the children of Ishmael live, and asked them, "Will you accept the Torah?" They asked, "What is written in it?" He said, "You shall not steal" (Exodus 20:15). They said to Him, "But that is our father's heritage to us, 'His hand will be against every man, and every man's hand against him' (Genesis 16:12). We cannot live without it." And so they did not accept the Torah. He went to the Ammonites and the Moabites and asked them, "Will you accept the Torah?" They asked, "What is written in it?" He said, "You shall not commit adultery" (Exodus 20:14). They said to Him, "But our ancestors all sprung from such illegitimate offspring, as it is said, 'Thus were both the daughters of Lot with child by their father' (Genesis 19:36). We cannot live without [adultery]." And so they did not accept the Torah.

He came to Israel and asked them, "Will you accept the Torah?" They responded, "Yes, indeed! All that the Lord has said will we do and obey" (Exodus 24:17). Yet after all these praiseworthy deeds, "I am the man that has seen affliction" (Lamentations 3:1).

—Lamentations Rabbah 3:1

VII

Rabbi Abba bar Kahana said, It is like a king who took a certain woman to be his wife. He wrote her a very large marriage contract. "So many bridal chambers will I make for you," he wrote her. "So many jewels will I bestow upon you, so much silver and gold will I give you." Then he left her for many years while he journeyed to a distant province. All this time her neighbors taunted her. "Has your husband not abandoned you?" they said. "Go! Take another man for yourself." The woman wept and sighed, but then she would go inside her bridal chamber, read her marriage contract, and console herself. Many days and years later, the king returned. "You amaze me!" he said to her. "How have you been able to wait for me all these years?" She replied, "My lord, O king! If not for the generous marriage contract you wrote me, my neighbors would indeed have led me astray."

So the nations of the world vex the children of Israel. "Your God no longer wants you," they say. "He has abandoned you, and removed His Presence from among you. Come! Join us, and we will appoint you rulers and commanders and generals." But the children of Israel enter their synagogues and houses of study where they read in the Torah, "For I will have respect unto you, and make you fruitful, and multiply you, and establish my covenant with you . . . and I will set my tabernacle among you, and My soul shall not abhor you" (Leviticus 26:9,11)—and so they console themselves. And in the future, when the redemption arrives, the Holy One, blessed be He, will say to Israel, "My children, you amaze me! How have you waited for me all these years?" They will reply, "Master of the universe! If not for the Torah you gave us, and the verse, 'For I will have respect unto you and I shall not abhor you,' which we read when we entered our synagogues and houses of study, the nations of the world would indeed have led us astray." This is what is written: "If Your law had not been my delight, I should then have perished in my affliction" (Psalm 119:92). And therefore it says, "This I recall to my mind, therefore I have hope" (Lamentations 3:21).[5]

—Lamentations Rabbah 3:21

VIII

It is written, "A song of Asaph. O God, the heathen are come into Your inheritance" (Psalm 79:1). A song! It should have said, A lament!

Rabbi Eleazar said, It is like a king who built a bridal chamber for his son. He fixed the chamber, plastered, cemented, and decorated it. Once, however, his son angered him, and the king destroyed the bridal chamber. The son's tutor sat down and began to sing. [A person] said to him, "The king has destroyed his bridal chamber. Yet you sit and sing!" The tutor replied, "This is why I sing: Because the king poured out his anger upon his son's bridal chamber—and not upon his son himself!"

So people said to Asaph, "The Holy One, blessed be He, has destroyed His Temple. Yet you sit and sing!" Asaph replied, "This is why I sing: Because the Holy One, blessed be He, poured out His anger upon trees and stone—and not upon Israel itself!" This is what is written: "And He has kindled a fire in Zion which has devoured its foundations" (Lamentations 4:11).[6]

—Lamentations Rabbah 4:11

IX

Rabbi Joshua of Sikhnin, in the name of Rabbi Levi, derived the solution [to the problem of what sort of tree was the tree of knowledge from which Adam and Eve ate] from its context.

It is like a king who had a son as well as many maidservants. The king commanded his son, "My son! Do not touch a single one of these maidservants!" What did the son do? He went and disgraced himself with one of the maidservants. When the king discovered this, he banished his

son from the palace. The son went around to the houses of all the maidservants, but not one would receive him, except—as you would expect—the maidservant with whom he had disgraced himself. She opened her door and received him.

So, after Adam had eaten from that tree, the Lord banished him from the garden of Eden. Adam went around to all the trees [asking them for leaves], but they would not receive him. What did the trees say? "Thief! You tried to deceive the Creator! You tried to deceive the Lord!" This is what is written: "Do not let arrogant feet crush me" (Psalm 36:11)—[the trees said,] "Do not bring against me that foot that transgressed in pride!" Or wicked hands expel me (Psalm 36:11)—[the trees said,] "Do not shake me with that hand! And don't take my leaves!" But as you would expect, that tree that gave him fruit also gave him its leaves, which is what is written, And they sewed fig leaves together and made themselves loin-clothes (Genesis 3:7). So what was the name of that tree [from which Adam ate]? The fig-tree.

—Pesikta de-Rav Kahana 20

X

It is like a king who married a woman and lived with her for many years. But he had no children from her. Finally, he said: "My daughter! Go, marry another man. Perhaps you will have children with him. And whatever precious objects I own in your house, take them when you leave." His wife replied: "If this is how it must be, let me make you a banquet, and let us feast and drink. *Then* I will leave you—and no one will say, 'Look! The king's wife! Because he hated her, he banished her from his house.' "

The king agreed, and she immediately prepared a banquet. The king ate and drank until he was drunk. At midnight the queen gave her servants orders, and they took the king as he lay asleep on his couch and brought him to her father's house. When the king awoke, he asked, "What place is this I am lying in?" "My father's house," the queen replied. "What am I doing in your father's house?" he asked. She responded: "Isn't this what you told me—'Whatever precious objects I own, take when you leave.' Nothing is more precious to me than you. Nothing delights me more than you do."

So the community of Israel said to the Holy One, blessed be He, when He asked them, "Whom do you wish me to bring back to life from his grave to go at your head to Babylonia?"[7] They replied: "You are the only one we want"—as it is said, "For You are our Father" (Isaiah 63:16). The Holy One, blessed be He, immediately responded, "Then I will be your companion. I will go up with you"—as it is said, "For your sake I have sent to Babylonia" (Isaiah 43:14).

—Pesikta Rabbati 141a

NOTES

1. Because Scripture writes that man "was created in the image of God" (Genesis 1:27), Rabbi Hoshaiah appears to believe that Adam so resembled His creator that the angels could not tell them apart. This parable is brought in reference to Genesis 1:26.

2. This verse is interpreted as though it were addressed to the angels. "A breath in his nostril" is taken to refer to the way a man breathes while he is asleep.

3. These last two lines might also be spoken by the man who makes the preceding statement.

4. Because the biblical script is unpointed and lacks vowelization, the vowels of a word can easily be repointed, thus changing one word into another—a technique the rabbis frequently exploit in midrash, as here, for the purposes of their interpretations. In this case, the noun *amo*, "his people," is read as *imo*, "with it," i.e., the soul.

5. "This" (*zot*) in Lamentations 3:21 is taken to refer to the Torah—a commonplace of rabbinic exegesis.

6. This verse is read, in effect, as "And He has kindled a fire in Zion which has devoured *only* its foundations."

7. That is, to exile in Babylonia, following the destruction of the Temple in 586 B.C.E.

2 ◆

TWO NARRATIVES ABOUT GOD

The following two narratives are preserved in Lamentations Rabbati, the amoraic midrash on the Book of Lamentations, as part of a *petihta*, or proem. The *petihta*, as its name suggests, was a sermon of introduction, originally perhaps to the weekly Torah reading in the synagogue or, as in this case, to the reading from the Book of Lamentations, which may possibly have been delivered on the Ninth of Av, the fast day in the Jewish liturgical calendar commemorating the destruction of the First and Second Temples.

The *petihta* in which these narratives are found is an exegesis of Isaiah 22:1–12. In its entirety, the *petihta* is extremely long and complex. For the last verse alone, Isaiah 22:12, three separate interpretations are offered, the final one being the lengthy passage containing the two narratives translated here. The complete passage, with both narratives, is found in only some of the manuscript traditions of the midrash, a fact which suggests that the textual sources and the history of transmission of this passage are equally complicated. Even in the manuscripts that preserve both narratives, the anonymous editor of the *petihta* did not distinguish between them. Indeed, from the way he combined the two, it appears that he considered them to be one continuous text.[1]

Close inspection immediately reveals, however, that the plots of the two narratives are independent of each other. Even more important, the portraits of God in the two narratives are so entirely different as to be almost incompatible. In the first narrative, God identifies Himself so totally with the Jews' catastrophe that, by the narrative's conclusion, He virtually claims to be its sole victim as well as chief mourner. In the second narrative, by contrast, He is portrayed as a distant, even indifferent, judge, who is moved to show compassion to the Jews only when the matriarch Rachel persuades Him that His motives are petty ones, unworthy of God.

The background to these remarkable narratives is unknown. Much lengthier and more fully developed than almost all other narratives in rabbinic literature, their characterizations of God are at once extreme and compelling, and highly problematic for any normative conception of divinity. For all their differences, both portraits derive from the paradox of the anthropomorphic imagination: Only the human image, in all its fallibility and mortality, could provide the rabbis with a model sufficiently complex to serve as the basis for their own attempts to imagine God's personality, so as to convey their own feelings about Him and His treatment of Israel.

The translation is based on the text of *petihta* 24, as reprinted in S. Buber's edition of Lamentations Rabbah (Vilna: 1899), pp. 25–28.[2]

Introduction and translation by
DAVID STERN

I

Here is another interpretation of "The Lord God of Hosts summoned on that day to weeping and lamenting, to tonsuring and girding with sackcloth" (Isaiah 22:12):

When the Holy One, blessed be He, sought to destroy the Temple, He said, "All the time that I am inside it, the nations of the world cannot harm the Temple. But I will turn my eyes aside and take a vow not to live in it until the end time. Let the enemies come and destroy the Temple!"

He immediately swore by His right hand and placed it behind Him, as it is said, "He has withdrawn His right hand in the presence of the enemy" (Lamentations 2:3). It was at that time that the enemy entered the sanctuary and burned it.

Once it had burned down, the Holy One, blessed be He, said, "I no longer have a residence on earth. I will remove My Presence, the Shekhinah, and ascend to my original habitation.[3] This is what is written: 'And I will return to My abode—till they realize their guilt, and they will seek Me' (Hosea 5:15)."

At that time, the Holy One, blessed be He, broke into weeping. He said, "Woe to Me! What have I done? I caused My Shekhinah to dwell below for Israel's sake, and now that they have sinned, I have returned to My original place. Banish the thought![4] I would have become a laughingstock for the gentiles, a thing of ridicule to human beings!"

At that moment, Metatron came and fell upon his face, and said: "Master of the universe! Allow me to weep! But You—do not weep!"[5]

The Holy One said to him, "If you do not leave Me alone to weep now, I will take Myself to a place that you have no permission to enter, and there I will weep, as it is said, 'If you will not give heed, My inmost self will weep in secret places because of your arrogance' (Jeremiah 13:17)."

The Holy One, blessed be He, said to the ministering angels, "Come!

49

Let us go, you and I, and see what the enemies have done in My house."
Immediately, the angelic host and the Holy One, blessed be He, went,
and Jeremiah went in front of Him.

As soon as the Holy One, blessed be He, saw the Temple, He said,
"Yes, indeed! This is My house. This is My resting-place. The enemy
came and did to it as it wished."

At that time, the Holy One, blessed be He, began to weep, saying,
"Woe to Me for My house! My children, where are you? My priests, where
are you? My lovers, where are you? What shall I do for you? I warned you.
But you did not repent!"

The Holy One, blessed be He, addressed Jeremiah, "I am like a man
who had a single son for whom he built a wedding chamber, and the son
died inside it. And yet you feel no hurt for Me, and none for My son!?
Go! Summon Abraham, Isaac, and Jacob and Moses from their graves—
they know how to weep!"

Jeremiah said, "Master of the universe! I do not know where Moses is
buried."

The Holy One, blessed be He, replied, "Go! Stand on the banks of the
Jordan, raise your voice, and shout, Ben Amram! Ben Amram! Arise!
And behold your flock whom the enemy has consumed."

Jeremiah immediately went to the Cave of Machpelah and said to the
patriarchs, "Arise! The time has come when your presence is requested
before the Holy One, blessed be He."

"Why?" they asked.

"I don't know," he replied—because he was afraid that they would say,
It was in your days that *this* happened to our children!

Jeremiah left them, and stood on the banks of the Jordan, and called
out: "Ben Amram! Ben Amram! Arise! The time has come when your
presence is requested before the Holy One, blessed be He."

Moses asked, "Why today is my presence requested before the Holy
One, blessed be He?"

"I don't know," Jeremiah answered.

Moses left Jeremiah and went off to the ministering angels, for he knew
them from the time of the giving of the Torah. "Heavenly attendants!" he
said to them, "Do you have any idea why my presence is requested before
the Holy One, blessed be He?"

"Ben Amram!" they said, "Don't you know that the Temple has been destroyed and the Israelites exiled?"

Moses cried aloud, and he wept until he reached the patriarchs, and they too immediately ripped their garments in mourning. They placed their hands upon their heads, and they cried out and wept all the way to the gates of the Temple.

As soon as the Holy One, blessed be He, saw them, then immediately "the Lord God of Hosts summoned on that day to weeping and lamenting, to tonsuring and girding with sackcloth" (Isaiah 22:12). If it were not explicitly written in Scripture it would be impossible to say it.

They went weeping from one gate to the next, like a man whose deceased kin still lies before him,[6] and the Holy One, blessed be He, lamented, saying, "Woe to that king who triumphed in his youth, and who failed in his old age."

II

Rabbi Samuel bar Nahman said: When the Temple was destroyed, Abraham came before the Holy One, blessed be He, weeping, tearing at his beard, pulling out the hair on his head, beating his face, ripping his garments, ash upon his head. He paced about the Temple, lamenting and crying out, and said to the Holy One, blessed be He, "Why am I different from every other nation and tongue that I have come to such shame and disgrace!?"

When the ministering angels saw Abraham, they too joined in lament, and standing in two rows, they said: "Highways are desolate, wayfarers have ceased, a covenant has been renounced, cities were rejected, mortal man was not considered" (Isaiah 33:8).[7]

What does the phrase "Highways are desolate" mean? The ministering angels said to the Holy One, blessed be He, "The highways to Jerusalem that You established so that pilgrims would never cease from them—how those highways have become desolate!"

"Wayfarers have ceased": The ministering angels said to the Holy One, blessed be He, "The roads on which the people of Israel came and went on holidays—how they have been made to cease!"

"A covenant has been renounced": The ministering angels said to the Holy One, blessed be He, "Master of the universe! That covenant has been renounced that was made with Abraham, their forefather, through whom the world was peopled and mankind came to acknowledge You as God supreme, Creator of heaven and earth."

"Cities were rejected": The ministering angels said to the Holy One, blessed be He, "You have rejected Jerusalem and Zion, and this *after* You chose them!" This is what is written: "Have You, then, rejected Judah? Have You spurned Zion?" (Jeremiah 14:19).

"Mortal man was not considered": The ministering angels said to the Holy One, blessed be He, "You did not even give the people of Israel the same consideration You gave the generation of Enosh, who were the first to worship idols!"

It was then that the Holy One, blessed be He, turned to the ministering angels and asked them, "What are you doing, composing laments on this matter and standing in rows?"

They replied, "Master of the universe! It is on account of Abraham, Your loving friend, who has come to Your house and lamented and wept! Why have You paid no attention to him?"

The Holy One replied, "Since the time my friend left Me to go to his eternal resting-place, he has not visited My house. And now, 'why should My beloved be in My house?' (Jeremiah 11:15)."

Abraham addressed the Holy One, blessed be He, "Master of the universe! Why have You exiled my children and handed them over to the nations, who murdered them in all kinds of horrible deaths? Why have You destroyed the Temple, the place to which I brought my son Isaac as a burnt offering to You?"

The Holy One, blessed be He, said to Abraham, "Your children sinned by transgressing against the entire Torah, against all twenty-two letters of the alphabet, of which the Torah is composed. This is what is written: 'All Israel has violated Your teaching' (Daniel 9:11)."

Abraham said to the Holy One, blessed be He, "Master of the universe! Who will offer testimony against Israel that they transgressed against Your Torah?"

He replied, "Let the Torah come and testify against Israel."

The Torah immediately came to be a witness against them. Abraham said to the Torah, "My daughter, are you really going to testify against Israel that they transgressed your commandments? Have you no shame in my presence? Remember the day that the Holy One, blessed be He, took you around to every nation and people, but no one wished to accept you—until my children came to Mount Sinai and accepted you and honored you. And now, are you about to testify against them on the day of their misfortune!?"

When the Torah heard this, she stepped to the side and did not testify against them. The Holy One, blessed be He, said to Abraham, "Let the twenty-two letters of the alphabet come and offer testimony against Israel."

The twenty-two letters immediately approached. The letter Alef was about to testify against Israel that they had transgressed against the Torah, but Abraham said, "Alef! You, the first of the letters, are about to testify against Israel on the day of their misfortune! Remember the day that the Holy One, blessed be He, revealed Himself on Mount Sinai and began with you, *Anokhi,* 'I am the Lord your God' (Exodus 20:2). No nation or people was willing to accept you—except for my children. And now you are about to testify against them!"

Alef immediately stood to the side and did not testify.

Then the letter Bet came to testify against Israel, but Abraham said, "My daughter, are you going to testify against my children? They are zealous for the five books of the Torah, and you are the Torah's beginning. This is what is written, *Bereshit,* 'In the beginning, God created' (Genesis 1:1)."

Bet immediately stood to the side and did not testify.

Then the letter Gimmel came to testify against Israel, but Abraham said to her, "Gimmel! Are you going to testify against my children that they transgressed the Torah? Does anyone except for my children perform the commandment of wearing fringes, *tsitsit*—the commandment that begins with you? For this is what is written, '*Gedilim,* tassels, you shall make on the four corners of the garment with which you cover yourself' (Deuteronomy 22:12)."

Gimmel immediately stood to the side and did not testify. And once the other letters saw that Abraham had silenced them, they too were embarrassed, and took themselves aside, and did not testify against Israel.

Abraham immediately commenced, saying before God, "Master of the universe! When I was one hundred years old, you granted me a son. And when he reached intellectual maturity, as a young man of thirty-seven years, then You told me, Offer him up as a burnt offering to Me. I made myself act without mercy for my son. I showed him no compassion. With my own hands I bound him. And will You not remember this for my sake and have mercy on my children?"

Isaac commenced and said, "Master of the universe! When father told me, 'God will see to the sheep for His burnt offering, my son' (Genesis 22:8), I did not hold back from Your command. I let myself be bound on the altar without resisting, and I stretched my neck out under the knife. Will You not remember this for my sake? Will You not pity my children?"

Jacob commenced and said, "Master of the universe! Did I not stay twenty years in Laban's house? And when I departed, Esau the wicked met me and sought to kill my children, but I offered to die in their place. And now they, my children, have been handed over to the enemy like sheep to the slaughter—after I raised them like little chicks, after I suffered the pains of child rearing on their behalf. For most of my life I suffered great trouble on their account. And now, You will not remember this for my sake and have compassion on my children!"

Moses commenced and said, "Master of the universe! Was I not a faithful shepherd for Israel for forty years? I ran in front of them like a steed in the desert, and when the time arrived for them to enter the land, You decreed that in the desert my bones were to descend. Now that they have been exiled, You have summoned me to lament and weep over them. That is how the folk saying goes: My master's good fortune is not good for me, but his bad fortune is bad for me."

It was then that Moses said to Jeremiah, "Lead me! I will go and gather them back. Let us see who will raise his hand against them."

Jeremiah replied, "It is impossible to walk on the road because of the dead."

Moses said, "Let us go nonetheless."

Immediately Moses went, with Jeremiah before him, until they reached the rivers of Babylon. When the Jews saw Moses, they said to each other, "Moses has risen from his grave to redeem us from the hands of our enemies."

A heavenly voice called out, saying, "This exile has been decreed by Me!"

Moses immediately said to the Israelites, "It is impossible to restore you. The decree has been issued. But God will restore you in the very near future."

And then he left them.

At that moment, the Israelites raised their voices in weeping so loud that it rose up to heaven. This is what is written, "By the rivers of Babylon, there we sat, sat and wept" (Psalm 137:1).

When Moses returned to the patriarchs, they asked him, "What has the enemy done to our children?"

He replied, "Some they killed. Others had their hands behind their backs. And still others were chained in iron fetters or stripped naked. Or they lay dead on the road, their carcasses given over to the birds of the heavens and the beasts of the earth. Or they were left exposed to the sun, hungry and thirsty."

Immediately, they all began to weep and lament [in Aramaic], "Woe for what has happened to our children! You are fatherless, like orphans! You must take your sleep at noontime, even in the heat of summer, without clothing and cover! You must walk over rocks and pebbles, stripped of shoes, without sandals! You must lug heavy burdens of sand! Your hands are bound behind your backs! You do not even have the luxury of swallowing the spit in your mouths."

Moses commenced and said, "You are accursed, O sun! Why did you not darken when the enemy entered the Temple?"

The sun replied, "By your life! Moses, faithful shepherd. How could I turn dark? They wouldn't let me. They wouldn't leave me alone. They lashed me with sixty whips of fire and said to me, Go forth and shine!"

Once more Moses commenced and said, "Woe for your splendor, O Temple! How has your splendor darkened! Woe that the time for its destruction arrived, the time for the sanctuary to be burned, for schoolchildren to be murdered, for their parents to suffer captivity, and exile, and death by the sword."

And again, Moses opened and said, "O captors! By your lives! If you come to kill, do not murder cruelly. Do not annihilate them entirely. Do not slay a son in his father's presence, or a daughter in her mother's. The day will come when the Lord of heaven will exact reckoning from you as well."

But the wicked Chaldeans[8] did not act as he requested. They set a child before its mother and then told the father, "Arise! Slay him." The mother wept. Her tears fell upon the child, and the father hung his head.

Again, Moses said before Him, "Master of the universe! You wrote in Your Torah, 'No animal from the herd or from the flock shall be slaughtered on the same day with its young' (Leviticus 22:28). And yet *they* have killed countless mothers with their children, and You have remained silent!"

At that moment, Rachel our mother leapt up before the Holy One, blessed be He, and said, "Master of the universe! You know full well that Jacob your servant loved me exceptionally, and that on my behalf he slaved seven years for my father. When those seven years were completed, and the time for my marriage to my husband had arrived, my father plotted to switch me with someone else for my sister's sake. It was a very trying thing for me to do, because I found out about the plot. I told my husband-to-be about it and gave him a secret sign so that he could distinguish between me and my sister. But then I had a change of mind. Feeling compassion for my sister, that she not be disgraced, I suppressed my desires. That night they substituted my sister for me and presented her to my husband in my place. I gave my sister all the secret signs I had entrusted to my husband, so that he would think that she was me, Rachel. What's more, I hid beneath the bed where he lay with my sister, and when he spoke to her, she was silent and I replied to his every word, so that he never recognized my sister's voice. I paid her kindness. I was not jealous, and I did not permit her to be disgraced or shamed. But You! eternally living King, Merciful One! Why are you jealous of idols that are without substance? Why have You exiled my children, to be slain by the sword and to be abused as the enemy has wished?"

Immediately, the compassion of the Holy One, blessed be He, was aroused. He said, "For your sake, Rachel, I will restore Israel to its place."

This is what is written: "Thus said the Lord: A cry is heard in Ramah—wailing, bitter weeping—Rachel weeping for her children. She refuses to be comforted for her children, who are gone" (Jeremiah 31:15). But it is also written there: "Thus said the Lord: Restrain your voice from weeping, your eyes from shedding tears; for there is a reward for your labor" (Jeremiah 31:16). And it is written: "And there is hope for your future— declares the Lord: Your children shall return to their country" (Jeremiah 31:17).

NOTES

1. For further discussion of the narratives and their textual history, see David Stern, *Parables in Midrash* (Cambridge: Harvard University Press, forthcoming), Appendix II.

2. Buber's text of the passage is, in fact, based on the Vilna edition of Midrash Rabbah; see his notes ad locum.

3. The Shekhinah is the technical name in rabbinic literature for God's immanent Presence in the world. According to some traditions, it accompanied Israel into exile; according to others, including this *petihta*, it returned to its original habitation in heaven following the destruction. Note, however, that despite God's initial statement, the Shekhinah does not actually leave the Temple until after it has been destroyed by the gentiles.

4. Hebrew *has ve-shalom* is usually translated as "God forbid," an impossible translation here, since it is God who is speaking. The thought that He banishes raises the possibility that He could have done otherwise.

5. Metatron is an archangel with a lengthy and complicated history in early rabbinic and mystical literature. In this narrative, he appears mainly as a defender of God's honor, the divine protocol officer.

6. This phrase is a technical term for the *onein*, the name in rabbinic literature for a mourner on the day that the deceased kin has died, before burial has taken place. The grief of the *onein* is considered to be so intense that rabbinic law excuses him from the obligation to perform the positive commandments of the law (e.g., praying).

7. From this point through the next five paragraphs, the ministering angels lament in midrashic fashion, that is, by expounding upon each phrase in Isaiah 33:8.

8. The Chaldeans are the Neo-Babylonian invaders who destroyed the First Temple in 586 B.C.E.

3 ◆

JONAH AND THE SAILORS
from *Pirkei de-Rabbi Eliezer*

Pirkei de-Rabbi Eliezer (The Chapters of Rabbi Eliezer) is a late midrashic-aggadic work that probably was composed sometime in the eighth century. Because the work contains a number of allusions to Islamic belief and shows its influence (sometimes in polemical terms), scholars believe that the final text was edited in a country that was part of the Islamic empire. No further facts about the work's literary history are known.

Pirkei de-Rabbi Eliezer is often described as an example of the genre known as the rewritten Bible. This genre consists of texts that present more or less independent stories that elaborate upon the biblical account. Although these tales draw on aggadot and midrashim from earlier commentaries upon the Bible, they weave these separate strands and patches of exegesis into the full cloth of whole narrative. This exegetical background is still visible in *Pirkei de-Rabbi Eliezer*, in the rabbinic comments that punctuate and interrupt the narrative. But the selection we have translated is also an excellent example of the way in which the work builds on the scriptural narrative.

Pirkei de-Rabbi Eliezer opens with a famous account of the education of Rabbi Eliezer ben Hyrcanus—hence the work's title—that culminates in a sermon Rabbi Eliezer preached before his father. That sermon praises God as Creator of the universe and then quickly evolves into an expansion of the Creation story. It supplies additional tales about the various events that occurred providentially on the different days of the week; these events correspond to the various creatures created on each day. Hence, on the fifth day, on which God created fish as well as the great sea monsters (Genesis 1:20–21), the author of *Pirkei de-Rabbi Eliezer* naturally recalls the greatest fish story in the Bible—the story of Jonah.

No critical text of *Pirkei de-Rabbi Eliezer* exists. This translation is based upon the available Hebrew text (Eshkol: Jerusalem: no date). An earlier English translation of the work was published by G. Friedlander in 1916.

Introduction and translation by
DAVID STERN

T he fifth day of the week was also the day on which Jonah fled from God's Presence.[1] Why did he flee? The first time God sent Jonah, he prophesied that the territory of Israel would be restored, and his words were fulfilled, as it is said, "It was he who restored the territory of Israel from Lebo-hamath to the sea of the Arabah, in accordance with the promise that the Lord, the God of Israel, had made through His servant, the prophet Jonah son of Amittai from Gath-hepher" (2 Kings 14:25). The second time God sent Jonah, he prophesied that Jerusalem would be destroyed. But after the Jerusalemites repented, the Holy One, blessed be He, acted with great kindness. He reconsidered His decree of doom and did not destroy the city. As a result, the Israelites called Jonah a false prophet.

Now the third time God sent Jonah to prophesy to Nineveh, he reasoned to himself: I know that these people are close to repenting. If they do, the Holy One, blessed be He, will aim His anger against Israel. It is bad enough that the Israelites call me a false prophet. Are the gentile nations to do the same? Let me flee to some place where His presence does not reach.[2] But where? The heavens? It is stated in Scripture that His Presence is there, as it is said, "His glory is above the heavens" (Psalm 113:4). Is there some place on earth? His Presence is everywhere, as it is said, "His presence fills all the earth" (Isaiah 6:3). I must flee to some place where His Presence has never been. Jonah went down to Jaffa, but he could not find a ship to board. The ship that he eventually boarded was already at sea, at a distance of two days' sailing from Jaffa. Why was this? To test Jonah. What did the Holy One, blessed be He, do? He brought a storm upon the ship and forced it to return to Jaffa. When Jonah saw the ship, he rejoiced, saying to himself: Now I know that my path has been laid straight before me.

"Let me sail with you," Jonah said to the sailors.

"We are going to the islands of the sea, to Tarshish," they told him.[3]

"I'll go with you," he answered.

Now seafarers usually pay their fare *after* they leave the ship. But Jonah was so delighted that he went and paid *beforehand,* as it is said, "Jonah started out to flee to Tarshish from the Lord's service. . . . He went down to Jaffa. . . . He paid the fare and went aboard" (Jonah 1:3).

They had sailed for a day when a storm struck them at sea from the east and from the west. Most ships go on their journeys and return safely, over quiet seas, but the ship that Jonah sailed on was in great distress, as it is said, "The ship was in danger of breaking up" (Jonah 1:4). Rabbi Hananiah commented: The sailors on the ship were of seventy different nationalities, and each one carried his native idol with him, as it is said, "In their fright, the sailors cried out, each to his own god" (Jonah 1:5). Prostrating themselves, they declared: "Let each person call in the name of his god. And the god who responds and rescues us in this distress—that one is God." Yet while each man called to his god, not one of them came to their aid.

Meanwhile, Jonah, who was in his own distress, had fallen asleep. The chief sailor came to him: "Here we are, hanging between life and death, and you sleep! From what nation are you?"

"I am a Hebrew," Jonah replied.

"We have heard that the God of the Hebrews is mighty," the chief sailor said. "Up, call upon Him! Perhaps your God will be kind to us,[4] and perform a miracle like the one He did for you at the Reed Sea."

Jonah said to the sailor, "I will not withhold the truth from you. I am to blame for this trouble. Heave me overboard, and the sea will be calmed"—as it is said, "He answered, 'Heave me overboard, etc.' " (Jonah 1:12).

R. Simeon commented: The sailors refused to cast Jonah into the ocean. But when they cast lots, the lot fell upon Jonah, as it is said, "They cast lots, etc." (Jonah 1:7). So what did they do? They took the cargo that was aboard and cast it into the sea in order to lighten the ship, but that did no good. They tried to row ashore, but they could not. What did they do then? They took Jonah and stood on the ship's deck and declared: "Lord, God of the universe! Do not make us shed innocent blood. We do not know who this man is."

"I am the cause of this distress," Jonah insisted. "Heave me overboard!"

They took Jonah and lowered him up to his knees into the ocean, and the sea quieted from its storm. But when they drew him back, the sea raged again. So they lowered him until his navel, and the sea's storm grew still; but when they lifted him out, it raged again. They lowered him up to his neck, and the sea quieted; but again, as soon as they had raised him, it raged. Finally, they lowered Jonah's entire body into the ocean. Immediately, the storm at sea ceased.

Rabbi Tarfon commented: The fish that swallowed Jonah had been assigned this task since the six days of Creation, as it is said, "The Lord provided a huge fish to swallow Jonah" (Jonah 2:1). Jonah entered its mouth the way a man enters a large synagogue. He stood there, and the eyes of the fish shone down upon him like two skylights.[5]

Rabbi Meir said: A precious stone was suspended in the fish's belly; it gave off light for Jonah like the sun at midday and it revealed to him everything that was in the depths of the ocean. About that precious stone, Scripture remarks, "Light is sown for the righteous" (Psalm 97:11).

The fish said to Jonah, "Do you not know that this is the day I am to be eaten by Leviathan?"[6]

"Take me with you," Jonah replied. Then he said to Leviathan: "It was for you that I descended into the ocean—to see the place of your habitation. For I am destined to take your tongue by a rope and to raise and sacrifice you for the great banquet of the righteous." Jonah showed the Leviathan his circumcised member, the sign of Abraham's faith. "Behold the covenant," he said. Leviathan turned and fled from Jonah a distance of two days' journey.

Jonah then said to the fish: "See! I saved you from the mouth of Leviathan. Now show me everything in the depths of the ocean."

The fish showed him the great river bearing the waters of Oceanus, as it is said, ". . . the deep engulfed me" (Jonah 2:6). Then it showed him the Reed Sea that the Israelites had crossed, as it is said, ". . . the weeds twined around my head" (Jonah 2:6). It showed him the places where the sea breaks, from which the waves depart, as it is said, ". . . all your breakers and billows swept over me" (Jonah 2:4); and the pillars of the earth and its foundations, as it is said, "the bars of the earth closed upon me forever" (Jonah 2:7); and Gehenna, as it is said, "You brought my life up from the pit, O Lord my God" (Jonah 2:7); and the nethermost underworld, Sheol, as it is said, "From the belly of Sheol I cried out, and You heard my voice" (Jonah 2:3). The fish showed Jonah the base of God's Temple, as it is said, "I sank to the base of the mountains" (Jonah 2:7)— from this verse we can deduce that Jerusalem is built upon seven mountains. And finally, the fish brought Jonah to the foundation stone of the world, set in the depths beneath the Temple of God, the place above which the sons of Korah stand and pray."[7]

"Jonah," the fish said, "you are now standing directly beneath God's Temple. Pray, and your prayers will be answered."

Jonah responded, "Wait here, right where you are, while I pray."

The fish stayed there, and Jonah began to pray to the Holy One, blessed be He: "Master of the universe! You are called He-who-lowers and He-who-raises. I have descended. Now raise me up. You are called He-who-causes-death and He-who-makes-live.[8] My soul has reached nearly unto death. Now revive me." But Jonah was not answered until out of his mouth came this promise: "What I have vowed I will perform" (Jonah 2:10). He said, "The vow I made to raise Leviathan and to sacrifice him in your presence I will fulfill on the day of Israel's deliverance."

The Holy One, blessed be He, immediately made a sign to the fish, and it cast up Jonah, as it is said, "The Lord commanded the fish, and it spewed Jonah out upon dry land" (Jonah 2:11).

The sailors, who witnessed all the miracles and great wonders that the Holy One, blessed be He, had performed for Jonah, immediately stood and cast their idols into the sea, every one of them, as it is said, "They who cling to empty folly foresake their own welfare" (Jonah 2:9). Then they returned to Jaffa and went up to Jerusalem where they had themselves circumcised, as it is said, "The men feared the Lord greatly; they offered a sacrifice to the Lord and they made vows" (Jonah 1:16).

But how could they offer sacrifice? Is it not true that sacrifices brought by gentiles are not accepted? The verse can mean only one thing: "sacrifice" is the blood of circumcision, which is like the blood of sacrifice. Each sailor vowed to bring his wife and entire household to worship the Lord of Jonah, and all of them fulfilled their vows. And because of these proselytes, the daily liturgy includes a prayer for the welfare of righteous converts.[9]

NOTES

1. For explanation of this opening statement, see the Introduction to this selection. The midrash knows that Jonah fled on the fifth day of the week because that is the day on which all the fish, including the one that swallows Jonah, were created.

2. The Hebrew literally reads, "to a place about which it is not said [in Scripture] that His Presence exists there."

3. See Isaiah 11:11.

4. Jonah 1:6.

5. Hebrew *afumiyot.* The meaning of this word is unclear.

6. For different traditions about Leviathan, see L. Ginzberg, *The Legends of the Jews* (Philadelphia: JPS, 1938, 1966), I:25ff. and notes.

7. These are the sons of Korah who were swallowed in the great earthquake along with their father; cf. Numbers 16. Here they are netherworld counterparts of the sons of Korah, an actual group of Levites who served in the Temple, to whom many hymns in the Book of Psalms are attributed.

8. The Hebrew for these titles, and for those in the previous lines, are *maaleh u-morid* and *meimit u-mehayeih.* Both phrases connote God's agency in the resurrection of the dead at the end time of the redemption.

9. This appears to be a reference to the thirteenth blessing in the daily Amidah prayer.

4 ◆

SEFER ZERUBBABEL

Sefer Zerubbabel, the *Book of Zerubbabel*, is perhaps the most influential of the medieval Hebrew apocalypses. Its picture of the last days made a deep impression on liturgical poets, on the authors of later apocalypses, and even on the followers of the messianic pretender Shabbetai Zvi a millennium later.[1]

An apocalypse is a work in which an angel, or sometimes God Himself, reveals secrets to a great figure of the biblical past. These secrets typically involve the contents of the heavens or the coming end of days, and the revelation usually takes the form of a guided tour of the heavens or the deciphering of a symbolic vision. The first apocalypses were written by Jews in the third century B.C.E., and the appeal of the genre was so great that well into the Middle Ages Jews and Christians continued to write apocalypses that drew on the forms, themes, and images established in much earlier centuries. One early Jewish apocalypse, the Book of Daniel, became part of the Hebrew Bible, while an early Christian apocalypse, the Book of Revelation, was canonized in the New Testament.

Sefer Zerubbabel was written against the background of the wars between Persia and the Byzantine Empire in the first several decades of the seventh century (604–30 C.E.). These wars touched Palestine and seem to have stirred messianic hopes among some Jews,[2] including the author of *Sefer Zerubbabel*, for whom the wars appear to be eschatological events leading to the appearance of the Messiah. The work mentions the defeat of the king of Persia and the subsequent victory of the Antichrist, Armilos,[3] who represents Christendom.

Sefer Zerubbabel takes its name from the seer to whom the secrets in the book are revealed. The historical Zerubbabel, the last descendant of the Davidic line to take a prominent part in Israel's history, was one of the leaders of the return of the exiled Jews to Jerusalem from Babylonia in the sixth century B.C.E. The prophets Haggai and Zechariah, who were his contemporaries, viewed him as a messianic figure chosen by God for his role in the rebuilding of the Temple (Haggai 2:20–23; Zechariah 3:8, 6:9–15). In keeping with the conventions of the apocalypse, which require a seer from the biblical past whose career often contributes to the message of the apocalypse, the anonymous author of *Sefer Zerubbabel* chose Zerubbabel as his hero and also anticipated the imminent arrival of another, more glorious, descendant of David, who would establish the Third Temple.

The revelations of *Sefer Zerubbabel* center on the course of events in the last days, from the apparent victory of the forces of evil led by Armilos to the ultimate triumph of the righteous. The revelations are made by an angel Zerubbabel meets during a vision that comes to him after he prays for knowledge about "the form of the eternal house." In the vision Zerubbabel is taken to the "city of blood," identified as Rome, which for our author meant Byzantium, the eastern Rome. He is eventually led to the "house of disgrace" (a church), a kind of antitemple. There he sees the beautiful statue of a woman (the Virgin Mary). With Satan as father, this statue gives birth to the Antichrist, Armilos. In the course of the events described by the angel the forces associated with Armilos and the antitemple come to rule the entire world. But in the end these forces are defeated, and at the conclusion of the work Zerubbabel has a vision of the descent of the heavenly Temple to earth. Now "the form of the eternal house" is revealed: unlike the Second Temple, it is made in heaven.

Many of the eschatological events of *Sefer Zerubbabel* derive from biblical prophecies,[5] and its language actively seeks to imitate the Bible through allusions and echoes, which are noted in the translation, as well as through direct quotations. But the Bible is not the only source on which the author of *Sefer Zerubbabel* drew. He was also heir to a varied body of rabbinic speculation about the Messiah and the coming of the messianic age.[6] Armilos, the central villain of *Sefer Zerubbabel*, does not appear in classical rabbinic literature, but he is a prominent figure in Jewish apocalyptic tradition from the seventh century on. His name may be a form of Romulus, and he is understood as the political and spiritual head of Rome, the evil empire.[7]

The most striking innovation in *Sefer Zerubbabel* is the role assigned to Hephzibah, the mother of the Davidic Messiah, in the events of the end. She defeats two kings with the help of her staff of wonders, and when the first Messiah, Nehemiah from the tribe of Ephraim, is slain, she guards the east gate of Jerusalem so that some of the Jews can remain in the city. Nowhere else in Jewish messianic speculation is the mother of the Messiah so important a figure, and even here her role has not been fully integrated into the traditional picture.[8] Despite the wide influence of *Sefer Zerubbabel*, Hephzibah disappears completely from the Jewish apocalyptic tradition; later authors must have been uncomfortable with a woman taking so prominent a part in the eschatological drama.[9]

Some scholars have proposed that the events described in *Sefer Zerubbabel* reflect a messianically motivated Jewish rebellion in Jerusalem and that Hephzibah represents an important female leader in this rebellion.[10] This claim seems overliteral, especially because *Sefer Zerubbabel* constitutes the only evidence for such a rebellion. I would suggest instead that the figure of Hephzibah should be understood as a counterpart to the figure of the Virgin Mary in contemporary Byzantine culture.

At the time *Sefer Zerubbabel* was composed, representations of the Virgin Mary were prominent among the palladia, or images, the Byzantines sometimes used to protect cities under siege or armies in battle. It is known that Heraklios, the emperor represented by Armilos in *Sefer Zerubbabel*, once carried a statue of the Virgin into battle with him.[11] If, as seems likely, our author was aware of this practice, the military role assigned to Hephzibah represents an attempt to offer a Jewish answer to the Virgin. It is clear, however, that the figure of the Virgin aroused strong but ambivalent feelings in our author. Thus, the stone statue is the mother of the Antichrist, but she is also surpassingly beautiful. Perhaps other Jews shared his feelings.

Like other medieval apocalypses, Christian as well as Jewish, *Sefer Zerubbabel* includes a number of blocks of traditional material that are only loosely integrated into the work. This becomes evident when the various manuscripts and printed editions are compared. In addition to the main plot sketched above, there are whole units, such as the signs of Armilos and the list of the ten kings, that are omitted in some versions or that appear in different places within the text.[12] The eschatological timetables are integrated in different ways into the various versions of *Sefer Zerubbabel*, and in some, including the manuscript translated here, the revealing angel is called both Michael and Metatron.[13]

It is often assumed that the simplest, clearest form of a work is the earliest. But in the case of *Sefer Zerubbabel* the core of the work draws on traditional materials that do not always fit together perfectly, and it may be that some of the simpler versions represent later attempts to eliminate these problems. I have chosen to translate the most inclusive form of *Sefer Zerubbabel*, which contains all the elements that become part of the tradition of medieval Jewish apocalyptic speculation. This form is found in a manuscript in the Bodleian Library. MS. Heb. d. 11 fol. 248r–251r,[14] which Israel Lévi published in 1914 in *Revue des études juives* 68, with variant readings drawn from printed editions and other manuscripts, and a French translation.[15]

This translation is based on a fresh examination of the manuscript through silver prints supplied by the Curators of the Bodleian. At a number of points it has been possible to improve on or correct Lévi's readings. I also consulted the printed editions edited by Adolph Jellinek (*Beit ha-Midrash* [1853–78; reprint, Jerusalem: Wahrmann, 1967], 2:54–57); S. A. Wertheimer (*Batei Midrashot*, 2d ed. [Jerusalem: Mosad ha-Rav Kook, 1954], 2:497–505); Yehudah Even Shmuel (*Midreshei Geulah*, 2d ed. [Jerusalem and Tel Aviv: Mosad Bialik, 1954], 55–88); and the translations of Lévi (cited above, as well as the continuation of his discussion in *Revue des études juives* 68 [1914], 108–21; 71 [1920], 57–65) and George Wesley Buchanan (*Revelation and Redemption: Jewish Documents of Deliverance from the Fall of Jerusalem to the Death of Nahmanides* [Dillsboro: Western North Carolina Press, 1978], 338–86). I also drew on the very helpful notes of Lévi and Even Shmuel. I have not indicated corrections of the obvious minor mistakes in the manuscript, but I discuss weightier changes in the notes. I would like to thank the Curators of the Bodleian Library for their permission to publish this translation.[16]

Introduction and translation by
MARTHA HIMMELFARB

T he word that came to Zerubbabel ben Shealtiel, governor of Judah, on the twenty-fourth day of the seventh month.[17] The Lord showed me this vision there. I was prostrate in prayer before the Lord my God during the apparition of the vision I saw on the Chebar (River).[18] When I said, "Blessed are You, Lord, who revives the dead,"[19] my heart groaned within me saying, What will be the form of the eternal house?[20]

The Lord answered me from the doors of heaven, "Are you Zerubbabel son of Shealtiel, governor of Judah?"

"I am Your servant," I said.

He answered me and spoke as a man speaks to a friend.[21] I heard His voice, but I did not see His form.[22] Then I went on to prostrate myself as at first. I finished my prayer and went to my house.

On the eleventh day of the month of Adar He spoke to me there, saying, "O Zerubbabel, my servant."

"I am Your servant," I said.

"Come to me," he said. "Ask and I will tell you."

"How shall I ask," I answered, "for my end draws near, and my days are numbered."[23]

"I will make you live," he said. "Be alive."

Then a spirit lifted me between heaven and earth[24] and led me about Nineveh, the great city,[25] which is the city of blood.[26]

"Woe is me," I said. "My heart has been false,[27] and my soul is very sad." Then I rose from my sorrow to pray and beseech the name of the Lord God of Israel. I confessed all my sins and transgressions, for my heart had been false. "O Lord," I said, "I have gone astray, I have sinned, I have transgressed, for my heart has been false. You, O Lord, are the God who made everything by the utterance of Your mouth, and by the word of Your lips[28] the dead will come to life."

Then He said to me, "Go to the house of disgrace, to the house of merriment." I went as He commanded. "Turn yourself this way," He said.

When I turned, He touched me, and I saw a man, despised and wounded, lowly and in pain.[29]

Now that despised man said to me, "Zerubbabel, what is your business here? Who brought you here?"

"The spirit of the Lord lifted me up," I answered, "and deposited me in this place."

"Fear not," he said, "for you have been brought here in order to show you."[30]

When I heard his words, I took comfort, and my mind was at rest. "My lord," I asked, "what is the name of this place?"

"This is Rome the Great, in which I am imprisoned," he said.

"My lord, who are you," I asked, "and what is your name? What do you seek here? What are you doing in this place?"

"I am the Lord's anointed, the son of Hezekiah,"[31] he answered, "and I am imprisoned until the time of the end." When I heard this, I was silent and I hid my face. His anger burned within him.[32] I beheld him[33] and was afraid.

"Come closer," he said, and my limbs trembled. He extended his hand and supported me. "Fear not," he said. "Do not be afraid in your heart." He strengthened me and asked, "Why did you fall silent and hide your face?"[34]

"Because you said, 'I am the servant of the Lord and His anointed, and the light of Israel,' " I replied. [Suddenly][35] he looked to me like a young man, a handsome and comely youth. I asked him, "When will the light of Israel come?"

As I was speaking to him, behold, a man with two wings came and said, "Zerubbabel, what are you asking the Lord's anointed one?"

"I am asking when the time of salvation will come," I answered.

"Ask me," he said, "and I will tell you."

"Who are you, my lord?" I asked.

"I am Michael,"[36] he answered. "I am the one who announced good news to Sarah.[37] I was the commander of the host of the Lord God of Israel who fought against Sennacherib and struck down 180,000 men.[38] I was the commander of Israel who fought the wars against the kings of Canaan.[39] And in the future I shall fight the wars of the Lord at the side of the Lord's anointed, that man who sits before you, against the king with the arrogant face[40] and against Armilos son of Satan, who came out from the statue of stone.[41] The Lord appointed me as commander of his people and those who love him to fight against the commanders of the nations."

Then Michael, who is Metatron, answered,[42] "I am the angel who led Abraham through all the land of Canaan and I blessed him in the name of the Lord.[43] I am the one who redeemed Isaac and cried over him.[44] I am the one who struggled with Jacob at the ford of Jabbok.[45] I am the one who led Israel in the wilderness for forty years in the name of the Lord.[46] I am the one who appeared to Joshua at Gilgal.[47] And I am the one who rained fire and brimstone on Sodom and Gomorrah.[48] For he put his name within me, Metatron, in gematria, the Almighty.[49]

"Now you, Zerubbabel, son of Shealtiel, son of Jeconiah,[50] ask and I shall tell you what will happen to your people at the end of days."

[Zerubbabel asked, "Who is this man here?"][51]

He answered, "This is the Lord's anointed, who is hidden in this place until the end time. This is the Messiah son of David, and his name is Menahem son of Amiel.[52] He was born at the time of David, king of Israel, and a wind lifted him up and hid him in this place until the end time."[53]

Now I, Zerubbabel, asked Metatron the commander of the Lord's host, ["What are the signs that Menahem son of Amiel will perform?"][54]

"The Lord will give Hephzibah,[55] the mother of Menahem son of Amiel, a staff for these acts of salvation," he said. "A great star will shine before her. All the stars will swerve from their paths. Hephzibah, the mother of Menahem son of Amiel, will go out and kill two kings whose hearts are set on doing evil.[56] The names of the two kings: Nof, king of Yemen, who will wave his hand[57] at Jerusalem. The name of the second, Iszinan,[58] king of Antioch. This war and these signs will take place on the festival of weeks in the third month.

"For this word is true. Four hundred and twenty years after the city and the Temple are rebuilt, they will be destroyed a second time.[59] And twenty years after the city of Rome has been built, after seventy kings corresponding to the seventy nations of the world have ruled over her, when ten kings have completed their reigns, the tenth king will come.[60] He will destroy the Temple, the regular offering will cease,[61] the holy nation[62] will be scattered, and he will give them over to the sword, to pillage and panic. Many of them will fall because they observe the Torah, so they will abandon the Lord's Torah and worship idols. And when they stumble, they will be helped with a little help.[63] From the day that the regular offering ceases and the wicked ones place him whose name is abomination in the Temple,[64] at the end of 990 years, the Lord's salvation will appear, when the shattering of the power of the holy people comes to an end,[65] to redeem and gather them by the hand of the Lord's anointed.

"Now the staff that the Lord will give to Hephzibah, the mother of Menahem son of Amiel, is made of almond wood, and it is hidden away in Rakkath, a city in Naphtali.[66] This is the staff that the Lord gave Adam and Moses and Aaron and Joshua and King David; it is the staff that blossomed and sprouted in the tent at the time it belonged to Aaron.[67] Elijah son of Eleazar[68] hid it in Rakkath, which is Tiberias. Also hidden away there is a man named Nehemiah son of Hushiel, son of Ephraim, son of Joseph.

Then Zerubbabel answered Metatron and Michael the commander,[69] "My lord, I would like you to tell me when the Lord's anointed will come and what will happen after all this."

"The Lord's anointed, Nehemiah son of Hushiel, will come five years after Hephzibah and gather all Israel as one," he said. "The children of Israel will remain in Jerusalem for forty years and offer sacrifice, and it will be pleasing to the Lord. Nehemiah will register Israel by families.[70]

"Then in the fifth year of Nehemiah and the gathering of the holy ones, Shiroi, king of Persia, will go up against Nehemiah son of Hushiel and Israel, and there will be great trouble for Israel. Hephzibah, the wife of Nathan the prophet, the mother of Menahem son of Amiel, will go out with the staff that the Lord God of Israel gave her. The Lord will give them a spirit of confusion,[71] and men will kill their neighbors and brothers. There the wicked one will die."

When I heard this, I fell on my face. "My lord," I said, "tell me what the prophet Isaiah meant when he said, 'There the calves graze, there they lie down and consume its boughs'" (27:10).

He replied, "The calf is Nineveh, the city of blood, which is Rome the Great."

There I continued to ask about the prince of the holy covenant.[72] He seized me and took me to the house of disgrace and merrymaking[73] and showed me a marble stone in the shape of a virgin. The beauty of her appearance was wonderful to behold.

"This statue is the wife of Belial," he said. "Satan will come and lie with her, and she will bear a son named Armilos. He will destroy the people. In the Hebrew language . . .[74] He will rule over all, and his dominion will reach from one end of the earth to the other. There will be ten letters in his hand.[75] He will worship strange gods and speak falsehood.[76] No one will be able to stand before him. He will slay by the sword anyone who does not believe in him, and he will slay many of them. He will attack the men of the holy ones of the Most High[77] with the help of ten kings, in might and great strength.[78] He will make war on the holy ones and destroy them. He will kill the Messiah son of Joseph, Nehemiah son of Hushiel, and sixteen righteous men with him. Then they will exile Israel to the wilderness in three groups.[79] But Hephzibah, the mother of Menahem son of Amiel, will stand at the east gate so that wicked man will not come there, in order to fulfill the verse, 'But the rest of the population shall not be uprooted from the city' (Zechariah 14:2).

"This war will take place in the month of Av, and there will be trouble in Israel such as there never was before. People will flee to citadels, mountains, and caves; no one will be able to hide from him. All the nations of the world will stray after him, except Israel, who will not believe in him. For forty-one days all Israel will mourn Nehemiah son of Hushiel. His corpse will be thrown down before the gates of Jerusalem and broken, but no wild beast will touch it, no bird or animal. Then the children of Israel will cry out to the Lord from great oppression and deep trouble, and the Lord will answer them."

When I heard the word of the Lord's prophecy, I was very troubled. I got up and went to the canal,[80] and I cried out there before the Lord God of Israel, the God of all flesh.[81] Then He sent his angel to me while the prayer was still on my lips, before I had completed it. The Lord sent His angel to me, and when I saw him, I knew that he was the angel who had spoken to me earlier. I knelt and bowed before him, and he touched me again as he had the first time. Then he asked, "What is troubling you, Zerubbabel?"

"My lord," I answered, "the spirit within me pains me."[82]

"Ask," Metatron said, "and I shall tell you before I leave you."

So I continued to question him. "My lord Metatron," I asked, "when will the light of Israel come?"

He said, "I swear by the Lord, who sent me and made me commander of Israel, that I shall tell you His deeds, for the Holy God told me, 'Go to my servant Zerubbabel, and tell him whatever he asks you.' "

Then Michael, who is Metatron, said, "Come here! Listen to all that I tell you. For the word I speak to you is true; it is from the words of the living God. Menahem son of Amiel will come suddenly in the first month, the month of Nisan, on the fourteenth day of the month,[83] and he will make a stand in the valley of Arbael[84] which belongs to Joshua son of Jehozadak the priest.[85] The sages of Israel who have survived will all go out to him, for only a few will survive the attack and pillage of Gog and Armilos and the plundering of the plunderers. Menahem son of Amiel will say to the elders and sages, 'I am the Lord's anointed. The Lord sent me to bring you good news and to save you from the hands of these enemies.' But the elders[86] will look upon him and despise him, for all they will see is a lowly man in worn-out clothes, and they will despise him as you did. Then his anger will burn within him. He will put on clothes of vengeance as a garment and wrap himself in a mantle of zeal.[87]

"Then he will go to the gates of Jerusalem, and Elijah the prophet will be with him.[88] They will awaken Nehemiah son of Hushiel and bring him back to life at the gates of Jerusalem. Then Hephzibah, the mother of the Messiah, will come and hand over to him the staff by which the signs were performed. The children of Israel and their elders will all go to see that Nehemiah is alive and standing on his feet. They will believe at once in the Messiah." Thus Metatron, the commander of the host of the Lord, adjured me, "In truth this matter shall come to pass, for there shall be peaceful understanding[89] between them, as in Isaiah's prophecy, 'Ephraim shall not envy Judah, and Judah shall not harass Ephraim' (Isaiah 11:13).

"On the twenty-first day of the first month of the completion of 990 years from the destruction of Jerusalem, there will be salvation for Israel from the Lord. Menahem son of Amiel, Nehemiah son of Hushiel, and Elijah the prophet will come and stand at the great sea and read from the Lord's prophecy. The corpses of all the children of Israel who threw themselves into the sea to escape their enemies will come forth,[90] and a wave will come up out of the sea, bring them to the surface, and cast them alive into the Valley of Jehoshaphat near the Valley of Shittim (Joel 4:18). For there the judgment of all the nations will take place.[91]

"In the second month, Iyyar, the congregation of Korah will come up to the plains of Jericho at the Valley of Shittim.[92] They will come to Moses, and the banner of the Korahites will be gathered in.[93]

"On the eighteenth day of the month mountains and hills will quake. The earth will be shaken, everything in it, and the sea and all in it.

"On the first day of the third month the dead of the wilderness will come to life,[94] and they will come in families to the Valley of Shittim.

"On the eighteenth of Sivan there will be a great earthquake in the Land of Israel.

"In Tammuz, the fourth month, the Lord God of Israel will descend upon the Mount of Olives, which will split[95] at His rebuke. The Lord will blow a great shofar.[96] All the strange gods and every temple of images and wall and cliff will fall to the ground.[97] The Lord will strike all their plunderers. He will fight against those nations. Like a warrior He will stir up His zeal.[98] Menahem son of Amiel, the anointed of the Lord, will come, and he will breathe on Armilos with his nostrils and slay him.[99] The Lord will lay each man's sword upon his neighbor's neck,[100] and there they will fall dead. Then the holy nation will go out to see the salvation of the Lord. With their own eyes[101] all the children of Israel will see the Lord, like a man of war with a helmet of salvation on His head, dressed in armor.[102] He will do battle against Gog and Magog[103] and against the forces of Armilos, and they will all fall dead in the valley of Arbael. Then all Israel will go forth to plunder their plunderers and despoil their despoilers for seven months.[104] But a fraction [of the enemy] will escape and gather at Zela ha-Eleph,[105] five hundred men, and a hundred thousand dressed in armor. [Against them] will be five hundred men of Israel, with Nehemiah, Elijah, and you, Zerubbabel, at their head. And [you] will kill all of them, for there one man shall pursue a thousand.[106]

"This will happen in the third war, for there will be three wars in the Land of Israel: one that Hephzibah will wage against Shiroi, king of Persia, another that the Lord God of Israel and Menahem son of Amiel will wage against Armilos and the ten kings with him and Gog and Magog, and a third at Zela ha-Eleph, which Nehemiah son of Hushiel and Zerubbabel will wage. This third war will take place in the month of Av.

"After all this has come to pass, Menahem son of Amiel will come, and Nehemiah son of Hushiel and all Israel will be with him. All the dead will come to life, and Elijah the prophet will be with them. They will go up to Jerusalem, and in the month of Av, during which they mourned Nehemiah and in which Jerusalem was destroyed, there will be great joy for Israel. They will offer sacrifices to the Lord, and the Lord will accept them. Israel's offering will be pleasing to the Lord as it used to be in ancient times.[107] The Lord will smell the sweet savor of His people Israel and rejoice greatly. He will bring down to earth the Temple that was built above, and the pillar of fire and the cloud of incense will ascend to heaven. Then the Messiah will set out on foot to the gates of Jerusalem, and all Israel will come after him.

"Then the Holy God will stand on the Mount of Olives. His awe and glory will rest upon the heavens and the highest heavens, over the whole earth and its depths, upon all walls, buildings, and foundations. Not a breath will be drawn, for the Lord God will reveal Himself before all on the Mount of Olives. The Mount of Olives will split beneath Him, and the exiles of Jerusalem will ascend to the Mount of Olives. Zion and Jerusalem will see and ask, 'Who bore us these? . . . and where were these?'[108] Then Nehemiah and Zerubbabel will answer Jerusalem, 'Here are your children whom you bore and who were exiled from you. Rejoice greatly, daughter of Jerusalem.' "[109]

Again I began to ask Metatron, the commander of the Lord's host, "My lord, show me Jerusalem, its length and width and construction." So he showed me the walls of Jerusalem round about it, walls of fire,[110] from the great wilderness to the Mediterranean Sea to the Euphrates River.[111] He showed me also the Temple building, and the Temple was built on five mountain tops that the Lord chose to bear His sanctuary, Lebanon, Mount Moriah, Tabor, Carmel, and Hermon.[112]

Then Michael answered,[113] "When 990 years from the destruction of Jerusalem have been completed, I will bring salvation to Israel."

Then he explained to me more about the word and the vision, for at the beginning he had said, "If you will inquire, inquire; come back again.[114]

"On the fifth of the week[115] Nehemiah son of Hushiel will come and gather all Israel together. On the sixth of the week Hephzibah, the wife of Nathan the prophet, who was born in Hebron,[116] will come and kill the two kings Nof and Esrogan.[117] In that year Menahem son of Amiel, the root of Jesse, will come forth, and ten kings will arise from among the nations. They will not be able to rule even a week and a half out of the year, year after year.[118]

"These ten kings will rise over the nations during seven years. Their names are as follows, according to their cities and in the order in which they arose:[119]

"The first king is Silqom, and the name of his city is Sepharad, which is Aspamia, the land of the sea. The second is Hertomos; his city is Gitnia. The third is Plios; his city is Plavis. The fourth is Galvas; his city is Galia. The fifth is Remoshdis; his city is Moditikha. The sixth is Moqlanos; his city is Italia. The seventh is Okhtinos; his city is Dormis. The eighth is Aplostos, from Aram-naharaim.[120] The ninth is Shiroi, king of Persia. And the tenth king is Armilos, son of Satan, who came forth from the stone statue of a woman. He will rule over all of them.

"He will come with the kings of Qedar and the children of Qedem[121] and start a war in the valley of Arbael, and the kingdom will be theirs. He will ascend in his strength and conquer the whole world. And from there, in Riblah,[122] which is Antioch, he will begin to plant the sacred posts of all the nations on the face of the earth and to worship their false gods, whom God hates. In those days there will be wages neither for men nor for beasts.[123] He will build four altars, and he will anger the Lord by his evil deeds. For forty days there will be an extremely severe famine on the face of the earth. Their bread will be mallow; they will pick leaves of bushes and broom for their sustenance.[124] On that day a fountain will come forth from the House of the Lord and water the Valley of Shittim.[125]

"This Armilos will then take his mother, the stone from which he was born, out of the house of disgrace of the scoffers. From all over, the nations will come to worship that stone, burn incense, and pour libations to her. No one will be able to look upon her face because of her beauty. Whoever does not bow down to her will die, suffering like an animal.

"This is the sign of Armilos: the hair of his head is colored like gold. He is green to the soles of his feet. The width of his face is a span. His eyes are deep. He has two heads. He will rise and rule the province with terror. Satan is the father of Belial. All who see him will tremble.

"Menahem will rise from the Valley of Shittim and breathe with his nostrils to slay him, as it is written, 'He shall . . . slay the wicked with the breath of his lips' (Isaiah 11:4). The kingdom will belong to Israel, and the holy ones of the Most High will receive the kingdom."[126]

These are the words Metatron spoke to Zerubbabel son of Shealtiel, governor of Judah, in the midst of the exile in the days of the kingdom of Persia. Zechariah son of Anan and Elijah wrote them down in complete exile.[127]

NOTES

1. For the influence of *Sefer Zerubbabel*, see Yehudah Even Shmuel, *Midreshei Geulah*, 2d ed. (Jerusalem and Tel Aviv: Mosad Bialik, 1954), 66, and Joseph Dan, *Ha-Sippur ha-Ivrit bi-Yemei ha-Beinayim* (Jerusalem: Keter, 1974), 43–46.

2. For the historical setting, see Salo W. Baron, *A Social and Religious History of the Jews*, 2d ed. (New York and Philadelphia: Columbia University Press and Jewish Publication Society, 1957–), 3:18–24. Further evidence that these events gave rise to messianic expectations is found in *Sefer Eliyyahu*, another medieval Hebrew apocalypse.

3. I spell Armilos with an *o* as in Greek, rather than a *u* as in Latin, because for the author of *Sefer Zerubbabel* Greek was the language of Christendom.

4. These messianic hopes in the early Second Temple period probably involved only the restoration of the monarchy and the Temple rather than the larger messianic agenda that develops later.

5. The books of Ezekiel, Zechariah, and Daniel are especially prominent. For a discussion of *Sefer Zerubbabel* as an interpretation of biblical texts, see Robert L. Wilken, "The Restoration of Israel in Biblical Prophecy: Christian and Jewish Responses in the Early Byzantine Period," in *"To See Ourselves As Others See Us": Christians, Jews, "Others" in Late Antiquity*, ed. Jacob Neusner and Ernest S. Frerichs (Chico, Calif.: Scholars Press, 1985), 443–71, esp. 453–61.

6. Among the features of the picture of the last days presented in *Sefer Zerubbabel* that are known from rabbinic literature are the Messiah descended from the tribe of Ephraim who falls in battle before the coming of the victorious Davidic Messiah (B. Sukkah 52a); the name of the Davidic Messiah, Menahem (P. Berakhot 2:4, B. Sanhedrin 98b); the birth of the Messiah long before his appearance and his occultation until the appropriate moment (P. Berakhot 2:4, B. Sanhedrin 98a); the place of hiding as Rome (B. Sanhedrin 98a; because of medieval censorship some printed editions substitute "city" for Rome); and the

suffering of the Messiah and his unprepossessing appearance (B. Sanhedrin 98a–b).

7. For a collection of texts about Armilos, see Raphael Patai, *The Messiah Texts* (Detroit: Wayne State University Press, 1979), 156–64. See also Dan, *Ha-Sippur ha-Ivrit*, 40–43.

8. Hephzibah fits only uneasily with the by now traditional picture of two Messiahs; she appears first with the Messiah son of Ephraim and only later with the Davidic Messiah, who is designated as her son. For a slightly different view of the lack of integration of Hephzibah and the Messiah son of Ephraim, see Dan, *Ha-Sippur ha-Ivrit*, 39.

9. On other mothers of the Messiah in earlier and later Jewish texts, see Patai, *Messiah Texts*, 122–30. None of them plays an active role in the unfolding of the messianic drama.

10. See Even Shmuel, *Midreshei Geulah*, 64–65; Baron, *History* 5:141.

11. This took place during Heraklios's effort to seize the empire from his predecessor Phokas. When Constantinople came under siege by the Avars during Heraklios's reign, the patriarch Sergios had pictures of the Virgin and the Christ child painted on the gates of the west side of the city. See Ernst Kitzinger, "The Cult of Images in the Age Before Iconoclasm," *Dumbarton Oaks Papers* 8 (Cambridge: Harvard University Press, 1954), 110–12, and references there. Israel Lévi in his groundbreaking study, "L'apocalypse de Zorobabel et le roi de Perse Siroès," *Revue des études juives* 71 (1920): 60, notes these uses of the image of the Virgin and relates them to the statue of the virgin in *Sefer Zerubbabel*, but he does not connect the figure of Hephzibah to the Virgin.

12. The signs of Armilos belong to a tradition of signs of the Antichrist that differ from each other in detail but not in general outline. They appear in a range of Jewish and Christian works. See Michael Stone and John Strugnell, *The Books of Elijah, Parts 1 and 2* (Texts and Translations 18, Pseudepigrapha Series 8; Missoula, Mont.: Scholars Press, 1979), 27–39.

13. This is true also of the text in S. A. Wertheimer, *Batei Midrashot*, 2d ed. (Jerusalem: Mosad ha-Rav Kook, 1954), where the angel identifies himself as "Metatron, whose name is Michael."

14. This is according to the present cataloging system. Lévi, "L'apocalypse de Zorobabel," refers to the manuscript as 2797.

15. The version in Even Shmuel, *Midreshei Geulah*, has the appearance of a critical edition, but as Baron (*History* 5:354 n. 3), writes, "somewhat arbitrarily rearranged, it is more readable than authentic." Even Shmuel has improved the logic of the work (according to his view) at many points without any textual warrant. Lévi's publication of the Bodleian manuscript is the closest thing to a critical edition, but his notes on variant readings are far from complete.

16. I would like to thank David Stern for his very helpful comments on the translation. I would also like to thank Richard Lim for the help he provided as my research assistant.

17. The formula "The word that came to . . ." and variants is common as an

introduction to prophecy. See, e.g., Hosea 1:1; Joel 1:1; Micah 1:1; Zechariah 1:1. The date of Zerubbabel's vision differs from edition to edition.

18. The identification of Zerubbabel as governor of Judah might lead to the conclusion that "there" means Judah, but the text goes on to place the vision at the river Chebar in Babylonia, site of Ezekiel's vision of the chariot throne of God (Ezekiel 1). There are some further indications later in the work that the author had in mind a Babylonian location for Zerubbabel's vision. After he hears of the death of the Messiah son of Ephraim, Zerubbabel goes to the canal (*amat ha-mayyim*), which appears to be a reference to the Chebar. The conclusion of *Sefer Zerubbabel*, "These are the words Metatron spoke to Zerubbabel son of Shealtiel, governor of Judah, in the midst of the exile," also points in this direction. By the time of Zerubbabel, Cyrus of Persia had already permitted the return of the Judeans to their homes. So it seems likely that "exile" here is meant in the geographical sense as Babylonia.

I would like to thank Mark Mirsky for his suggestions about this question.

19. This is the second of the eighteen benedictions, which constitute the central prayer of every service.

20. "Eternal house" is a rabbinic term for the Temple.

21. See Exodus 33:11.

22. Cf. Deuteronomy 4:12, "You heard the sound [literally voice] of words but perceived no shape." "Shape" here is *temunah*; "form" in the text translates *mareh*.

23. See Lamentations 4:18.

24. See Ezekiel 8:3.

25. See Jonah 3:3.

26. The phrase appears in Ezekiel 22:2, 24:6,9; Nahum 3:1.

27. See Hosea 10:2.

28. See Psalm 17:4.

29. The description of the despised man draws on the description of the suffering servant in Isaiah 53:3–5. In the classic rabbinic description of the suffering Messiah (B. Sanhedrin 98a), Rabbi Joshua son of Levi meets the Messiah, who is sitting among the poor and sick at the entrance to the city of Rome, binding and unbinding his wounds, as he waits for the time he is to manifest himself. (Because of medieval censorship some editions of the Talmud read "city" for Rome.) The language of Isaiah 53 does not appear in this passage, but later in the same discussion (B. Sanhedrin 98b), the rabbis quote Isaiah 53:4 as a source for a name of the Messiah.

30. See Ezekiel 40:4. In Ezekiel, these words are spoken by the angel who guides Ezekiel about the eschatological Temple with instructions to pay close attention.

31. The name Menahem son of Hezekiah appears in B. Sanhedrin 98b as a name for the Messiah. Lamentations 1:16 is used as a prooftext for the name Menahem; see also P. Berakhot 2:4 and Lamentations Rabbah 1:51. There are rabbinic traditions that God considered appointing Hezekiah, the righteous king of Judah, as Messiah (see B. Sanhedrin 94a, Song of Songs Rabbah 4:8:3). As a

descendant of David, Hezekiah would seem an appropriate choice for father of the messiah. But the passage in P. Berakhot and Lamentations Rabbah places the birth of Menahem at the time of the destruction of the Second Temple, so that King Hezekiah could not possibly be the father.

32. The manuscript reads, "My anger burned within me." But why should Zerubbabel be angry here? My translation follows the reading of Wertheimer's text. This reading seems to be supported by a later passage in the work, in which Menahem son of Amiel announces to the sages of Israel that he is the Messiah. They look at him and see only a lowly man in worn-out clothes. Then "his anger burned within him," apparently in reaction to the failure of the sages to recognize his true status. It seems likely that the passage here is another instance of the Messiah's anger at such a failure.

33. Hebrew *ashurenu*, probably an allusion to Balaam's prophecy of the star from Jacob (Numbers 24:17), where this rare root appears in the identical form. This prophecy was understood as a prophecy of the Messiah.

34. Cf. Daniel's reactions to the angels who appear to him and to their words to him (Daniel 8:15–19, 10:8–11).

35. "Suddenly" is lacking in our manuscript, but it appears in Jellinek's text.

36. The angel Michael makes his first biblical appearance in the Book of Daniel, where he is identified as "the great prince in charge of your people" (12:1; see also 10:13, 21), who is engaged in battle against the angelic princes of the nations. Thus the military aspect of most of the deeds Michael here claims to have performed.

37. According to Genesis 18:10–15, it is God Himself who gives the news to Sarah. But B. Baba Metsia 86b and parallels (see Louis Ginzberg, *Legends of the Jews*, 7 vols. [Philadelphia: Jewish Publication Society, 1909–38], 5:236–37 n. 147) attribute the announcement to Michael.

38. See 2 Kings 19:35–37, and the parallel in Isaiah 37:36–38, where the number of Sennacherib's men is 185,000. The angel there is not identified by name. Some traditions say that it was Michael (e.g., Exodus Rabbah 18:5); others, that it was Gabriel (e.g., B. Sanhedrin 95b). (For a listing of other passages that make these identifications, see Ginzberg, *Legends* 6:362 n. 55.)

39. See Joshua 5:13–15, where the angel calls himself "commander of the host of the Lord."

40. See Daniel 8:23.

41. Hebrew *tsalmah*, apparently the feminine of *tselem*, "image," "statue," but a word probably invented by the author.

42. The manuscript reads, "Then Michael answered Metatron and said . . ." In his edition Lévi ("L'Apocalypse de Zorobabel," *Revue des études juives* 68[1914]: p. 133, n. 17) suggests the reading represented in my translation. This wording actually appears farther on in the manuscript (249v). The strange reading here is perhaps the result of the copyist's confusion at an attempt to integrate two different names and two different sets of claims for the revealing angel.

The first set of claims requires Michael's role as commander of the heavenly host. The name Metatron is more closely associated with the second set of claims, which requires an angel with God's name (see note 33 below). Metatron is frequently referred to as the lesser YHWH, the bearer of the name of his master, and Gershom Scholem has suggested that Metatron acquired this designation from the angel Yahoel, whose own name does indeed contain the ineffable name of God (*Jewish Gnosticism, Merkabah Mysticism, and Talmudic Tradition*, 2d ed. [New York: Jewish Theological Seminary, 1965], 43).

The identification of Metatron with Michael is no innovation. Metatron gradually replaces Michael as the name for the dominant figure in the angelic hierarchy in the talmudic period (Scholem, *Jewish Gnosticism*, 43–51). Metatron does not, however, usually take over Michael's military role.

43. I do not know which biblical passages our author has in mind, nor can I locate a tradition that it was an angel who led Abraham about the land of Canaan. Even Shmuel suggests (*Midreshei Geulah*, 2d ed. [Jerusalem and Tel Aviv: Mosad Bialik, 1954], 73) that this claim is based on joining Joshua 24:3, "I took your father Abraham from beyond the Euphrates and led him through the whole land of Canaan," with Psalm 91:11, "For He will order his angels to guard you wherever you go." But the verse from Psalms is usually applied to Jacob (see Midrash Psalms to 91:11).

44. According to Genesis 22:11–19, it is "the angel of the Lord" who calls to Abraham from heaven to tell him not to slaughter Isaac and then to bless him. Midrash Vayosha identifies this angel as Michael. A tradition that the ministering angels cried as Abraham took the knife in his hand to slaughter Isaac appears in Genesis Rabbah 56:7 and parallels (see the edition of Theodor-Albeck).

45. See Genesis 32:22–32. Jacob's mysterious antagonist is called both "man" (vv. 24–25) and "God" (by Jacob, v. 30). According to Genesis Rabbah 77:3, he is "the prince of Esau." Midrash Abkir quoted in Yalkut Shimoni 132 identifies him as Michael.

46. See Exodus 23:20–23.

47. Joshua 5:13–15. Michael makes a similar claim for himself above.

48. The peculiar language of Genesis 19:24, "And the Lord rained upon Sodom and Gomorrah sulfurous fire from the Lord out of heaven," leads to several interpretations in Genesis Rabbah 51:2. One takes the second Lord of the verse as Gabriel. Another claims that "and the Lord" always signifies the heavenly court, here acting together with God, represented by the second "Lord." A third interpretation insists that the two "Lord"s are simply a manner of speaking. These interpretations may be responding to interpretations like that of Justin Martyr, *Dialogue with Trypho* 56, who took the verse as evidence that there are two Lords, God and Christ. The views in Genesis Rabbah that "Lord" is used to denote a specific angel or the heavenly court are close to the view implicit in the claim here.

49. Gematria is a form of numerology in which Hebrew words are compared on the basis of the equivalent numerical value of their letters. The letters of the name Metatron (*mttrwn*) add up to 314, as do the letters of the Almighty (*shdy*), a divine name that appears in the priestly source in the Torah and in biblical

poetry. This gematria makes sense of the claim that Metatron is the bearer of the divine name, a claim obviously true for Yahoel, but not at all obvious for Metatron.

I would like to thank David Satran of the Department of Comparative Religion of the Hebrew University for helping me to make sense of this passage.

50. The manuscript reads, "whose name is Jeconiah." In using "son of," I follow the reading of Jellinek's and Wertheimer's texts (Adolph Jellinek, *Beit ha-Midrash* [1853–78; reprint, Jerusalem: Wahrmann, 1967], 2:54–57; S. A. Wertheimer, *Batei Midrashot* 2d. ed. [Jerusalem: Mosad ha-Rav Kook, 1954], 2:497–505). This genealogy appears to reflect a combination of the identification of Zerubbabel in Haggai and Ezra-Nehemiah as son of Shealtiel with 1 Chronicles 3:17–19, where Shealtiel is called son of Jeconiah. In Chronicles, however, Zerubbabel is son of Pedaiah.

51. I supply this question from Wertheimer's text.

52. As we have seen, the name Menahem for the Messiah is traditional. But as far as I know, the name Menahem son of Amiel appears outside of *Sefer Zerubbabel* only in works that show the influence of *Sefer Zerubbabel*, like *Otot ha-Mashiah* and the *piyyut* of Eleazar Kallir, "Ba-Yamim ha-hem."

53. See P. Berakhot 2:4, Lamentations Rabbah 1:51.

54. Again I supply Zerubbabel's question from Wertheimer's text.

55. The name means "my delight is in her." It is the name of the mother of the wicked king Manasseh in 2 Kings 21:1. It appears also as a title for Zion at its restoration in Isaiah 62:4.

56. This echoes Daniel 11:27.

57. *Henif*, which I have translated "will wave," plays on the name Nof. Waving the hand is an act of vengeance in Isaiah 11:15 and Zechariah 2:13.

58. This name differs considerably from text to text. Later in the text the second king is called Esrogan. It is possible that Iszinan (*yszynn*) reflects the name of Vespasian, the Roman emperor responsible for the destruction of Jerusalem. If so, the association with Antioch is puzzling. Lévi reads here *ysrynn*, which is closer to Esrogan (*srwgn*), but I do not think he is correct.

59. This is the destruction of the Second Temple. Like other texts of the rabbinic tradition, our author's chronology of the Second Temple period is not very accurate.

60. To say that the chronology is confusing would be an understatement. Even Shmuel suggests emending "20" to "720" to get back to a reasonable date for the founding of Rome. See Daniel 7:24–27 for the picture of ten kings of the last world kingdom.

61. See Daniel 11:31.

62. See Daniel 8:24.

63. See Daniel 11:34.

64. "Him whose name is abomination" appears to be a reference to "the appalling abomination" that desolates of Daniel 11:31, 12:11.

65. See Daniel 12:7.

66. See Joshua 19:35.

67. See Numbers 17:23 for Aaron's staff. The author of *Sefer Zerubbabel*

seems to have drawn on a variety of traditions about staffs. One tradition provides a genealogy for Moses' staff that takes it all the way back to Adam (Yalkut Shimoni 173). Another equates Aaron's staff with that of Moses. This staff is said to have been handed down in Judah from king to king until the destruction of the Temple, when it was hidden away for the "king Messiah" (Numbers Rabbah 18:23). For these and other traditions about staffs, see Ginzberg, *Legends* 6:106–7 n. 600.

68. The treatment of Elijah as the son of Eleazar, one of the sons of Aaron, presupposes the identification of Elijah with Phinehas son of Eleazar. Phinehas is zealous in opposing the sins of the Israelites with the women of Moab. For his zeal he is granted a "pact of friendship" (Numbers 25). Elijah too is said to be zealous on God's behalf (1 Kings 19:10, 14). Further, the language in which God grants the covenant suggested to the rabbis that Phinehas was immortal (Numbers Rabbah 21:3 and elsewhere). Elijah, of course, never dies, but ascends to heaven in a fiery chariot (2 Kings 2:11). Although the identification of Elijah with Phinehas is often assumed in later literature, it is less common in earlier texts. It may be implied in Pseudo-Philo's Biblical Antiquities 48, and it is explicit in Targum Jonathan to Exodus 6:18, and in *Pirkei de-Rabbi Eliezer* 47 (chap. 29 assumes the identification). For full references, see Ginzberg, *Legends* 6:316–17 n. 3; many of these passages do not make the identification explicitly as Ginzberg claims.

69. Note the change to the third person for Zerubbabel, who until now has spoken in the first person. Note also the awkward use of both names for the angel.

70. See Ezra 2, 1 Chronicles 10, and 2 Chronicles 23–27, for the process, Ezra 2:62, and 2 Chronicles 31:16–19 for the phrase.

71. See Isaiah 19:14.

72. The phrase "prince of the holy covenant" echoes Daniel 11:22, "prince of the covenant," and Daniel 11:28, 30, "holy covenant."

73. "The house of disgrace," as above, is a church.

74. The ellipsis indicates the existence of a problem in the manuscript. Lévi suggests that the intention of the text is to provide a Greek etymology for Armilos, "destroyer of the people," and that the text should read "in the *Greek* language" ("L'apocalypse," 68:152 n. 6).

75. With the omission of a single y, the word *letters* becomes *signs*. In light of the signs of Armilos' appearance given later in the text, this may be a better reading, though in our version of the text the signs do not number ten. It is also possible that "ten letters" refers to the name of the emperor represented by Armilos. But that emperor is usually taken to be Heraklios, whose name does not contain ten letters.

76. My translation takes the reading of the manuscript, *le-zekher*, as a corruption of *ve-kazav*, an allusion to Daniel 11:27, *kazav yedaberu*, "they will speak falsehood."

77. See Daniel 7:27, the people of the holy ones of the Most High.

78. See Zechariah 4:6.

79. Perhaps the three groups reflect the picture presented in Zechariah 13:7–9,

although there is no indication in *Sefer Zerubbabel* that only a third of the people is saved.

80. Presumably the Chebar. See note 18 above.

81. See Jeremiah 32:27.

82. See Job 32:18.

83. This date is the eve of Passover, the great holiday of redemption.

84. The valley of Arbael is located between Tiberias and Sepphoris (Yehudah Even Shmuel, *Midreshei Geulah*, 2d ed. [Jerusalem and Tel Aviv: Mosad Bialik, 1954], 81), and is associated with the coming of redemption in a number of rabbinic sources (see, e.g., Song of Songs Rabbah 6:10).

85. Joshua son of Jehozadak appears in Haggai and Zechariah 3; he was the high priest who was Zerubbabel's contemporary.

86. The margin adds, "and sages."

87. See Isaiah 59:17.

88. Elijah is regularly associated with the coming of the Messiah in Jewish tradition because of Malachi 3:23, "Lo, I will send the prophet Elijah to you before the coming of the awesome, fearful day of the Lord."

89. See Zechariah 6:13.

90. See the midrash in B. Gittin 57b, in which Jewish children throw themselves into the sea to escape their captors and quote the verse from Psalm 68:23: "The Lord said, 'I will retrieve [them] from Bashan, I will retrieve [them] from the depths of the sea.' "

91. Joel 4:2, 12 picture the final judgment of the nations taking place in the Valley of Jehoshaphat; Jehoshaphat means "the Lord judges." In 4:18 Joel describes the Valley of Shittim watered by a fountain that emerges from the Temple at the time of this judgment. In the new JPS translation, the Valley of Shittim is called the Wadi of the Acacias.

92. We have moved from Joel's Valley of Shittim in Jerusalem to the Shittim of Numbers 25:1, Joshua 2:1, 3:1, and Micah 6:5, on the border of the holy land. This Shittim is not called a valley; it seems to have become one here by association with Joel. Elsewhere in the Bible (e.g., Numbers 33:49) it is called Abel-shittim.

93. Banner is a term used in the Book of Numbers in the description of the Israelites' camp as they travel through the wilderness. The Korahites were swallowed by the earth as punishment for the rebellion against Moses (Numbers 16). Their emergence from the depths of the earth is associated with the dawning of the messianic age (see the references in Ginzberg, *Legends* 6:103–5 nn. 586, 590).

94. These are the Israelites who left Egypt and died in the wilderness during the forty years of wandering.

95. See Zechariah 14:4.

96. See Isaiah 27:13.

97. See Ezekiel 38:20.

98. See Isaiah 42:13.

99. See Isaiah 11:4.

100. See Judges 7:22.

101. See Isaiah 52:8.

102. See Isaiah 59:17.

103. See Ezekiel 38–39. For the rabbis Magog, the land of Gog according to Ezekiel, becomes a second prince paired with Gog. The war of Gog and Magog is the eschatological war.

104. See Ezekiel 39:10. The period of seven months is the time for burial of these bodies in Ezekiel 39:12, 14.

105. Joshua 18:28 mentions this place as part of a list. Both RSV and JPS translate as two separate places, Zela and Eleph, although the Hebrew certainly lends itself to the understanding in *Sefer Zerubbabel*.

106. See Deuteronomy 32:30. As Even Shmuel (*Midreshei Geulah*, 88) notes, Joshua 23:10, which describes the few pursuing the many in the course of a victory for Israel, would be more appropriate here than Deuteronomy 32:30, which refers to Israel's defeat.

107. See Malachi 3:4.

108. See Isaiah 49:21. The second question is an adaptation rather than an exact quotation of the verse.

109. See Zechariah 9:9.

110. See Zechariah 2:9.

111. This is probably a somewhat confused reference to Deuteronomy 11:24.

112. Also according to Midrash Psalms 68:9, the eschatological Temple rests on five mountaintops. The plurality of mountain tops derives there from a superliteral reading of Isaiah 2:2, "And it will come to pass at the end of days that the house of the Lord will be established on the top of the mountains." But Midrash Psalms lists only four of the five mountains: Tabor, Carmel, Sinai, and Zion (= Moriah). Mount Sinai does not appear in *Sefer Zerubbabel*, which adds Lebanon and Hermon.

113. Notice the change of name for the angel, who was called Metatron in the paragraph above. The scribe was troubled by this, so the margin offers, "Again he swore."

114. See Isaiah 21:12; here the first clause has been changed from plural to singular.

115. "Week" here means a week of years, or seven years, as in Daniel.

116. The Hebrew of the manuscript, *ha-noldah*, makes it clear that it is Hephzibah who was born in Hebron. According to Wertheimer's text, it is "Nathan son of David" who was born in Hebron. 2 Samuel 5:14 reports the birth of a number of sons to David *after* he left Hebron for Jerusalem; one is named Nathan. As far as I know, this son is nowhere identified with Nathan the prophet.

117. At the first mention of Nof and Esrogan (= Iszinan), Hephzibah kills them before Nehemiah makes his appearance.

118. As the translation suggests, this passage is extremely unclear.

119. The names of both kings and cities have been garbled in transmission. Thus the abundance of marginal alternatives and variations from text to text.

120. Aram-naharaim is the term for Mesopotamia in the priestly source in Genesis.

121. "Qedem" means east. Lévi ("L'Apocalypse" 68:158 n. 18) suggests that this is a reference to the Arabs.

122. Riblah is mentioned in 2 Kings 25:6 as the place where Nebuchadnezzar sat in judgment on Zedekiah, king of Judah. According to the version of Midrash Abba Gorion in Salomon Buber's *Sifre de-Agadta al Megillat Esther* (Vilna: Wittwe et Gebrueder Romm, 1886), Nebuchadnezzar attempted unsuccessfully to ascend the throne of Solomon there (p. 4). It may be that our author intends the reference to Riblah to place Armilos in a line that includes such world rulers as Nebuchadnezzar. B. Sanhedrin 96b equates Riblah with Antioch.

As it stands, the passage is confused. "From there" is odd following "the whole world." It is possible that in the background there lies an event of the author's own time that took place at Antioch.

123. See Zechariah 8:10.

124. See Job 30:4.

125. See Joel 4:18.

126. See Daniel 7:18.

127. The parallel in Wertheimer's text reads, "Zechariah son of Iddo and Elijah the prophet." Thus the sentence is not a colophon (as Even Shmuel thinks [*Midreshei Geulah*, 88]), but an attempt to explain how Zerubbabel's vision came to be recorded when Zerubbabel is nowhere in the Bible represented as an author. The expression "complete exile" appears in Amos 1:6, 9, where it means the exile of an entire people. Here it seems to mean something like "when things were at their worst."

5 •

MIDRASH ON THE TEN COMMANDMENTS

"Midrash on the Ten Commandments" is a medieval compilation, structured loosely on each of the Ten Commandments (Exodus 20:1ff.). It represents the transition in Jewish literature from interpretation of Scripture to pure fiction, in a more modern sense of the term. It was probably completed by the beginning of the eleventh century, somewhere in Iraq. There are numerous versions of this work, some having as few as thirteen and others as many as forty tales. The present translation is based upon the text edited by Galit Hasan-Rokem, *Midrash Aseret ha-Dibrot (Nusah Verona) 5407 [1647]* (Jerusalem: Akademon, 1971).

Despite its name, it is a genuine story anthology, one of the first of its kind in Jewish literature. Many of its tales are of non-Jewish origin, bearing features found in the tales of many other cultures around the world: deathbed admonitions, pirate abductions, exiles, disguises, talking animals, talismanic powers, buried treasures, amorous seductions. One tale, that of the man who meets Leviathan and receives the power to communicate with animals, is largely a variant of the Greek myth of Melampus.

The literary quality of this collection is uneven. Some details of the stories are undoubtedly offensive to modern readers. Rabbi Meir's mishap with a lion is narrated in a gruesomely deadpan manner, worthy of the brothers Grimm. There is a blatant male chauvinism to some of the tales, of a type that must be taken for granted if the material is to be approached on its own terms. And in other ways, the narrative art is deficient. Inconsistencies abound, details hang in the air, emphases sometimes seem skewed, and motifs from other tales are often grafted clumsily onto the work to no apparent advantage. If Hebrew literature could be compared to, say, Russian literature, the anonymous author-editor of this work would be a kind of Lermontov: ground breaking, fanciful, inventive, possessing a flair for the surprise and the exotic, filled with rich convolutions of fictional time and space, but not producing the finest specimens of the storytelling art. There is an instinctually mottled quality, an almost willful inclination toward noncomparable episodes—thus, perhaps, a kind of modernism—that exercises a fascination of its own. But, in that our midrashist challenges the *mashal* genre by adding an interest in narrative unfolding for its own sake, he manifests the early stages of a trend that found a richer expression in such works as "The Alphabet of Ben Sira," "The Tales of Sendebar," "The Gests of Alexander of Macedon," and "The Maaseh Book," as well as in the Hasidic legend, the symbolic stories and dream visions of Nahman of Bratslav, the parables of Kafka, and the fiction of Agnon and Singer. "Midrash on the Ten Commandments" stands at the threshold of a renascence of the story in Jewish life. For this reason, if for no other, it is worth our attention today. And certain of its passages, such as the portrait of Israel at Sinai, the neatly calculated meanderings of the man who met Leviathan, or the domestic apocalypse of the man with three unsavory daughters, achieve a mastery that any storyteller would envy.

Most of all, the collection elicits fascination for its elusively irreverent and satirical tone. Behind a veil of orthodox exhortation, it portrays unapologetically sordid or extreme behavior: familial treachery, uxoriousness, false accusation, random violence, sexual chauvinism, idolatry, adultery, materialistic rapacity, divine refusal, horrific divine castigation; in general, something akin to the Hobbesian state of nature—paradoxically introduced by an idyllic picture of a transfigured Israel receiving the Torah. Moses in midrash is made to ask: "*This* is Torah, and *this* is its reward?" As is frequent in satire, the moralist and the immoralist merge in the one editor, and we cannot say to which vision he is more drawn.

In the following translation (representing selections from midrashim on the five odd-numbered commandments), I have, for the most part, kept to the rather wooden quotational structure of dialogue in a midrashic story ("He said to her: X. She said to him: Y.") to preserve the stylistic simplicity typical of these tales even where they attain sophisticated complexity of plot.

Introduction, translation, and notes by
JOEL ROSENBERG

FIRST COMMANDMENT:
I AM THE LORD YOUR GOD.[1] (Exodus 20:2)

When it emerged from the mouth of the Holy One, blessed be He (may His name be exalted!), bolts of lightning and thunder issued from Him, firebrands on His right side and His left. In that hour no human being breathed. No bird chirped. No lion roared. No cattle lowed. No ass brayed. The world seemed uninhabited.

And the word went forth from the mouth of the Holy One, blessed be He, and went like someone walking about in the world. The divine speech turned into seventy languages, for all the world to hear. As it is said: "All the kings of the earth shall praise You, O Lord, for they have heard the words you spoke" (Psalm 138:4).[2]

When Israel heard the divine speech, they were knocked back twelve miles, and the Israelites' souls departed from them. As it is said: "I was faint because of what he said" (Song of Songs 5:6).[3] Torah said before Him,[4] "Master of the universe,[5] to whom would You give me—the living or the dead?" He said to her, "To the living." She said before Him, "Master of the universe, look! They're all dead!" God said to her, "I will revive them." As it is said: "You released a bountiful rain, O God! When Your own land languished, you sustained it" (Psalm 68:10).

But the Israelites were still unable to stand upon their feet, and the Holy One, blessed be He, sent to each and every one of Israel two angels, one to lay his hand upon his heart so that his soul would not depart and the other one to lift his head up to behold his Creator. And the Holy One, blessed be He, gave permission and ability for them to look upon Him, and His voice went out and traveled around to each one's ears, and said to them, "Will you receive upon yourselves the Torah, which has in

it two hundred forty-eight positive commandments?" And the Israelites answered, "Yes!" And the speech came forth again from God's mouth, and went around to each one's ears, and said, "Will you receive upon yourselves the Torah, which has in it three hundred sixty-five negative commandments?"[6] And the Israelites answered, "Yes!" And the divine speech reemerged from the ear and kissed them upon their mouths. As it is said: "Oh, give me the kisses of your mouth!" (Song of Songs 1:2).

Whereupon, the Holy One, blessed be He, opened up for them the seven heavens, the seven layers of the deep, and the seven layers of the earth, and they saw, each with his own eyes, that there was none other than He. And He said to them: "See now, that I, I am He, and there is no god beside Me. I deal death and give life; I wounded and I will heal" (Deuteronomy 32:39).

A tale is told of a certain crippled Jew who heard people saying that there was a heathen shrine in a certain place, and any lame person who went there was cured immediately. The Jew said, "I will go there; perhaps I will be cured—even I." He went there and spent one night with other handicapped people who had been there. And it happened that at midnight, when all of them were sleeping, the Jew lay awake and saw a certain demon coming out of the wall. In his hand was a flask of oil, and he was anointing the sick, but left the Jew alone. The Jew said to him: "And why haven't you anointed me?" He replied, "If you are Jewish, why have you come here? Can a Jew traffic in idolatry? Don't you know that heathen rites have nothing real in them? It is for this reason that I am misleading them, so they will cling to error, and they'll have no portion in the world to come. But you, why have you run to alien worship instead of standing up to pray before the Holy One, blessed be He, who is the one to cure you? You should know that by tomorrow your time had come to be healed, but because you have done this, you will never find a cure. Therefore, do not trust in any mortal being, but rather in the Holy One, blessed be He—for He, this kingly God, is a physician who heals for free!"[7]

THIRD COMMANDMENT:
DO NOT TAKE THE NAME OF THE LORD
YOUR GOD IN VAIN. (Exodus 20:7)

Do not let an oath be continually on your lips, for great punishment awaits one who abounds in oaths and is filled with violence. A plague shall not be lacking from his house. And one who swears falsely cannot be cleared of guilt, as it is said: "And I will draw near to you for judgment, and I will be a swift witness against the sorcerers, the philanderers, and those who swear falsely by my Name" (Malachi 3:5).

When Naaman (a general from Syria, a leper cured by the prophet Elisha) came to Elisha (in gratitude for the cure), he brought an offering and said, "Now I know there is no God in the whole world except in Israel! So please accept a gift from your servant" (2 Kings 5:15). But Elisha said, "As the Lord lives, whom I serve, I will not accept anything." And he urged him to take it, but he still refused. Then Gehazi (Elisha's assistant) swore to Elisha by a prophet's donkey, swearing falsely, and was driven out of the world. As it is said: "And Gehazi pursued after Naaman and said to him,[8] 'My master has sent me to you, that you may send to two youths who have come to him (from a prophetic order) a talent of silver and two sacral garments.' " (Naaman) replied, "Swear an oath and take them." He swore an oath and took. But *what* did he take? He took upon himself the leprosy of Naaman, which clung to him and to his offspring forever. And our rabbis of blessed memory have said, "A person is obligated to guard his lips from oath-making, for whoever accustoms himself to oath-making will find that there are times when he does not wish an oath but his tongue has habituated him to one, even in a case where he is definitely not permitted to make one."

A tale is told of a certain man who placed a gold dinar in trust with a certain widow. She placed it in a jar of flour and kneaded it into a single loaf, and gave it to a pauper. After some days, the owner of the dinar came and said to her, "Give me my dinar." She replied, "May I enjoy death if I have profited in any way from your dinar!" Not many days passed when one of her sons died, and when the sages heard of this matter they said, "And if this one, who swore truthfully, could lose her sons—for one who swears falsely, how much the more so!"[9]

A tale is told of a certain pious man who had never in his lifetime sworn falsely. He was an exceedingly rich man, and in the hour of his death he called to his son and said to him, "My son, beware never to swear an oath at all, for all of this wealth that I leave to you I was able to acquire only by guarding my tongue from an oath. Not even a truthful oath have I sworn. For this, the Holy One, blessed be He, made me successful in all of my business endeavors and in all that my hands have made." And his son answered him, saying, "I will uphold your wishes and will not swear at all." And when the pious man died, deceivers descended upon his surviving son and requested from him a lot of money, saying that his father owed it to them—but if he were to swear an oath, he could depart freely. The survivor said to himself, "If I swear to them, I will profane the heavenly Name and make null the wishes of my father. Better that I should pay them whatever they ask from me and not swear."[10] He went and paid to the deceivers all the wealth his father had left him, until he was left a poor man without a shred. With all of this, he continued to follow the commandments and uphold the wishes of his father and honor the students of the sages.

Finally, a certain deceiver came and said to him, "You still owe me one dinar." He replied, "I beg of you, look at me, I do not have left the sustenance for even a single moment, and it is known to God that if I had anything, I would pay you!" He replied, "Come, swear an oath to me that you have nothing to pay me." And he led him to the house of a judge, who said to him, "Pay him his dinar, or swear that you have nothing." He said to them, "I will not swear!" The judge said to the deceiver, "Either he will pay, or he will be imprisoned."

In the jailhouse at that very hour, the bereaved man wept and said, "Master of the universe, it is revealed and known before You that I have nothing at all, for if I had in my hand anything at all, I would pay. May Your name be praised forever, for of all the silver and gold that I had in great abundance, I have been stripped bare. And now I sit in thirst and want, but if they should demand any more from me, I wouldn't care—for naked I emerged from my mother's womb, and naked I'll return to it. Blessed be the name of the Lord, from now and evermore!"

What did his saintly wife do? She was ashamed to request alms, so she took in linens to wash, to redeem her husband from the deceivers and to feed and support him and his children. One day she and her children were standing at the seashore, and they saw a ship coming. They awaited it until it drew near to them. When the ship's captain saw that she was a beautiful woman, he desired her in his heart, and said, "She is from a family of kings!"

He asked her, "Why do you wash clothes?" She told him everything that had happened to her and her husband. He said to her, "I'll give you a gold dinar to wash my clothes." And she took the clothes to wash, and took the gold dinar from his hand and gave it to her oldest son to rescue her husband from the hands of the deceivers.

Meanwhile, the ship's captain repaired his mast, and when the saintly woman came to return his clothes, he took her by force and fled. Her sons saw her, and began yelling and crying, "Woe to us! Our mother! What will we do?" They returned to their father and gave him the dinar and told him how their mother was captured. He tore his garments and mourned. Then he paid out the dinar and went out from the prison. He said to himself, "What will I do? If I return to my house, I shall die in the evening, or more deceivers will come to me and do to me as the others have done. Better that I should go to another place." And he wept a great deal, and said, "See, O Lord, take note of how I and my sons are left like orphans without any sustenance in the world!" All of them wept together until their strength gave out from weeping so much and so bitterly, and they went off.

From gate to gate they traveled until they arrived at a great river close to the sea—but there was no passage. What did he do? He took off his clothes and took his youngest son, placed him on his shoulders, and eased himself into the river. When they reached the depths of the river, the waters welled up, and the man was about to drop his son. But God appointed for them a great fish, and he and his young son perched upon it, and with its help they crossed back to dry land.[11] Walking naked before his son, he reached a town. But meanwhile, back on the other shore, his other sons, weeping and wailing among themselves, were discovered by a brigand boat and taken captive.

When the townspeople saw the pious man walking naked, they asked him, "Where are you from?" He said, "I am a poor Jew." They said, "What are your skills?" He said, "I know how to read and write." They replied, "We don't want anything like that.[12] If you wish to feed our cattle, you can dwell with us, and we'll give you a good wage." He said to them, "Yes, I'll do it." So they gave him their flocks, and he pastured them faithfully and honestly. They warned him, "Be careful not to go near this river, which is exceptionally deep. If any of the sheep fall in, they won't come out." He said, "I'll do as you say."

One day he was sitting at the riverbank, and he remembered all the wealth and money that his father had left him. He wept bitterly. "Why do I stay alive, now that my wife is taken captive and my sons have been exiled, and I have been left by myself? It is better for me to die than to live!" He rose to throw himself into the river, but saw that it had snakes and scorpions in it. When he saw the bodies of those slain by them, he was struck by fear and turned back. As he turned, he heard a voice calling him and, wheeling, he saw the figure of an angel, who said, "Come here. How many days and years has this treasure been guarded for you! Take from this that I have kept for you, for your destined time has arrived to ascend to greatness because you kept the wishes of your father and have never sworn an oath!" Immediately, he revealed to him the treasure and said to him, "Go, buy this river from the lord of the country, and afterward build on this spot a great city."

And so he did. The man went to the lord of the country and said to him, "My lord, may it be your wish to sell me this river from such and such place to such and such place." The lord replied, "Fool! What could you do with it?" He said, "Even so, sell it to me!" Thereupon, the river was sold to him at a high price and transferred to him immediately. The lord wrote him a bill of ownership, signed by witnesses as an everlasting and irrevocable purchase. The man immediately set about hiring laborers and built upon the riverbank a great city with huge palaces. He was made king of the city, and his fame spread far and wide. People came from everywhere to carry on business, and he paid honor to all wayfarers, and his fame spread still farther, and still more people gathered to his town.[13]

One day, there came the boat that had captured his sons. When the pious man saw his sons, he brought them into his palace without revealing who he was, and gave them treatment befitting freemen.[14] He invited, as well, the men of the boat to dine with him. Meanwhile, there came the boat on which his wife had been taken captive. He invited all of the boatsmen to dine with him. But the boat's captain said to him, "My lord king, I can't leave this boat, for my wife is here." The king said, "Look, I have two trustworthy youths who will guard it." The youths (his sons)[15] went off to the boat, and the captain went to the feast.

The youths said to each other, "Woe to us, for this boat looks like the one on which our mother was captured!" And they wept into the night.[16] But their mother said to them, "Why are you weeping?" They told her, "We remembered that on a ship such as this our mother was taken captive." Immediately, she recognized them, and she wept the entire night but did not say anything to them.

In the morning the captain returned and saw her anguished of spirit, and said to her, "What is the matter with you?" She replied, "Could you not go off without leaving these shameless souls to sport with me?"[17] He went immediately to the house of the king and said to him, "My lord king, did you have only these scoundrels to send to my boat, so they could play around with my wife all night?" Immediately, the king called to them and said to them, "Is there any truth to what I have heard—that you have acted foully with this man's wife all the night?" They replied, "God forbid that we should do such a thing! Let this man's wife come and bear witness about us, and if she confirms this report, kill us immediately!" They brought the woman before the king, and the king said to her, "My daughter, do not deny anything; do not be afraid to tell me everything." Suddenly, she threw herself upon her face to the ground, and said to him, "My lord king, give me permission, and I will tell you something!" The king said, "Speak." She said to him, "I beg of you, my lord king, ask them where they are from." Thereupon, they told him all that had happened to them, after which the woman rose and embraced them and kissed them, and she said, "As your soul lives, my lord king, they are my sons!" And she cried out, weeping, and told him the entire story. When the king heard her words, he immediately recognized that they were his children and she his wife. The king said to the ship's captain, "Tell me the truth. How did this woman come into your hand? If you do not tell me the truth, I will cut off your head!" He replied, "My lord king, I captured her by the seashore as she was washing clothes, and as your soul lives, my lord king, I have not touched her nor lusted after her at all! Now, do with me whatever you please." Right away, the king replied, "Go in peace back to your land." And the king said, "Blessed is He who rewards them that fear Him, and blessed is He who returns what is lost to its owners!"

And the king remained with his wife and his sons in great wealth. And our rabbis of blessed memory have said, "And if, for this one, who kept only a single wish that his father commanded him, the Holy One, blessed be He, bestowed so much reward, all the more so one who keeps many commandments: the Holy One, blessed be He, will repay him many thousandfold."[18] As it is said: "He shows kindness to the thousandth generation, etc." (Exodus 20:6). Thus it is said: "Do not take the name of the Lord your God in vain."

FIFTH COMMANDMENT:
HONOR YOUR FATHER AND YOUR MOTHER.
(Exodus 20:12)

The Holy One, blessed be He, said, "The father who begot you, honor him! The house in whose midst you slept, honor it as you would honor Me for it is enough that they nurtured you! Support them in old age, for they were my partners when you were formed." One who fears the Holy One, blessed be He, will honor his father and his mother to the best of his wealth and ability. And how should one fear a parent? Let him not cross in front of him, nor sit in his place, nor speak out of turn before him, nor conceal anything from him, nor argue with him. And Rabbi Johanan has said, "Whoever despises his father and his mother and mocks them will not merit a grave. Birds of the sky will eat his flesh, as it is said: "The eye that mocks a father disdains the homage due a mother—the ravens of the brook will gouge it out, young eagles will devour it" (Proverbs 30:17).

A tale is told of a certain man who commanded his son in his hour of death, saying to him, "All of your days, cast your bread upon the waters, and do not eat of it by yourself." When his father died, the son fulfilled his command, and a certain fish became accustomed to approach his bread and eat it, until that fish grew very big and would pursue the other fish and eat them.[19] When all of the fish saw this, they went to the abode of Leviathan[20] and said to him, "Our lord, a certain fish has grown big among us, and we cannot survive around him." He sent for him and said to him, "Why have you grown bigger than your companions?" He replied, "A certain man comes to my abode and casts his bread before me, and I eat it." He said to him, "Go, and bring him to me, and we will see if your words are true." Thereupon, the fish went and brought him before Leviathan. He said to him, "Why do you cast your bread upon the waters?" He replied, "My lord, thus has my father commanded me, and I am fulfilling his command." He said to him, "You have fulfilled the command of your father?" He replied, 'Yes." He said to him, "Open your mouth." He opened his mouth, and he spit into it three times. Immediately, there rested upon him the spirit of wisdom and understanding, and he knew and understood the voices of the beasts and birds, and he knew seventy languages.[21] Afterward, he commanded the fish to bring him back to the dry land. He went and brought him out to the dry land.

And he was tired from having entered into the belly of the fish, and he lay down there, and two birds flew down. One said to the other, "I'll go and pluck out his eyes." His companion replied, "Look, this man is very clever. Do not touch him!" But he said to him, "Yes, I will." He went and bit him on his feet and did not fear him. But when he approached to pluck out the man's eyes, the latter reached out his hand and grabbed him. The other bird, who was the mother of this one, said to the man, "If you let go of my child, I'll show you a great treasure that King Solomon has stored away, upon which is a great crown." When the man heard this, he understood her words and said to her, "Show me, and I'll let your child go." He grabbed her wings and flew off with her. Soon she set him down at that treasure, whereupon he let go of her child. And when he let him go, the mother began striking her child and said to him, "Why didn't you believe me? Didn't I tell you not to descend upon him, for he is clever, and he descended upon you and grabbed, and you have caused this wealth to be revealed!" She struck him too hard and killed him. Immediately, she went and brought a marsh reed, and placed it over his mouth. Thereupon, his soul returned to him. A certain man saw the effects of this marsh reed, and said, "Certainly this reed can revive the dead."[22] He took the reed and said, "Now I will go to Jerusalem and revive the dead there with this." When he was on the road to that place, he came upon a lion that had died from a plague. He touched him with the reed, and the lion rose upon his feet and ate him.

The man to whom the treasure had been revealed returned home and rented donkeys to bring the treasure back home. He led them to the hiding place and loaded them with silver and gold, as much as they could carry. Now, among those donkeys was a certain one who was disreputable and evil of deeds. He said to his companions, "If you listen to me, we'll play a trick upon this fellow so that he'll lose all of the treasure, for he has burdened us excessively." His companions replied, "How can we do that?" He said to them, "Watch me, and do the same. When I enter the city, I'll fall down midway through the gate, and people will come to help, and they'll see the silver and the gold and will steal everything from him." His companions replied, "We are afraid because this man is clever. If we do this thing, he will beat us with the staff that is in his hand and drive us out of the world, with none to help us." He said to them, "Watch what I do; if they run to assist me, you fall down, too, and all the treasure will be lost."

Now the man understood this, kept quiet, and waited to see what would happen. When he entered the city, the donkey fell down at the gate. People came to assist him. "I beg of you, don't help me," he said, "for I recognize his mischief." What did he do? He took the staff that was in his hand and smacked him a good one on his head, his flanks, and his back—great whacks,[23] until the donkey got up by himself, and his companions said, "Had we listened to your advice, we'd have been punished like you." Thereupon, the man returned with his treasure to his house and stored it away.

"How did you get all this treasure?" his wife said to him. "Why should you ask me this?" he replied. "The Holy One, blessed be He, gave it to me." But she pressed him day and night to tell her, until finally he promised to tell her the next night.

That same day the man entered the place where his horse was kept and saw the beast weeping. Along came a rooster to the horse's fodder, to eat of the barleycorns. It saw the weeping horse and asked, "Why do you cry?" The beast replied, "Because my master vowed to his wife to tell her this night how he came into possession of all this wealth, and she will not be able to conceal the matter; she will tell her women neighbors, and they will tell their husbands, and they will kill him and take his treasure."

The rooster answered, "Don't I have ten wives, and are not all of them afraid of me? Now, see what I do." He took a barley branch, and with it summoned his wives. They all came immediately and ate. Afterward, he shouted at them, and immediately they all ran away. "See, they are afraid of me," said the rooster. "So also should our master do with his wife, that she might fear him." The man heard all of these words and understood. When his wife said to him, "Tell me where all this wealth came from," he struck her hard, and she said, "Don't beat me anymore, and I won't ask you for anything else!"

Who brought about a glorious state[24] such as this? Wisdom. As it is said: "Wisdom preserves the life of him who possesses it" (Ecclesiastes 7:12)—provided one upholds the commandments.

SEVENTH COMMANDMENT: DO NOT COMMIT ADULTERY. (Exodus 20:13)

Do not associate with philanderers, and do not desire any manner of adultery, for by the sin of adultery, captivity came into the world. Whoever commits adultery ends up engaged in idolatry. Whoever has never cast his eye upon the wife of another man, the Holy One, blessed be He, joins with Him to make him holy, and He will give no permission to the evil urge to overcome another man's wife.

A tale is told of Rabbi Matthiah ben Heresh, who once was sitting and occupied with Torah. And he was so handsome that the light of his face was like the sun, and its features like those of the ministering angels, with their expression of heavenly awe.[25] He had never once cast his gaze upon a woman. Now, as he sat occupied with Torah in the house of study, Satan espied him and was kindled with interest in him. He thought, "Is it possible that a fine man like this would not sin?"

So he went up to the heavens and stood before the Holy One, blessed be He. He said, as he stood before Him, "Master of the universe, Matthiah ben Heresh, what is he in Your sight?" He replied, "He is a thoroughly just man." He said to Him, "Give me permission, and I will lead him astray." The Holy One, blessed be He, replied, "Go."[26]

He went and found him sitting occupied with Torah. What did he do? He appeared to him in the guise of a woman whose beauty was unequaled in all the world. She came and stood in front of him. When he saw her, he turned his eyes away. And when he saw that she could appear wherever he turned his glance, he thought, "I'm afraid that the evil urge will overcome me!" What did he do? He said to his sons, "Go fetch me a fire and some nails." He then placed the nails in the fire until they grew red-hot, and with them he blinded his eyes.[27]

When Satan beheld this, he was frightened. He went up before the Holy One, blessed be He, and he said, "Master of the universe, here is what happened. . . ." God replied, "Did I not tell you that you could not have any power over him?" That same hour, the Holy One, blessed be He, called to the archangel Raphael and told him, "Go, cure the eyes of Matthiah ben Heresh!"

Raphael came before him. He asked Raphael, "Who are you?" "I am Raphael the angel," he replied, "the Holy One, blessed be He, has sent me to heal your eyes." He said to him, "I'm afraid lest the evil urge conquer me." Raphael went up before the Holy One, blessed be He, and said, "Here is what Matthiah has said to me. . . ." The Holy One, blessed be He, replied, "Go, and say to him that I'll guarantee that the evil urge will never conquer him." And the angel went to him immediately and cured his eyes.

Whence our rabbis of blessed memory have said, "Whoever does not cast his eye upon another man's wife will not be conquered by the evil urge."

A tale is told of Rabbi Meir,[28] that he used to go up to Jerusalem on each and every festival. And he would stay at the home of Judah the Cook.[29] The wife of this cook was a beautiful woman, and she was extremely conscientious about honoring Rabbi Meir whenever he came up to see them. In time, the wife of the Rabbi Judah died, and he married another woman.

He told her, "If a certain disciple of the sages by the name of Rabbi Meir should come to visit, be careful to treat him respectfully, bringing him home and satisfying all of his needs." She replied, "I'll do as you say."

When the pilgrimage season came around,[30] Rabbi Meir came to Jerusalem, where he went to stay at the house of Rabbi Judah the Cook. Rabbi Judah's wife came before him, and Rabbi Meir said to her, "Call the wife of Rabbi Judah the Cook." She replied, "Sir, his wife has died, and he has married me." Thereupon, Rabbi Meir wept, and he turned away to go. She quickly grabbed Rabbi Meir by his garment and said to him, "Sir, my husband has already requested that I should care for your honor even more than his first wife did." Rabbi Meir said to her, "I do not have permission to enter his house unless he give it." Rabbi Meir went out of the house and found Rabbi Judah the Cook. He gave him greeting, and Rabbi Judah said to him, "Sir, my first wife has by now died, and this one is more zealous for your honor than her predecessor." Whereupon, Rabbi Meir went into the house, and the wife brought before him food and drink. He ate, and she served before him.

Now, Rabbi Meir was a handsome young man, and she cast her gaze upon him and gave him so much to drink that he soon did not know his right from his left.[31] She suggested that he lie down, and when he did so, she went and lay with him until dawn. From his great drunkenness, he was not aware of her lying down or her rising up,[32] and he sported with her the entire night.

In the morning Rabbi Meir got up and went to the synagogue to pray. When he returned to the house, she brought before him food and drink, as before, in ministering to his needs. And she bantered and joked in his presence as if Rabbi Meir were a young man to flirt with. And Rabbi Meir wondered to himself, Why is she so brazen in front of me? He looked at the ground and did not wish to gaze upon her. She said to him, "Look at me! Didn't you play the whole night with me? And now, you're ashamed of me!"

"God forbid!" Rabbi Meir said. "No such thing has ever happened!"

"If you don't believe me," she replied, "the sign of it is on your flesh."

Rabbi Meir realized that he had lost his senses with her, and he grew extremely morose, and wept and cried out, saying, "Woe is me that I have lost the Torah that I have learned, and now what remedy do I have?" He resolved to go to the head of the rabbinical community[33] and confess his transgression before him. Whatever he requires me to do, I'll take upon myself.

He made his way home, crying out the whole way, rending his garments and casting ashes on his head. And all his relatives went out to meet him, and asked him, "What happened to you?" He said to them, "Here is what happened. . . ." They asked him, "What is in your heart to do?" "I'll go to the head of the rabbinical community," he replied, "and whatever judgment he renders concerning me I'll take upon myself." "But it was an unintentional error," they said, "and the Holy One, blessed be He, will forgive you. Don't listen to your own voice of conscience casting aspersions on yourself." "If I listen to you," he replied, "the Holy One, blessed be He, will never forgive my sins, for it says: "He who covers up his faults will not succeed" (Proverbs 28:13).

Thereupon, he went off to the house of the head of the rabbinical community, and he stood before him. "What do you seek, wise man?" he was asked. "O everlasting luminary," he replied, "here is what happened to me . . . , and for this reason I've come before you. For whatever you tell me, whether for death or life, even to feed me to the lions, I will take upon myself." He replied, "Let me first do some research into your case."

The next day, he came before him. The jurist said to him, "I have done research into your case, and we have seen fit to feed you to the lions." Rabbi Meir replied, "I accept upon myself the judgment of Heaven. Give the word concerning me as you have spoken." Thereupon, the sage called his son, who in turn summoned two Israelite strongmen. He told them, "Take this fellow to a place in the forest where the lions are found, and bind his hands and feet, and leave him there. And you, wait in the treetops to see what happens to him. If they eat him, bring me the bones, and we will offer great lamentation because he has taken upon himself the judgment of Heaven."

Immediately, they took him out to the forest and the place of the lions, bound him hand and foot, and themselves ascended into trees. At midnight along came a lion, sniffed his aroma, but went off on his way. They went before the magistrate and told him, "A lion came along, sniffed him out, and went on his way." "Do the same thing to him again," he replied.

The next day, at midnight, a lion came along, growling around him and sniffing him, but went away. And they told the matter to the sage. "Do it again," he replied, "If, on the third day, at night, they don't touch him, bring him to my place, for there is no judgment of Heaven against him."

And so they did.[34] At midnight, a lion came along, growling and roaring around him, who planted his teeth into him, pulled out a rib from his back, and ate from it. The next day, they went and told the sage. He said, "Bring him to me. In that the beast has eaten only an olive-bulk, it is as if he had eaten him all."[35] Thereupon, they went to get him and brought him before the sage, who ordered the physicians to heal him.

When Rabbi Meir went back to his house, an oracular voice[36] went out and said, "Rabbi Meir, who has been commanded to obtain life in the world to come, is designated fit to do so. Let a man be warned not to touch another man's wife!"

A tale is told of two sisters who resembled one another.[37] One of them committed adultery. The thing came to the attention of her husband, and he decided to take her to the priest to have her drink the bitter waters of the adultery ordeal (see Numbers 5:11–31). What did she do? She went to her sister, and said to her, "My husband suspects me, and I know that he intends to make me drink the bitter waters. Now, we look a lot alike, and you are my bone and flesh. Be a loving sister, and cover my shame and disgrace, for you also will bear it otherwise. So, make ready and go with my husband and drink the bitter waters—for you are innocent, and there is no impurity in you!" And her sister replied, "I'll do as you ask."

That night, the two of them spent the night together, and the next day, the look-alike rose early to go off with her sister's husband to the priest. There, the priest gave her the poisonous brew to drink, and it had no effect on her, for she was innocent. When she returned, she encountered her sister, and the latter came up and threw her arms around her and kissed her, for she felt great love for her and great happiness, and she said to herself, "From now on, I'll have many lovers!"

But it was the Lord's wish that the following should happen. At that moment, just as she kissed her sister, she smelled the aroma of the bitter waters, and immediately her face went green, her belly swelled up, and she fell to her knees and keeled over dead.

She had acted in secret, and the Holy One, blessed be He, brought her back out in the open. Had she said, "I am impure," they'd have torn up her wedding document, and she'd go forth unmarried. And had she said, "I am pure," they'd have brought her to Nicanor Gate, and there made her drink. And were she to have proved pure, she would be visited with something good—were she barren, she would become pregnant; were she to have birth pangs, she'd be given a painless birth; were she to have only girl children, she'd be made to bear males; and were she to bear ugly children, she'd be given to bear handsome children. But if she were impure, she would be punished in accord with the nature of her offense. If she had stood in open view of a man, the priest would stand her at Nicanor Gate, that her disgrace might be viewed. If she had gestured to a man with her fingers, her nails would be torn off. If she had adorned her head for a man, the priest would remove it from her and place it under her feet. If she had set her hair for a man, the priest would cover her coiffure. If she had put mascara on her eyes, her eyes would be made to swell. If she had rouged her face, her face would be made to turn green. If she had bound herself with straps for a man, the priest would have an Egyptian rope strapped around her breasts. If she had fed a man delicacies, her barley offering would be fed to cattle. If she had given him fine wine to drink in a silver cup, the priest would give her the bitter waters to drink in a cup of clay. If she performed the foul deed of adultery in secret, the Holy One, blessed be He, would bring upon her recompense in the open, for she is an adulteress and stubborn of spirit. Therefore, the Holy One, blessed be He, commanded in his Torah: "Do not commit adultery."[38]

NINTH COMMANDMENT: DO NOT BEAR FALSE WITNESS AGAINST YOUR NEIGHBOR. (Exodus 20:13)

Lest your children learn how to bear false witness. And our rabbis of blessed memory have said,[39] "Four classes of people do not greet the Shekhinah (the Divine Presence): the class of scoffers, the class of hypocrites, the class of liars, the class of those who recount evil gossip. The scoffers, for it says, "He extended his hand to scoffers" (Hosea 7:5).

The class of hypocrites, for it says, "A hypocrite will not come before him" (Job 13:16). The class of liars, for it says, "One who utters lies cannot stand in my sight" (Psalm 101:7). The class of those who recount evil gossip, for it says, "For You are not a God who delights in wickedness, evil does not dwell with You (Psalm 5:5). What does "evil does not dwell with you" mean? You are just, O Lord, and evil does not dwell in Your abode. Therefore, a person is required to guard his tongue from evil gossip.

A tale is told of a certain man who had three daughters. One of them was lazy, one was a thief, and one engaged in evil gossip. And he saw them grow old in his household. No man wanted them because of their bad reputation. One day a friend who came to stay as a guest in his house saw his daughters, who were growing old in his household, and told him, "I have three sons, and if it pleases you, give them to me as wives for my sons." "My daughters are not fit for your sons," he replied. "Why?" the man asked. "Because they have a terrible and shameful reputation," he replied, and spelled out the details.

"Even so," the man said, "give them to my sons!" Right away, he married them off to the man's sons. How did the man accomplish this? The lazy one he sat upon a bed and appointed servants to minister before her, telling them, "Do not neglect to do anything for her!" The thief he gave in trust all his money and said to her, "Whatever you'll do, is done." For the one who engaged in evil gossip, her father-in-law rose early each day and greeted her with a kiss, sat her down next to him, and said, "My daughter, what is your inclination? If you wish to ask anything of your husband, tell me, and I'll talk with him, and he'll perform your wish." But she would not tell him anything.

After some days, their father came to inquire about their welfare. Here is what happened. The women were living with their husbands, and the father went first to the house of the lazy daughter, and said to her, "My daughter, how are you with your husband?" "May a blessing come upon you, father," she answered, "for you have given me to a man who does for me so many good things. He has appointed servants and handmaidens to minister before me, and they don't let me do anything." He praised them and left and went to the house of the one who was a thief, and said to her, "My daughter, how are you with your husband?" She gave as good a report as the first one. And he praised the Lord and went out from there and went to the house of the daughter who engaged in evil gossip. When she saw her father, she began to cry, and said to him, "Father! It is the custom in this world for a person to give his daughter to one man, and you have given me to two, a father and a son! If you don't believe me, hide in this room and you'll see the truth." She quickly hid him in the room, and her father-in-law came to inquire of her welfare, as was his custom. She told her father-in-law, "Go away, don't touch me, and don't talk to me!" "Have I come for any evil deed?" he asked. "God forbid! Such a thing has not occurred to me!" When her father saw him, he came out of his hiding place, and, rising up over him, slew him. Afterward, the people of the house came running up to him, and they killed him. And she cried out and wept, and they turned on her and killed her. Whence are we accustomed to say, "The evil tongue kills threefold—the one who wields it, the one who receives it, and the one about whom it speaks." And our rabbis of blessed memory have said, "There is nothing harder for the world than the evil tongue. Therefore (God) commanded us: "Do not bear false witness against your neighbor."[40]

NOTES

1. We translate the four-letter divine name (the Tetragrammaton) as "Lord," and the pious Jew truncates the name in Hebrew writing to a letter *h* (he). Miracle stories abound in midrash about magic effected by wielding the sacred four letters (yod/he/vav/he) in their "correct" (presently unknown) pronunciation. The name is written out fully in biblical or liturgical texts, but those who read it aloud substitute *Adonai* (Lord) in devotional circumstances, *Adoshem* or *Hashem* ("the Name") in everyday uses. The unpronounceable letters are seen as the ground of all Creation, as the root and structure of all divine self-unfolding. For God to be, as it were, on a first-name basis with a people was seen as no small event (see Exodus 3:13–16).

2. The psalmist may not have known that there were 70 kings, corresponding to the 70 languages of the world; the midrashist, apparently, did. Actually, there are 159 nations represented at the U.N., some 2,800 identified languages, and about 1,400 languages into which the Bible is translated. The world may have been even more complex in the midrashist's day, but he thought in astrologically round numbers.

3. The lore and literature on the Song of Songs, from ancient times to now,

is enormous. Song of Songs began as a garland of secular love lyrics, lush and ribald of imagery, portraying the romance of King Solomon and a shepherd maiden. King Solomon is traditionally held to be the author, but he is more like a figure in a masque than a flesh-and-blood inventor. Jews of later times made the poem an allegory of God and Israel (just as Christians made it one of Christ and the church), and the Jewish mystics read it audaciously as a map of the body of God. In Kabbalah, the God addressed in prayer is spoken of as male; the itinerant Presence (Shekhinah) made luminous through prayer is spoken of as female. This midrashist, however, is not a kabbalist, though the interpretation he offers was also used by kabbalists: the maiden is Israel, and her breathlessness at meeting her lover is equated with the swooning of Israel before Sinai.

4. Torah in midrash and Kabbalah is the primordial daughter of God, a figure of Wisdom who antedates Creation and is its nurse and blueprint. She sits before the Throne of Glory and pleads repeatedly for Israel (see Genesis Rabbah 1:1).

5. Hebrew *Ribbono shel Olam* (Yiddish *Ribboyne sheloylem*) is usually the way God is addressed directly in a story; the "Holy One, blessed be He" (*Ha-Kadosh Barukh Hu*, or simply HKBH) is used when speaking in the third person.

6. The number 365 equals, of course, the number of days in the solar year; 248 equals the number of parts of the human body (B. Makkot 23b). This gnosis, which etches the entire ritual life of the Jew onto the life of the solar and the human body, the crowning creations of heaven and earth, respectively, is very ancient and had a long history beyond its use here.

7. The situation is a double bind. Apparently, the lotion proffered heals the body but destroys the spirit. The Babylonian mythic hero Adapa was wisely inclined to turn down a goblet of the same stuff. The crippled Jew, of course, does not refuse; he is refused. Two lines of his fate cross in a single instant: one favorable (a place in the world to come), one unfavorable (no cure of the body). Precisely by coming here has he sealed his own fate. (Some centuries later, a Hasidic master would tell his followers, "You shouldn't trust in miracles. Pray!") Ironically the whole thing is made known to him by one of the very beings whose existence (though taken for granted here) the Jew is supposed to repudiate. Even the nonexistent gods and godlets believe in God. But why was the Jew's soul spared? Because he was a Jew? Or because he had done acts of piety, unmentioned in this story, that now stand to his credit? The text never tells us. The sole indication that he has clung to his Jewishness despite himself is the fact that he suffers from insomnia at a pagan shrine.

8. What follows is not a quotation from the biblical account but a paraphrase, probably made from memory. The biblical account makes no mention of Gehazi swearing an oath. The midrashist may have been thinking of verse 16, where Elisha swears by the life of God (there, apparently, an irreproachable act), or he may have invented the detail about Gehazi swearing in order to set him in sharper contrast to his more saintly master.

9. The widow's act is technically a theft and a violation of a trustee relation, but these are committed for the sake of charity. None of the details of this brief episode has a rational explanation, nor is there any clear-cut way to sort out the

rights and wrongs of the woman's action or its apparent divine recompense. The sages' "explanation," by relating the event to the Third Commandment, is appropriately off the point. The total montage thus supplies, perhaps inadvertently, an accurate portrait of the difficulty in the relation between legality, morality, and divine justice.

10. The man's decision not to swear in court litigation is in conflict with Jewish law, which does permit a truthful oath in a court of law, especially in a case such as this. In this collection, all of the examples of pious adherence to one of the Ten Commandments are exaggerated cases (see note 19 below).

11. So according to one version of the text, which reads *dag* (fish). Other versions read *daf* (leaf), *saf* (window sill or bowl) (= *suf* [reed]?).

12. No doubt a common event in the experience of the medieval Jew.

13. One version of the text condenses all that follows into a single sentence, "And finally, the Holy One, blessed be He, wrought a miracle for him and returned to him his wife and his children, and he made them princes and sultans, and that righteous man gave alms, and thanks, and praise to the Holy One, blessed be He, who had repaid him his reward (of piety) in full" (A. Jellinek, *Beit ha-Midrash*, 1853; reprint, Jerusalem: Wahrmann, 1967, 1:73).

14. For this motif (delay of a family reunion through the dissembling of one of its members) compare the Joseph story, Genesis 42:5ff. The difference here is that the man acts not to test his kin but to expose the captain.

15. This is clear from what follows, but it was in no way anticipated by the sentences that precede. It is as if the sons had long been part of his palace household.

16. The narrator is fond of this classically Jewish gesture as a way of indicating agitation; lamentation in response to crisis occurs several times in this story. It was not, apparently, an expression of passivity. Note that the wife, though lamenting, can dissemble like her husband and not reveal her identity. Intrigues of delayed recognition are contagious in this story.

17. Without much prior indication, the wife suddenly metamorphoses into a Shakespearean schemer. The point of this false accusation is probably to provide a pretext for her removal to the palace. (That she should be left on the ship in the first place seems to be taken for granted by our narrator.) The irony of a mother accusing her sons of molesting her was probably not lost on the reader.

18. This point contradicts the earlier mention that the man also "followed the commandments, and . . . honored the students of the sages." Figures in midrash who are praised for observing a *single* commandment are often subjected to mild ridicule, as if to suggest that single-minded pursuit of a moral precept out of proportion to the moral system as a whole is a kind of demonic obsession to be shunned, rather than an ideal to be emulated. The hero of this story and his family, however, seem to remain idealized figures throughout, despite the extreme nature of his obedience to the Third Commandment. So the tag line, following the rabbinic logic of *de minore ad maiem*, fits better with the next story in our translation, where the hero is more clearly a satirical figure whose pious observance of *one* commandment has by no means shaped him into a noble personality. For a

deeper understanding of the function of "demonic" characters in literature, see Angus Fletcher, *Allegory: Theory of a Symbolic Mode* (Ithaca, N.Y.: Cornell University Press, 1964), 50ff.

19. This clearly marks the story as satire. "Cast your bread upon the waters," as the second clause suggests, means that one should feed the *poor*. Our protagonist, however, takes it quite literally. For the original context of the expression "cast your bread . . . ," see Ecclesiastes 11:1.

20. Leviathan enters Jewish tradition via Job 40:25–32. He is the same as Lothan in Canaanite myth. Cf. Psalm 104:26. The name is possibly derived from a Semitic root meaning "coiled." Midrash made Leviathan into king of all sea creatures, God's viceroy for the oceans, and devourer of every sea creature whose appointed end had come (Midrash Jonah, ed. Jellinek, 1:98). Leviathan is also the world's largest bathtub plug: he sits across the hole that leads down to Tehom, the torrential waters of the underworld. Certain hours of the day, however, he is on call as God's house pet, sporting with the Master of the universe like a puppy. In our story he is represented, in good rabbinical fashion, as presider in a court of law. According to legend, at the End of Days, the flesh of this loyal servant will be fed to the righteous in the world to come. See Louis Ginzberg, *Legends of the Jews* (Philadelphia: Jewish Publication Society, 1909–1953), 1:27–28; 5:41–46.

21. Analogously for Melampus, "his ears having been licked clean by a grateful brood of young serpents" (Robert Graves, *The Greek Myths* [New York: George Braziller, Inc., 1957], 72c; Apollodorus 1.9.11). At this point, the story seems to shift gears and enter a fairy-tale, or *Märchen*, mode. This new phase will consist of three episodes, each demonstrating how the man averted disaster by his knowledge of communication with animals. This knowledge was classically attributed to King Solomon (cf. 1 Kings 5:9–14; also see 3:4–28; Ecclesiastes 1:12–18) and is a common motif in the wisdom literature of the ancient Near East. I am grateful to poet-translator-anthropologist David M. Guss for pointing out to me the connection with Melampus. On the notion of "seventy" languages, see n. 2, above.

22. The Talmud (esp. B. Sanhedrin 96b–99a) abounds with lore about the coming of the Messiah and the resurrection of the dead. But messianic activists were looked at with a baleful eye. "Blast the bones of those who calculate the end!" cries Rabbi Samuel bar Nahman, a third-century Palestinian teacher, "for if the appointed time arrives and it hasn't yet come about, they will say it will never come." Our story's digression is borrowed from Leviticus Rabbah 22:4. It is actually a digression within a digression and serves as addendum to the aftermath of the man's confrontation with the birds, as a kind of inverse mirror: a bird kills and revives her child, a man revives a lion and it kills him. This structure is called chiastic (a b b' a'): kill/revive/revive/kill. In the end the dead stay dead, and the animals multiply.

23. Though reminiscent of the biblical Balaam episode (Numbers 22:2–24:5; see esp. 22:21–31), this detail conflicts with both the letter and the spirit of Judaism regarding the treatment of animals. See Noah J. Cohen, *Tsa'ar Ba'ale Hayim: The Prevention of Cruelty to Animals* (New York: Feldheim, 1976).

24. Hebrew *kavod* (glory, honor). This theosophically and eschatologically weighted word is probably used here facetiously—the story has lost all connection with the theme of honoring one's parents.

25. The handsomeness of the protagonist is a frequent motif in stories involving sexual temptation. Cf. Genesis 39:6ff., and John D. Yohannan, *Joseph and Potiphar's Wife in World Literature: An Anthology of the Story of the Chaste Youth and the Lustful Stepmother* (New York: New Directions, 1968).

26. Cf. Job 1:6ff.

27. Again, the manner of obeying the commandment is extreme. See note 10 above, and Joseph Dan, *The Hebrew Story in the Middle Ages* (in Hebrew) (Jerusalem: Keter, 1974), 83–84. The story about Rabbi Matthiah is already found in older midrashim (Tanhuma, ed. S. Buber, B. Hukkat 66a; cf. Yalkut Shimoni on Genesis, 161). Rabbi Matthiah was a second-century Palestinian teacher who fled to Italy during the Bar Kokhba wars (ca. 135 C.E.), though he is said to have returned to his native land out of homesickness. This did not deter him from eventually settling in Rome, where he is said to have founded a great yeshiva (B. Sanhedrin 32b). His most famous legal decision is the ruling that all Sabbath prohibitions may be overruled to save a human life (Mishnah Yoma 8:6). His most famous saying is "Be a tail to lions, and not a head to foxes" (M. Avot 4:15), the reversal of a Roman proverb (see P. Sanhedrin 4:10; B. Sanhedrin 37a).

28. Rabbi Meir was a contemporary of Rabbi Matthiah's and also from Palestine. He was at the center of the politics and cultural life of his generation, though he experienced, for a time, political exile, and, later, factional opposition within the reconstituted Sanhedrin after the Roman wars. He was known for his political moderation and cosmopolitan affinities. He was the only one among his colleagues to maintain contact with the alleged heretic Elisha ben Abuya (known as Aher, "the Alien") after his ostracism from the rabbinic community. Rabbi Meir was a compiler of a legal collection that two generations later would be the basis for the Mishnah, the first great postbiblical Jewish law code. He is also reputed to be the author of three hundred fox fables, of which only three are preserved (B. Sanhedrin, 38b). He was a fierce partisan of learning and study and is believed to have been sufficiently punctilious in matters of ritual purity as to have merited the rare rabbinic epithet *holy*. His wife Beruriah is said to have been a scholar in her own right, and a woman who bore the death of her two children with grace and courage. Rabbi Meir is said to have rescued Beruriah's sister from a brothel, though, according to Rashi (B. Avodah Zarah 18b), poor Meir suffered the seduction of Beruriah herself by one of his rabbinical colleagues. The amorous peccadillo ascribed to Meir by our story seems a purely medieval invention, prompted by his reputation for piety and ritual perfection. He is thus a kind of inverse of many of the other protagonists in this collection. Their distinction is a single commandment followed; his, a single commandment *not* followed. For a list of versions of this story, see M. J. Bin-Gorion, *Mi-Mekor Yisrael: Classical Jewish Folktales* (Bloomington, Ind.: University of Indiana Press, 1976), 3:157 n. 34.

29. Or Rabbi Judah the Butcher (*tabbah*). A variant of this story (see Bin-Gorion, *Mi-Mekor Yisrael* 2:580–82, 3:1,507 n. 35) deals instead with a Rabbi

Judah of Tiberias. Not much seems to be known about either figure, assuming they are not fictional creations. Rabbis are sometimes known by their secular trade (e.g., Rabbi Johanan the Sandalmaker), a reflection of the fact that the earliest generations of rabbis pursued ordinary professions and exercised their rabbinical (chiefly juridical) functions as an avocation. (Maimonides, in turning down a community stipend, preferring instead a highly demanding career as a physician, paid his respects to an ancient custom that had in his day become an exception, at least among the Oriental rabbis.) Judah the Cook's designation as "Rabbi," however, may derive from his association with Rabbi Meir, who was known as no friend of the unlearned (see B. Pesahim 49b).

30. Three times in the year—Passover, Shavuot (Pentecost), and Sukkot (the Feast of Booths)—a Jew was expected to "appear before the Lord God" (Exodus 23:17) to present a festival offering. In the days when the Temple stood, this was taken to mean an appearance in Jerusalem. The practice was discontinued after 70 C.E., though the three pilgrim festivals remain the core of the Jewish calendar.

31. Cf. the similar phrasing in Jonah 4:11.

32. Cf. the similar phrasing in Genesis 19:33, 35, and (in a very different context) Deuteronomy 6:7 (the Shema).

33. Hebrew *rosh yeshivah*, literally "a head of an academy," who in this context seems to have had a local governing authority (see B. Berakhot 57a).

34. It is a typical folktale pattern that things happen in threes. Note the increase in ferocity of the lion in each respective instance.

35. An olive-bulk was the minimum quantity affixed by rabbinic law for defining whether or not food has been eaten (Mishnah Kelim 17:8; cf. Mishnah Berakhot 7:1, Mishnah Kilayim 8:5, Mishnah Hallah 1:2, Mishnah Pesahim 3:2, et al.). The use of the expression here must be understood tongue in cheek, in keeping with the bawdy and satirical overtones of the story. Though the ostensible reference is to Rabbi Meir's *rib*, another anatomical part may be hinted at.

36. Hebrew *bat kol* (literally daughter of a voice), "echo." This device is invoked frequently in talmudic and midrashic stories where the intervention of Heaven is required to resolve an insoluble human predicament or to comment on the justice of an action taken. "After the last prophets died out, the Holy Spirit was removed from Israel, but still they make use of the *bat kol*" (B. Yoma 9b). Cf. B. Berakhot 3a, B. Pesahim 94a. See also p. 163 below (*Midrash Eleh Ezkerah*, n.9).

37. For a list of variants of this story, see Bin-Gorion, *Mi-Mekor Yisrael* 3:1,510 nn. 90, 91, and cf. 2:626–28.

38. The foregoing passage is mostly a paraphrase and condensation of the talionic punishments enumerated in Mishnah Sotah 1:5–6, 2:1. In the present story, the echo of mishnaic language effects a certain eery eloquence and conveys rather transparently the male anxieties aroused by thoughts of a woman's infidelity. The retributive ecstasy suggested by this chilling passage is qualified considerably in its original mishnaic context; there, the mishnaic editor balanced its apparent vindictiveness toward the woman with a passage referring to analogously karmic punishments of men: "Samson went after what his eyes saw—therefore the

Philistines put out his eyes. . . . Absalom gloried in his hair—therefore he was hanged by his hair. And in that he came upon his father's ten concubines, they thrust ten spearheads into his body. . . . And in that he stole away three hearts— that of his father, that of the court, and that of Israel— . . . three darts were thrust into him" (Mishnah Sotah 1:8).

39. B. Sotah 42a.

40. A tale that swallows its tail—a classic self-consuming artifact. One is amazed that after an exposition so leisurely, the story is sped up to a Keystone Kops pace and abruptly collapsed into a proverb. Warnings against an "evil tongue" grew still more intense in the centuries that followed this midrash. In the nineteenth century it was the basis of an ethical movement motivated by Rabbi Israel Meir ha-Kohen (known as the Hafetz Hayyim, after Psalm 34:13), who regarded gossip about and even praise of a person as illegitimate discourse, analogous to breaking the Ninth Commandment. It seems as if the midrashist himself (herself?) suddenly grew demure about talebearing.

6 ◆

THE TALE OF THE
JERUSALEMITE

"The Tale of the Jerusalemite," "Maaseh Yerushalmi," is one of the masterworks of medieval Hebrew fiction. Though traditionally attributed to Abraham, the son of the great Maimonides, little is actually known about its history. Modern scholars have disputed the time and the place of its composition. Moses Gaster, who first published an English translation in 1931 and acclaimed the work "one of the earliest fairy-tales accessible to European readers" (*Folklore* 42 [1931]: 157), dated it to thirteenth-century Egypt. Joseph Dan (in *Ha-Sippur ha-Ivrit bi-Yemei ha-Beinayim*) has suggested that it may have derived from an Ashkenazic (German) locale in the twelfth or thirteenth century. Finally, and most likely, Jehuda Zlotnik, who edited the critical edition of the text, has placed the work in Babylonia during the geonic period, in the ninth or tenth century. Wherever it originated, though, the tale was widely disseminated in medieval Jewish centers, a testimony to its popularity as well as to the appeal of its universality.

In genre, "The Tale of the Jerusalemite" resembles the exemplary anecdotes found in such other collections of medieval Hebrew narrative as "Midrash on the Ten Commandments." Like the much briefer narratives in that collection, this tale about a nameless Jerusalemite is recounted under the pretense of illustrating or exemplifying a moral—in this case, the punishments that will befall a son who disobeys his father's commands.

And like the narratives in "Midrash on the Ten Commandments," "The Tale of the Jerusalemite" far exceeds its moral justification.

The translation is based upon the Yemenite manuscript published by Jehuda L. Zlotnik in *Maaseh Yerushalmi* (Jerusalem: The Palestine Institute of Folklore and Ethnology, 1946), with notes by Zlotnik, a preface and additional notes by Raphael Patai, M. Grunwald, and S. Assaf. Many of the comments to this translation are drawn from those notes.

Introduction by
DAVID STERN

Translation by
DAVID STERN *and* AVI WEINSTEIN

There once lived a great merchant who had a single son. He taught his son Torah, Mishnah, and Talmud and gave him a wife, who bore children to the son during his father's lifetime.

When the time came for the merchant to die, he summoned all the elders of the town. "You know that I own a large amount of property," he said to them. "My wife, according to the terms of her marriage contract, will receive from my estate more than one hundred measures of silver. The rest of my wealth I leave to my son—if he follows the command I now set before him in your presence. But if he disobeys my last will, I consecrate my property to heaven."

He called his son at once and announced before the elders: "My son! You know how much property I own—silver, gold, precious stones, and pearls. I earned them toiling on journeys over land and sea. How many tribulations I endured on the oceans! Swear to me by the strictest of oaths that you will not endanger yourself on the sea. For I am about to leave you sufficient wealth—for you, for your children, for your children's children. But if you violate this oath, then I consecrate all my property to heaven."

The son swore before the town's elders that he would never go to sea. After some time the father died, and the son sat and studied Torah in obedience to his oath.

Two years later a ship came to port in that very town. When the sailors went ashore, they asked if the merchant was still alive. The people told them, "The merchant died, but he left behind a son who is wealthy and a scholar."

"Please show us his home," the sailors asked. They entered the house to greet the son. "Are you really the child of that great merchant who journeyed in trade to the ends of the earth?"

"I am the son of that man," he replied.

"If so," they said, "tell us what instructions your father gave you about the properties and securities he owned abroad at the time of his death."

"He gave me no instructions about what he owned. He only bound me by oath never to go to sea."

"If it's true that he did not leave instructions about his deposits or property abroad," responded the sailors, "then he must have been feeble when he died. Everything on this ship, the silver, the gold, the pearls— all of it belonged to your father, who left it with us in trust. Even though he has died and left no instructions, we could never, heaven forbid, betray his confidence. For we are trustworthy men, and we worship the Lord in heaven.[1] We do not covet the money of others, for—the Lord be praised— we have much wealth of our own. Come now with your servants, and take everything in the ship. It is all yours." The merchant's son happily went to the ship and brought all the money to his house. He invited the sailors home as well and made a feast and celebration.

The next day the sailors declared, "Your father was known to be a wise and clever man. When, at the time of his dying, he made you swear never to go to sea, he could not have been in his right mind. In truth, the oath he made you swear has no substance, for your father still owns property and securities ten times greater than what we have brought you. How could he ever make you swear and lose that property? He must have been demented. Listen to us. Request permission from the king and from the sages. Come away with us, buy the merchandise found in our country, make a great profit on it, and return home happy with the money your father deposited in our homeland."

The son replied, "My father has already made me take an oath never to go to sea. I will not violate this oath. As for his not giving me instructions about the money abroad, he must have had my own welfare in mind, not wanting me to wish to go to sea to bring the money home. You see, I cannot break the oath."

The sailors asked, "Did your father love you more than himself? Yet he went to sea all his life until he had become very rich. No! He must have been unbalanced. The oath has no substance, for even 'Job did not speak with knowledge' (Job 34:35). It would be best for you to have the oath nullified and come with us."

In the end, the sailors so pressed the son and distracted him from his right mind that he gave in, feeling compelled to accompany them and bring back the money. What did he do? He went and purchased a great store of merchandise and left with the sailors on their ship.

As they sailed in the ship on the great sea, God was incensed at his going,[2] for the man had broken his oath and his father's commandment. And the Lord cast a mighty wind upon the sea, and there was such a great tempest in the sea that the ship was wrecked.[3] And all the sailors who had misled the man and turned his mind to embark upon the sea, to transgress the oath and his father's commandment, were drowned. But the Lord, blessed be He, made a sign to the celestial officer in charge of the sea. He cast the man onto dry land, naked and barefoot at the ends of the earth, in a place uninhabited by mankind. In this way, the man would now suffer in his lifetime the punishment for the sin that he had committed.

The man, once he came to dry land and saw himself naked and barefoot, recognized that this was God's wrath and that the day of his judgment had arrived.[4] The man lifted his eyes to heaven and surrendered to divine judgment. Then he began to walk along the seashore in hopes of finding shelter or something to eat or wear, for he was as naked as when he came forth from the womb.[5] After he had walked a whole day, he came upon a tree whose foliage overspread the seashore. The man thought to himself, Some person has planted this tree. He began to look for its roots, but he did not find them until it was dark, for they lay at a distance of forty parasangs. Realizing that he had nothing to eat or wear, he rose and covered his body with the tree's leaves in order to protect himself from the cold of the night.

It was midnight[6] when he heard the roar of a lion. The man understood that a lion was approaching to eat him. As it drew nearer, the man, terrified that he was about to be eaten for having broken his father's oath, raised his voice, crying to God, the Lord of Israel, to protect and show him mercy, not to rage in anger against him, and not to punish him with a death so unnatural.[7]

What did the man do? He grabbed the leaves and climbed up one of the branches of the tree. When the lion came, it saw nothing and went away.

The man thanked the blessed Lord for saving him from the lion. He decided to climb higher up the tree, hoping to find something to eat, for he was starved. And when he had climbed all the way up, he discovered a great bird, which is called the Kifufa.[8] As soon as the bird saw the man, it opened its beak to eat him. The man sought to flee. But the Lord, may He be blessed, set wisdom in the man's heart. He mounted the bird, and once he was on top, the Kifufa became so frightened it did not move or stir from its place the entire night. The young man, also afraid, prayed to the blessed Lord to save him, holding on to the bird's feathers with both hands. And while the man could not descend from the bird, the Kifufa was also terrified, for it did not know who was mounted on its back.

At daybreak the Kifufa saw the man, but it was still terrified. All day, until evening came, the bird flew in a panic, carrying its passenger across the sea to the ends of the earth. The man looked down as he passed over the ocean, and afraid he was about to fall, he prayed to the blessed Lord to rescue him. In the night the Kifufa passed over a certain province, flying close to the ground. The man heard the voices of children reading the section of the Torah that begins, "These are the rules that you shall set before them. When you acquire a Hebrew slave . . ." (Exodus 21:1–2). Hearing this, the man said to himself: This province must certainly have Jews living in it. I will throw myself down there. Perhaps they will pity me. If not, I'll sell myself as a slave. And so he threw himself down and landed at the gate of the synagogue in that town. The Kifufa went on its way, but the man, once he had fallen, could not move for two days. He had nearly been crushed by the force of the fall; besides, he was very weak since he had not eaten for two days.

At last, he rose to his feet and walked toward the gate of the synagogue. But he found it closed. The man shouted, "Open the gates of righteousness for me!"[9]

A boy came out of the synagogue. "Who are you?" he asked.

The man replied, "I am a Hebrew, and I worship the Lord God of heaven."[10]

The boy went and told the rabbi, who told him to open the door. When the rabbi saw that the man had no clothes, he asked what had happened, and the man told the rabbi his entire story, beginning to end, all the troubles he had suffered. The rabbi responded, "Everything that has happened to you is trivial in comparison with what you are now about to suffer here."

"But aren't you Jews?" the man asked. "Are not the children of Israel a merciful people, descendants of merciful ancestors? And particularly to someone like myself, an impoverished man, lacking everything, naked, barefoot?"

"Don't waste your words," the rabbi said. "You can't be saved from death."

"Why do you say such things?" the man implored.

"This is not a town of humans but of demons," answered the rabbi. "These boys are the children of demons. They are all about to gather to pray at this moment. When they see you, they'll kill you."

As soon as the man heard this, he fell panic-stricken before the rabbi as though to kiss his feet, and he begged him for advice as to how he could be delivered from death. For he was learned in Torah and pious except for the time he sinned by following the counsel of men who misled him into transgressing his father's oath.

As the rabbi listened, he was overcome with pity for the man. "You are a scholar of Torah, a learned man," the rabbi said. "Since you show regret for what you have done, you deserve mercy. And because you kissed my feet and fell before me, I will make an effort to save you."

What did the rabbi do? He took the man to his house, fed and clothed him, and let him sleep there, and all night the demons did not sense his presence. The next day the rabbi said to him, "Come with me to the synagogue. Sit beneath my robe, but don't say a word until I speak to them on your behalf." They went to the synagogue, and the man sat hidden in the rabbi's robe. At daybreak, the demons came to the synagogue like fiery torches. The man heard the roar of thunder and lightning and shrieks of terror everywhere, and was left in such dread he could hardly breathe. And then the demons, just like Jews, began to recite the preliminary prayers, the psalms of praise.

One demon, however, was standing near the rabbi. He said to his fellow demon, "I smell a human."

Then the two of them heard the voice of the man in their midst, and they said, "Here he is, sitting next to the rabbi!" Yet because the man was

127

under the cloak of the rabbi, whom they treated with respect, the demons did not harm the man.

The rabbi, though, immediately realized that the man's presence had been detected. Waiting until the preliminary prayers had been completed, he told the prayer leader, "Stop the prayers! Let me speak!"

"Speak, our teacher," the demons responded. "Your servants are attentive."

"I beg you," the rabbi said to them. "Do not harm this man. He has come beneath the shelter of my roof."[11]

"And what is this mortal to us?" they responded. "What reason has he for being here?"

The rabbi told them his entire story from beginning to end, but the demons answered, "How can we spare a man as wicked as this, who disobeyed both his father's commandment and a sacred oath? Such a man deserves to die."

The rabbi replied, "The man has already taken his punishment through the troubles he has suffered. He is a Torah scholar, moreover, and it is only right that his knowledge of Torah protect him. If he truly deserved death, then the Lord, blessed be He, would not have saved him from the lion, from the sea, from the Kifufa, and from the many other calamities he faced."

"Yet that is all the more reason for him to be executed now," the demons countered, "precisely because he is a Torah scholar who did not obey his father's commandment and broke his oath. Even the crimes he committed unintentionally should now be treated as though they were done willfully.[12] There is only one reason God has saved him from everything until now: that he might die an unnatural death at our hands."

The rabbi said, "It would not be right for you to execute him without a proper trial. He is, after all, a man learned in Torah. Now do what I say. Let the prayer leader announce that no demon shall harm the man during the prayer service. Immediately after the service we will take him to King Ashmadai, who will judge whether or not the man shall be executed."

The demons responded unanimously, "What you propose to do is good."[13] They immediately ordered the prayer leader in the synagogue to announce that no demon was to harm the man until the king of the demons had judged him. After prayers they brought the man before

Ashmadai. "O king, our lord," they said, "this man has sinned against God, he has broken his oath, and he did not keep his father's commandment. The following things have already happened to him, but we did not wish to execute him before we had brought him to you, for he is a scholar of Torah."

When the king heard this, he summoned the members of his court. After telling them what the man had done and what had subsequently happened to him, he gave them the following charge: "Render a just verdict in the morning.[14] His case must be thoroughly researched, for he is a Torah scholar; therefore judge him according to the laws of the Torah of Moses."

The members of the court adjourned, investigated the case, and issued their verdict—the man must die. For it is written, "Cursed be the man who dishonors his father and mother" (Deuteronomy 27:16)—and this verse refers to a person who makes light of his father's honor, just as this man broke his father's oath. And he who is accursed is guilty of death. From where do we know this? From the case of Jonathan, the son of Saul, who was accursed.[15]

The members of the court returned to King Ashmadai and reported their verdict that the man be executed for the stated reasons. Ashmadai said to them, "Be lenient in judgment. Leave it overnight. For it is said, '. . . the congregation shall judge . . . and the congregation shall protect . . .' (Numbers 35:24–25).[16] Even Moses, their teacher, hesitated to pronounce judgment upon the man who gathered wood on the Sabbath, since the law for that transgression was not explicitly stated."[17]

The members of the court replied: "We will do as you say. For you are our lord, and we look to you for guidance."

The king said, "The man will come with me tonight. No one shall harm him until his verdict has been made clear."

And so it was.

At that time Ashmadai asked the man if he had studied Torah and Talmud. He ordered that a Bible, Mishnah, and Talmud be brought before the man, and then they examined him and found that he was wise and expert in every subject. When Ashmadai saw this, he said, "Now I know that you are a truly wise man. You have found favor in my eyes. Swear to me that you will live here and instruct my children in what you know, and I will protect you from the demons' hands. For I know that they will make a pact to kill you."

The man took an oath to that effect. The king then said, "Let me teach you the correct arguments to plead tomorrow. When they say you are guilty of death, respond by saying that you yourself are a judge and a learned man. You wish to review the case and to examine the arguments. They will come to me, and I will save you."

The next day the members of the court came before King Ashmadai and told him, "We have no cause to acquit him."

The man spoke up in response, "Mine is a court greater than yours. I wish to examine the case for myself."

They replied, "No man admits to his own guilt." Immediately they took counsel among themselves. "The best thing we can do," they said, "is to follow the words of King Ashmadai. For he studies every day in the celestial academy, and then descends and teaches in the academy below, and so he is expert in the laws of heaven and earth."

They came to Ashmadai and asked him, "What is your verdict?"

Ashmadai responded, "The man has not committed a transgression justifying the death penalty. For whatever he did was not rebellious or belligerent or malicious. Other men incited him. They misled him, and as the rabbis say, 'The Torah absolves a man who acts under duress.'[18] From where is this law derived? From the verse '. . . and do nothing to the girl' (Deuteronomy 22:26). You know that the Lord put those other men to death while at sea, yet He saved this man!" When the court heard this, they declared the man innocent.

Afterward, Ashmadai took the man home and set his son before him. They studied the Pentateuch, the Prophets, and the Writings, the Mishnah, and Gemara. The man was shown great honor, and by the end of three years Ashmadai's son had mastered the entire Torah. During this time one of the king's provinces rose in rebellion. King Ashmadai assembled his legions, and he appointed the man over his house and property, entrusting him with the keys to the treasury. The king, after ordering the entire household to do nothing without his permission, showed the man all the treasuries. There was, however, one door that he pointed out to him to which he did not give the man the key. "You may enter every one of my treasuries except for this one," the king told the man. He then departed to lay siege to the rebellious province.

One day the man happened to pass the door that Ashmadai had commanded him not to enter. The man asked himself, What could there be in this treasury that is not in the others? Why did Ashmadai command me not to enter it? The man went up to the entrance. The daughter of Ashmadai was seated on a golden throne. Seven maidens danced and frolicked before her. And she was shapely and beautiful.[19]

When she saw the man, she called out, "Enter." The man entered and stood before her. "Fool!" she said to him. "First you disobeyed your father's command, and now you've disobeyed the command of my father, the king. Besides, what business have you with women? I hope you know that you are going to die today. My father already knows that you have entered this house. Look! Here he comes with his sword in his hand, drawn to kill you."

Hearing this, the man fell at her feet, kissing them, and weeping and pleading with her to save him from her father as he might be slain. For he had not entered the house for licentious purposes; his intentions had not been evil. Observing this, Ashmadai's daughter said to the man, "Since you are a scholar, your modesty will save you today. But leave the house. When my father arrives and asks why you entered and disobeyed his command, and when he seeks to kill you, tell him, 'My lord, please understand that I entered that house only because I am in love with your daughter. I ask you, Give her to me as a wife.'

"Your words will win approval in his eyes, I know. He will give me to you. Since the day you arrived, he has had his eye upon you, to marry me off to you, because you are a scholar of Torah. But it is not our custom for a female to woo a male, and for a great king like him to ask a man to marry his daughter is insulting."

When the man heard her words, he was delighted. Indeed, he was still thinking about it as he left the house and Ashmadai arrived, his sword drawn. He asked the man: "Why did you disobey my commandment? The day of your doom has come! I shall exact payment for all you have done."[20]

"Heaven forbid! O king!" the man replied. "I entered the house only out of desire for your daughter. I beg you! Give her to me as wife. I am in love with her."

Hearing this, Ashmadai rejoiced. "I will happily give her to you," he told the man. "But you must wait until I return from war." Then he added, "From now on you have my permission. You can enter my daughter's house, frolic together, and woo her as you wish."

Ashmadai at once returned to battle, captured the province, and destroyed it. He announced to his legions, "Accompany me to my daughter's wedding! I am marrying her to a special man, a scholar and a sage."

What did they do? The soldiers gathered all the beasts and fowl they had found in the wilderness, more animals than they could count, and brought them to the banquet. Ashmadai presented the man with a sum of money so great he could not measure or count it. The two of them, with all of Ashmadai's princes and servants present, wrote up the marriage contract. Then Ashmadai made a great feast, distributing gifts worthy of a king.

In the evening the king gave his daughter to the man as is customary in all lands. When the man and his new wife entered their chamber, she said to him: "Don't think in your heart that you are a human and I am a demon. For I possess everything you could ever find in a woman; I lack nothing. But take care! Do not approach me if you do not desire me. I love you as if you were my own eye. I will never leave you. But swear to me about the matters I have just told you."

The man swore to her. He put the oath in writing and signed it. Afterward, he had intercourse with her and she conceived a son by him. The man had the infant circumcised on the eighth day, in accordance with the law of the Torah, and named him Solomon, after King Solomon.[21] And so the man lived for two years.

One day the man was playing with his son Solomon in the presence of his wife, the daughter of Ashmadai. Suddenly, the man let out a painful sigh. "Why do you sigh?" his wife asked.[22]

He replied, "I sighed for the wife and child I left behind in my former land."

"What do you lack here?" she retorted. "Do you not find me beautiful? Is it money or honor you want? Tell me, and I will fulfill your wish."

The man answered her, "It's not that I lack anything here. But when I see my son Solomon, I remember my other children."

She said: "Didn't I once tell you not to take me as a wife if my love was not engraved in your heart? Now here you are, pining away, thinking of the past and your first wife. Don't do it again."

"I won't," he answered.

Several days later, though, he sighed again. She said to him, "Will you never stop sighing for that first wife of yours and her children? If this is how it must be, I will take you to them. But you must fix the length for your journey and the time for your return."

"You set the time," he replied.

"I will give you a year to go and return," she said.

"I will do that," the man agreed.

"Swear to it," she responded. He took an oath, sealed it in writing with his signature, and gave it to her. And she kept all the oaths to serve as written testimony for herself.

What did she do? She invited all her servants and prepared a great banquet. After they had eaten and drunk their fill, she announced: "My husband and master longs to see the wife and children he once had in that other place. Which one of you has the strength to take him there?"

One demon replied, "I will take him—in twenty years!"

Another spoke up, "I will take him—in ten!"

Still another volunteered, "I will do it—in one year!"

Then one demon, crippled and blind in an eye, declared, "I'll deliver him in a day."

"May your strength increase!" she said to that demon. "But take special care that you inflict no injury upon the man, not even a blemish.[23] Carry him gently, for he is your master and a scholar of Torah; he doesn't have the strength to endure misfortune."

"I will do as you have spoken," replied the demon.

To her husband she then said, "Be careful. Don't provoke this demon. He is easily angered, and on account of his anger he is blind."

"I will do nothing to anger him," the man replied.

"Go in peace," she said. "But take care of your oath."

What happened to the man? The demon took him on his shoulders, brought the man to his town, and left him safely outside it on a mountaintop. At daybreak the demon took on human form, and the two of them entered the city. They met a certain gentile, a former acquaintance of the man. "Are you really that man?" the gentile asked him. "The man who went to sea in the ship that sank?"

"Yes," the man replied.

"Let me go and tell your wife," the gentile said. "She has lived like a widow for so many years."

He went and reported the news, and the man's relatives and acquaintances rejoiced greatly. They all came out, and he told them what hardships had happened to him on the way, and how the Lord had delivered him.[24] The man prepared a great banquet for all his relatives and acquaintances, and after they had eaten and drunk, the man asked the blind demon who had brought him there by order of Ashmadai's daughter, "Why are you blind?"

The demon replied, "Doesn't it say in Scripture, 'He who guards his mouth and tongue guards himself from trouble' (Proverbs 21:23)? Why must you embarrass me in public? Did not our sages state, 'He who embarrasses his fellow man in public loses his place in the world to come' (B. Baba Metsia 59a)?"

The man tried to provoke the demon a second time. "Why are you a hunchback?" he asked him.

The demon answered, "It's already been stated in Scripture, 'As a dog returns to its vomit, so a dullard repeats his folly' (Proverbs 26:11). But I will tell you the true answer to your first question, as to why I'm blind in one eye: because I am bad tempered. One day I was quarreling with a friend, and he stabbed me with a knife and took out my eye. And to your question as to why I'm a hunchback—go ask the artisan who fashioned me."[25]

"I have offended you," the man said. "Forgive me."

"I will never forgive that insult," the demon answered.

"Give him food and drink," the man ordered his servants.

"I will never eat or drink anything of yours," the demon said. "Have them recite grace, and let me return home."

After they recited grace, the demon asked the man, "What do you want me to tell my mistress, your wife?"

The man replied, "Tell her that I will never return to her. She is not my wife. I am not her husband."

"Don't say that," the demon said to the man. "Don't break your oath."

"I'm not concerned about the oath I swore to her," the man answered. He brought out his first wife and embraced and kissed her in front of the demon. "This is my wife," said the man to the demon. "This woman was created in God's image and likeness, while your mistress is a demon. You can tell her that I will never return."

Once he saw this, the demon departed, went back to his mistress, and told her everything the man had done to provoke him. "But how is my master and husband?" she asked him.

"Why do you ask about a man who does not love you?" the demon replied. "He despises you, he says that he will never return to you. He says that you are not his wife, and that he is not your husband!"

"I don't believe a word you've said," she answered. "Everything he's done he did only to provoke you. I know him. He is a scholar of Torah, and he won't break his oath. Let me wait until the appointed time; then we'll see what will happen."

Once the appointed time for the man's return arrived, she summoned the servant, "Go, bring my master and husband."

The demon said to her, "I already told you what he told me to tell you—that he will never return."

She answered, "When he said that to you, the appointed time had not yet arrived. But now go and tell him that the time of his oath has come and that he must return to me."

The demon went and told the man as she had commanded, "My mistress asks about your welfare. She also warns you to return to her, for the time of your oath has arrived."

The man replied, "Go and tell her that I do not want her greetings and that I will never return."

When the demon heard this, he returned to his mistress to report her husband's words, and she told the entire story to her father, Ashmadai, and asked his advice as to what should be done, according to the law. Her father replied, "Perhaps he doesn't want to return with your blind servant because he quarreled with him. Perhaps he feels it is beneath his honor to be escorted by a blind hunchback. Try this. Send venerable emissaries, and let them caution him about his oath."

So she did. The emissaries went and cautioned him, but the man told them, "I will never return."

"But you are a scholar of Torah!" they said to him. "How can you break your oath? The time has passed that you yourself stipulated. Not only are you transgressing the prohibition, 'You shall not swear falsely by My name' (Leviticus 19:12); but you are also forfeiting the positive injunction, 'If a man marries another [wife], he must not withhold from [his first wife] her food, her clothing, or her conjugal rights' (Exodus 21:10)."

The man answered them just as he had the first messenger, and they reported his response to their mistress. But she, thinking that perhaps the past emissaries were not sufficiently impressive, sent additional messengers to admonish him; these were even more venerable than their predecessors. But when the messengers went and warned him, he told them, "Don't waste your words.[26] I am never going back to her."

They returned to their mistress. "Don't send more messengers," they said. "He has no desire for you."

When she heard this, she went and told her father and asked his advice as to what she should do, according to the law. Her father replied, "I will gather all my legions and go to him. If he wishes to return, good; if not, I'll kill him and all his townsfolk."

Ashmadai's daughter responded, "Heaven forbid! You, my lord, cannot go in your majesty. Send your emissaries with me, as many as you see fit, and I will go to him. Perhaps he will show me favor and return."[27]

The king consented and sent his legions along with her to the man's town. In addition, she took with her Solomon, their son. They arrived in the middle of the night. The soldiers wished to enter the town immediately to slay the man and everybody else in the town, but she would not let them go in and spill innocent blood. "It's nighttime," she said. "When people are asleep, as they all are now, they entrust their souls to the Holy One, blessed be He, as you know. So long as their souls are in His hand, blessed be He, we cannot harm them. Let us do the following and not sin. We will wait until daybreak to enter the town. If they listen to us, good; if not, we will know what to do."

The legions responded, "Our mistress! Do as you think best."

She then told her son, Solomon, "Go to your father. Tell him that I have come for him and that he should return with me and not break his oath."

The boy went and found his father asleep in bed. He immediately woke him. Trembling, the man stood up. "Who are you?" he asked. "You've awakened me from my sleep."

The boy replied, "I am your son, Solomon, your child by the daughter of King Ashmadai."

The man immediately began to shake in fear, but he embraced and hugged the boy. "Why have you come here?"

Solomon replied, "My mother, your wife, came here to pay the respect due you, to have you return with her and uphold your oath. She has sent me to give you warning."

The man said to the boy: "Please tell her that I will never return. She is not my wife. I am not her husband. I am a human, she is a demon. One is unlike the other. The two can never be united."

The child answered his father, "With all due respect to your honor, what you say is in error. All the time you spent with us the demons never harmed you; in fact, they treated you with great respect on account of your wife, and she, my mother, also honored you. My grandfather, Ashmadai, appointed you as a prince and officer over the demons, and he commanded them to do your will. So why do you scorn her? Why do you despise her and not remember the kindness she did you when she saved you from my grandfather, Ashmadai? He, too, did you a kindness by saving you from the demons—and not after twelve months, either! O my master, my father! Heed my voice, and it will go well with you.[28] Return to my mother. Fear no injury or plague."

The man replied, "Solomon, my son, I don't want to hear any more about this. I will never return to her. All those oaths I swore under duress, out of fear that the demons might slay me. The oaths have no substance, for the Torah absolves those who act under compulsion."

"I beg you!" the boy pleaded. "Do not destroy yourself willfully!"

"Leave!" his father said. "Don't talk nonsense to me."

The son returned and told his mother everything. Hearing the words of her son, Solomon, she said, "I will not kill him before I have warned him publicly, not until I hear his answer and what the community and its court say. If they convene a trial, fine. If not, I will exact revenge from all of them." She approached the synagogue and announced to her soldiers and officers, "Wait here for me, outside the synagogue, while I go inside and hear how he responds."

She entered and waited until the congregation had completed the preliminary prayers. Then she said to the prayer leader, "Wait! I wish to interrupt the prayers to speak."

"Speak," the prayer leader said to her.

"Gentlemen!" she addressed the congregation. "You know that I have been embittered by this man, this Jerusalemite, the son of Salmon.[29] This man fell among us because of his sins, but my father did him an act of kindness by saving him from the demons who had condemned him to death. Then I saved him from my father, who wished to kill him because the man disobeyed his command. My father presented me to him as wife and appointed him to be a prince and ruler over all his legions. The man married me according to the laws of Moses and Israel, and wrote me a marriage contract for a large sum, and swore that he would never leave me. After some time, though, the man longed to see his first wife and children, and he swore a solemn oath that he would return to me after twelve months. Look! Here are the oaths in his own handwriting, and with his signature. Yet now he wishes to repay my goodness with evil. He doesn't want to return. I demand that you ask him why he has done this. Render a just verdict this morning.[30] Just examine the documents."

The judges said to her, "Rise, you and the defendant." The two of them stood before the judges. "Why have you broken your oath?" they asked the man. "Why have you not returned to her, after she has done so many good things for you? After all, you can't absolve yourself from the oath."

The man replied, "Your honors! All those oaths, you should know, were made under duress. For I knew that if I didn't do as they wished, they would kill me. Therefore I have asked to be free of these oaths, and all of them have been absolved. It is not natural for a human to marry a demon and to have from her demon progeny. I want only to live with my first wife, who is a human like me, and to engage with her in the commandment to be fruitful and multiply. For it is written in Scripture, 'The Lord God said, "It is not good for man to be alone; I will make a fitting helper for him" (Genesis 2:18).' But that one is not a helper fitting for me. That is the reason I do not want to return to her. Let her go and marry a demon like herself. Let one race remain with its own. And I will live with my wife, the wife of my youth."[31]

Ashmadai's daughter said to the judges: "Do you not acknowledge that a person who hates his wife must write her a writ of divorce, [even if] it is stated in Scripture, 'For I detest divorce, said the Lord, the God of Israel' (Malachi 2:16)?"[32]

The judges replied, "That is true and correct. For so the law requires."

"If so," she responded, "let him write me a writ of divorce and pay me the compensation in my marriage contract." She took out her marriage contract, and the judges found recorded in it a sum of money so large it was beyond counting.

"Either pay her the money," they said to the man, "or return to her."

The man responded, "Here! All my money is yours. Let me give her a writ of divorce and her compensation from the marriage contract. I will never return to her."

The judges said, "You must either free her with a writ of divorce and pay her the complete sum in the marriage contract or give her permission to do as she wishes."

The man answered, "I will pay only according to the custom of my land."

The judges responded, "You have already obligated yourself to everything written in the marriage contract."

Ashmadai's daughter addressed the court, "You have provided me with a fair and lawful hearing. There was no favoritism in your decision. But I don't want him to live with me against his will. He has already rejected me. Allow me one thing: Let me kiss him before I return home alone."

The judges turned to the man: "Do as she wishes. Let her kiss you, and she will absolve you of everything that we have obligated you to do."

She rose at once, and kissed him, and strangled the man to death. "This is your reward," she told him, "for transgressing your father's command, for breaking three oaths, and for mocking me. You wished to abandon me in a state of living widowhood.[33] Now your first wife and I will both be widows. As the proverb says, Whoever wishes to steal my husband—let *him* suffer an unnatural death. Now he will never give pleasure or joy, neither to me nor to that wife of his."[34]

Following this, she addressed the townsfolk, "If you do not wish me to avenge myself upon you, then take my son, Solomon, and marry him to the daughter of the greatest man of the generation, and appoint him your leader and ruler. For he is one of you, and he should live among you. Now that I have slain his father, there is no gratification for me in watching him live with me; he will only remind me of transgression and disappointment. But I will give him a bequest of money large enough that he will never want for anything, and you shall order the others to give him his share of his father's inheritance."

The court did all this. The people in the town accepted Solomon. They made him their leader and ruler, and he reigned over them. His mother returned to her home, to her father's house, as in her youth.[35]

Accordingly, a son should always obey his father's commands and must never break an oath. As it is stated in Scripture, "For the Lord will not clear one who swears falsely by His name" (Exodus 20:7).

NOTES

1. Jonah 1:9.
2. Cf. Numbers 22:22, a reference to God's reaction when the prophet Balaam goes off to prophesy against Israel.
3. Jonah 1:4.
4. Jeremiah 46:21.
5. Job 1:21.
6. Exodus 12:29.
7. In the Hebrew this passage is in indirect, not direct, speech.
8. The name of this mythical bird is a mystery. It is mentioned nowhere else, though mythical birds are not uncommon in rabbinic and medieval Hebrew narratives.
9. Psalms 118:19.
10. Jonah 1:9.
11. Cf. Genesis 19:8, where Lot uses the same words to protect the angels who have come to visit him from the evil Sodomites.
12. This claim derives from B. Baba Metsia 33b, where it is specifically applied to scholars of Torah who, because of their learning, are considered to possess greater culpability in cases where they transgress the law. Cf. also Mishnah Avot 4:13.
13. Deuteronomy 1:14.

14. Jeremiah 21:12, which reads in the JPS translation, "render just verdicts morning by morning."

15. For the story of Jonathan, see 1 Samuel 14.

16. For the traditional rabbinic interpretation of these verses, see Mishnah Sanhedrin 1:6. Their meaning here remains, however, slightly unclear.

17. Cf. Numbers 15:34.

18. B. Nedarim 27a.

19. Genesis 29:17, where this phrase describes Rachel's beauty.

20. This line conflates phrases from Jeremiah 50:31 and Obadiah 1:15.

21. There is no explanation in the narrative for why he names his son Solomon. There may perhaps be a buried allusion here to the legend that the queen of Sheba, whom Solomon married, was a demoness.

22. Ezekiel 21:12.

23. Cf. Genesis 22:12, where these words echo the angel's instructions to Abraham not to sacrifice Isaac.

24. Exodus 18:8.

25. For this expression, see B. Taanit 20b.

26. Cf. 1 Samuel 2:3.

27. Cf. Genesis 32:21.

28. Jeremiah 38:20.

29. The text here reads literally "this man Dihon ben Salmon." The name Dihon appears nowhere else in this text and scholars have debated its meaning inconclusively. My translation follows a suggestion made by M. Grunwald (in a note in Jehuda L. Zlotnik, *Maaseh Yerushalmi* [Jerusalem: The Palestine Institute of Folklore and Ethnology, 1946], 104) that the word might be derived from the Arabic *dihkhan*, "a man from a city," referring here specifically to the city of Jerusalem. Salmon is mentioned in Ruth 4:21 as the father of Boaz, but I would like to suggest that the name here might be understood as cognate to Solomon; hence the man's son by Ashmadai's daughter is named after his grandfather.

30. Jeremiah 21:12, but see note 14 above.

31. Isaiah 54:6, where this phrase is used by God as an affectionate name for Israel.

32. The text here is difficult, and it is not clear how exactly the verse from Malachi is being understood; the bracketed words are my addition. In P. Kiddushin 1:1, the Malachi verse is used as a proof that gentiles do not require divorces in the same way that Israelites do.

33. 2 Samuel 20:3.

34. My translation follows Zlotnik's reading of the proverb; see his discussion in *Maaseh Yerushalmi*, 43.

35. Leviticus 22:13, where this phrase is used in reference to a priest's daughter who has been widowed.

7 ◆

MIDRASH ELEH EZKERAH
or *The Legend of the Ten Martyrs*

Midrash Eleh Ezkerah ("These I Will Remember") takes its title from Psalm 42:5, "These I will remember, and my soul melts within me"—a verse that traditionally served the rabbis as an occasion to commemorate the victims of the Jewish War in 68–70 C.E. as well as the martyrs of later persecutions. Elsewhere the midrash is known as "The Legend of the Ten Martyrs," and its account of the execution of the ten greatest sages of Israel is among the central traditions of Jewish martyrological literature in the early Middle Ages.

The idea that ten sages were collectively executed by the Roman emperor is a legend conflated from several earlier martyrological sources. Talmudic and midrashic literature both narrate the separate deaths of sages who defied the edicts promulgated by the Roman emperor Hadrian against the Jews of Palestine following the brutal defeat of the Bar Kokhba revolt in 135 C.E.; these edicts included prohibitions against the study of the Torah and the observance of Jewish law. Some of these accounts have been incorporated into our midrash, as have different versions of the martyrdom of sages believed to have died by Roman execution. But the lives of the ten sages cited in our midrash actually span a number of generations in the first two centuries of the common era. While a list of ten martyrs and the phrase "ten martyrs" (*asarah harugei malkhut*) are mentioned in rabbinic texts (Lamentations Rabbah 2:2 and Midrash

Psalms 9:13), the earliest narrative about their deaths to anticipate our midrash is found in the early mystical-gnostic text, Heikhalot Rabbati, which recounts the martyrdom of Rabbi Ishmael and Rabbi Akiba, two eponymous heroes of early Jewish mysticism. The scholars of today agree that the legend of the ten martyrs began to take shape within these mystical circles, and the imprint of its origins is still visible in our midrash, whose lengthiest portion is devoted to the description of Rabbi Ishmael's ascent to heaven to learn whether the decree against the sages has been issued by God.

The legend of the ten martyrs is not, however, a mystical document, not even mystical hagiography. As martyrology, it shares more in common with pagan and early Christian martyrological literature than it does with other kinds of rabbinic writings of the period. Because of its legendary character, it is impossible to say exactly when the legend took on its present form. In the course of the Middle Ages it became the paradigmatic account of *kiddush ha-shem*, "sanctifying the name of God," as the rabbis called martyrdom. In Germany and northern France, particularly during the harrowing Crusader massacres in the eleventh and twelfth centuries, later Jewish martyrs evoked the ten sages as their exemplary predecessors and even cited the midrash as legal precedent. The theme of the ten martyrs became the frequent subject of liturgical poems, two of which are still recited to this day, *Eleh Ezkerah* on Yom Kippur and *Arzei ha-Levanon Adirei ha-Torah* on the Ninth of Av.

The prevalence of the legend of the ten martyrs in medieval Judaism and its literature testifies to a growing obsession in that culture with martyrdom as the ultimate act of religious devotion. In the classical period of rabbinic Judaism the idea of *kiddush ha-shem* was not particularly glorified. Because they recognized the futility of opposing Rome on the political or military front, and since they understood that the survival of Judaism was predicated upon living to observe the law rather than dying for its sake, the rabbis discouraged both martyrdom and the kinds of actions that would inevitably lead to it. Still, the fact that some of the most eminent sages in the Talmud had died the death of martyrs could not be avoided, and still less so as martyrdom became an increasingly inescapable reality of Jewish history. Yet death does not hold quite the same transfiguring, otherworldly beauty in our midrash as it does in, say,

Christian martyrologies of the period. The sages can hardly be said to have sought out their martyrdom, and their corpses were more likely to be thrown to the dogs than buried. If, for Jews, the event of martyrdom came to symbolize absolute devotion to the pursuit of holiness, its narration became the occasion for explaining why the kind of suffering epitomized by martyrdom seemed to be a fate reserved exclusively for the holiest members of the community.

Midrash Eleh Ezkerah is preserved in numerous versions. The present translation is based on the most complete one in Adolph Jellinek's *Beit ha-Midrash* (1853; reprint, Jerusalem: Wahrmann, 1967), 2:64–72; in the same anthology, Jellinek published two other versions (in 6:19–30 and 31–35), references to which are made in the notes. After this translation was completed, a critical synoptic edition entitled *Die Geschichte von den Zehn Märtyrern* was published by Gottfried Reeg (Tübingen: 1985). Although the translation was not redone, Reeg's edition was consulted in the course of revising the original translation for republication in this book.

The conflated legend in our midrash preserves at least three different explanations for the martyrdom of the ten sages. The first explanation, offered by the parable with which the midrash begins, attributes the tragedy to the behavior of those Jews whose pride and arrogance were not sufficiently chastened by the destruction of the Temple. A second explanation traces the sages' martyrdom to their own decision to teach Jewish law to the Roman emperor. While this rationale is only suggested in our version of the midrash, it is explicitly stated in version 2: "If Israel had not taught the Roman emperor the Torah, they would never have found themselves in such straits" (Jellinek, *Beit ha-Midrash* 6:19)—an idea that is not without some historical truth, inasmuch as participation in larger cultural spheres, inevitable and well intentioned as it may originally have been, did culminate for the Jews in disaster. Finally, the martyrdom of the sages is explained as an act of atonement—not for the sages' own sins, though, or for those of their generation—but for the capital transgression committed long ago by the brothers of Joseph, the fathers of the tribes, as they are called. They kidnapped their younger sibling and sold him to the Ishmaelites who, of course, eventually brought him to Egypt, where he rose to become Pharaoh's vizier and the ultimate savior of his family.

145

The role this transgression plays in our midrash is not easy for us to accept. Even among the rabbis there were some who objected to the primeval sin, never atoned and implicating all Israel (inasmuch as virtually all Israel descends from the fathers of the ten tribes), on the basis of Deuteronomy 24:16, "Parents shall not be put to death for children, nor children be put to death for parents." The meaning of this transgression committed by Joseph's brothers, however, is not the kind of original sin we might imagine it to be; nor is it a Kafkaesque specter hovering over all Jewish history. Rather, the transgression served the rabbis as a mode of rationalizing the suffering they endured by connecting the travail of their existence with the national past: "In every generation the death of ten men is required in order to atone for this sin, and it still has yet to be properly atoned for" (Midrash Psalms 1:13).

Introduction and translation by
DAVID STERN

When the Holy One, blessed be He, created the trees, they grew haughty because they were so tall, and they raised themselves ever higher and higher. But once the Holy One, blessed be He, created iron, the trees humbled themselves, saying, "Alas! The Holy One, blessed be He, has created the intrument that will fell us."

Likewise, after the destruction of the Temple, the arrogant members of that generation boasted, "So what if the Temple has been destroyed! There are still sages among us, and they can instruct the world in the study of the law and the observance of the commandments."

Thereupon, the Holy One, blessed be He, set it in the mind of the Roman emperor to study the Torah of Moses directly from the sages and the elders. The emperor began with the Book of Genesis, and he studied until he reached the chapter in Exodus that begins, "And these are the rules" (Exodus 21:1). When he came to the verse, "He who kidnaps a man—whether he has sold him or is still holding him—shall be put to death" (Exodus 21:16), he immediately ordered his palace to be filled with shoes,[1] and summoned the ten foremost sages of Israel. They came before him, and he seated them upon thrones of gold, and said, "There is a grave matter of law about which I must question you. Tell me the law, only the law, and the truth."

"Speak," the sages said.

"If a man has kidnapped one of his brothers from the children of Israel and treated him cruelly and sold him," the emperor asked, "what is the law concerning that man?"

"According to the Torah," the sages answered, "that man must surely die."

"If so," the emperor said, "you are guilty of death."

"Tell us why," they asked.

"Because of Joseph," the emperor answered, "whom his brothers

147

kidnapped and sold. If his brothers were still alive, I would judge them. Since they are not, you will bear the sin of your forefathers."

The sages beseeched the emperor, "Grant us three days' reprieve. If we can find a merit by which to acquit ourselves, then good. And if we can't, do as you wish."

They agreed upon this. The sages departed and persuaded Rabbi Ishmael, the high priest, to pronounce the Ineffable Name and thereby ascend to heaven in order to learn whether the decree against them had been issued by the Holy One.[2]

Rabbi Ishmael purified himself through ritual immersion. He wrapped himself in his prayer shawl and in his phylacteries and distinctly pronounced the Ineffable Name of the Lord. Immediately, a wind bore him to the sixth heaven. There he met the angel Gabriel who said to him, "Are you Ishmael in whom your God prides Himself every day? Because He has a servant on earth who so resembles His own brilliant countenance!"

Ishmael replied, "I am that man."

Gabriel questioned him, "Why have you ascended here?"

He answered, "Because the wicked kingdom has decreed that ten sages of Israel must die. I have therefore ascended to learn whether that decree has gone forth from the Holy One, blessed be He."

Gabriel asked, "If the decree has not been signed, can you nullify it?"[3]

"Yes," Ishmael answered.

"How?" Gabriel asked.

"[By pronouncing] the Ineffable Name."

"Blessed art thou, children of Abraham, Isaac, and Jacob!" Gabriel immediately exclaimed. "For to you the Holy One, blessed be He, has revealed matters He has not disclosed even to the angelic host."

It was said about Rabbi Ishmael, the high priest, that he was one of the seven most handsome men in the world,[4] and that his face resembled an angel's. When Rabbi Yose, Rabbi Ishmael's father, reached the last days of his life, his wife said to him, "My dear husband and master, why do I see that many people manage to have children, while we have not? For we have no heir, neither a son nor a daughter."

Rabbi Yose replied, "The reason is this: When other men's wives leave the ritual bathhouse, they watch themselves very closely. If anything unseemly happens to them, they return to the bathhouse and immerse a second time, and so they succeed in having children."

His wife said, "If this is what has prevented me, then I promise to be very scrupulous in these matters."

The next time she went to immerse herself, after she left the ritual bathhouse, a certain dog crossed her path. So she returned to the bathhouse, and reimmersed herself. [But when she left] the dog crossed her path again; she returned once more and reimmersed herself. Eight times this happened, until the Holy One, blessed be He, said to Gabriel, "How much trouble this righteous woman takes upon herself! Go and appear to her in the form of her husband."

Gabriel immediately went and sat at the door of the ritual bathhouse, where he appeared to the woman in the form of her husband, Rabbi Yose. He took her [by the hand] and led her home. That same night she conceived Rabbi Ishmael, and he was as handsome as Gabriel himself.

For this reason, Gabriel encountered Rabbi Ishmael when he ascended to heaven. The angel said to him, "Ishmael, my son, I swear to you that I overheard from behind the heavenly partition that ten sages are to be handed over to the wicked kingdom to be executed."

"For what cause?" Ishmael asked.

"[As atonement] for the transgression Joseph's brothers committed when they sold him. Every day Justice argues in accusation before the Throne of Glory,[5] saying, 'Have you written in Your Torah a single superfluous letter? And yet, the fathers of the tribes sold Joseph, and You have still not punished them or their descendants!' It has therefore been decreed that ten sages must be handed over to the wicked kingdom to be executed."

"And till now," Rabbi Ishmael asked, "the Holy One, blessed be He, could find no way to exact punishment except through our lives?"

Gabriel answered, "I swear to you by your own life, Ishmael, my son! From the day his brothers sold Joseph [until now] the Holy One, blessed be He, has not found ten men in a single generation so righteous and pious as the fathers of the ten tribes. Because of this, the Holy One, blessed be He, will exact payment through your lives. But the truth is with you."

When Samael, the wicked angel, realized that the Holy One, blessed be He, was about to seal His signature upon the decree to hand over the ten sages to the wicked kingdom, he rejoiced and boasted, "I have triumphed over the archangel Michael."

The Holy One, blessed be He, thereupon burned with anger against Samael, and said, "Samael! If you wish, you may release the ten sages from death, or you must agree to suffer leprosy for all time to come. But one of these [decrees] you must accept."

Samael the wicked replied, "I refuse to release those ten sages from death. Let me accept the other decree just as you have spoken."

The Holy One, blessed be He, immediately raged in fury, and even before Samael had finished speaking, He summoned Metatron, the master scribe and archangel, and commanded him, "Write this and seal it: For six whole months, plague and leprosy, tumors, sores, burning inflammations, jaundice, every sort of evil boil shall afflict Edom the wicked.[6] Brimstone and fire shall fall upon man and beast alike, on their gold, their silver, and all they own, until a man shall say to his neighbor, 'I will give you Rome and everything in it for free!' and the other will answer him, 'What do I need these things for? There is no profit in them for me.' "

When Rabbi Ishmael heard this decree, his mind was finally set at rest. He was strolling to and fro in heaven when he saw an altar next to the Throne of Glory. "What is this?" he asked Gabriel.

"An altar for sacrifice," the angel told him.

"What sort of sacrifice do you offer upon it each day?" Ishmael asked. "Are there bullocks and sacrificial animals here?"

"Every day we sacrifice the souls of the righteous on this altar," Gabriel answered.

"Who offers the sacrifices?" Ishmael asked.

"The archangel Michael," Gabriel responded.

Rabbi Ishmael thereupon descended to earth and told his fellow sages that the decree against them had already been issued, written down, and sealed. On the one hand, his colleagues felt that they had been wronged to have such a grievous decree issued against their lives. On the other hand, they rejoiced that the Holy One, blessed be He, had judged them to be equal to the fathers of the tribes in righteousness and piety.

This was the order in which the sages sat in pairs: RABBI ISHMAEL and RABBI SIMEON BEN GAMALIEL; RABBI AKIBA and RABBI HANINA BEN TERADION; RABBI ELEAZER BEN SHAMMUA and RABBI YESHIVAV THE SCRIBE; RABBI HANINA BEN HAKHINAI and RABBI YUDA BEN BABA; RABBI HUTZAPIT THE TRANSLATOR and RABBI YUDA BEN DEMA.

The Roman emperor now entered, followed by all the noblemen of Rome. He addressed the sages, "Who shall be executed first?"

Rabbi Simeon ben Gamaliel spoke, "I am patriarch, son of a patriarch, descendant of David, the king of Israel, may he rest in peace. I shall be executed first."[7]

Rabbi Ishmael the high priest spoke, "I am high priest, son of a high priest, descendant of Aaron the priest. I shall be executed first—and not see my colleague die."

Said the emperor, "This one has said, 'I shall be executed first,' and this one has said, 'I shall be executed first.' If so, cast lots between them."

The lot fell upon Rabbi Simeon ben Gamaliel. The emperor ordered his head cut off, and his servants decapitated Rabbi Simeon ben Gamaliel. Then, Rabbi Ishmael the high priest took the head, and, placing it between his thighs, he lamented with a bitter heart, "Where is Torah? Where is its reward? Here lies the tongue that once explained the Torah in seventy languages! And now it licks the dust!"

So Rabbi Ishmael mourned and wept over the body of Rabbi Simeon ben Gamaliel. The emperor said to him, "What is this? You, an old man, weeping over your fellow sage! You should be weeping over yourself!"

Rabbi Ishmael replied, "I *am* weeping over myself! For my fellow sage was greater than I in knowledge of Torah and wisdom. And now he has joined the heavenly academy before me. This is why I am weeping."

While Rabbi Ishmael was still giving voice to his grief, weeping as he lamented, the daughter of the emperor looked out her window and saw how handsome Rabbi Ishmael the high priest was. Compassion for him seized her, and she sent to her father asking him to grant her one request. He sent back to her, "My daughter, whatever you ask I shall do—so long as it does not concern Rabbi Ishmael and his colleagues." She sent back, "I request you to allow him to live." The emperor replied, "I have already taken an oath." She responded, "Let me then request that you order the skin stripped off his face, that I may have it to use instead of a mirror to look upon myself."[8]

The emperor immediately ordered his servants to strip the skin off Rabbi Ishmael's face. When they reached the spot on his forehead where he used to place his phylacteries, Rabbi Ishmael groaned with such terrible bitterness that the heavens and the earth trembled. He groaned a second time, and the Throne of Glory trembled. The host of angels spoke before the Holy One, blessed be He, "A righteous man like this, to whom You have revealed all the mysteries of the upper world and the secrets of the lower one—shall this man be murdered cruelly by so wicked a man? *This* is Torah? *This* is its reward?"

The Holy One, blessed be He, answered, "Leave him to his fate. The merits of his deeds shall stand for the generations following him." Then He added, "What can I do to help my children? The decree has gone forth, and there is no one to annul it."

An oracular voice declared from heaven, "If I hear one more word in protest, I shall destroy the entire universe and return it to chaos and void!"[9]

When Rabbi Ishmael heard this, he became silent. The emperor said to him, "Until now you never wept or cried out. Yet now you do!"[10]

Rabbi Ishmael replied, "Not for my own soul am I crying out—but for [the privilege of observing] the precept of laying phylacteries [upon my forehead], which now is lost to me."

"Yet you still trust in your God!" said the emperor.

"Let Him kill me if He will," said Rabbi Ishmael. "I shall still hope in Him."[11] Thereupon, his soul departed from Rabbi Ishmael.

Next they brought forth Rabbi Akiba, the son of Joseph. Rabbi Akiba was able to offer interpretations for the crowns upon the letters of the Torah, and he revealed meanings in the Torah just as they had been transmitted to Moses at Sinai.[12] When they brought him forth to be executed, a letter to the emperor arrived informing him that the king of Arabia had invaded his territory. The emperor hastened to depart and ordered that Rabbi Akiba be imprisoned until his return from war. After he returned, he ordered Rabbi Akiba to be brought forth, and they carded his flesh with steel combs. Each time the steel comb entered his flesh,

Rabbi Akiba proclaimed, "Righteous is the Lord. The Rock!—His deeds are perfect; yea, all His ways are just; a faithful God, never false; true and upright is He."[13]

An oracular voice came forth and declared, "Blessed are you, Rabbi Akiba. For you were righteous and just, and now your soul has departed you, righteous and just."

After he died, Elijah the prophet, of blessed memory, took Rabbi Akiba's corpse on his shoulders and carried him a distance of five parasangs. On the way, Elijah met Rabbi Joshua the Grits Dealer.[14] He asked Elijah, "Are you not a priest?" Elijah answered, "The corpse of a righteous man does not impart impurity."[15] Rabbi Joshua the Grits Dealer accompanied Elijah until they came to a certain cave of extraordinary beauty. They entered the cave and found inside it a handsome bed and a burning candle. Elijah, of blessed memory, lifted Akiba by his head, and Rabbi Joshua the Grits Dealer took him by his feet, and they laid the body upon the bed. For three days and for three nights the angelic host wept over Rabbi Akiba. Afterward, they buried him in that cave, and the following day Elijah, of blessed memory, took Rabbi Akiba and brought him to the heavenly academy where he interpreted the meaning of the crowns upon the letters of the Torah. And all the righteous and pious souls gathered to hear Rabbi Akiba's interpretations.

After Rabbi Akiba, Rabbi Hanina ben Teradion was brought forth.[16] It was said about Rabbi Hanina ben Teradion that his behavior was equally becoming to the Holy One, blessed be He, and to his fellow men. Never did a curse against his neighbor rise upon his lips. When the Roman emperor forbade the study of Torah, what did Rabbi Hanina ben Teradion do? He arose, convoked public assemblies, and sat in the marketplace of Rome, where he taught and occupied himself with interpreting Torah. The emperor commanded that Rabbi Hanina be wrapped in the scroll of the Torah and burned. The executioner seized Rabbi Hanina. He wrapped him in the Torah scroll, kindled the fire, and took tufts of sheep's wool that he had soaked in water and placed them upon Rabbi Hanina's heart so that he would not die too quickly.[17] Rabbi Hanina's daughter was standing nearby, and cried to her father, "Oh, oh, father! Must I watch you [die] this way?"

He answered her, "It pleases me, my daughter, to have you see me now."

His students stood next to him, and asked, "Our teacher, what do you see?"

He replied, "I see scrolls of parchment aflame and letters flying up [through the air]." Then he began to weep, and his students asked him, "Why are you weeping?"

He answered, "If I alone were being burned, it would not grieve me. But the scroll of the Torah is now being burned with me."

The executioner addressed Rabbi Hanina, "Rabbi! If I were to remove the tufts of wool from above your heart and let you die quickly, would you promise to bring me to eternal life in the world to come?"

Rabbi Hanina answered, "Yes."

The executioner said, "Swear to me." Rabbi Hanina took an oath, and as soon as he had, the executioner fanned the flames, removed the tufts of wool, and Rabbi Hanina's soul departed him. Likewise, the executioner threw himself upon the flames and was consumed by the fire.

An oracular voice thereupon declared, "Rabbi Hanina and his executioner have both gained entrance to eternal life in the world to come."

About this incident, Rabbi Judah lamented, "Some men gain eternal life for themselves in a single moment, like that executioner, while others work all their lives to win this reward and then lose it in a single moment, like Johanan the high priest, who served in the high priesthood for eighty years and became a Sadducee at the very end of his life."[18]

Next they brought forth Rabbi Yuda ben Baba.[19] From the time he was eighteen years old until he was eighty, Rabbi Yuda never tasted the pleasure of sleep for longer than a nap.[20] The day he was brought forth for execution was a Friday, late in the afternoon, and Rabbi Yuda beseeched his captors, "Wait for me just a little until I fulfill one precept the Holy One, blessed be He, has commanded me."

They said to him, "You still trust in your God?"

He answered, "Yes."

"Does this God in whom you trust," they asked Rabbi Yuda, "still have any strength left him?"

"Great indeed is the Lord," he replied, "and very exalted, and to His greatness there is no end of searching."[21]

"If your God still has strength," they asked, "then why has He not saved you and your colleagues from this kingdom?"

Rabbi Yuda answered, "A great and awesome king requires our deaths. He has merely handed us over to your ruler so as later to requite our blood from his hands."

Those men went and told the emperor what Rabbi Yuda had said. The emperor summoned him and asked, "Is it true or not what my men have told me you said?"

Rabbi Yuda replied, "It is true."

The emperor said, "How insolent you people are! You stand upon the threshold of death, and you still keep up your insolence!"

Rabbi Yuda responded, "O Caesar! Wicked man! Son of a wicked man! Did the Lord not see His Temple destroyed, His righteous and pious servants murdered? And yet He did not make haste to avenge them at once."

Rabbi Yuda's students said, "Our teacher, you should have flattered the emperor with words of cajolery."

He answered, "Have you not learned that any one who flatters a wicked man is destined to fall into his hands?" Then he said to the emperor, "By your life, Caesar, permit me to fulfill one commandment. Its name is the Sabbath, and it is [like] the world to come."

The emperor replied, "Was it to fulfill *this* request I agreed to listen to you?"

Rabbi Yuda at once began to sanctify the Sabbath with the verses, "The heaven and the earth were completed," and so forth (Genesis 2:1ff.). He uttered them in a pleasing and loud voice, and all who stood around him were amazed. But when he reached the end of the last verse, "Which in creating God had done," they did not let him complete it. The emperor ordered that Rabbi Yuda be executed, and his servants executed him. Rabbi Yuda's soul departed him just as the sage pronounced "God."

An oracular voice came forth and declared, "Blessed art thou, Rabbi Yuda! You resembled an angel, and your soul departed you with the name of God."

The emperor gave his servants commands. They cut Rabbi Yuda's limbs apart and threw them to the dogs, and Rabbi Yuda was never brought to funeral or given burial.

After him, Rabbi Yuda ben Dema was brought forth.[22] That day was the eve before the holiday of Shavuot,[23] and Rabbi Yuda said to the emperor, "Upon your life! Grant me a short reprieve until I can fulfill the commandments of Shavuot. Allow me to sanctify the day in order to praise the Holy One, blessed be He, who gave us the Torah."

The emperor said to him, "Do you still hold trust in the Torah and in the God who gave it?"

"Yes," Rabbi Yuda replied.

"What reward will you receive for this Torah of yours?" the emperor asked.

"It is what David, may he rest in peace, said," the sage answered. "How great is Your goodness, reserved for those who fear You."[24]

The emperor exclaimed, "No fools in this world are like you people— if you believe in a world to come!"

"And no fools in the world are there like *you*," Rabbi Yuda responded, "who deny the Eternal Lord. Oh, oh! The shame, the disgrace *you* will feel when you see us united with the Holy Name in light eternal, while you reside in the lowest, deepest depths of hell!"

The emperor burned with anger against Rabbi Yuda and ordered that he be tied by the hair upon his head to the tail of a horse and dragged through Rome in all its expanse. After this was done, he gave orders for the sage to be cut up, limb by limb.

Elijah, of blessed memory, then came, gathered Rabbi Yuda's limbs, and buried him in a certain cave near the river that descends to Rome. For thirty days the Romans all heard the sound of lament and weeping from inside that cave, and they went and informed the emperor.

He said to them, "Even if the entire universe were to be turned back to chaos and void I will not rest, not until I have satisfied myself with those ten sages just as I have sworn to do."

One of the wise men of Rome happened to be present, and he said to the emperor, "My lord, O Caesar! Recognize the folly of your acts, how completely you have erred in sin by sending forth your hand against the people of God without compassion. Know that a bitter end awaits you, for it is written in the Jewish Scriptures, 'God is compassionate and gracious, slow to anger'; yet it is also written there, 'But He instantly requites with destruction those who reject him.' "[25]

When the emperor heard this, his anger burned against that elder and he ordered him to be strangled to death. When the elder heard this, he immediately rushed to circumcise himself, and once he had been strangled, his corpse vanished and could not be discovered anywhere.

The emperor was seized with violent trembling.[26] Nonetheless, he did not relent in his anger, and his hand was still stretched forth.[27]

Rabbi Hutzapit the Translator was brought out next.[28] About Rabbi Hutzapit, it was said that he was a hundred and thirty years old the day he was brought to be executed, yet he was so handsome in appearance he resembled an angel of the Lord of Hosts. [The emperor's] men went and told him about Rabbi Hutzapit's beauty and old age, and said, "We beseech you, our lord, pity this old man."

The emperor asked Rabbi Hutzapit, "How old are you?"

The sage answered, "Tomorrow I will be a hundred and thirty years old. Allow me, I beseech you, to complete my days."

The emperor asked, "What difference does it make if you die today or tomorrow?"

Rabbi Hutzapit responded, "The chance to observe two more precepts."

"And which commandment do you wish to observe now?" the emperor asked.

"The recitation of the Shema in the evening and in the morning," Rabbi Hutzapit replied, "whereby I will crown as king over me the name of the great, awesome, and sole Lord."

The emperor exclaimed, "Shameless and greedy people! How long will you trust in your God? He has no power to rescue you from my hands. My ancestors destroyed His Temple. They strewed the corpses of His servants around Jerusalem. No one was there to bury them. And now your God Himself is old, He has no more strength to save you. For if He had any strength, would He not already be avenging Himself, His people, His Temple, as He once did to Pharaoh, Sisera, and all the kings of Canaan?"

When Rabbi Hutzapit heard this, he let out a terrible cry of lament,

seized his clothes, and rent them in mourning over the blaspheming of the blessed Name and its shame. "Woe unto you, Caesar," he said. "What will you do on the final day when the Blessed One judges Rome and your gods?"

The emperor said, "Am I to haggle with this man forever?" He commanded that Rabbi Hutzapit be executed, and his servants stoned him to death and hung him. Later, the emperor's officers and counselors came and beseeched him to permit Rabbi Hutzapit to be buried because they had taken pity upon the sage's elderly age. The emperor allowed the sage to be buried, and Rabbi Hutzapit's students came and buried him, making a great and solemn lament over their teacher.

Next they brought forth Rabbi Hanina ben Hakhinai.[29] That day was Friday, the Sabbath eve, on which Rabbi Hanina used to sit in fasting from the time he was twelve until now, when he was ninety-five. His students asked him, "Our teacher, do you wish to taste something before your execution?"

He said, "All my life until now I have fasted [on this day], never eating or drinking. And now that I do not know where I am going, you tell me to eat and drink!" He began to recite the blessing that sanctifies the Sabbath day, "The heaven and the earth were completed,"[30] until he reached "and He made it holy," but even before the sage was able to complete that verse, he was executed.

An oracular voice came forth and proclaimed, "Blessed are you, Rabbi Hanina ben Hakhinai! For you were holy, and now your soul has departed you in holiness just as you pronounced the word 'and He made it holy.' "

After Rabbi Hanina, they brought out Rabbi Yeshivav the Scribe.[31] It was said that Rabbi Yeshivav was ninety years old on the day he was brought forth to be executed. His students came and asked him, "Our teacher, what will be the fate of the Torah?"[32]

Rabbi Yeshivav replied, "It is destined that the Torah will be forgotten from Israel because this wicked nation has shamelessly plotted to destroy our most precious jewels [the sages] among us. If my death could only serve as atonement for our generation! Yet I behold [this vision]: No street in Rome will be without a corpse slain by the sword. For this wicked nation is fated to shed the innocent blood of Israel."

His students asked, "And what will be our fate, our teacher?"

He answered, "Hold fast to each other. Love peace and justice, perhaps there will be hope."

The emperor asked Rabbi Yeshivav, "Old man, what is your age?"

Rabbi Yeshivav replied, "This day I am ninety years old, and even before I came forth from my mother's womb, it was decreed by the Holy One, blessed be He, that my colleagues and I would be handed over into your hands so as to avenge our blood from them."

"And does there exist another world [when this act of vengeance against me will take place]?" the emperor asked.

"Yes," the sage answered. "And woe to you! Woe to your shame when He will requite the blood of His righteous creatures from your hands."

The emperor commanded, "Quickly kill this one, too. And let me behold the power and strength of this God. Let me see what He will do to me in another world." So he commanded, and they burned Rabbi Yeshivav to death.

Rabbi Eleazar ben Shammua was brought forth next.[33] On that day, it was said, Rabbi Eleazar was a hundred and five years old, and from his infancy until the end of his life no one had ever heard him utter a frivolous word; nor had he once quarreled with his neighbor, not in word or in deed. He was a humble and modest man, and he had fasted for eighty years of his life.

The day of Rabbi Eleazar's execution was Yom Kippur. His students came to him and asked, "Our teacher, what is it you behold?"

He answered, "I behold Rabbi Yuda ben Baba whose bier is raised aloft, and the bier of Rabbi Akiba ben Joseph is next to it. The two are disputing with each other over a point of law."

"And who is there to decide the law between them?" Rabbi Eleazar's students asked.

"Rabbi Ishmael the high priest," he replied.

"And who wins the dispute?" they asked.

"Rabbi Akiba," the sage said, "because he has toiled with all his strength over the Torah." Then he said to them, "My children, I also behold the soul of each and every righteous creature purifying itself in the waters of Shiloah in order to enter the heavenly academy in purity this day and to hear the sermons that Rabbi Akiba ben Joseph will preach on the matters of the day. Each and every angel will bring golden thrones upon which the righteous souls will all sit in purity."

The emperor ordered the sage to be executed. Then an oracular voice came forth and proclaimed, "Blessed are you, Rabbi Eleazar ben Shammua! You were pure and your soul has departed you in purity."[34]

NOTES

1. This seemingly bizarre act on the emperor's part makes more sense in light of the gloss in *Midrash Eleh Ezkerah* version 2 (Jellinek, *Beit ha-Midrash* [1853; reprint, Jerusalem: Wahrmann, 1967], 6:19–20). After he studies Exodus 21:16, this text tells us, "the emperor went and plastered the walls of his house with shoes. He then sent for Rabbi Simeon ben Gamaliel and his colleagues and said to them, 'If a man kidnaps another man from among the children of Israel and sells him, what is the law concerning that man?' They replied, 'He is guilty of death.' The emperor said, 'If so, you are guilty of death. Prepare yourselves to accept the judgment of heaven.' They asked him, 'On account of what?' The emperor answered, 'Because of Joseph's brothers who sold him, as it is written, "And they sold Joseph" (Genesis 37:28), and it is also written, " because they have sold the virtuous man for silver and the poor man for a pair of shoes" ' (Amos 2:6). It was for this reason that wicked man plastered the walls of his house with shoes: in order to make the sages recognize what his brothers had sold Joseph for, as it is said, 'a pair of shoes,' that is, for the money a pair of shoes costs." While Genesis 37:28 states merely that Joseph was sold to the Ishmaelites for twenty pieces of silver, the legend that the money was used to buy shoes is an ancient one, attested to both in Targum Pseudo-Jonathan, the Palestinian Aramaic translation of the Bible, *ad* Genesis 37:28, and in The Testaments of the Twelve Patriarchs, Zebulun 4, in both apparently on the basis of a traditional association of Amos 2:6, and possibly Amos 8:6, with the Joseph story.

2. Rabbi Ishmael ben Elisha is among the most prominent members of the second generation of tannaim. He lived in the first half of the second century in the Common Era and is traditionally believed to have been the founder of one of the two important exegetical schools of his age, his sole rival being his contemporary, Rabbi Akiba. Rabbi Ishmael is also an eponymous hero of the early mystical Heikhalot literature, which, as noted already in the Introduction, is one of our earliest sources for the legend of the ten martyrs. The Ineffable Name of God he is said to have pronounced here is presumably the Tetragrammaton, which, in mystical literature, is attributed with extraordinary, supernatural powers.

According to rabbinic sources, the knowledge of the correct pronunciation of the Tetragrammaton was possessed only by the high priest, who was permitted to pronounce it solely on such rare occasions as Yom Kippur during the special ritual sacrifice ordained for that day. The second-century rabbi Ishmael ben Elisha was not, however, high priest (since that position had ceased to exist with the destruction of the Temple in 70 C.E.), and it is likely that the later rabbinic tradition confused him with another, earlier Ishmael ben Elisha who was high priest. In B. Berakhot 7a this Ishmael ben Elisha reports, "Once I entered the Holy of Holies to burn the incense, and I saw Akatriel the Lord of Hosts [Akatriel being one of God's names] seated upon the high and exalted throne. He said to me, 'Ishmael, my son, bless me.' I said to Him, 'May it be Your will that Your pity will conquer Your anger and that Your mercy will rule over Your judgment, and that You will act with Your creatures according to the principle of mercy and allow them the benefit of judgment.' He nodded His head to me in consent." For some discussion of this confused identification, see A. J. Heschel, *The Theology of Ancient Judaism* (in Hebrew) (London: Soncino, 1962), 1:xxxvii n.3, and literature cited therein. As Dr. Eliezer Slomovic has pointed out to me, the fact that God calls Ishmael "my son" here may have something to do with the tradition in our text connecting the sage with Gabriel.

3. This passage is problematic, since usually a decree is not valid until it has been signed. Cf., however, Numbers Rabbah 11:6 and Rosh Hashanah 18a.

4. The six other handsome men in the world are, according to version 2 (Jellinek, *Beit ha-Midrash* 6:23), Adam, Jacob, Joseph, Saul, Absalom, and Rabbi Abahu.

5. Justice, literally the principle of justice *(midat ha-din)*, is a concept that first appears in rabbinic literature as an attribute of God alongside His parallel attribute of mercy *(midat ha-rahamim)*. In later rabbinic literature these two attributes come increasingly to be seen as virtual hypostases of the divine power, almost as independent forces in heaven, and by the fourth century the principle of justice is described as a kind of prosecuting angel whose role in heaven resembles the one Satan serves in the Book of Job, as an antagonist of mankind. The Throne of Glory *(kisei ha-kavod)*, upon which God sits, is a frequent subject of the Heikhalot literature, which records the songs sung by the heavenly creatures who bear it. In our text the throne appears to be little more than a synecdoche for God.

6. The biblical nation of Edom, by tradition believed to have descended from Esau, was identified with Rome in rabbinic typology; for a thorough discussion of the identification, see Gerson D. Cohen, "Esau as Symbol in Early Medieval Thought," in *Jewish Medieval and Renaissance Studies*, ed. A. Altmann (Cambridge, Mass.: Harvard University Press, 1967, 19–48). Samael is the angel identified with Satan, at least from the third century on, and he is also represented as the guardian angel of Rome, and therefore as the antagonist of Michael, the guardian angel of Israel. It has been suggested that his name means "the blind angel" (see Gershom Scholem, *Kabbalah* [New York: 1974], 385–88). Metatron (or Matatron) is identified, in Heikhalot traditions as well as in the Book of Jubilees, with the

biblical figure Enoch who "walked with God" (Genesis 5:22). According to these traditions, Enoch ascended to heaven and was changed into an angel in addition to becoming the master scribe who recorded the deeds of mankind; see Scholem, *Kabbalah,* 377–81.

7. Two sages by the name of Simeon ben Gamaliel are prominent figures in early rabbinic history, both of whom occupied the office of patriarch, or *nasi,* the official presidency of the Sanhedrin. Recognized by the Roman government as the head of the Jews, the patriarch held religious and political authority over the internal affairs of the Jewish community, outside Palestine as well as inside. The position was a hereditary one, and the patriarchs, scions of the family of Hillel, claimed that Hillel himself was descended from the house of David, a claim that, true or not, bolstered the legitimacy of their own line. Rabbi Simeon ben Gamaliel mentioned in our text is probably Simeon ben Gamaliel II, who lived in the first half of the second century and was one of the few survivors after the Romans destroyed the house of the patriarch in revenge following the Bar Kokhba revolt. It is possible, however, that our legend has confused him with Simeon ben Gamaliel I, the *nasi* during the time of the destruction who was traditionally believed to have died a martyr (B. Semahot 8).

8. Rabbi Ishmael's face was apparently so brilliant the emperor's daughter could see her own reflection in it. Version 2 (Jellinek, *Beit ha-Midrash* 6:24) adds the following note, a slightly garbled version of the account in B. Avodah Zarah 11b: "The brilliant countenance of Rabbi Ishmael is still preserved in Rome in the wicked kingdom of Edom. Once every seventy years a man is brought forward, placed upon [the shoulders of] a cripple, and dressed in the clothes of Adam [e.g., skins of animals]. Then they place the skin of Rabbi Ishmael over his face, hang a tablet weighing four zuz upon his neck, and a public announcer proclaims before him, 'Let him who can see, see. If he will not see it now, he never will.' And he completes the proclamation, 'Woe to this one [e.g., the cripple]! So this one [e.g., the healthy man carrying the cripple] shall rise!' And may the Holy One, blessed be He, utterly destroy Edom the wicked, in order to fulfill what is written, 'I shall unleash my revenge on Edom . . .' " (Ezekiel 25:14). This apocryphal account is very possibly based upon the kinds of circus festivals the Roman emperors used to stage, but the significance of the spectacle described in it is far from clear. For some discussion of its historical context and meaning, see Saul Lieberman, *Greek in Jewish Palestine* (New York: Jewish Theological Seminary, 1942), 145 n. 7, and literature cited therein.

9. Hebrew *bat kol,* literally a voice, reverberating sound, or echo. Such oracular voices are frequently cited in rabbinic literature and are the principal means by which divine revelation has occurred since prophecy ceased. On the use of the term and its meaning, see Saul Lieberman, *Hellenism in Jewish Palestine* (New York: Jewish Theological Seminary, 1950), 194–99. Note that in the context of our text, the oracular voice appears almost as the public voice of God; it seems to contradict the more private statement God makes immediately before the *bat kol* speaks.

10. The text here is problematic since we have just been told that Rabbi

Ishmael has ceased to cry out; it would therefore be more logical for the emperor to ask him why he has stopped.

11. Job 13:15.

12. Rabbi Akiba (50–135 C.E.) is among the most prominent members of the second generation of tannaim, and the subject of many tales and legends in rabbinic literature. He was especially celebrated for his unique powers of interpretation whereby he endeavored to exploit the significance of virtually every word, and sometimes letter, in the Torah. The crowns cited in our text are the decorative flourishes scribes traditionally make upon the letters of the Torah; however, no interpretations for these crowns are actually preserved in rabbinic literature, and the claim made in our text, which is repeated elsewhere about Rabbi Akiba, is probably a rhetorical exaggeration. Aside from his scholarly accomplishments, Rabbi Akiba was also famous for encouraging the Bar Kokhba revolt. According to one source, he proclaimed Bar Kokhba to be the Messiah (Lamentations Rabbah 2:2). After the Hadrianic persecutions, he was imprisoned by the Romans for teaching Torah and eventually executed. For a different account of his martyrdom, along with his famous interpretation of Deuteronomy 6:5 as he was dying, see J. Berakhot 9:5.

13. Deuteronomy 32:4.

14. Rabbi Joshua the Grits Dealer (ha-Garsi), Akiba's student, attended his teacher while he was in prison (about which, see B. Eruvin 21b) and was present when Tinneius Rufus condemned Akiba to death. For a slightly different version of the story of his meeting with Elijah, see Midrash Proverbs 9:2.

15. According to mishnaic laws of ritual purity, a priest is forbidden to pollute himself by coming in contact with a human corpse, "the father of all impurity." Hence Rabbi Joshua's question, which Elijah answers by claiming that the corpse of a righteous person does not communicate impurity even to a priest like himself, presumably because the purity of righteousness overpowers any impurity brought about by death. According to the medieval German tosafists (B. Yevamot 61a and B. Baba Metsia 114b), what Elijah meant was that because Rabbi Akiba was a martyr and other Jews hesitated to bury him out of fear of the Roman government, it was permissible even for a priest to bury him, so great is the commandment of burying the dead.

16. Rabbi Hanina, or Hananiah, ben Teradion, head of the yeshiva at Sikhnin in the Galilee, was among the more illustrious sages of the second century C.E. According to the account in Mishnah Semahot 8:9, he and Rabbi Judah ben Baba, after hearing of Rabbi Akiba's martyrdom, together prophesied that Judea would soon be filled with corpses, a prophecy that was fulfilled shortly later with Rabbi Hanina's own death. For much the same account of his martyrdom as in our text, except that it takes place in isolation, see B. Avodah Zarah 17b–18a.

17. In other words, the executioner intended the wet tufts to prolong Rabbi Hanina's agony.

18. Rabbi Judah, also known as Rabbi Judah the Prince or simply as Rabbi, was patriarch in the latter half of the second century and the beginning of the third, and was responsible for the final redaction of the Mishnah. Johanan the

high priest is the Hasmonean king John Hyrcanus (134–104 B.C.E.), who appointed himself to the high priesthood. The Sadducees were the rivals and opponents of the Pharisees from whom the rabbinic sages claimed their own ideological descent.

19. Rabbi Yuda, or Judah, ben Baba (Bava), a second-century sage, was known for his exceptional piety: "All his deeds were for the sake of heaven." After the crushing of the Bar Kokhba revolt, he forbade the popular use of foliatum, aromatic oil of spikenard, as a sign of national mourning, and he also continued to ordain scholars in defiance of the Hadrianic prohibition. For a different account of his martyrdom, after he was discovered performing the ceremony of ordination, see B. Sanhedrin 14a.

20. Hebrew *sheinat sus,* "the sleep of a horse," which the rabbis defined as sixty winks (B. Sukkah 26b).

21. Psalm 145:3.

22. Rabbi Yuda, or Judah, ben Dema (Tema) lived in the middle of the second century.

23. Shavuot, Pentecost, is one of the three pilgrimage holidays. It occurs in the late spring, seven weeks after Passover. According to tradition, it celebrates the giving of the Torah to Israel at Sinai.

24. Psalm 31:20.

25. Exodus 34:6; Deuteronomy 7:10.

26. For this expression, compare Genesis 27:33.

27. Cf. Isaiah 5:25, 9:11, 16, 20, 10:4; Exodus 6:6; and Deuteronomy 4:34.

28. Rabbi Hutzapit the Translator (*ha-Meturgeman*)—so called because he was the official "mouthpiece" for Rabban Gamliel of Yavneh and transmitted the sage's opinions to the public—lived at the beginning of the second century. According to late traditions, his body was defiled in the public market and the sight of his mutilated corpse caused the apostasy of Elisha ben Abuya.

29. Rabbi Hanina, or Hananiah, ben Hakhinai was a student of Akiba's and lived in the late second century.

30. Genesis 2:1ff.

31. Rabbi Yeshivav the Scribe, a colleague of Akiba's, lived in the latter half of the second century.

32. The text reads *torah mah tehei aleinu,* a very problematic phrase; I have translated *aleinu* as *aleiha,* on the basis of Esther Rabbah 7:18 and B. Nazir 50a.

33. Rabbi Eleazar ben Shammua, one of Akiba's last pupils, was ordained by Rabbi Yuda ben Baba and lived in the middle of the second century; it is doubtful whether he was actually martyred.

34. I wish to record a special debt of gratitude to Dr. Eliezer Slomovic who generously discussed several problems of translation with me, and supplied me with a number of the references in these notes, particularly those in notes 2, 3, and 32 above.

8 ◆

THE ALPHABET OF BEN SIRA

"The Alphabet of Ben Sira," an anonymous medieval work, has been preserved in several versions, which differ in both major and minor details. A composite text, its core is a series of twenty-two aphorisms arranged in alphabetical order and organized into a rough narrative. In most versions this alphabet is preceded by the fantastic and provocative story of the conception and birth of Ben Sira and his early education. The final section of the work deals with Ben Sira in the court of the Babylonian king Nebuchadnezzar and consists of another series of twenty-two episodes. These comprise the various ordeals that Nebuchadnezzar sets for Ben Sira and the stories, many of them animal fables, that Ben Sira tells Nebuchadnezzar in answer to various questions posed by the king.

Based on internal evidence, "The Alphabet" was composed in one of the Muslim countries sometime during the geonic period, possibly as early as the eighth century. The fact that this work originated in a non-Christian country strongly militates against the theory that the account of the miraculous birth and prodigious childhood of Ben Sira was intended as a parody on the life and childhood of Jesus as found in the Infancy Gospels or as found in their Jewish version, *Toledot Yeshu*. The Jews of a non-Christian country had neither the need of nor the interest in such an enterprise. So we must look for its source elsewhere.

"The Alphabet" is composed in the style of an aggadic midrash and treats various biblical characters and rabbinic motifs irreverently, at times almost to the point of inanity. This fact has led some scholars to conclude that the work was composed as an antirabbinic tract intended to disparage the genre of aggadah. In fact, parts of "The Alphabet" clearly parody not merely the genre of aggadah but specific passages in the Talmud and midrash. Indeed, "The Alphabet" may be one of the earliest literary parodies in Hebrew literature, a kind of academic burlesque—perhaps even entertainment for rabbinic scholars themselves—that included vulgarities, absurdities, and the irreverent treatment of acknowledged sancta.

"The Alphabet" was read as popular entertainment in most rabbinic communities throughout the Middle Ages. In some quarters, however, it enjoyed an unusual respectability. The famous thirteenth-century tosafist Rabbi Peretz of Corbeil, France, used the account of Ben Sira's conception as a source to demonstrate the halakhic permissibility of artificially inseminating a woman with her father's sperm (as cited by the Taz in the *Shulhan Arukh*, Yoreh Deah 195:7). Admittedly, this case was exceptional. As a rule, the work was treated in high rabbinic circles with deprecatory neglect—even while some scholars had no objections to savoring its contents.

The present translation is based upon the version first published by M. Steinschneider and reprinted in Eisenstein's *Otsar Midrashim* (1915; reprint, Israel: no publisher, 1969), 1:43–50.

Introduction by
NORMAN BRONZNICK

[Editor's note: Since the time the translation was completed, a critical edition of "The Alphabet" was published by Eli Yassif under the title, *Sippurei Ben Sira* (Jerusalem: Magnes, 1984). Yassif's edition includes two parallel recensions of the text. While it has not been possible to retranslate "The Alphabet" from either of those recensions, the original translation by Norman Bronznick has been revised in the light of the critical edition, and the notes redrawn according to Yassif's exhaustive annotations.]

Translation by
NORMAN BRONZNICK
with DAVID STERN *and*
MARK JAY MIRSKY

It is written, "Who does great things without limit and wonders without number" (Job 9:10). Come and see how great are God's deeds. If Scripture says, "Who does great things without limit," why does it add "and wonders without number"? And if it says, "and wonders without number," why must it say "Who does great things without limit"?

How did the sages of blessed memory explain this? The phrase "Who does great things without limit" refers to all the creations in the world, while "and wonders without number" was said about those three persons who were born without their mothers having slept with a man.[1] These were Ben Sira, Rav Pappa, and Rabbi Zera. All three were perfectly righteous men and great scholars of Torah. It is said about Rabbi Zera and Rav Pappa that in their entire lives they never engaged in trivial conversation. The never slept in the house of study—not regular sleep nor even a nap. And no one arrived at the house of study before them. They were never found sitting in silence, but they were always occupied in study, and they never failed to perform the sanctification of the Sabbath day. They never gave a bad name to their fellows, nor did they honor themselves by disgracing others. They never went to bed cursing their colleagues. They never looked into the face of a wicked person, nor did they accept gifts. And they were generous men, thereby fulfilling the verse "I endow those who love me with substance; I will fill their treasuries" (Proverbs 8:21).[2]

How did their mothers give birth to Rabbi Zera and Rav Pappa without having intercourse with their husbands? It is said that they once went to the bathhouse, Jewish semen entered their vaginas, and they conceived and gave birth. Yet neither sage knew who his father was. Ben Sira, however, knew the identity of his father and how his mother had given birth to him without lying with her husband.

It is said that Ben Sira's mother was the daughter of Jeremiah. One day Jeremiah went to the bathhouse and found wicked men from the tribe of Ephraim who, he saw, were all masturbating. For the entire tribe of

Ephraim of that generation was wicked. As soon as he saw them, Jeremiah began to admonish them. They immediately rose against him: "Why do you admonish us? 'As the way to Beer-sheba lives' (Amos 8:14), you will not leave this place until you join us."

"Leave me alone," cried Jeremiah. "I swear to you I will never reveal this."

"Did not Zedekiah see Nebuchadnezzar eating a hare," they responded, "and swear to him, by divine decree, that he would never reveal it! And yet, he broke his oath.[3] You will do the same. If you now join us, fine. If not, we will sodomize you just as our ancestors used to do in their idol worship. For if they did this with idols, you can be certain we will do it to you."

In fear and dread, Jeremiah acquiesced. As soon as he left the bathhouse, though, he cursed his day, as it is said, "Cursed be the day on which I was born" (Jeremiah 20:14). Jeremiah went and fasted on this account two hundred and forty-eight days, the number of days corresponding to the limbs in the human body. As for that righteous man's semen, the drop was preserved until Jeremiah's own daughter came to the bathhouse, and it entered her vagina. Seven months later[4] she gave birth to a baby boy who was born with teeth and with fully developed powers of speech.

After she gave birth, Jeremiah's daughter was ashamed, for some people said she had conceived because she had been promiscuous. But the boy opened his mouth and said to his mother, "Why are you embarrassed by what people say? I am Ben Sira, the son of Sira."

"Sira, who is he?" she asked.

"Jeremiah," the child replied. "He is called Sira because he is the officer over all officers,[5] and he is destined to give names to every officer and king. If you compute them, the numerical values of the letters in Sira and in Jeremiah are equal."

She said to him, "My son, if this is true, you should have said, I am the son of Jeremiah."

"I wanted to," he answered, "but it would have been unseemly to suggest that Jeremiah cohabited with his daughter."

"My son," she said, "it is written, 'That which has been is that which shall be' (Ecclesiastes 1:9). But who ever saw a daughter giving birth by her father?"

"My mother," the child answered, " 'there is nothing new under the sun' (Ecclesiastes 1:9). For just as Lot[6] was perfectly righteous, so is my father perfectly righteous.[7] Just as a similar occurrence happened to Lot under duress, so too it happened to my father."

"You amaze me," she said. "How do you know such things?"

"Don't be amazed by what I say. There is nothing new under the sun. Jeremiah, my father, did the same thing. When his mother was about to give birth, my father opened his mouth and called out from his mother's belly, 'I will not come out until you tell me my name.'

"His father opened his mouth and said, 'Come out and you will be called Abraham.'

"My father replied, 'That is not my name.'

"His father said, 'You will be called Isaac.' And his father tried the name Jacob, and the names of all the sons of Jacob, the fathers of the twelve tribes, and the names of all the men of that generation. But each time my father said, 'That is not my name.'

"Finally, Eliyahu, the prophet Elijah of blessed memory, appeared and said, 'You will be called Yirmiyah, Jeremiah, for in your days God will establish a foe who will raise [yarim] his hand over Jerusalem.'

"My father said, 'That is my name! And you, Eliyahu, because you told me my name, I will also be called by your name. From your name, I will take the ending yahu, and I will be called Yirmiyahu.'

"Just as Jeremiah came out from the womb with the power of speech, so I have emerged with the power of speech. Just as he came forth with the power of prophecy—as it is said, 'Before you came forth out of the womb, I sanctified you; I have appointed you a prophet unto the nations' (Jeremiah 1:5)—I, too, have emerged from the womb with the power of prophecy. As he left his mother's belly with his name, so have I; and as he composed a book arranged in alphabetical acrostics, the Book of Lamentations, I too will compose a book in alphabets. So do not be amazed by my words."

"My son," his mother said to Ben Sira, "don't speak, for the evil eye may fix its power over you."

"The evil eye has no authority over me. Besides, do not try to talk me out of doing what my father did. To me applies the proverb, 'The ewe takes after the ewe, and the son follows the deeds of his father.' "[8]

"Why do you interrupt me, my son?" his mother asked.

"Because you know that I'm hungry, and you give me nothing to eat."

"Here, take my breasts. Eat and drink."

"I have no desire for your breasts. Go and sift flour in a vessel,[9] knead it into fine bread, and get fatty meat and aged wine—and you can eat with me!"

"And with what am I to buy these things?"

"Make some clothes and sell them. That way you will fulfill the verse, 'She made a linen garment and sold it' (Proverbs 31:24). And if you also support me, you will fulfill the verse, 'Many daughters have done valiantly, but you surpassed them all' (Proverbs 31:29)."[10]

Ben Sira's mother made clothes and sold them and brought him bread, fatty meat, and aged wine, and so supported him for one year. At the year's end, he said to her, "Take me to the synagogue."[11] She took him to a teacher who had seven daughters. Ben Sira sat next to him and said, "My master, teach me Torah."

Said the teacher, "You cannot be taught, for you are still too young. Our sages of blessed memory stated, 'At the age of five years a child begins to study Bible' (Mishnah Avot 5:24)."

"But have you not learned," Ben Sira asked, " 'The day is short, but the work is great' (Mishnah Avot 2:20)? And you tell me to sit and not to study because I am too young! In the cemetery I can see children younger than I who are dead. Who knows what will be, whether I shall live or die?"

The teacher retorted, "How dare you instruct me! Our sages of blessed memory declared, 'Whoever teaches the law in the presence of his teacher is deserving of death' (B. Berakhot 31b)."

Ben Sira replied, "You are not yet my teacher, for so far I have learned nothing from you."

א The teacher said to him, "Say alef."[12]

Said Ben Sira, "Abstain from worrying in your heart, for worry has killed many."

The teacher was immediately thrown into a panic. "I don't have a worry in the world," he said, "except for the fact that my wife is ugly."

ב "Say bet," he said to Ben Sira.

"By a beautiful woman's countenance many have been destroyed, and numerous are all her slain ones."

The teacher said to Ben Sira, "Are you telling me this because I revealed my secret and told you that my wife is ugly? Do you find it wrong that I told you my secret?"

ג "Say gimmel!"

"Give over your secrets to one in a thousand even if your friends are many."

Again the teacher said to Ben Sira, "To you alone, to no one else, have I revealed my secret. Advise me about what I am going to tell you. I want to divorce my wife on account of an especially beautiful woman who lives in my courtyard."

ד "Say dalet."

"Defend yourself from a woman of charm as you would before flames of a burning coal."

"But what can I do?" asked the teacher. "Every time I enter the house she flaunts herself in front of me. I can't take my eyes off her, she is so attractive."

ה "Say hey."

"Hide your eyes from a charming woman lest you be caught in her snare."

"My child," the teacher said, "in what snare will I be caught? If it is some kind of witchcraft she might practice on me, I know that she will never use such craft against me. For her first husband had a thin beard, but mine is thick."[13]

ו "Say vav."

"Vexation will fall on the man who follows his eyes' desire; let him know they are the children of harlotry and that nothing good will come from them."

ז "Say zayin."

"Zero be your scorn for the thin-bearded or thick-bearded man, for you know not what has been decreed for you."

The teacher said, "I do not wish to take your advice. I plan to marry her. I have seven daughters, and she has one, and they will support me in dignity."

ח "Say het."

"Cherished by every person are male children, but woe to the father of females."

"But I have seven daughters," the teacher objected. "And they spin and do all the housework for me. They are like a lush olive tree in my home, like a beautiful garden. How can you say to me, 'Woe to the father of females'?! If there were no females, where would males come from?"

"Poor man!" Ben Sira replied. "You comfort yourself with worthless consolation. For the sages stated, 'Happy is the man whose children are male, and woe to the father of females' (B. Pesahim 65a), and accordingly I spoke to you. Furthermore, when a female comes forth from the belly of her mother into the air of this world, the heavens, the earth, the stars, and the constellations—everything that has been created in the world— mourn that this has happened. But when a son comes forth into the air of the world, the entire universe rejoices. If a man has a baby girl and you ask what the wife of that man gave birth to, he tells you with a weak voice and a heavy head and downcast eyes, 'A baby girl.' But if it is a baby boy, he answers brightly, 'She gave birth to a son,' and he speaks strongly, enunciating clearly, and with his eyes raised high."[14]

ט "Say tet!" said the teacher.

"Treasure of no value is a daughter to her father; because of fear for her, he does not sleep at night."

י "Say yod."

"Yea, her custodian will certainly not sleep. When she is a child, he fears she will be molested; when she is a girl, that she will be raped; and when she has reached her adolescence, that she will be promiscuous."

"Everything you have said is true," said the teacher.

כ "Say kaf."

"Come her marriage, you worry the most—that she will not have sons. And when she grows old, you fear that she will engage in witchcraft."[15]

ל "Say lamed."

"Let not your youth pass away in sleep, and in old age do not marry an elderly woman. For an old woman saps your strength even if you are a young man, while a young virgin increases your strength and potency."

מ "Say mem."

"Moist and sweet and invigorating are the juices of a young woman. But those of an old woman are bitter as gall; they sap your potency, like a well whose waters were drawn out by the wind."

נ "Say nun."

"Never tie yourself to an evil woman whose tongue tyranizes you. An evil woman is like a mad dog; even when she is locked behind doors, she barks at everything."

ס "Say samekh."

"Scribes and scholars should marry virgins, not women who have had intercourse. For the juices of a virgin will be yours alone to enjoy; those of a woman not a virgin have already been drained by a stranger, not you."

ע "Say ayin."

"Eye not a widow; covet not her beauty in your heart. For her children are the offspring of harlotry."

פ "Say pe."

"Protect yourself from evil companions. Do not travel with them; avoid going with them, for you may be snared in their trap."

צ "Say tsadi."

"Store away money in your lifetime, my son; hide it well. Don't give it to your heirs until the day you die."

ק "Say kuf."

"Keep your money for yourself and a good wife who fears God, and have many sons, even a hundred."

ר "Say resh."

"Run away from wicked neighbors, and don't be counted in their company. For their feet run to evil, and they rush to shed blood. Similarly, have compassion for your neighbors, even if they are wicked. Share your food with them, for when you appear in court, they will give testimony about you."

ש "Say shin."

"Shun quarrels with your neighbors, my lord. Listen to my words; turn your ear to my speech. Even if you should see something evil in your neighbors, do not malign them with your tongue."

ת "Say tav."

"Troves of gold buy for yourself, anything that is money. But never tell your wife where your wealth is, not even if she is a good woman."

The teacher said to Ben Sira, "The laws of nature have to be changed for you."

" 'There is nothing new under the sun,' " replied Ben Sira. "For Jeremiah taught Baruch ben Neriyah the same way, and the laws of nature were not changed.

"Jeremiah said to Baruch, 'Say alef.'

" 'Alas!' Baruch replied, 'Lonely sits the city' (Lamentations 1:1).

"Jeremiah said, 'Say bet.'

" 'Bitterly she weeps in the night' (Lamentations 1:2), Baruch answered.

"And so they continued through the entire alphabet, as you can see in the Book of Lamentations."[16]

It is said about Ben Sira that he mastered the Book of Leviticus in one day. The teacher said to him, "The laws of nature have to be changed for you."

Ben Sira answered, " 'There is nothing new under the sun,' for Jeremiah did likewise. Furthermore, it is written, 'And Benaiah ben Yehoiada the son of a living man' (2 Samuel 23:20). Was everyone dead, and only he alive? But 'living' must mean that he was alive in the study of Torah, for he mastered the Book of Leviticus in one day."[17]

It is also said about Ben Sira that during that year he mastered the entire Pentateuch. The following year he mastered the Bible, the Mishnah, the Talmud, the halakhot, and the aggadot. During the third year he studied the fine points in the interpretation of the biblical laws and in the rabbinic enactments; in the fourth year, the different languages spoken by palm trees, the ministering angels, and the demons, as well as fox fables. During the sixth year he mastered Sifra, Sifrei, and Tanna de-Bei Eliyahu. By the seventh year there was not a major or minor subject that he had not studied.

Come and see how great was the wisdom of Ben Sira. They would bring him a measure of wheat and he would tell them, "Count the wheat in this measure, and you will find exactly this number of grains."

His fame spread through the world until Nebuchadnezzar, king of Babylon, heard of his wisdom. From whom did he hear? From his own wise men! When Nebuchadnezzar's wise men heard of Ben Sira's wisdom, they said, "Woe to us! Nebuchadnezzar will now destroy us. Let us defame Ben Sira before the king. He will summon him, and we will ask Ben Sira a difficult question concerning something we know but he does not. If he does not give the correct answer, we will have him killed."

They did this. They told the king, who sent for Ben Sira. Then he asked the wise men, "What question do you wish to put to him?"

They replied: "What are *oy* and *nehi?*[18] If he knows, fine. If he does not, we shall put him to death."

One thousand horsemen, who proved their courage by cutting off their fingers and by uprooting a tree as they rode,[19] were called to bring Ben Sira. The horsemen spoke in unison to the king: "Our lord! We will go anywhere in the world you wish to send us, but do not make us go to a Jewish sage. He will destroy us as Elisha did the troops of Aram."[20]

Nebuchadnezzar wrote down for them: "And the beasts of the field also have I, [God], given [Nebuchadnezzar] to serve him" (Jeremiah 27:6). Then he told them, "When Ben Sira speaks to you, go and inform him of this sign that his God promised me, and he will come with you." And he wrote it down for them in a letter. But when the horsemen came to Ben Sira and showed him the letter, he told them, "He did not send you for me but for a hare that I own." At once, he took a hare and wrote down on its head, "Here is a beast of the field. Let it serve you."

Said Nebuchadnezzar: "How was the hare's hair shaven clear as parchment? This cannot be done with a razor of iron or of anything else. I see that its flesh is still within it, whereas it is impossible for parchment to retain the flesh within it." He could not figure out how this had been done, so he immediately sent another troop to Ben Sira with this note: "If you do not want to come in my honor, come in honor of your hare." Ben Sira was quickly mollified and agreed to go.

When he made this journey, Ben Sira was seven years old. The wise men of Nebuchadnezzar immediately gathered and asked him the question, "What are *oy* and *nehi?*"

Ben Sira replied, "When you heard about me, you had *oy*. And now, if I kill you, there will be *nehi* for you."

"Explain precisely what *nehi* and *vey* are."[21]

Ben Sira answered: "There are two kinds of *vey* with different meanings. If a man goes and grabs a dog and holds him by the ear, *vey* to him for certain. But if a lion comes upon a man before he has a chance to save himself from being bitten by a snake, then you have a case of *oy* and *nehi.*"

When they heard this, the wise men became frightened. But they hid their terror and said, "We do not know what you are saying. Demonstrate *vey* and *nehi* before our eyes." Ben Sira immediately went and took a crystal with two openings, and caught three snakes and three scorpions. He placed the scorpions in the bottom opening and the snakes in the upper one. Then he closed the crystal and came before the king. The wise men asked, "What is in the crystal?"

"Look for yourself," he answered. One of them put his hand in the upper opening of the bowl. Feeling snakes, he called out, *"Vey!* What is this?" Then he put his hand in the bottom opening. A scorpion struck him, and he called out, *"Vey!"* and *"Nehi!"*

"Now you know what *vey* and *nehi* are," Ben Sira said. "You have seen them for yourselves."

The wise men trembled in fear and fell upon their faces. Then the king told them, "We agreed that if Ben Sira did not know what *vey* and *nehi* are, you would have him executed. But since he did know, you are now liable to the death sentence you wished to pronounce upon him."

The wise men answered, "The king can do to his servants as he wishes."

He immediately handed them over to Ben Sira, who said, "Did you not bring me here for the purpose of *vey* and *nehi?"* He cast them into a lion's den where they died with *vey* and *nehi.*

Then the king took Ben Sira and sat him upon a golden throne and placed a crown on his head. "I will enthrone you because you are fit to be a king."

"My lord," Ben Sira replied, "I cannot. I am too young, as well as not qualified to reign over Israel since I am not of the seed of David."

"But Jehoash became king at the age of seven," Nebuchadnezzar protested. [22]

"He was of royal seed."

"I see that you are not willing," said the king. "But stay here with me in my kingdom, for I wish to ask you about everything I see in the world that I do not understand."

179

"My lord," Ben Sira said, "ask whatever you desire, and I will explain everything you wish."

The king then asked him twenty-two questions, all of which Ben Sira answered. These were the questions:

I. First, he asked him how he had shaved the hare's head.

"With a lime solution," Ben Sira answered.

"Of what kind?"

Ben Sira replied, "A depilatory solution of lime, composed of lime and arsenic. Solomon used his wisdom to invent this solution in the days of your mother, the queen of Sheba. When she came bearing gifts to Solomon in order to observe his wisdom, he found her very attractive and wanted to sleep with her. But Solomon discovered that she was very hairy.[23] He took lime and arsenic, minced the lime by hand with a knife, crushed the arsenic, and mixed them together in water, and so made a depilatory solution of lime. Then he smeared her with the solution and bathed her, and the hair fell off. He had intercourse with her right away. And she said to Solomon, 'I did not believe all these things until I saw them with my own eyes.' "[24]

Nebuchadnezzar asked Ben Sira, "How do you know all this?"

"I am a prophet," he answered. "The Holy One, blessed be He, reveals to me all that is unknown."

II. "If what you say is true, itemize all the trees in my garden."

"There are thirty kinds of trees in your garden.[25] The fruits of ten are eaten as they are: apples, figs, sycamore fruits, citrons, grapes, quinces, pears, terebinth berries, peppers, and lemons. In another ten, only their insides are eaten while the outside is discarded: pomegranates, nuts, almonds, pistachios, pignolias, melons, poppy seeds, coconuts, querumins. And in the last ten, only their outsides are eaten: dates, olives, carobs, peaches, crab apples, jujubes, plums, cherries, medlars, and sebestens."

The king asked, "Who planted them?"

"Adam took them from the Garden of Eden. He did not go out from there until he took them with God's permission. He also took all kinds of spices and medicines—thirty types!"

The king exclaimed, "Either you saw them in my garden, or someone told you about them!"

III. "If you wish," Ben Sira replied, "blindfold me. Go out with your troops, divided them into units, and I will tell you in which unit you are to be found."

Nebuchadnezzar did this. He covered Ben Sira's eyes and left him with a guard who could be trusted. A unit passed with such noise and sounds that the earth quaked. The trustworthy guard asked, "Is the king in this unit?"

Ben Sira replied, "No."

Another unit passed with great tumult and horsemen running on all its sides. The guard asked, "Is the king in this unit?"

Ben Sira responded, "No."

A third unit passed with songs and every kind of music. "Is the king here?" the guard asked.

"He is not," answered Ben Sira.

Then a fourth unit passed in silence; not even the footsteps of the horses could be heard, only a gentle stillness. "Is he here?" the guard asked.

"Yes, he is facing me," Ben Sira responded. They uncovered his eyes, and he saw the king standing right next to him.[26]

"Tell me how you penetrated this great secret," the king said to Ben Sira.

He replied, "You so prided yourself on your kingship that you compared yourself to God, about whom it is said, 'Behold God passes with the sound of a gentle stillness' (1 Kings 19:11–12). There the King of Kings is seen sitting on a high and lofty throne."

"Are you likening me to your God?" asked Nebuchadnezzar.

"Nothing about you resembles Him," Ben Sira answered, "except that in your arrogance and enormous insolence you compared yourself to the kingship of God. Therefore His wrath is upon you."

"If His wrath is upon me, why did He exalt and magnify me in the world and place everything beneath my authority?"

Ben Sira replied, "If the Holy One, blessed be He, wishes to humiliate someone, He first elevates and then lowers him, as it is said, 'Should you nest as high as the eagle, from there I will pull you down' (Jeremiah 49:16)."

The king at once responded: "If you become my son-in-law and take my daughter as wife, I will make you king in my place."

"I am a human being," Ben Sira answered. "I cannot marry an animal, for it is said, 'Their flesh is as the flesh of asses' (Ezekiel 23:20)."

When the king heard Ben Sira abusing and reviling the nations of the world, he became very angry and asked his wise men, "Tell me what we can secretly feed him so as to make him die."

"We do not know," they answered. The king immediately put them to death.

IV. Then he said to Ben Sira, "Let me ask you about something. If you tell me, I'll give you silver the weight of a buffalo and no end of gold. I have a friend whom I hate even though he loves me. I wish to kill him in a way he won't suspect, say, with a food he might eat and then die from having eaten."

Ben Sira immediately realized that he was the one the king wished to kill. "I will tell you a parable," he said. "Nimrod had an exceedingly beautiful horse.[27] The other horses said to it, 'Let us cut off your head, and we will give you a house full of straw and barley.'[28] The horse, who was clever, understood what they wanted to do to him, and said, 'Fools!

If I let you cut off my head, who will eat the straw and barley?"[29] Similarly, you desire to kill me. But if you kill me, who will get the silver and gold the weight of a buffalo?"

"I swear by the life of Chemosh[30] that I will not kill you," said Nebuchadnezzar.

"Then I will tell you," Ben Sira said. "Give him egg yolks without salt to eat for ten days, and he will die."[31]

The king thought that he was lying. So he brought a man and fed him the egg yolks; and the man died. The king said to Ben Sira, "If you eat this in my presence, I will let you go."

"I cannot eat what you prepare with your hands," Ben Sira said. "Let me prepare it myself, and I will eat it."

What did Ben Sira do? He hid some salt and ate it with the egg yolks for a whole month. "Why did you lie to me?" asked the king.

"I made thin slices out of the yolks," answered Ben Sira.[32] "I crushed them a bit, and put something in them."[33]

The king immediately did the same, but he became ill. "Cure me," he said to Ben Sira. Ben Sira wrote an amulet for the king, and he recovered. "Why did you seek to kill me?" he asked Ben Sira.

"The ancient proverb states, 'Out of the wicked comes forth wicked ness' (1 Samuel 24:14)," Ben Sira answered. "If someone wishes to kill you, slay him first."[34]

V. Soon afterward the young son of the king took ill. Said Nebuchadnezzar, "Heal my son. If you don't, I will kill you." Ben Sira immediately sat down and wrote an amulet with the Holy Name, and he inscribed on it the angels in charge of medicine by their names, forms, and images, and by their wings, hands, and feet. Nebuchadnezzar looked at the amulet. "Who are these?"

"The angels who are in charge of medicine: Snvi, Snsvi, and Smnglof.[35] After God created Adam, who was alone, He said, 'It is not good for man to be alone' (Genesis 2:18). He then created a woman for Adam, from the earth, as He had created Adam himself, and called her Lilith. Adam and Lilith immediately began to fight. She said, 'I will not lie below,' and he said, 'I will not lie beneath you, but only on top. For you are fit only to be in the bottom position, while I am to be in the superior one.' Lilith responded, 'We are equal to each other inasmuch as we were both created from the earth.' But they would not listen to one another. When Lilith saw this, she pronounced the Ineffable Name and flew away into the air. Adam stood in prayer before his Creator: 'Sovereign of the universe!' he said, 'the woman you gave me has run away.' At once, the Holy One, blessed be He, sent these three angels to bring her back.

"Said the Holy One to Adam, 'If she agrees to come back, fine. If not, she must permit one hundred of her children to die every day.' The angels left God and pursued Lilith, whom they overtook in the midst of the sea, in the mighty waters wherein the Egyptians were destined to drown. They told her God's word, but she did not wish to return. The angels said, 'We shall drown you in the sea.'

" 'Leave me!' she said. 'I was created only to cause sickness to infants. If the infant is male, I have dominion over him for eight days after his birth, and if female, for twenty days.'[36]

"When the angels heard Lilith's words, they insisted she go back. But she swore to them by the name of the living and eternal God: 'Whenever I see you or your names or your forms in an amulet, I will have no power over that infant.' She also agreed to have one hundred of her children die every day.[37] Accordingly, every day one hundred demons perish, and for the same reason, we write the angels' names on the amulets of young children. When Lilith sees their names, she remembers her oath, and the child recovers."

VI. Some days later the king said to Ben Sira, "I have a daughter who expels a thousand farts every hour. Cure her!"

Ben Sira replied, "Send her to me in the morning with her attendants, and I will heal her." The next morning, she came with her attendants. When Ben Sira saw her, he began to act as though he were very angry.

"Why are you angry?" she asked him.

"Your father decreed that I must expel one thousand farts in his presence tomorrow and the following day. I am afraid he may put me to death. He gave me an extension of three days, but I still do not know what to do."

"Do not worry," she said. "I will go in your place and expel one thousand farts in front of him for both of us."

"If that is the case," replied Ben Sira, "stay here with me for three days and don't break wind, so that the farts will be ready on the third day." Every time a fart was about to come, the king's daughter stood up on one foot and stretched her eyes wide, as Ben Sira told her to do, and she contained herself and closed her "mouth" slowly, until the breaking of wind stopped completely. After three days no farts came out from her behind. On that day Ben Sira took her to her father, saying, "Go and expel one thousand farts for your father." She stood before the king, but she was unable to break wind even once. The king stood up and kissed Ben Sira.

VII. He questioned Ben Sira, "Why were farts created?"

"If not for breaking wind, a person would have diarrhea and defecate in his clothes. But when a person feels that he is about to fart, he goes and attends to his needs so that he will not be embarrassed and sit in filthied clothes."

VIII. "Why are there two hairs in each follicle on a man's body but only one hair in each of the follicles on his head?"

"God created one hair for each follicle in the head, for had He created two hairs for each follicle, his two eyes would grow dim.[38] The same goes for the world. Were two rain drops to come from one cavity, the world would be destroyed because there would be more water than in the Flood. For every affliction, God has created the remedy with it."

"Fortunate are you, my son, that God revealed all this to you."

IX. "Why were mosquitoes created? They exist in the world for only a day, then they perish while others are created."

"For the sake of the one mosquito that is destined to punish the wicked Titus.[39] The rest were created in order to keep alive the offspring of the ravens. When their offspring emerge from the eggs and enter their nest, the parents flee and abandon them.[40] But the offspring cry to God, as it is said, 'And to the young ravens which cry' (Psalm 147:9), and He leads mosquitoes to their mouths, which they eat and live on for three days. After these three days the offspring turn black and their parents return. Thus God creates the remedy prior to the disease."

X. "Why has God created in His world wasps and spiders, which only cause harm and do nothing beneficial?"

"David, king of Israel, peace to him, was once sitting in his garden and saw a wasp and a spider fighting. A fool came with a stick in his hand and separated them.[41] Said David to God: 'Sovereign of the universe! What good comes from these creatures of Yours? The wasp eats honey, ravages, and produces no benefit. The spider spins all year but never wears its web. The mindless fool harms other creatures; unaware of Your oneness and power, he does nothing beneficial for the world.' God replied, 'David, you deride these creatures! There will come a time when you will need them, and you will understand why they were created.'[42]

"When David was hiding in a cave from King Saul, God sent a spider, which spun a web across the cave's opening and closed it. When Saul came, he saw the web and said, 'Surely no one has gone inside; if anyone had, he would have torn the web to pieces.' Saul went away without going inside. When David came out of the cave, he saw the spider and kissed it, saying, 'Blessed be your Creator and blessed be you. "O Sovereign of the universe! Who can do according to Your works and according to Your mighty acts?!" (Deuteronomy 3:24). For all Your deeds are fitting.'

"And in the presence of Achish, David pretended he was crazy.[43] Achish's own daughter happened to be a mad fool. When the courtiers brought David to Achish, he said: 'You mock me! You have brought this one to me because my daughter is a fool. Don't I already have enough madmen?!'[44] They immediately released David. He fled and thanked God for His deeds, saying, 'There is benefit in everything that He created in the world.'[45]

"When David found Saul resting at noon, Abner was lying at one entrance to the barricade with his head at the other entrance and his legs lifted high. David came, entered between his legs, and took a cruse of water.[46] But when he wanted to exit, Abner stretched his legs and covered the entrance with them. They appeared to David as two large pillars, and he prayed to God, 'My God, my God, why have you forsaken me?' (Psalm 22:2). Right there God performed a miracle for him, sending a wasp, which stung Abner in his legs so he straightened them. David came out and praised God. So, you see, it is not proper for a man to deride God's works."

XI. Nebuchadnezzar asked Ben Sira, "Why does the ox not have hair under its nose?"

"Joshua was a stout man when the Israelites and Joshua were encircling Jericho in order to bring it down, and they brought him first a horse to ride, then an ass, and then a mule, but all of them died under him. Finally, they brought Joshua an ox, and it managed to carry him.[47] When Joshua saw this, he kissed the ox on its nose, and that is why it has no hair."

XII. "Why does the cat eat the mouse rather than other rodents?"

"At first, the cat and the mouse were friends. But one day the mouse went and slandered the cat before God, saying, 'Sovereign of the universe! The cat and I entered into a partnership, but I have nothing to eat.'[48] God said to the mouse, 'You slandered your friend only in order to eat him. Now he shall eat you, and you shall be food for him.' Asked the mouse, 'Sovereign of the universe! What have I done?' God replied: 'O you unclean rodent! Have you not learned from the sun and the moon? They were equal in size and appearance, but after the moon spoke ill of the sun, I diminished her light and added it to the sun.[49] You, too, spoke ill of your friend so that you could eat him. Therefore he shall eat you.'

" 'Sovereign of the universe!' said the mouse. 'If so, I and my seed will perish.'

"God replied: 'I shall recompense you as I have the moon.'[50]

"The mouse immediately went and bit the cat on its head. Then the cat jumped, cast the mouse onto the ground, and bit it; and the mouse died. At that moment the fear of the cat fell upon the mouse, and as a result, the cat eats mice."[51]

XIII. "Why does the donkey urinate in the urine of another donkey, and why does it smell its own excrement?"

"When God created all living things, the donkey asked itself: 'Why do the horse, the mule, and many other creatures have relief from work, while we must work generation after generation without rest?[52] Let us pray to our Creator that He give us relief. If not, we will stop procreating.'

"The donkeys prayed, but their prayers were not answered. God, however, said to them: 'When your urine flows as rivers and a water mill can be made thereby to turn, and when the odor of your excrement is like the aroma of spices, I will give you your reward.' That is why they smell their excrement and urinate as they do.' "

XIV. "Why are the cat and the dog enemies?"

"When the cat was created, he went into a partnership with the dog. They hunted together and ate. It happened that three days passed without either one finding anything to eat. The dog said to the cat: 'How long shall we go hungry? You go to Adam and stay with him in his house, where you will eat until you are full, and I will chase lizards and insects. That way we shall both eat and stay alive.' The cat said to the dog, 'Let us take an oath that both of us will not go to the same master.' The dog replied, 'Well spoken.' They immediately took the oath. The cat went to the house of Adam, where he found mice, which he ate until he was full, while the rest of the mice fled. When the man realized that the Holy One, blessed be He, had provided him with a great remedy, he gave the cat lodging in his house, food, and water to drink.

"What did the dog do? He went to the wolf and asked him, 'May I lodge with you for the night?'

" 'Yes,' the wolf replied.

"They went to sleep in a cave, but later the dog heard the sound of animal feet. He woke the wolf. 'I hear the sound of robbers,' the dog told the wolf. 'Go and drive them off,' said the wolf. But the animals rose up against the dog in order to kill him. He fled and went to the ape, but the ape drove the dog away. Then he went to the sheep, who received him. As he lay with the sheep, the dog heard the sound of footsteps. 'I hear the sound of robbers,' he said. 'Go outside,' the sheep answered. The dog went out and barked. 'A sheep must be over there,' said the wolves, and they went and found the sheep and devoured it.

"The dog fled from lodging to lodging, unable to find a resting-place anywhere. He finally went to Adam, who received him. The dog and Adam lay down in the lodge together. At midnight, the dog said to Adam, 'I hear the sound of footsteps.' Adam got up, took his spear, and went with the dog to give chase to the wild animals until they drove them away. Then they returned home together. Adam said to the dog, 'Come to my house and live with me. You will eat my food and drink what I drink. The dog went with him.'

"When the cat heard the voice of the dog, he came out and said to him, 'Why have you come to my place?'

"The dog answered, 'Adam brought me.'

"Then they began to quarrel. Whereupon Adam asked the cat, 'Why do you quarrel with him? I brought him home because I saw he is clever, "all heart."[53] But don't worry,' Adam told the cat, 'you, too, can stay with me, just as you are accustomed.'

"The cat protested. 'My lord! The dog is a thief. Is it proper to dwell with a thief?' And to the dog, the cat said, 'Why have you broken your oath?'

"The dog replied: 'I will not enter your dwelling place. I will not eat what is yours. I will not hurt you in the least.' But the cat would not listen, and they began to quarrel. Seeing this, the dog fled to the house of Seth and stayed with him. The dog tried to make peace with the cat, but the cat would not agree. And to this day they remain enemies. As the parents, so the children, whether they are beasts, animals, or men. Speakers of proverbs say about them, 'A sheep takes after a sheep.' "

XV. "Why does the dog acknowledge its master while the cat does not?"

" 'Whoever eats anything from which a mouse has eaten will forget his learning' (B. Horayot 13a). Surely, then, a cat that eats the mouse itself will not know its master."

XVI. "Why does the mouth of the mouse appear to be sewn?"

"During the time of the Flood all kinds of creeping animals and insects, male and female, entered the ark. One day, the mouse and its female were sitting near the cat. The cat said: 'I remember that my father used to eat the mouse and its offspring. It is therefore permissible for me to eat them as well.'

"The cat immediately tried to eat the mouse, but it fled, searching for a hole in which to hide. At first, it could not find a hole, but a miracle took place, a hole was found, and the mouse entered. The cat wished to follow, but it could not because the hole was too small. So the cat put its paw inside to pull the mouse out, but the mouse opened its mouth. The cat pulled the mouse's cheeks by its nails, and half a span of its mouth was torn off.

"After the cat had gone away, the mouse came out of the hole and went to Noah. 'Righteous man!' the mouse said. 'Be charitable, and sew up my cheek, which the cat, my enemy, tore.'

"Noah replied, 'Go and bring me hair from the pig's tail.' The mouse went to the pig and found it asleep, and stole some hair from its tail. Then the mouse returned to Noah, who sewed its mouth up. To this day, the stitch is still visible."[54]

XVII. "Why does the raven walk unsteadily?"

"Once the raven saw the dove walking gracefully, with a step lovelier than that of any other bird. Since the dove's step pleased him, he said to himself, I will walk just like her. But while he nearly broke himself in two trying to learn to walk like the dove, the other birds made fun of him. Embarrassed, the raven said, 'I will go back to my original step.' But when he tried to return to it, he could not. He had forgotten the way he used to walk. The raven wobbled. He could not walk in his original step or in the new one. The proverb says about him: He who seeks more than he has will be left with less. The raven was left with nothing."

XVIII. Nebuchadnezzar asked Ben Sira, "Why does the raven copulate by mouth?"

"The sages of Israel have argued about the question," Ben Sira replied. "There are those who say that because the raven copulated in the ark, he was created odd. Others say that because he is wicked, a thief, and a pest, the raven was made different from all other creatures. A wise man once came to the sages as they were arguing over this question, and said: 'I will give you a proof of your words.

" 'When Noah was in the ark, he wanted to send the raven to see whether the waters had gone down, but the raven ran away from Noah's presence and hid beneath the wing of the eagle so that Noah could not send it. They searched for the raven, and after they found it beneath the eagle's wing, Noah said, "Wicked one! Go out of the ark and see if the waters on the earth have diminished."

" 'The raven said to Noah, "Of all birds you could find no one but me?"

" 'Noah replied, "I have authority only to send the birds whose initial letters of their names spell *ay*, that is, the letters ayin and yod, which must mean the birds called *orev*, 'raven,' and *yonah*, 'pigeon.' "

" ' "So why send the raven and not the pigeon?" asked the raven.[55]

" ' "Because there is a city by the name of Ai," Noah answered, "and its inhabitants are destined to kill Yair, who declared that the raven is unfit to be eaten while the pigeon is fit."[56]

" 'The raven brazenly replied, "The only reason you are sending me is so that I will be killed and you will be able to have intercourse with my wife. That is the only reason you made every creature come into the ark with its mate."

" 'Noah immediately responded by cursing the raven, "May you be cursed by that very thing that you slander me with. May you never copulate with your female except through your mouth."

" 'All the animals in the ark answered, "Amen!"

" 'The raven exclaimed, "Why have you cursed me? I will take you to court!"

" 'Noah replied: "Because you are a lecher, a fool, and you cast aspersions upon the innocent. Wicked thing! I do not cohabit with my own wife, who was created in my image and in my likeness, and who is permitted to me. So why should I ever cohabit with your female, who is not in my likeness and who is forbidden to me as well?"[57]

" ' "Why did you call me a lecher?" asked the raven.

" ' "You are truly a lecher, judging by your own words," Noah responded.[58] "It is not I who have given you a bad name." '

"And since that time, the raven copulates by mouth as a result of Noah's curse."

XIX. "Why are all the species in the world found in the sea except for the images of the fox and the weasel?"[59]

"Because the fox is clever. After the Holy One, blessed be He, created the angel of death, the angel looked at the other creatures and said to God, 'Give me permission to slay them.' To which God replied, 'You have power over all creatures except for the offspring of the bird Milham, the phoenix, who will never taste death.'

"Said the angel, 'Sovereign of the universe! Because they are righteous, set them apart—so they will not learn the ways of the other creatures and sin before You. Do not let them taste sin.'

"The Holy One, blessed be He, immediately gave permission, and the angel built a large city for the offspring of the phoenix and brought them there. He engraved on the door of that city the following: A decree has been issued that neither my sword nor the sword of others shall have power over you. You shall not taste death till the end of all generations.

"Afterward, the angel of death returned, and God told him, 'Cast one pair of each of the creatures into the sea. Over those that remain you may have power.'[60]

"The angel cast a pair of each species into the sea, and sank them. What did the fox do upon seeing this? He stood up and cried. The angel of death asked him, 'Why do you cry?'

" 'For my friends whom you cast into the sea,' replied the fox.

" 'And where are your friends?' asked the angel.

"The fox stood up near the seashore. Seeing the shadow of the fox in the sea, the angel of death thought that he had already cast a pair of foxes into the sea. He therefore told him, 'Leave this place.' The fox fled immediately. The weasel met him, and the fox told him all that had happened and what he had done. The weasel went, did the same thing, and also escaped.

"A year later Leviathan gathered all the creatures in the sea, but the fox and the weasel were missing because they had not entered. When Leviathan sent for them, he was told what the fox and weasel had wisely done. He was also told that the fox was exceedingly clever. When Leviathan heard of the fox's wisdom, he grew envious and sent large fish with orders to trick the fox into coming. The fish went and found the fox strolling by the seashore. Seeing the fish amusing themselves along the shore, the fox became curious and waded in. They asked, 'Who are you?'

" 'I am the fox,' he replied.

" 'Then you surely must know that a great honor awaits you, and that we have come for you.'

" 'What is it?' the fox asked.

"The fish replied, 'Leviathan is sick and about to die, and he has decreed that no one should be king in his place except the fox, because he has heard that you are wiser and more knowledgeable than all other creatures. Come with us. We are his emissaries, and we have come in your honor.'

" 'But how can I go below the sea without dying?' asked the fox.

"To which they replied, 'Ride on top of one of us, and he will carry you above the sea. Not a drop of water from the sea will touch even the bottoms of your feet. When you arrive at the kingdom, we shall lower you—how, you cannot understand now—and you will reign over all. You shall be king, happy all your lifetime. You will no longer need to seek food or to fear that evil beasts larger than you will try to devour you.'

"When the fox heard their words, he believed them and rode on top of the back of one of them over the sea. But as soon as the waves swept over him, he began to regret what he had done and realized that he had lost his wits. Woe is me! he thought. What have I done? The fish have played a trick on me equal to all the tricks I have played on other creatures. Now that I have fallen into their hands, how can I save myself? So he said to the fish, 'Now that I have come with you, and that I'm in your domain, tell me the truth. What do you want with me?'

"They replied: 'We shall tell you the truth. Leviathan heard that you are famous for being exceedingly wise, and said, "Let me slit his belly and eat his heart so that I will become wise." '

" 'Why did you not tell me the truth?' asked the fox. 'I would have brought my heart with me, and then I could have given it to King Leviathan, and he would have honored me. Now you will be in trouble.'

" 'Is your heart not with you?' they asked.

" 'No,' the fox answered. 'For our custom is to leave our heart in our residence when we travel. If we need it, then we fetch it. If not, it remains at home.'

" 'What shall we do now?' the fish asked.

" 'I lodge near the seashore. If you wish, bring me back to the place you took me from, I will take my heart and come with you, and then I will give it to Leviathan. He will honor me and you. But if you bring me as I am, heartless, Leviathan will be angry, and he will devour you. As for me, I have no fears, for I will tell him, "My lord, they did not inform me in advance. When they told me about you, I asked them to bring me back so that I could take my heart, but they refused." '

"The fish immediately thought, That makes sense. They returned to the place by the seashore from which they had taken the fox. He climbed off the fish and danced, rolling himself in the sand.

" 'Take your heart quickly and let us go,' they said.

" 'Fools! Go away! Had I not had my heart with me, I would not have entered the sea with you. Is there a creature that walks about without having his heart with him?'

" 'You played a trick on us!'

" 'Fools! I have already played a trick on the angel of death, and I can certainly play one on you.'

"The fish returned in shame and told Leviathan. He said to them, 'Verily, he is smart, and you are fools. About you speaks the proverb, "The smugness of the thoughtless shall destroy them" (Proverbs 1:32).' Then Leviathan ate them. And since that time, every species, including man and his wife, are to be found in the sea—except for the fox and the weasel."

XX. "Why does the angel of death have power over all creatures except for the offspring of the bird Milham?"

"Not only over the offspring of the bird Milham does the angel of death not have power. He also does not rule over the descendants of Jonadab. And there are those who say that certain individual persons entered paradise alive."

XXI. "Who are those persons?"

"Enoch; Serah, the daughter of Asher; Bityah, the daughter of Pharaoh; Hiram, king of Tyre; Eliezer, the servant of Abraham; Eved-Melekh, the Ethiopian; the servant of Rabbi Judah; Jabez; Rabbi Joshua the son of Levi; all the children of Jonadab; and the seed of the bird Milham."

"Why?"

"Let me tell you. Enoch—because he was the most righteous man in his generation and no one was like him—lives in paradise. Eliezer, the servant of Abraham, is the son of Ham, who was Noah's son. When Eliezer heard about the curse on his father, he handed himself over to

Abraham; he was righteous and therefore he lives in paradise. Serah, the daughter of Asher, brought Jacob the news that Joseph was alive. Jacob said to her, 'The mouth that brought the good tidings to me that Joseph is alive shall not taste death.' Bityah, the daughter of Pharaoh, raised Moses our master from his infancy, [and she lives in paradise] so that people cannot ask, What was her reward for this act? Eved-Melekh, the Ethiopian, is there because he saved Jeremiah from the pit of mire. The servant of Rabbi Judah the Prince, because he was righteous, humble, and lowly of spirit. And Jabez is also in paradise, because he was more righteous than everyone in his generation.

"Rabbi Joshua the son of Levi was perfectly righteous as well as a friend of the angel of death. Once he said to the angel of death, 'Show me paradise.'

" 'Happily!' the angel responded.

"As he went along with him, Rabbi Joshua said, 'I am afraid of you. You may slay me with your sword without meaning to. If you like me and want me to come with you, hand your knife over. I will hold it while we walk. Then you can courteously show me paradise, while I view its chambers from the gate.'

" 'Fine,' said the angel, and he immediately took Rabbi Joshua to paradise.

"What did Rabbi Joshua do? He stood in the doorway of paradise and looked. Suddenly, he jumped into paradise, holding in his hand the knife of the angel of death, which he held for seven years, until the Holy One, blessed be He, said to him: 'Rabbi Joshua the son of Levi, you have done a great deed. Now return the knife to the angel of death.'

"When Rabbi Joshua jumped into paradise in the presence of the angel of death, the angel cried out loudly and sought to destroy the world, but God silenced him. After seven years Rabbi Joshua returned the knife.

"Hiram, king of Tyre, was brought by God into paradise because he built the Temple and was at first God-fearing. He remained alive in paradise for a thousand years. Later, however, he became arrogant and said, 'I am a god,' as it is said, 'Because you have been so haughty and have said, I am a god' (Ezekiel 28:2). He was then driven out of paradise, and he entered hell.

"The descendants of Jonadab, the son of Rechab, entered alive because he had fulfilled all that is written in the Book of Jeremiah.[61] He was righteous, he chastised the people of Israel,[62] and he therefore lives in paradise.

"As for the offspring of the bird Milham, when Eve ate from the tree of knowledge and also gave of it to her husband, and he ate with her, she became envious of the other creatures and gave them all to eat. But when she saw the bird Milham and told it, 'Eat of this, of what your friends ate,' Milham replied: 'Is it not sufficient for you that you have sinned against God, may He be blessed, and caused others to die? Yet now you come to beguile me into breaking God's command, that I may eat and die! I won't listen to you.' Then he admonished Eve and all the creatures. Instantly, a heavenly voice addressed Eve and Adam: 'You were commanded, but you disobeyed and sinned. And you came to the bird Milham, but Milham refused because it feared me even though I had not commanded it. Even so, it observed my decree. Because of this, neither Milham nor its offspring will ever taste death.' "[63]

XXII. "Why does the eagle fly close to heaven, higher than all the other birds?"

"When the eagle emerged from the ark, the female eagle stood before a bird that she wanted to eat. All the animals said, 'The one who wishes to eat its friend is liable to death.' They struck her, shaved her wings, and cast her into a lion's den. But God watched over the eagle, and the lions did not kill her.

After a year the eagle's wings grew back, and she flew off. The other birds met and sought to kill her, but the raven saved her from their hands by its cunning; then it copulated with the eagle, which conceived and gave birth to a baby eagle. That is why the raven is called Orev—because it mingled, *iyrev*, its semen by the abundance of its whoring in every direction.[64] And when the birds searched for the female eagle, a miracle took place. The Holy One, blessed be He, caused His Presence to rest on her in order that His creature not be destroyed, and He gave her strength to fly higher than all the birds. The eagle is therefore called Nesher because God came to dwell, *hishrah*, upon her.[65] This is why the eagle flies so high in the sky that her enemies can never capture and kill her and thereby cause a species of the Holy One's creatures to disappear from the world."

Nebuchadnezzar said to Ben Sira, "Blessed is He who gave of His wisdom to those who fear Him, and revealed to them hidden and profound matters."

NOTES

1. There is no such reference in the extant midrashic literature. As for the possibility of conception by artificial insemination, see B. Hagigah 15a.

2. Most of these qualities are attributed to various sages in the Talmud (B. Megillah 28a).

3. Cf. B. Nedarim 65a.

4. To be born in the seventh month after conception is considered a mark of greatness. See Midrash ha-Gadol to Exodus 2:2, where it states, "All prophets were born in the seventh month after conception."

5. The name Sira is thus explained as a superlative form of the Hebrew word for an officer, which is *sar*.

6. See Genesis 19:30–38.

7. Saul Lieberman in his *Tosefta ki-Fshutah,* Megillah (Part V, Order Mo'ed) (New York: Jewish Theological Seminary, 1962), 1,214, notes that nowhere in Jewish sources is Lot referred to by the epithet "righteous." There is, however, some basis in the midrash for such an appellation, where it is stated that whoever feeds the needy is called "righteous" (Tanhuma, Noah 5) and Lot was such a person (cf. Genesis 19:1–22). Cf. Genesis Rabbati, ed. Albeck, 92 and n. 25.

8. Cf. B. Ketubbot 63a.

9. I am following Lieberman's suggestion in his *Shekiin* (Jerusalem: Wahrmann, 1970), 34, that the Hebrew *tarnegola* does not mean a hen but a kind of pot. This suggestion seems to be correct because otherwise the Hebrew *tarnegol* (rooster) or *tarnegolet* (hen) would have been used and not the Aramaic *tarnegola* in a text that is composed in Hebrew.

10. These verses are taken from the chapter in Proverbs praising the *eshet hayil*, or woman of valor, the ideal wife of rabbinic tradition.

11. In talmudic times the synagogue served as a schoolhouse for children in elementary school.

12. In Hebrew, this proverb begins with the letter alef. Each one of the proverbs that follow begins with the subsequent letter of the Hebrew alphabet.

13. Apparently, the witchcraft that his fancied paramour might practice against him is for the purpose of keeping him in her sexual clutches (cf. note 15 below). What is not altogether clear is the teacher's reason for his conviction that

this will not occur. The implication seems to be either that witchcraft is ineffective against a thick-bearded person or that such a person is endowed with an overabundance of sexual prowess—thus, his wife need not use witchcraft to assure the full satisfaction of her sexual needs.

14. According to Yasif (206, n. 1), the last misogynous speech of Ben Sira is a later addition to the text, and missing from all manuscripts.

15. The close association of women with sorcery is already intimated in the Bible. While the biblical legal code is generally formulated in the masculine gender, the law regarding sorcery is put in the feminine gender: "You shall not suffer a sorceress to live" (Exodus 22:17). The rabbis were quick to note that the law applies equally to the sorcerer, and they explained that the Bible mentions the sorceress in particular because it was more common for women than it was for men to engage in the practice of sorcery (B. Sanhedrin 67a).

Oddly enough, the verse regarding the sorceress appears in the Bible right after the laws governing seduction and is immediately followed by the law concerning sleeping with an animal. This prompted the medieval exegetes (e.g., Hizkuni to Exodus 22:17) to conclude that sorcery is part of this complex because it was used as an instrument for inducing fornication.

This interpretation finds corroboration in the juxtaposition of harlotry and witchcraft elsewhere in the Bible (2 Kings 9:22; Nahum 3:4). The famous medieval exegete David Kimhi, commenting on Nahum 3:4, states that the two go together because the harlot is wont to employ witchcraft in addition to cosmetics in order to entice her lovers. This is also implied in the mishnaic observation "The more wives, the more sorcery" (Mishnah Avot 2:7), as correctly explained by Rabbi Jonah Gerondi, in his commentary thereto, that each woman, especially the unloved one, will resort to sorcery to gain and keep her husband's affection.

Sorcery was used not only as an instrument for securing sexual favors but also for the reverse effect. Often a jilted lover or a disappointed suitor would employ sorcery to prevent the consummation of the marriage of his or her loved one to another person. According to Targum Jonathan to Deuteronomy 24:6, the upper and lower millstones represent, respectively, the groom and bride, and the Deuteronomy verse prohibits the use of sorcery for holding back the groom and the bride from consummating their marriage. To avoid such a risk, the Talmud (J. Ketubbot 1:1) permits the changing of the wedding day of a virgin, which in talmudic times was typically on a Wednesday, in order to confound any act of sorcery aimed at thwarting the consummation of the marriage.

In the light of the foregoing, a father's fear, as stated in "The Alphabet," that his married daughter would practice sorcery in her old age is a real one. As the married daughter ages and loses her feminine charms, she might be tempted to resort to sorcery either to gain her husband's affection or, if that was unsuccessful, at least to prevent him from being enticed by other women.

16. Cf. Jeremiah 36:4–7 and Lamentations Rabbah, ed. Buber, 43.

17. Cf. B. Berakhot 18b. Leviticus is considered to be the most difficult book in the Pentateuch because it contains most of the biblical laws.

18. In biblical Hebrew, used primarily in Jeremiah, *nehi* means a cry of anguish.

It is perhaps because he identifies Sira with Jeremiah that the author of "The Alphabet of Ben Sira" made use of this word, rather than any of its synonyms, for a cry of anguish.

Taken as it reads, the entire passage seems to be inane. The question that Ben Sira is asked, instead of being the stumper one would expect, turns out to be so simplistic that anyone with a minimum of intelligence could easily have supplied the appropriate answer. Apparently, however, the wise men tried to use negative psychology in order to confound Ben Sira. By asking Ben Sira an absurdly simplistic question, the wise men expected Ben Sira, whose wisdom was being put to the test, to conclude that the question contained some deep, concealed meaning; he would thus be misled into providing a farfetched and incorrect answer, which would then justify the wise men's demand for Ben Sira's execution. As it turns out, Ben Sira does not fall into the trap, but supplies, with a vengeance, the simple but correct answer, all to the discomfiture of the wise men.

19. These acts were used by Bar Kokhba to test the bravery of his would-be soldiers (J. Taanit 4:8).

20. See 2 Kings 6:15–18.

21. The scribe of this manuscript was inconsistent and interchanged the biblical *oy* with its rabbinic equivalent *vey*. Other manuscripts maintain the biblical *oy* throughout the passage.

22. Cf. 2 Kings 12:1.

23. This passage is clarified in the light of a well-known rabbinic tradition, according to which the Jewish women, up to the time of Isaiah (when they became sinful), had virtually no pubic hair (B. Sanhedrin 21a). Interestingly enough, one who has coitus with a woman with pubic hair is viewed as risking castration by having his genital organ become entangled in the hair (B. Sanhedrin 21a and B. Gittin 6b). The Talmud interprets the phrase *pathein yeareh* (Isaiah 3:17) to mean that as a result of the women's sinfulness, God "will afforest with hair their pubic regions" (B. Shabbat 62b). For this reason, as well as for the sake of beauty, women in talmudic times were in the habit of shaving their pubic hair (B. Nazir 59a).

24. This last line paraphrases 1 Kings 10:7, the statement the queen of Sheba makes to Solomon after she witnesses all the wonders of his court.

25. There are many variants in the manuscripts in the naming of the trees, and there are difficulties in ascertaining the identities of some of them. The translation follows, in the main, Immanuel Loew, *Die Flora der Juden* (1928–1934; reprint, Hildesheim: G. Olms, 1967), 4:162–66. The text on which this translation is based lacks the name of one of the trees in the second category; the text also includes translations of the names into Judeo-Arabic (which have not been translated here).

26. Cf. B. Berakhot 58a, where the same story is told about the talmudic sage Rabbi Sheshet.

27. For Nimrod, the biblical character, see Genesis 10:9.

28. According to the Oxford manuscript, the horse, on account of his beauty, behaved arrogantly, and that is why his fellow horses disliked him.

29. Cf. Sifrei, Numbers 95, ed. Horowitz, p. 95.

30. This is the biblical name of Moab's deity (1 Kings 11:7).

31. According to the Jerusalem and Oxford manuscripts, Ben Sira advised the King to feed his intended victim the whites of eggs. Our text, however, has the correct version, which is, apparently, based upon the talmudic claim that eating egg yolks without the whites will result in chronic constipation (B. Shabbat 108b).

32. In the Ben-Yehudah dictionary, p. 5979, the Hebrew word, *kalshit*, is rendered as a "thin solution," which is contraindicated by the use of the plural as well as by the statement that follows in the text that he crushed them, an act that is hardly applicable to a solution. Our rendering of this hapax legomenon has its basis in a geonic use of the verb *k-l-sh*, which Ben Yehudah misinterprets to mean "to spread," but, as dictated by the context, means "to split."

33. According to the Budapest manuscript, he put coriander and salt into the mixture.

34. Cf. B. Sanhedrin 72a.

35. For an analysis of these names, which make their first recorded appearance in this work, see Joshua Trachtenberg, *Jewish Magic and Superstition* (1939; reprint, N.Y.: Atheneum, 1970), 101, 102. According to him, these names were probably pronounced as Sanvi, Sansanvi, Semangelaf. They were portrayed in amulets as birds, a sample of which is used as an illustration on the soft-cover edition of Trachtenberg's book.

It was customary in eastern Europe to post these names on the walls of the room in which the newborn slept to protect it from demonic harm. See Jacob Reifman, *Ha-Karmel*, 2:125.

36. It is self-evident why Lilith has no power over a male baby past the eighth day, since on this day the child undergoes the rite of circumcision. But it is not clear why Lilith's power ends on the twentieth day after the birth of a female. Trachtenberg's suggestion (*Jewish Magic*, 37) that this may have originated in a period when the girls had an initiatory rite on that day lacks support in the sources. In the Oxford manuscript, the reading is twelve days instead of twenty.

37. According to a midrashic tradition, Lilith is so cruel as to destroy her own offspring (Numbers Rabbah 16:25).

38. Cf. B. Baba Batra 16a.

39. For Titus, cf. B. Gittin 56b; for the ravens, cf. B. Ketubbot 49b and Leviticus Rabbah 19:1.

40. Because they are white, the baby ravens do not look like ravens.

41. The translation here follows Yassif's texts (*Sippurei Ben Sira* [Jerusalem: Magnes, 1984], 237–38). Steinschneider's text (in Eisenstein, *Otsar Midrashim* [1915; reprint, Israel: 1969]) reads: David "saw a wasp consuming a spider. Then a fool came . . . and banished the wasp and the spider."

42. For the beneficial use of folly, cf. Midrash Psalms 34:1; for the spider, cf. Targum to Psalm 57:3.

43. Cf. 1 Samuel 21:11–16.

44. 1 Samuel 21:16.

45. Midrash Psalms 34:1.

46. Cf. 1 Samuel 26:7–12.

47. The probable reason for having Joshua ride an ox is the fact that the tribe of Ephraim, to which Joshua belongs, is compared to an ox (Deuteronomy 33:17). Also, according to rabbinic tradition, the coins issued by Joshua had the form of an ox on them (Genesis Rabbah 39:11).

48. For good sense here, I am following the Oxford manuscript.

49. Cf. B. Hullin 60b.

50. In compensation for its diminished light, the moon received the accompanying light of the stars that appear in the night (Genesis Rabbah 6:4).

51. A similar account is recorded by Rabbi Moses ha-Darshan (eleventh century) in his Genesis Rabbati, ed. Albeck, 59.

52. Ginzberg in *Legends of the Jews* (Philadelphia: Jewish Publication Society, 1928; repr. 1956), 5:54, 55, takes the Hebrew word *revah* to mean "reward," which makes little sense in this context. It should be rendered, instead, as "rest" or "repose," which explains the nature of the donkey's complaint since, as reputed, it is subjected to ceaseless toil.

53. The Hebrew word *kelev* (dog) is taken as a blend of *kol* and *lev*—"all" and "heart" or "mind"—meaning, in effect, "all mind."

54. Rabbi Moses ha-Darshan (eleventh century) records this story in Genesis Rabbati, ed. Albeck, 59, with the difference that the mouse in his account is told to fetch Noah a hair from the cat's tail, which it does when the cat is asleep.

55. The translation here follows Yassif, *Sippurei Ben Sira*, 246–47.

56. Cf. B. Sanhedrin 44a, 100a. The inhabitants of Ai were sinful people who detested anyone who proclaimed the laws of the Torah.

57. Cf. B. Sanhedrin 108b for the various details in this entire passage.

58. This is based on a talmudic principle that the leveling of a false charge against one's fellow is prima facie evidence that its author is guilty of the very same crime.

59. Cf. B. Hullin 127a, where the weasel is mentioned as the only exception. The meaning of the Hebrew *demut* is "likeness," "form," etc. I have rendered it as "species," which, etymologically, means "outward appearance," "shape," "form." For the correctness of this translation, cf. Tanhuma, Vayikra 8, and the use of *demut* at the conclusion of this work.

60. According to the Budapest manuscript, the sea was to serve, like Noah's ark, as a place of protection for each species against the ravages of the angel of death. Thus, the fox, who by his cunning avoided having a representative of his species in the sea, outsmarted himself and worked, in the end, to his own detriment.

61. Our text, stating that "he wrote all the words in the Book of Jeremiah," is obviously corrupt and I have, therefore, followed the text as it appears in the Budapest manuscript.

62. Cf. Jeremiah 35.

63. For the immortality of the phoenix, cf. Genesis Rabbah 19:5. But there, as well as in all other rabbinic sources, it is called *Hol*. Only in this work is it

called *Milham*. For all the human beings who were translated alive into paradise, cf. Derekh Erets Zuta, end of chap. 1, and see Higger's edition for parallels.

64. One of the basic meanings of the Hebrew root of *orev* is "to mix." Hence, the miscegenetic nature of the raven is rooted in its very name.

65. The anonymous author of this work associated the Hebrew *nesher* with the root *sh-r-h*, "to dwell." The idea that the Divine Presence dwells on the eagle is to be taken in the sense that the eagle enjoys special divine protection. This is in accordance with the Maimonidean view that the term *Shekhinah* may refer to its manifestation "in some object which is constantly protected by Providence" (*Guide of the Perplexed*, p. 1, chap. 25).

9 ◆

PARABLES FROM SEFER
HA-BAHIR

Sefer ha-Bahir, literally "the book of brilliance," is the first literary work
to develop the mystical concepts and symbolism that come to fuller
expression in later Spanish kabbalistic works like the *Zohar.* As with so
much in Jewish mysticism, nearly all we know about *Sefer ha-Bahir* derives
from Gershom Scholem who has discussed at length the difficulties
connected to the *Bahir:* its mysterious appearance in southern France in
the twelfth century; its problematic place in the history of Kabbalah; and
the convoluted and often unresolved questions concerning the work's text
and plain meaning. About its literary character, Scholem has written that
the book is "devoid of a literary structure. . . . Everything seems to have
been jumbled together haphazardly."

These difficulties notwithstanding, several things can be said about the
Bahir. As Scholem has noted, the book is written in imitation of the form
of a classical midrash with homiletical expositions of scriptural verses.
These homilies frequently employ techniques of classical midrashic exegesis—puns and wordplays, interpretations of verses through other verses,
gematriot, and other still more obscure hermeneutical techniques. Among
all these midrashic borrowings, however, the parable holds arguably the
most prominent position. There are some forty-five parables in the *Bahir,*
and they touch upon the most profound and original aspects of the work's
mystical theology. Scholem has attempted to sketch that theology: it is

essentially Gnostic in character and is predicated upon the identification of Torah with the Gnostic Sophia, or Wisdom-figure, who is exiled in this world from the pleroma or divine realm of fullness of being. Readers interested in the *Bahir's* Gnostic mysticism should consult Scholem's lengthy treatment of the book in *Origins of the Kabbalah* (Philadelphia: Jewish Publication Society, 1987). In our notes, we make reference to Scholem's discussions in that book in the case of each parable.

As narratives, the parables in the *Bahir* are most interesting not for their underlying theological content, which usually can be understood only by a reader who already possesses the theological code, but for their literary transformation of the midrashic parable into an esoteric form and their use of imaginative narrative as a medium for mystical expression. In their diction and themes, the parables of the *Bahir* closely resemble classical midrashic parables about kings and consorts, royal courts, and wayward children. Yet the anonymous author of the *Bahir* radically transformed the midrashic parable into a quintessentially private literary form simply by dropping the *nimshal*, the so-called explanation, which in rabbinic literature nearly always accompanies the *mashal* and supplies the reader with the information necessary for interpreting and applying the parable's message. In the *Bahir*, no such explanatory aid facilitates the reader in understanding the parables, while the narratives themselves become increasingly more bizarre, less naturalistic, more distantly mimetic. At the same time, the brief narratives in these parables carry an enormous load of imaginative power, which makes them quite unlike anything else in medieval Jewish literature. In their themes of exile, absence, and unsatisfied longing, these parables look forward to the more contemporary parables of Kafka and Agnon. Through the distorting lens of historical retrospection, they bear an unsettling modernity.

There exists no critical text of the *Bahir*. Scholem supposedly prepared a critical text of the Hebrew original, which, unhappily, he never published, though he did put out a German translation of the text entitled *Das Buch Bahir* (Leipzig: W. Drugulin, 1923). The English translation by Allan Arkush of *Origins of the Kabbalah* (mentioned above) contains many passages from the *Bahir*, presumably translated from Scholem's German translation. My translation is based upon the edition of the Hebrew text of the *Bahir* by Ruben Margalioth (Jerusalem: Mossad Harav Kook, 1951);

as Scholem noted, the edition is far from satisfactory, but it is the only one available. I have also consulted Arkush's versions and leaned upon Scholem's interpretations.

Introduction and translation by
DAVID STERN

I

Why does the first word in the Torah, *bereshit*, begin with the letter bet? So that it would begin with a *berakhah*, a blessing. And what is our source for calling the Torah a blessing? It is said, ". . . and full of the Lord's blessing, take possession of the sea and the south" (Deuteronomy 33:23). The word *sea* always points to the Torah, as it is said, "Its measure . . . is broader than the sea" (Job 11:9). What, then, does the phrase "and full of the Lord's blessing" teach us? That the letter bet, every place it appears in the Torah, designates a blessing, as it is said, *bereshit*, "in the beginning" (Genesis 1:1)—*reshit*, "beginning," is actually wisdom, as it is said, "the beginning, *reshit*, is wisdom, the fear of the Lord" (Psalm 111:10).[1] We also know that wisdom itself is a blessing, for it says, "And God blessed Solomon"[2] and "The Lord had given Solomon wisdom" (1 Kings 5.26).

It is like a king who wed his daughter to his son, and gave her to him in marriage. The king said to his son: "Do with her as you wish."[3] (Par. 3)

II

"What is a *patah?*" [his students asked Rabbi Akiba].[4]

"An entrance," [he replied].

"Which entrance?"

"The entrance on the north, which serves the entire universe. From that gate through which evil went forth, good comes out."

"What is good?"

Rabbi Akiba answered [his students] with a sneer: "Haven't I already told you? The small *patah.*"

"We forgot," his students said. "Teach us again."

Rabbi Akiba began to instruct them: "It is like a king who had a throne. Sometimes he took it in his arms. At other times he placed it on his head."

"Why did he do this?" the students asked.

"Because it was so beautiful," Rabbi Akiba replied, "and it saddened him to sit upon it."

They asked, "And where on his head does he place the throne?"

Rabbi Akiba answered, "In the open letter *mem*,[5] as it is said, "Truth springs up from (*mem*) the earth; justice looks down from (*mem*) heaven" (Psalm 85:12).[6] (Par. 37)

III

And what is the function [of the letter *bet*]? A parable.

What is it like? It is like a king who had a daughter. She was fine and beautiful, lovely and perfect, and he gave her as wife to the son of a king. The king garbed her, and gave her a crown, jewelry, and bestowed her upon the prince with a great sum of money.

Could the king live without his daughter? You answer, No. Could he spend all his time with her? You answer, No. What, then, did he do? He placed a window between himself and his daughter. Whenever his daughter needed the king, or he needed to see her, they communicated through the window.

That is what is written: "The royal princess, her dress embroidered with golden mountings, is led inside to the king" (Psalm 45:14–15).[7] (Par. 54)

IV

What is the meaning of the verse ". . . make it known in these years" (Habakkuk 3:2)? The prophet meant: I know that You are the Holy Lord, for it is written, "Who is like You, majestic in holiness?" (Exodus 15:11)— and that holiness exists in You and that You exist in holiness.[8] Nonethe-

less, make it known in these years. What does "make it known" signify? That "You, Lord, should be merciful," as it is said, "God looked upon the Israelites, and God knew" (Exodus 2:25).

What does "He knew" mean? It is like a king who had a lovely consort, and he had many sons by her whom he loved and raised. But they turned to evil ways, and the king grew to hate them and their mother. She, then, went to her sons and said, "Why are you doing this, making your father hate me as well as you?"

Finally, they repented of their evil ways and once again obeyed their father's wishes. When their father saw this, he returned to loving them just as he had in the beginning, and he remembered their mother as well, as it is said, "God looked upon the Israelites, and God knew" [meaning that He remembered], as it is said, "make it known in these years" [which really means "remember"].[9] (Par. 76)

V

What is our source for knowing that Abraham had a daughter? It is written, ". . . and the Lord had blessed Abraham with [a daughter whose name was] Everything" (Genesis 24:1);[10] it is also written, "Everything who is called by My name, whom I have created, formed, and made for My glory" (Isaiah 43:7).[11]

Now was this blessing a daughter or not?

A parable. It is like a king who possessed a servant who obeyed his master perfectly and completely. He tested him through several trials, and the servant withstood all of them. The king asked himself, What can I give this servant or do for him? "I will commend him to my older brother," he said, "to advise, protect, and honor him." The servant went off with the older brother and learned his ways, and the brother grew to love him dearly and came to call him his friend, as it is written, ". . . seed of Abraham, my friend" (Isaiah 41:8).[12]

The brother asked himself: What can I give this servant or do for him? Here is a beautiful crown[13] I have made with precious and unique gems. This is a treasure [fit] for a king, but I will give it to this servant, and he will merit it instead of me.[14] That is what is written: "And the Lord blessed Abraham with *kol*," that is, everything.[15] (Par. 38)

VI

What is the meaning of the phrase "the Presence of the Lord" [in Ezekiel 3:12, "Blessed be the Presence of the Lord, in His place]? A parable. It is like a king who kept a special consort[16] in his chambers. All his troops delighted in her. And the consort had sons, and every day they came to greet the king and to bless him. "Our mother—" they asked, "where is she?" The king replied, "You cannot see her now." They answered, "Blessed is she wherever she may be."[17]

And what does Scripture mean when it writes, "in His place"? It means that no one knows where His place is. A parable. It is like the daughter of a king who came from afar, and no one knew where she had come from. But when they saw that she was a woman of strength and beauty whose every deed was done with dignity, they said, "She surely was taken from the side of the light, for through her deeds the world is enlightened." They asked her, "Where are you from?"

"From my place," she replied.

"If so," they said, "the inhabitants of your place must be great men. Blessed are you, and blessed is your place!"[18] (Pars. 131–32)

VII

For what reason does Scripture say, "Keep My Sabbaths . . ." (Leviticus 19:30)? Why does it not say "My Sabbath"?

A parable. It is like a king who had a beautiful bride, and every week he invited her to be with him for a day. The king also had handsome sons whom he loved. He said to them, "This being her situation, you, too, rejoice with her on the day of my rejoicing. For I exert myself for your sakes. And you glorify me as well."[19] (Par. 181)

NOTES

1. This verse is usually translated as "the beginning of wisdom is the fear of the Lord."

2. This quotation is not found in any biblical verse.

3. For discussion of the parable, see Scholem, *Origins of the Kabbalah* (Philadelphia: Jewish Publication Society, 1987), 91–93. The king is, of course, God; the son is Solomon; and the daughter is Wisdom (Sophia), which God grants Solomon.

4. The˙ *patah* is the short vowel *a*. In replying to the students, Akiba punningly revocalizes the word to read *petah*, an "entrance." The short *patah* to which Akiba later refers is the segol, the short vowel *e*, which in par. 36 is described as indicating the south side of the world, which is open to good and evil (Scholem, *Origins*, 60 n. 15).

5. According to Scholem (*Origins*, 60), the open mem, as opposed to the closed final mem, is a symbol of the feminine.

6. The closing exegesis plays upon the double appearance of the letter *mem* in *mei* in the two places indicated in the verse in Psalms. The king's placing of the throne upon his forehead and arms seems to allude to the ritual of tefillin, or phylacteries, and recalls the talmudic aggadah according to which God wears tefillin (B. Berakhot 6a). While Scholem notes that the meaning of this parable is "utterly enigmatic," the king's affection for the throne carries a moving pathos about it.

7. Here, again, the daughter represents the lower Sophia, a Gnostic figure identified by the *Bahir* with the Torah. Elsewhere in the *Bahir* the letter bet is described as the union of the masculine and the feminine, a union that, situated at the very beginning of the Torah, also enacts the primordial act of creation. For discussion, see Scholem, *Origins*, 170–71.

8. The precise meaning of the Hebrew is unclear.

9. Compared with the other parables in this section, this parable is relatively exoteric in meaning. The consort who is alienated from the king symbolizes the common Gnostic theme of the alienation of Sophia from the pleroma, or divine fullness of the Godhead. It would seem from the parable that the children of Israel bear responsibility for that alienation but also possess the capacity for correcting it through repentance. According to the exegesis, the story of God's deliverance from Egypt is allegorized in terms of the Gnostic doctrine.

10. "Everything," the Hebrew *kol*, in Genesis 24:1 is taken here as the daughter's name, a midrashic exegesis that derives from B. Baba Batra 16b, though in the talmudic passage, Abraham's daughter's name is given as *ba-kol*, "with everything."

11. Here, too, "Everything" translates from the Hebrew *kol*.

12. The Hebrew word translated as "friend" is *ohavo*, which in rabbinic parables usually refers to the king's special friend, adviser, or counselor.

13. *Keli*, literally "a utensil"; my translation follows the classical commentators who interpret it as the crown, possibly of the Shekhinah, in which the ten *sefirot* (= gems) are embedded. Abraham's virtue is generally associated with deeds of loving-kindness and charity.

14. Literally "in his place."

15. For discussion, see Scholem, *Origins*, 87–88. The parable reinterprets the talmudic midrash on Genesis 24:1 so that Kol, Abraham's daughter, is now made out to be not a mere mortal but the Shekhinah.

16. Hebrew *matronita,* sometimes translated as a great queen or lady.

17. The troops here refer to the angels; the sons, to Jews who pray to God every day. The consort is the Presence, or *kavod,* of God, a feminine symbol for a grammatically masculine subject. The king's final statement plays on the phrase *mimkomo,* "in [or from] His [its] place."

18. For discussion, see Scholem, *Origins,* 94ff. A translation of the entire context in which these parables are found is printed in Joseph Dan, ed., *The Early Kabbalah,* trans. Ronald C. Kiener (New York: Paulist, 1986), 57–69. As both Scholem and Dan note, the two parables contradict each other in a sense: according to the first, God's glory, the lower Sophia, is invisible; according to the second, she is visible. The phrase "the side of the light" refers to the Gnostic pleroma.

19. For discussion, see Scholem, *Origins,* 158–59.

10 ·

NARRATIVE FANTASIES FROM SEFER HASIDIM

Rabbi Judah the Hasid, or "the Pietist," (d. 1217) was the founder of pietism, or Hasidut, an original religious doctrine that transformed Judaism in the Rhineland towns of Speyer, Worms, and Mainz during the thirteenth century. One of the main literary vehicles for Judah's religious teachings was the exemplum, the narrative tale illustrating a religious truth. Judah's writings are peppered with narratives, short and long. This is most evident in his summa, *Sefer Hasidim* (The Book of Pietists), a work he composed for the religious guidance of his followers. It contains almost two thousand thematically arranged passages of biblical commentary, rabbinic homily, and exemplary tales.

Judah was primarily a religious thinker and leader, not a folk artist or court poet. The tales he collected, refashioned, or wrote himself served theological and didactic purposes in his writings. A charming anecdote, an animal fable, a demonic tale were of interest to Rabbi Judah primarily because they revealed to the pietist an otherwise hidden aspect of the Deity or of His infinitely demanding religious program. Like his Christian contemporary Caesarius of Heisterbach, Judah often drew his tales from a common reservoir of Germanic and other folklore that reflects a belief in supernatural creatures who can affect, even possess, human beings.

Some narratives that Judah refashioned, like The Judgment of Saadiah (no. 12), he borrowed from such well-known story cycles as those about the wisdom of Solomon. Others, like the story about the herder who could not pray properly (no. 2), are found elsewhere in medieval Christian and Muslim sources. Still others, like The Three Confessing Jews (no. 3), Judah himself probably invented.

Scholars disagree as to what extent Judah was a literary as well as a religious innovator. Yet while they were certainly crafted with religious aims in mind, Judah's exempla portray real human conflicts over religious principles. The modern reader feels part of the tension Judah and his first readers experienced as they struggled with the pietist revision of Judaism. But are these narratives truly "fantasies"? The term is, in part, appropriate only from a modern perspective, especially when it is used to refer to such stories as those about religious conflict (nos. 1–5) and reward and punishment (nos. 7–10) in which the supernatural also figures. To Rabbi Judah and his medieval audience, communication with spirits of the dead, visions, and dreams of divine import were reality, not fantasy. To a modern reader, in contrast, they are fantasies in a twofold sense: first, they run counter to our sense of reality; second, even the religious and literary universe reflected in these narratives is, for us, a creation of the imagination.

But would Judah the Pietist, despite his openness to experiences that we today dismiss as fantastic, have called these narratives fantasies? Perhaps. For Judah surely recognized that he stood in a long line of Jewish religious thinkers who developed their own private vision—their fantasy, as it were—of what Judaism means, and then read their vision in and out of the sacred texts of their tradition. Like every traditional religious culture grounded in sacred writings and rites, Judaism enables an innova-tive initiate to legitimate a subjective, or fantastic, insight by making it appear as the objective meaning of the Word. In this way, a new idea is clothed in an ancient form in order to appear old. The misreading is a rereading of *the* reading—which happens to be exactly what the Hebrew term for Scripture, *mikra,* means.

In this way, Judah expressed his innovative fantasy of Judaism through אמשל? the underlined exemplum. And what better way could he have done it than by couching the most radical statements he could make in the narrative genre par excellence of classical rabbinic literature? This religious and literary sleight of hand asserts that a transformation of tradition itself is being carried out by means of traditional modes. By using the traditional form of the exemplum to legitimate his fantastic understanding of Judaism, Judah made his private vision part of tradition itself—an extension of midrash, of Torah, even of the will of God.

We may today enjoy these fantasies in ways that Judah and his first readers could not. Judah's religious view of the world precluded frivolous activities like idle talk, even with one's own children, let alone storytelling for amusement. Yet if we allow ourselves to enter his imaginative universe sympathetically, we may emerge understanding one way a Jewish thinker linked his personal religious sensibility with the tradition he inherited.

The narratives translated in the following pages are part of a translation-in-progress of the complete *Sefer Hasidim*, which will be published in the Yale Judaica series. The translation is based on the Parma manuscript (hereafter referred to as P), found in the Biblioteca Palatina, Hebrew MS 3280, which I have published in a facsimile edition (Jerusalem: Zalman Shazar Center, 1986). This is a unique manuscript, arranged in numbered paragraphs, which I have listed in my notes. References are also made in the notes to the edition of *Sefer Hasidim* edited by Jehuda Wistinetzki, with additions by Jacob Freimann (Frankfurt am Main: Wahrmann, 1924) (hereafter referred to as W); and to the Bologna edition of 1538 (hereafter referred to as B).[1]

Introduction and translation by
IVAN G. MARCUS

I

For this[2] is like a man who had several daughters. When men sought to marry them, their father married them off. But one daughter remained at home, unsought in marriage.

She said to her father, "You taught my sisters respectable skills, like weaving and embroidery. This is why everyone jumped [to marry] them, that is why they were wed. But why did you give me a skill [that keeps] everyone away from me—sewing mourning clothes and shrouds?[3] If my skill lay in making festive clothes, I would be married, too, like my sisters!"

Her father said, "I will sing your praises to all, and they will be attracted to you."

This is what such tractates in the Talmud as Tractate Minor Festivals said to God, "Master of the universe! Why does no one spend time studying me as they do other tractates?"[4]

The Holy One, blessed be He, replied, "It has already been stated: 'It is better to go to the house of mourning, than to go to the house of feasting; for that is the end of all men, and the living will lay it to his heart.' "[5]

II

A man should perform every religious commandment that he can, and what he cannot perform, he should think of performing.[6]

This lesson can be likened to this story: Once there was a man who was a cattle herder and did not know how to pray properly. Every day he said, "Master of the universe, You know full well that even though I normally charge everyone else a fee, if you had animals and gave them to

219

me to guard, I would guard them for free—because I love You." And he was a Jew.[7]

One time a scholar was out walking and found the cattle herder praying in this way. He said, "Fool! Do not pray that way."

The herder replied, "How then[8] should I pray?"

The scholar immediately taught him the required blessings, the Shema reading, and the Tefillah prayer[9] so that the herder would no longer pray as he had before.

After the scholar had left, the herder forgot everything that he had been taught. He did not say the prayers that the scholar had taught him.

But he was also afraid to say the prayer he formerly said because the righteous scholar had so forbidden him.[10]

In a dream at night[11] the scholar saw himself being told, "If you do not go and tell the cattle herder to pray as he did before you met him, beware the misfortune that awaits you. You have robbed Me of a man who deserves the world to come."[12]

The scholar immediately went to the cattle herder and asked, "What prayers are you saying?"

He replied, "None at all. I forgot the prayers you taught me, and you told me not to say 'If He had animals . . .' "

The sage responded, "I dreamed such and such. Say what you used to say."

This is the case of a man who had no Torah and no good deeds. Yet he merely thought of performing good deeds and God counted it as a great thing. For "the Merciful wants the heart."[13] That is why a man should think good thoughts toward the Holy One, blessed be He.

III

Three men came before sages[14] to confess to them. The sages were to instruct them in the good and correct path. But [each] sage[15] was not certain what he should say to them.

The first man said to the sage, "My father told me that he was very poor, destitute in fact, with children to support. And yet there was no evil impulse[16] in him to steal or cheat.

"At night, though, he used to go to a place where he knew money was hidden.[17] When he saw the money, he took it out, but immediately he used to return it to its hiding place. His evil impulse would then attack him. It said, 'Are you not poor? Do you not lack a protector to help you support yourself, your wife, and children? Don't worry about anyone discovering you. The owner of the money does not know. He'll never find out who took it.' [My father] used to do this every day solely in order to withstand the trial of the evil impulse." So spoke the first young man.

Then he addressed the sage, "I wish to ask you this question concerning my father and his son.[18] My father did this for many years until he moved to another land and became wealthy. *He* has already been delivered[19] from this act. But I still do it. Will my father receive a punishment or a reward? And must I, since I still do it, receive a penance? Did I sin? Or will I receive a reward?"

The second man said to the sage, "I am a man who gets into fights over nothing.[20] Every day a certain man insults me. He curses me and does everything he can all day long to abuse me publicly. But he has relatives in town, and so I am afraid to answer him back. Moreover, my evil impulse is still not powerful enough to make me fight with him. When he travels from town, *I* go armed; he does not, and I fight with him. I taunt him, and he taunts me back still more. He curses me, and this truly infuriates me because he does it all the time—even when I am the only other person present. He makes me so angry, I insult him solely to get him to curse and insult me in response. I even draw my sword against him, but he doesn't care. I get no pleasure from the fight because my heart[21] is not in it.

"Sometimes I intentionally fight with him when we are alone in the forest in order to arouse my evil impulse. It will dupe me[22] and make me want to kill him. Then, even if he were about to kill me, I would not be afraid of him. My only thought would be that now, finally, I am able to avenge myself for what he did to me in town. But because I am powerless to gain vengeance in town, because my evil impulse can arouse me only when I am solitary in the field, I often go walking in the field alone on the chance that I might meet him, and thereby arouse my evil impulse and be avenged. And yet, even if I do manage to arouse it, I still hold my temper. May the Holy One, blessed be He, count my self-restraint as a religious act.

"My father acted the same way for several years. This is why I am asking you: Is it counted as a virtuous deed, as a religious act? In regard to myself, did I act correctly by holding my temper, or must I confess for having brought myself to the point of sinning by drawing my sword, insulting and cursing him, so that he would fight with me? Or do I merit a reward for performing a religious act?"

The third man said to the sage, "I loved a woman who was married to another man. I loved her so much I could have died. When her husband had journeyed to a distant land, I spent time alone with her. She, too, loves me deeply. I embraced her and kissed her and fondled her all over her body. But I did not have intercourse with her. To me, all our kisses and embraces were no more than those between two men or two women. For my evil impulse did not participate in this deed. My purpose in doing it was only to arouse my evil impulse. My heart was hot as when fire ignites flax. Like a fire,[23] it burned with desire to have intercourse with her. My evil impulse for her attacked me only when I embraced and fondled her.

"For a considerable time,[24] I carried on this way. I could have done to her anything I wished because the two of us were living together in the same house during the time her husband journeyed to a distant land. He could not prevent me from doing to her anything I wanted, even from having sexual intercourse. Nevertheless, for the sake of the Holy One, blessed be He, I refrained from sex. I did not refrain from embracing or kissing her. Still, I did not enjoy doing those things because my heart was intent on having intercourse.[25] For several years I acted this way, in order to receive a reward.

"My father did the same thing. The single difference between us was that in his case the woman was married as well as a minor. My father also did the same thing with his mother-in-law and with his wife's sister during his wife's lifetime." The young man concluded, "I am asking you the following question: Must I repent and do penance for this? Does my father, even if he acted for the sake of Heaven? Or will we receive a reward since we were saved[26] from sinning?"

The sage replied, "Go to the Head of the Academy. Ask him." And he sent them to the Head of the Academy.

They said to the Head, "So-and-so, the sage, sent us to ask you about such-and-such a matter," as we have written above. But they did not reveal to the Head of the Academy that they were actually confessing their own sins; they told him that their cases concerned other men.

The Head of the Academy of the Diaspora responded, "You require a penance for the sins you committed. For we are commanded to purge those who act sinfully, and you have come very close to sinning intentionally. Still, your reward depends on the Holy One, blessed be He. As our sages said,[27] 'A person is supected of sinning only if he actually committed a sinful act, or actually entertained a sinful thought, or was pleased when others did.' All the more does limited culpability apply to those who merely thought of committing a sin and afterward restrained their passion."

The Head of the Academy, however, became concerned that they[28] might cause others to sin if he did not tell them that they required atonement and repentance. He said to them, "For the sins you have committed you need to atone[29] by means of a penance I will give you. The penance will be appropriate to the number of days you sinned and to the fact that you violated the sages' prohibition against being alone[30] with a married woman." And so he gave them penance for their sins and ordered them not to continue to do those sinful things.

IV

A story about a son who truly honored his father:[31] His father said to him, "You honor me now, during my lifetime. But honor me after I am dead, too. I command you to put aside your anger for one night; check your temper, and say nothing."[32]

After his father died, the son traveled far away and left his wife pregnant, although he did not know this. He stayed away for a considerable time,[33] and when he returned to the town, he arrived at night.

He went up to the room where his wife usually slept, and he heard the sound of a young man kissing her. At once, he drew out his sword and wanted to kill them. But then he remembered his father's command, and he returned the sword to its sheath.[34]

Then he heard her saying to the young man—it was her son[35]—"It has been many years since your father left me. If he only knew a son had been born to him, he would return to arrange your marriage."

When the father heard this, he spoke, " 'Let me in, my own, my darling!' (Song of Songs 5:2). Blessed is the Lord, who curbed my anger. And blessed is my father, who commanded me to curb my anger 'one night' so that I did not kill you and my son."

They rejoiced greatly and made a banquet for everyone present, who were all happy.

V

Once there was a rich man. He had many servants, and they used to steal his money.[36] The rich man's son knew this, and he said to his father, "Are they not robbing you of everything? Why don't you stop them?" But the father did not believe his son. Instead, he became angry with him. When the son saw that the servants were still robbing his father, the son said, "I will rob my father of all that remains. If I don't take it, they'll rob him of everything. My father will be left completely impoverished, with nothing but disgrace."

And so he robbed his father. His intention was that once his father was impoverished, he would support him and care for him, since his father would be left without the money the servants had also stolen from him.

The son said to the sage, "When I saw that they were robbing him, I said to myself, If I wait until they steal everything, my father will be left in disgrace."

The sage replied, "Tell your father that you robbed him of the rest of his money. He will forgive you. Then return everything you took."

The son said, "If I tell my father, he will suspect me of robbing *all* of his money [including the amount the servants stole]. He will curse and never forgive me. Yet if I give him back what I stole, he will say, 'I will never forgive you until you return *all* of it.' He won't believe me."

The sage said, "Return it nonetheless."

The son answered, "But if I return it, the servants will only continue to rob my father. The Creator Himself knows I did not steal the money because I needed it but only because I knew *they* would steal everything. So I said, Better that I should steal it in order to protect my father. I knew he would become impoverished. If I return everything, the servants will steal it. Yet he already suspects me of stealing what they stole, and he won't believe me."

The sage said, "If that is the case, you should support him. He lacks sufficient common sense to look out for himself. Just spend the money as though he still had it. You acted prudently. It is good that he benefit from his money even if it is in your possession, and that it support him in his old age."

VI

A man should not invite women into his house lest he have sinful thoughts about them.[37] He should not live in a house where wicked men live because either they will make him take oaths [in vain] or he will make them. If he has children, they may learn from the wicked people's behavior. A man should not live in a neighborhood where large families live because they will not heed criticism. For the family will cover up their wrongdoing so as not to be embarrassed before the other members of their family in the same town.[38] Consequently, you will always be quarreling and arguing with them. Do not live in a town where the only way to make a living is through trade, because then a man will not be able to study Torah regularly. He should not live in a town with wicked people who are gluttons or drunkards, nor in a town led by more than one ruler, as it is said, "When there is rebellion in the land, many are its rulers" (Proverbs 28:2).

Go and learn from a gentile prince.[39] Once there was a ruler in whose territory people gathered at a large fair. They came from everywhere, and all on the same day. Many prostitutes also flocked there, and the prostitutes had a madam.

The ruler said to his servant, "Take a large sum of money and hire all the prostitutes because tomorrow people will come to the fair. After you have hired all of them and given them everything they want, put them all in a house, prepare a comfortable bed for each, give them food, drink, and wool to work, and guard them until the fair is over. Then send them home."

The servant went and spoke to the madam, "I will give your women everything you wish—above and beyond what you would normally earn." And he gave her everything she stipulated. He brought the prostitutes to a house and guarded them there. When the fair was over, he brought them back to town.

He did this every time there was a fair that attracted prostitutes. And how much more so should a Jew, who must keep his distance from those who sin! Therefore God commanded: "There shall be no harlot of the daughters of Israel" (Deuteronomy 23:18). And it is written, "Visit your neighbor sparingly" (Proverbs 25:17). Consider: If there are two friends in business together, and one of them has a beautiful wife, better that he should come to your house [than you to his].

VII

For[40] there is a story about a pietist who asked in a dream question[41] who would sit next to him in paradise. The pietist was shown[42] a young man in a distant land.[43] The next day he prepared himself and went to see the young man. He searched for him carefully, and when he approached the area where the man lived, he asked after him. Everyone was shocked, "Why are you looking for that man? He is extraordinarily wicked!"

When the pietist heard this it saddened him. Still, he continued on to the man's house. But the man threw him out, heaped insults upon him, struck him on the face, and removed his pants. He said, "Come in now, if you still want to!" The man and his friends laughed at the pietist, but he paid no attention to them and entered the house.

The wicked man brought the pietist to a room near a chamber used by prostitutes. During the night the man gathered all the prostitutes in town and went with them to the chamber, which was near the room of the pietist. The wicked man gave the prostitutes much wine; they became drunk, and he danced before them all night until they were dead drunk and had fallen asleep. He then left the room and went away.

227

The pietist saw all this and wept. The next day he prepared to return home. Before he departed he asked the man, "By your life! Tell me, have you ever in your life done anything good? For I have seen in a dream that you will sit near me in paradise. But you do such wickedness! How can it be possible that you will sit there with *me?*"

The man replied, "Everything you have seen I have done intending to do good. I only pretend to be a wicked man. Consequently, the truly wicked men tell me about the prostitutes they have hired. Then I secretly go and offer the prostitutes more money so that they will come with me. And they believe I have intercourse with them because they get drunk during the night. Also, I told my mother to come during the night and drag me out by my hair. So if they should ask the next day, 'Why didn't you sleep with us?' I can answer, 'You know my mother attacked me.' Meanwhile, I prevent the wicked men[44] from sinning. I don't care if people suspect me. I forgive them for doing it."

VIII

The story of a man who was riding alone at night.[45] The moon was shining as he rode in the desert. He suddenly saw a large convoy of many wagons. There were people sitting on the wagons, and others pulling them. As he approached, the man realized that some of the people were dead.

He asked them, "How is it that some of you are pulling the wagons all night and others are sitting on them?"

They replied, "It is because of our sins. When we were alive in that other world, we consorted with women and virgins. Now we pull a wagon until we are so exhausted we can pull no longer. Those riding on the wagons then get off, and we get up to rest. Then they pull us until they are exhausted. Afterward, they do the same."[46] That is what is said, "Behold, I[47] will make it creak under you, as a cart creaks that is full of sheaves" (Amos 2:13). And it is written, "Woe unto them that draw iniquity with cords of vanity, and sin as it were with a cart rope" (Isaiah 5:18).

The righteous hit the men who pull the wagons the way a driver strikes an animal harnessed to a wagon,[48] as it is said, "He is like the beasts that perish" (Psalm 49:13).

Thus we learn: Whoever acts like an animal during his lifetime must work like an animal in the other world. Whoever oppresses or terrorizes people during his life is oppressed in [that other][49] world like an animal—even a man who merely abuses his animal.

IX

A certain Jew took a long journey. Another Jew saw in a dream that angels were weighing the Jew who had gone on the journey in one pan of a scale against his sins in the other pan.[50] The sins were heavier than the Jew himself, and they said, "Because his sins weigh more, the man does not deserve a portion in the world to come."

Other angels came along and said, "You did not weigh him properly." They placed the skins of foxes and other animals[51] on the man. Now he was heavier and they said, "Look! He deserves the world to come."

Now the second man—the dreamer—thought that the man in the dream was still alive. But while he dreamt, the man who was being weighed died. The angels said, "The skins placed on him were skins he contributed to the tax fund, and it is written, 'I will also make your officers peace, and charity your magistrates' (Isaiah 60:17)." When the community decrees that everyone, on penalty of excommunication, must contribute a certain amount to the tax fund, if a man contributes honestly, it is considered as if he gave it as charity.[52] And the reason they weighed his body is because it is written, "Tekel, you have been weighed in the balance and found wanting" (Daniel 5:27). Another explanation is because the man worked hard with his body to do acts of piety.

X

A tale about a pietist.[53] In the summer, he used to lie down on the ground among fleas, while in the winter he put his feet in a container filled with water until they froze in the ice.

His friend asked him, "Why do you act this way? Is it not written, 'And surely your blood of your lives will I require' (Genesis 9:5)? Why then do you endanger your own life?"

The pietist replied, "I have never committed a [serious][54] sin, but I must have transgressed minor ones. True, for those I do not *have* to impose on myself penances. But the Messiah suffers for the sins of Israel, as it is said, 'But he was wounded because of our transgressions' (Isaiah 53:5). Men who are truly righteous [willingly] undertake acts of suffering. I want no one but myself to suffer for my sins. In addition, I will perform an act of kindness for others. For many persons benefit when the righteous suffer. For example, take Rabbi Eleazar, the son of Rabbi Simeon, and our Holy Rabbi [Judah the Prince]—the world benefited from their suffering as though they had inflicted it upon themselves.[55] [This is the meaning of] 'Assuredly I will give him the many as his portion' (Isaiah 53:12)."

His students said to the pietist, "Still, we[56] are afraid that you will be punished and die." One student thought to himself, Since he imposes penances on himself, it is possible he may die. For the student had seen the penances. Sometimes his teacher threw fire upon his skin, and afterward, he had to recover in bed. The student said to him, "Look how you are neglecting the study of Torah. That is a sin."

After the pietist died, the student became worried that his teacher's penances might be considered a sin in the other world. He lay down on the pietist's grave and asked him to say in a dream if he was receiving a reward for his penances.[57]

The pietist appeared and said, "Come with me! I will show you." And he brought the student to paradise.

The student asked, "Where is my place?"

The pietist replied, "In 'that place.' But if you perform more acts of virtue [you] will be high up."[58]

"Where is your place?" the student asked.

"In 'that place' high up," the pietist answered.

"Show me."

"You cannot see it yet," the pietist responded. "You have not performed enough acts of virtue even to glimpse my place."

Though he did not get to see his teacher's place, the student rejoiced over the great illumination there and the pleasant aroma.[59] And he did learn that his teacher was not being punished.[60]

XI

This also applies to the case of a man who lived in a certain town where his children died. People could not support themselves in that town, and this man was being punished for causing his children to die [by staying there]. And let no one object, "Had they lived elsewhere, they would have died anyhow." A dangerous place is different.[61]

For there once was, in the land of the Hungarians, a town to which Jews came. They moved their homes from the area where they had lived before and built them in another place. Then people began to die. Nearly everyone died.

The Jews fasted, but it did no good. Finally, the cantor traveled out of his distict and encountered a great army. He saw their commander riding on a lion with a bridle in its mouth, and the bridle was actually a long snake.

The old man knew at once that these were spirits.[62] He greeted them, and they returned his greeting.

The commander said to the old man, "Return to that town and tell the Jews to leave that place. My great army and I are about to perform a *danse* [*macabre* (?)][63] there."

Before he left them, the army wished to injure the old man. But the commander ordered them not to.

He said to the old man, "Go to the Jews. Tell them to leave that area. If they do not, I will kill them all."

The old man—that is, the cantor[64]—said, "I am afraid your army will harm me."

The commander ordered one of the spirits standing before him to escort the old man to the town so that the other spirits would not injure him.

The old man reached the town and told the townspeople what the commander of the spirits had told him. He himself left the town at once.

This story proves that even though these people fasted, they benefited only after they left that dangerous place.

XII

For there once was a story involving Rabbi Saadiah, the son of Joseph the sage.[65] A man traveled with his servant and took along a great sum of money. His wife, whom he had left behind, was pregnant.[66] Sometime later the master died and left all his money unclaimed. The servant immediately took possession of the property and said, "I am his son."

When the son to whom the master's widow had given birth grew up, he learned that his father had died, and he proceeded to claim the property the servant had seized. Meanwhile, the servant married into an aristocratic family, a fact which made the son fear for his life if he dared to challenge the servant.

The son took lodging with Rabbi Saadiah, who brought him food. But he refused to eat until he had told Rabbi Saadiah what had happened. Saadiah advised him to speak to the king. So the son went and, in tears, pleaded with the king until he sent for Rabbi Saadiah to judge the case.

Rabbi Saadiah ordered blood [belonging to the son and to the servant] let into cups. He then took a bone of the son's father,[67] and placed it in the servant's cup. But the blood was not absorbed by the bone. He then took the bone and placed it in the blood in the son's cup, and the blood was absorbed by the bone. This was because the two were one body.[68]

NOTES

1. I am also preparing a new synoptic critical edition of the Hebrew text. Readers interested in further discussion of German Hasidut and *Sefer Hasidim* may refer to my "Penitential Theory and Practice Among the Pious of Germany," (Ph.D. diss., Jewish Theological Seminary of America, 1974); Haym Soloveitchik, "Three Themes in the *Sefer Hasidim*," *AJS Review* 1 (1976), 311–57; Ivan G. Marcus, *Piety and Society: The Jewish Pietists of Medieval Germany* (Leiden: Brill, 1981). For the narratives, see Joseph Dan, "Rabbi Judah the Pious and Caesarius of Heisterbach: Common Motifs in Their Stories," in *Studies in Aggadah and Folk-Literature*, ed. J. Heinemann and D. Noy (Jerusalem: Magnes, 1971), 18–27. For hagiographical traditions about Judah the Pietist and his father, see M. Gaster, *Maaseh Book* (1934; reprint, Philadelphia: Jewish Publication Society, 1981), 317–96. In addition, I wish to acknowledge the Hebrew studies on these narratives by Joseph Dan and Tamar Alexander, who have provided many of the insights in

my notes. A monograph by Tamar Alexander on some of these stories will be published by J. C. B. Mohr in the near future.

2. This exemplum (P 1) is found in the introductory section of *Sefer Hasidim*, called *Sefer ha-Yirah* (The Book of the Proper Fear of God) and ascribed to Judah the Pietist's father, Samuel the Pietist. In it the author stresses that pietism requires doing religious duties other Jews despise: burying an unclaimed corpse (*met mitsvah*) or studying the parts of the Talmud that deal with burial and mourning, such as Tractate Minor Festivals (Moed Katan). Reward in the hereafter, he claims, will be proportional to the difficulty of the act, as promised in Mishnah Avot 5:23: *le-fum zaara agra*, (the reward for a commandment is commensurate with the trouble it takes to perform it).

3. The Hebrew is truncated and is best understood without emendation.

4. The Babylonian Talmud includes thirty-seven tractates, of which Minor Festivals (Moed Katan) is one. As the story suggests, it is hardly the most famous or studied.

5. Ecclesiastes 7:2. The point of the exemplum is not exactly congruent with the argument being made. Although "all" pietists should study the despised tractate, still, within the exemplum, the unmarried daughter just wants some suitors. It is also not obvious that fathers teach their daughters weaving and embroidery, but the gender of the Diety is masculine and must correspond to a father, not a mother. In general, exempla in the book do not seem to correspond to the point being made except in a general, partial way.

6. This exemplum actually spans three sections, P 4, P 5, and P 6. The frame in paragraph 4 ("A man should . . . think of performing") and at the end of paragraph 6 ("This is the case . . ." to the end) are designed to create a new "subtext" resulting from the dissonance between the exemplum itself and the religious-ideational context in which it is placed. Using an international motif attested to in Christian and Muslim sources (as well as in later Hebrew literature), the author appears to contradict such pietistic values as the requirement for complicated prayers extending well beyond the minimal Jewish liturgy and the strong opposition to anthropomorphic views about the Diety. The text of the exemplum seems to prove that sincere and loving intentions are sufficient, and that God can be portrayed in the most anthropomorphic terms. The introductory rubric and the conclusion, however, set up a tension between text and context: only if a person is incapable of doing the rigors of pietistic Judaism are sincere thoughts better than doing nothing.

7. This gloss is one sign that the author knew that the original tale was not about a Jewish protagonist.

8. P reads *ela* (then) and not *eilav* (to him), as in Wistinetzki.

9. These prayers are the core of the daily evening and morning liturgy.

10. The use of the term *tsaddik* (a righteous man) in connection with the scholar is ambiguous. On the one hand, a learned person who teaches a Jew how to pray is righteous. On the other hand, in our story, the scholar may appear to the herder to be righteous, but the reader knows that he is acting incorrectly.

11. The biblical phrase *halom lailah* (a dream by night), rather than the simpler

halom, may echo the biblical divine warnings in Genesis 20:3 (God warns Abimelech not to harm Sarah and Abraham) and Genesis 31:34 (God warns Laban not to harm Jacob). In both cases, the narrator is critical of the recipient of the dream. This overtone reinforces the problematic status of the "righteous" scholar in our exemplum and heightens the irony (cf. 1 Kings 3:5).

12. Cf., for example, B. Sanhedrin 91b: "[A teacher] who holds back (*mana*) from a student knowledge of [even] one religious law (*halakhah*) is considered to have robbed him (*gazal*) of his ancestral inheritance." This dictum, too, suggests an implicit critique of the scholar. In the exemplum, the scholar's instruction of the liturgically correct prayers is what keeps the herder from saying his simple prayer and, in turn, from earning his reward in the world to come. By twisting the talmudic statement and using the same language (both use the verbs *m-n-'* and *g-z-l*), the scholar is criticized, not praised.

13. The phrase is found in Rashi (Rabbi Solomon, son of Isaac of Troyes, d. 1105) on B. Sanhedrin 106b.

14. Source: P 52–53. In *Sefer Hasidim*, the sage (*hakham*) is a Jew learned in the demands of pietism who serves as an adviser to pietists. When pietists or would-be pietists require atonement, they confess to the sage, who intuitively knows the appropriate penance they should perform. The sage himself cannot effect divine forgiveness in a sacramental way. He is merely the vehicle through which the penitent learns how to behave in order to merit divine forgiveness directly from God. This mode of ascetic atonement does not, despite appearances, seem to have been influenced by Christian practice. It has had a major influence on Jewish piety down to the present time.

15. The text shifts from the plural in the rubric to the singular, which continues throughout the rest of the narrative.

16. The "evil impulse" of the heart (see Genesis 6:4, 8:21, and the near personification in Genesis 4:7) is a classical rabbinic construct, which attempts to provide a metaphysical and psychological description of how people defy God's will. See Solomon Schechter, *Aspects of Rabbinic Theology* (New York: Schocken, 1961), 242–92, for the rabbinic sources. As in rabbinic thinking, German Jewish pietism maintained that man has a good impulse and an evil impulse and that the former can control the latter. Unlike rabbinic sources, however, the pietists gave a greater positive role to the evil impulse than did the earlier midrash (cf. Genesis Rabbah 9:7). For them, the evil impulse provides opportunities for reward. By resisting it, one earns a greater reward than by obeying God's will when the trial is not present. The three-part fiction found in paragraphs 52 and 53 is among the most original exempla in the book and dramatizes a new religious problem that pietists faced: Can one intentionally subject oneself to a trial (in their terms: incite the evil impulse) even if one commits a minor sin in the process? Does the risk of possibly earning a great reward from successfully resisting the stimulated evil impulse justify the certainty of committing a minor sin? For a talmudic precedent for subjecting oneself to temptation in order to resist succumbing to sin, see B. Avodah Zarah 17a–b. The story involves prostitutes. Cf. below nos. 6 and 7.

17. Cf. B. Baba Metsia 42a for places to hide money.

18. P reads *beni* (my son), which is a scribal error for *beno* (his son). Wistinetzki does not note the emendation.

19. P reads *nuzzal*, not *nizzal*.

20. The text is corrupt but seems to be based on a combination of phrases from Jeremiah 15:10 and the rabbinic idiom for gratuitous hatred *(sinat hinam)*. P reads, *ani riv u-madon ish hinam u-ve-khol.* . . . W's reconstruction in his n. 1 is the opposite of the required sense. The protagonist *is* easily angered. This vulnerable condition is parallel to the first case (poverty) and the third (sexual opportunity). Despite these conditions, the protagonists' evil impulses are dormant and require contrived stimulation.

21. The heart is the seat of the evil impulse. See the biblical verses cited in note 15 above.

22. The verb alludes to Eve's defense that "the serpent duped me" (Genesis 3:13). Unlike Eve, however, the pietist intends to resist the temptation of the evil impulse/serpent.

23. See B. Taanit 12b and Jeremiah 20:9. In each allusion the pietist, who is actually sinning with a married woman, compares himself to two acts of piety: fasting and uttering a divine prophecy. These overtones heighten the tension in the exemplum between potential virtue and actual sin.

24. The phrase *yamim ve-shanim* (literally days and years) seems based on 1 Samuel 29:3, which is a crux. The allusion to David's loyalty/disloyalty, however, is appropriate. In the biblical account Achish of Gath vouches for David's loyalty, but the Philistine officers suspect him. In the exemplum, the protagonist's loyalty is divided between his hope of serving God while at the same time disobeying him. The phrase is also used in no. 9.

25. In P there is no letter *vav*, but the word still should be read *livol* (to have sexual intercourse), not *la-baal* (on the husband).

26. P, which reads *nuzzalnu*, was miscopied, and W's emendation is almost correct but is not necesssary.

27. See B. Moed Katan 18b which is abbreviated and paraphrased, not quoted.

28. P reads *yahtiu*, which is the plural. W's copyist had it in the singular (or did W himself "correct" it?). The difference: the three penitents will mislead, the sage will mislead others unless he gives them penances. In either case, the responsibility falls on the sage to avoid the unwanted consequences. He gives the penitents the appropriate penances.

29. The reconstruction avoids the awkwardness of a sudden shift in the text from the third to the first person, not uncommon in *Sefer Hasidim*.

30. The ending is anticlimactic and incomplete: a relatively minor sin is singled out for the third penitent while the sins of the first two are omitted.

31. This relatively simple suspense story (P 126) can be contrasted to the middle section of no. 3 and to no. 5. Here the pietistic element defines an additional dimension to the religious duty of honoring one's father (Exodus 20:12). Unlike those exempla, whose very rubric announces a conflict of principles, this one proceeds on the assumption that the son is virtuous. A parallel text, with minor variations, is found in B 655.

32. This enigmatic deathbed command is unclear to the son and to the reader. Ahead lies a trial, but the son in no way contributes to its happening. Even the married son's disappearance is a contrived device to enable the unknown son to grow up. It is not a source of religious judgment. (Cf. no. 12.)

33. See 1 Samuel 29:3. As in no. 3 (note 24), the allusion to David is apt. The son will eventually face a choice between giving loyalty to his dead father and succumbing to a jealous fit. The details of the situation differ but the tension between a positive and a negative evaluation of the protagonist is similar.

34. Cf. with no. 3.

35. The resolution comes first for the reader, then for the son.

36. The conflict in this exemplum (P 1730) involves another boundary situation for the pietist. Can one steal from one's father and be suspected of sinning in order secretly to help him? A parallel text (B 585) diverges significantly enough in two places to be considered a different recension of the story.

37. Source: P 57–58. Instead of looking for temptations, the pietist is supposed to do everything possible to avoid them. No temptation was so alluring for the pietist as sexual relations with a woman other than his wife. The parallel in B 179 has some variants, including the omission of the line about trade.

38. On the power of large families, Cf. no. 2 (P 52) and B. Shavuot 39a.

39. The exemplum reduces the tension by making the protagonist a non-Jew. Cf. no. 7.

40. This exemplum (P 80) illustrates a principle discussed in the preceding section of *Sefer Hasidim:* how a pietist should risk being suspected of sinning while he secretly performs a religious act. The tension in this exemplum, unlike the simpler narrative in no. 6, derives from the conflict in the "wicked pietist." Tamar Alexander has suggested that this exemplum operates on two levels. It can be read as a narrative about appearances and then reread as another story about reality. The pietist version of this exemplum is unique in creating a literary tension that reflects the religious problem in pietism of the hidden righteous man who appears to sin.

41. On divination by dreams, see Joshua Trachtenberg, *Jewish Magic and Superstition* (New York: Behrman, 1939), 241.

42. Cf. the motif of divine communication with that in no. 2 (the scholar's dream).

43. Cf. no. 3 (end) and no. 4 for the use of this motif.

44. B 623 reads the end of the exemplum in the feminine, possibly a different version rather than an error of transmission.

45. This exemplum (P 63) involves a vision, not a dream. The difference lies in whether or not the protagonist is sleeping.

46. B 169 glosses (?): "they get up and rest," which is only implied by P.

47. P and B omit the word *anokhi* from the verse.

48. P and B agree (against W's unmarked emendation or copyist's error): *ve-ha-agalah* (and the wagon).

49. So B. The word apparently fell out of P by assimilation to the previous word.

50. Source: P 124. On weighing people in the pans of a scale to assess their relative merit, see the rabbinic version that compares Rabban Johanan ben Zakkai's five disciples in Mishnah Avot 2:8. In contrast, the German pietists developed an elaborate system of penances designed to approximate the amount and quality of deserved divine punishment; Rabbi Eleazar of Worms, Judah the Pietist's disciple, called this "a penance of weighed suffering." The parallel text in B 654 has minor variants.

51. Cf. Genesis 27:11–16, where Jacob gets Isaac to give him the blessing of the firstborn son by disguising himself in animal skins.

52. See B. Baba Batra 9a, where the verse containing the word *tsedakah* (meaning "righteousness" and "charity") is taken to mean that giving under governmental duress can be considered charity. See, too, 2 Kings 12:16.

53. This exemplum (P 1556), about an ascetic pietist who suffers for his generation, is unique for its overt messianic associations. Generally, the German pietists do not exhibit a collective sense of Jewish history or of cosmic processes like those presupposed in messianic speculations. Personal, not national, redemption is constantly on the pietists' minds, and this motif is also the real focus of the present exemplum. The religious boundary question being examined here is whether extreme asceticism, even if it verges on suicide, is a sin or a part of pietism. Cf. B. Taanit 11b.

54. So B, which balances "minor ones" but may simply be a gloss.

55. See B. Baba Metsia 84b–85a on the sufferings these sages endured.

56. B has it in the singular to make it agree with what follows. It is not clear if there is a shift of protagonists from "friend" to "students" to "student" or not. Cf. no. 3.

57. Cf. no. 7.

58. B reads, "*It* will be high up."

59. So B. The line fell out of P because the scribe skipped from "there" to "there" and omitted the phrase in between.

60. The last line is not found in B, raising some doubts about the outcome of the student's inquiry.

61. This exemplum (P 1871) is preceded by several warnings similar to this one, all to the effect that if a series of people die unexpectedly in a certain place, the inhabitants of the place should leave or bear the guilt of any future deaths. A parallel text is found in B 478, which becomes an entirely different narrative just before the word "Hungarians." For "dangerous places," cf. B. Pesahim 8b; B. Yoma 11a; B. Berakhot 3b.

62. Hebrew *shedim*. See Trachtenberg, *Jewish Magic*, 29–34.

63. See Philippe Ariès, *The Hour of Death* (New York: Knopf, 1981), 116–18.

64. Perhaps this is a sign that a non-Jewish story about an "old man" has been transformed into a Jewish one. The seam shows.

65. This exemplum (P 291) about the affinities between father and sons is introduced to explain why sons should fast annually on the day their fathers died. It has a long and multifaceted history that is associated with "wisdom of Solomon" exempla. Saadiah was the head of the talmudic academy of Sura in Baghdad in

the early tenth century and was renowned for his great learning. He influenced the German pietists' speculative theology, which is perhaps why this story is connected with his name.

66. Cf. no. 4.

67. The Hebrew is difficult: *etsem le-umat etsem*. It is usually taken to mean "the bone" [of the son's father]. Does it mean a bone corresponding to the father's bone? (See Trachtenberg, *Jewish Magic*, 196.) Or perhaps it is trying to say "two corresponding types of bones."

68. I especially wish to thank Raymond Scheindlin and Edith Pintel for their help in reading these texts with me.

11 ◆

LOVE IN THE AFTERLIFE
A Selection from the *Zohar*

The *Zohar* is the most important text of Jewish mysticism, unique in its influence on Jewish thought, law, and apocalyptic dreaming. It claims to be the document of a second-century talmudic sage, Rabbi Simeon ben Yohai. This attribution, challenged even in the thirteenth century when the *Zohar* appeared, was contradicted in the twentieth by Gershom Scholem, who held it to be the pseudonymous work of Moses de Leon, a Spanish Jewish author.

Why should it be so crucial whether the *Zohar* was written in the second century or the thirteenth? The reason is that its fantasies have so broadened the spectrum of Jewish dream life, that it has engendered a reverence as deep and holy as the oldest sources of Jewish literature. Rabbi Pinehas of Koretz, a famous Hasidic saint (d. ca. 1791) is said by Scholem to have praised and thanked God because he was not born until the *Zohar* was known to the world: "den der Zohar hot nimch derhalten bei Yiddishkeit [for the *Zohar* has helped me to remain a Jew]."

Whoever was the author of the *Zohar*, the antiquity of its sources is unmistakable. And what it has chosen to tell from the treasure of Jewish stories about the Bible, as well as how it does so—setting the narrative in a mighty stream of men ascending and descending between an ideal Palestine and the heavens—is certainly the issue. The promise of a future world, limned in gratified desire and a present wave of converts brought into existence through that hallowed sex, is a marker in the common endeavor of women and men to imagine the world to come.

In the passage translated, the *Zohar* posits a luminous planet in which the dead wake up in bodily form, fly back and forth between Rabbi Simeon's academy on earth and heavens filled with sexual joy. It is a new world, yet a very old one, recalling the flights of angels to the earth and its daughters before the Flood, although in the *Zohar* it is scholars—not fiery messengers—who are the heroes. The darkened atmosphere in Rabbi Simeon's yeshiva and the skies above emphasizes the dramatic effects of light and masks the radical nature of the questions under debate. Woven together in just this short excerpt are opinions about the status of pious women in the afterlife, the sexual nature of life there, and the suffering inflicted on the pious in this world. Unifying all of these themes is the celestial light that issues as seed from the pious in the act of coupling and as the flow of the soul when it is struck by suffering in this world. This light, which descends to form the souls of proselytes to Judaism, ascends in the sufferings of the pious.

This is no ordinary light. Many of the seemingly obscure moments in the *Zohar* can only be understood in the "light" of Neoplatonic philosophy, which posited a spiritual light that had substance. Maimonides refers to such light in his chapter on prophecy, when he speaks of the phenomenon of the prophetic vision. What do the prophets see—hallucination or reality? They see reality, but reality as bodied forth in atoms of this spiritual light. Such is the substance of the bodies of the dead in Dante's *Purgatorio.*

In the *Zohar,* which can be translated as "Brightness" or "Enlightenment," light is always a principal actor, shimmering through the book's language, lending it clarity even when initially the thought seems murky. The *Zohar*'s idea of what might take place in a Jewish paradise stands, even for us today, as a compelling vision, with its dream of extending the messianic promise of Judaism throughout the world via the converts, the followers of Abraham and Sarah; its emphasis on light as a purifier, and on sexual joy; its presentation of Torah scholarship among women as well as men, and of the dead sitting at study; and its ambiguous portrayal of the Holy One, the Unknown, laughing, sporting, in sexual play among the righteous!

Gershom Scholem talked about the deliberately nonsensical in the *Zohar*, about names that can be read in whimsical or funny ways. Like the laughter in Dante's *Commedia*, it reminds us that the human voice will often flirt with absurdity in speaking of spiritual vision.

The passage translated here, which we have called "Love in the Afterlife," is part of a lengthy section that describes an ascent of Rabbi Simeon ben Yohai, the early talmudic sage who is the central figure in the *Zohar*'s narrative, to the Heavenly Academy. The passage is found in *Zohar Be-Midbar* (Numbers) Shelah Lekha. The translation is based upon the edition of R. Margalioth (Jerusalem: Mossad Harav Kook, 1984), 3:332–35.

Introduction by
MARK JAY MIRSKY

Translation and annotation by
YAAKOV ELMAN,
with MICHAL GOVRIN
and MARK JAY MIRSKY

A s the members of the Academy sat, they remarked, "Look, the night has darkened." One of them said, "Rabbi Simeon, O holy pious one, Light of the world, take a book from this case, take a lamp, write these words. The time has come when each of us must visit his grave, until midnight. For then, the Holy One, blessed be He, enters His garden to disport with the righteous, and each one flies there. Since they have given us permission to complete the gift they sent you, tomorrow we will be back."[1]

They flew.

Rabbi Simeon burst into tears and groaned.

He began by saying, " 'Let her be as the loving hind and pleasant roe. Let her breasts satisfy you at all times. And be ravished always with her love.'[2] Torah, Torah, light of all the worlds. How many seas and rivers and sources and springs spread out from you on all sides. Everything from you! All upper and lower beings exist by your merit. Spiritual light radiates from you! Torah, Torah, what can I say to you? You are 'the loving hind and the pleasant roe.'[3] The above and the below are your lovers. Who merits to suckle properly from you? Torah, Torah, the sport of your Master! Who can reveal or tell your mysteries and hidden things?"[4]

He cried and put his head between his knees and kissed the dust.

Meanwhile, he saw around him images of the colleagues.[5] They said to him, "Do not fear, son of Yohai, do not fear, Holy Lamp. Write, and rejoice in your Master's joy."

He wrote down all the things he heard that night. He repeated, memorized, and did not forget a word. That lamp burned before him all night until the day. When morning came, he lifted his eyes and saw one light burning in the heavens. He lowered his eyes below. He turned upward as before and in all the heavens saw light shining. And rising in the light was the image[6] of the Temple in various guises. Rabbi Simeon rejoiced and at that moment, this light was hidden.

Meanwhile, the two messengers came. They found him with his head between his knees. They said to him, "Peace on the Master. Peace to the one whom the Upper and the Lower regions wish to greet. Rise!" Rabbi Simeon rose and rejoiced in them.

"Have you not seen what your Master did to gratify you?" they asked. "You have seen the light of the Temple in the heavens."

"I saw," he said to them.

"At that moment," they said, "the Deep released the Temple, and the Holy One, blessed be He, brought it through the Great Sea; and from its light, the heavens lit up."

They said, "The Head of the Yeshiva[7] greets you, and he knows that we are messengers to you."[8]

And many new 'old things' were innovated in Torah that night.

"Please," he said to them, "tell me one of them."

"We have not been given permission under the terms of our coming to you. But one new matter can now be disclosed to you.

"The Head of the Yeshiva recited a homily on the verse, 'Now the Lord said unto Abram, "Go forth from your native land, etc." (Genesis 12:1).'[9] This is because light like this shone on him. One who does not obtain merit in one place should go and take himself to another place. Let him obtain merit there. So with wood that burns and from which a light does not ascend and shine, let them shake it and light will ascend and shine from it.

"We were prepared to hear [the rest of his sermon] but because we had to come to you, we did not wish to delay."

Rabbi Simeon rejoiced.

They said to him, "O holy pious one, every word in the Torah contains within itself minute words, and these minute words, how great and elevated they are beyond measure! For in them there is no ambiguity but the clear meaning of the Torah—properly understood.

"It was at this moment that the Head of the Yeshiva explained hidden matters about this—the root of a soul, as to why it does not shine in one place while it merits to shine in another.[10] And until now we did not merit to hear his words, because we had [first] to come to you.

"We were worthy to hear another matter from him. A spirit that goes naked in that world without children—his wife is made the vessel through which he is built up.[11] What is the reason? His wife is the lamp that is lit by him. The two of them constitute one lamp, and one light proceeds from the other. So if one goes out, it is relit from its very own light—because they were one light.[12]

"Now Rabbi, let us return to earlier matters. When we go back to our place, we will get permission from the Head of the Yeshiva in regard to the matters that we will receive from him, and we will tell you. Your portion is worthy, for you are worthy of hidden light from all sides, from above and below, from this world and the other world."

Rabbi Simeon said, "There is one thing I wish to know—if you can make it known to me. Women—are they worthy to rise above into that world? What is it like for them there?"

"O Rabbi, Rabbi!" they said to him. "About this a great secret is [known] to us; but so as not to give away the hidden things of that place, let this one go and get permission, and we will tell you."

At that moment, one of them flew—was hidden from sight, went on his way.

After a while he returned, saying, "I was prepared to enter, but all of them were in a circle judging the case of a person who was standing at the gates of the Garden of Eden, and the cherubim seized him and would not allow him to go in there. He was in pain among them and cried out near the door. The righteous ones within heard his cries. Now all the members of the Yeshiva are gathering to approach the King Messiah to look into his case.

"I came to let you know, for my colleague has to go there since a call has been passed to all members of the Yeshiva to gather now before the Messiah."

He took a note and gave it to Rabbi Simeon. He said, "Look at what is here until we return." The two of them flew away.

Rabbi Simeon took the note and all that day saw what he saw of the secrets there. At night, he saw a lamp, sleep fell upon him, and he slept until morning. When the day became light, he rose. And the note flew away from him. But look—the two of them were coming.

"Rise, Rabbi, your portion is worthy—rise! Because of you we were worthy to see several hidden upper things. How much joy seized us when they gave us permission to reveal to you all that you wish. The Head of the Heavenly Academy came out to us and said, 'Greet the son of Yohai. The place of Bar Yohai—has it not been kept empty several days? No one will approach it. He is worthy.'

"Rabbi, Rabbi, when we flew from you, we went and saw all the members of the Yeshiva had gathered in a certain hall,[13] where the Messiah is, and they were judging the case of that man who was standing by the gate. His name we are not permitted to reveal."

Rabbi Simeon was grieved by this.

"Do not be grieved. Tonight in your dream you will know it. But they judged his case as the Messiah decreed. They decided that the man must remain outside in his pain for forty days. At the end of forty days they will give him pain through judgment, the pain of Gehenna, an hour and a half.

"And all this because, one day, one of the colleagues was explaining matters of Torah. When the colleague reached a certain matter, *this man* knew that the speaker would stumble upon it. He said to his colleagues, 'Be silent. Say nothing.' Because the colleagues were silent, the speaker stumbled on that matter and was embarrassed. The shame that *this man* caused have they judged with this harsh judgment. For the Holy One, blessed be He, does not want to leave a debt[14] in Torah, even by a hair's breadth.

"They judged him, all the members of the Yeshiva departed, and I asked permission, for the son of Yohai had asked this question. Because of this they showed me what I did not know before. O Rabbi! Six halls they showed me, with so many different pleasant things, in the place where the veil is drawn in the Garden. For from that veil onward, men do not enter at all.

"In one hall is Bitya[15] the daughter of Pharaoh and several tens of thousands and thousands of women who have merit along with her. Each one of them merits wide places of light and pleasantness without bound. Three times a day the call goes out, 'The image of the faithful prophet, Moses, is coming!' Bitya goes to the place where her curtain is, sees the image of Moses, and bows to him, 'Happy is my portion that I raised this light.' And this is why her pleasure is greater than everyone else's.

"She returns to the women and they occupy themselves with commandments of the Torah. All of them are in the forms they took in this

world, in garments of light like the garments of the men, but theirs do not shine as much. They occupy themselves with commands of the Torah they were not worthy to fulfill in this world and with the reasons behind them. All of these women who sit by Bitya the daughter of Pharaoh are called tranquil women because they never suffered the pain of Gehenna, not a moment.

"In another hall is Serah[16] the daughter of Asher and several tens of thousands and thousands with her. Three times a day they call out to her, 'Here comes the image of the righteous Joseph,' and she rejoices. She goes to her curtain, sees the light of the image of Joseph, rejoices, bows to him, saying, 'Worthy is the day that I brought your tidings to my grandfather.' Afterward she returns to the rest of the women, and they occupy themselves with praises of the Master of the world and exalt His Name. Each one of them has several places and joy. After this they return and occupy themselves with the commandments of the Torah and the reasons behind them.

"In another hall is Jochebed, the mother of the faithful prophet Moses, and several thousands and tens of thousands with her. In this hall they do not call out at all. But three times every day she thanks and praises the Master of the world, she and all the women who are with her. Every day they sing the Song of the Sea.[17] And she alone recites the verse, 'And Miriam the prophetess took the tambourine in her hand, etc.' (Exodus 15:20–21). All these righteous ones in the Garden of Eden listen to her pleasant voice, and several holy angels thank and praise her with the Holy Name along with her.

"In another hall is Deborah. She too, and all the women with her, render thanks and sing the song she recited in this world.[18] O Rabbi, O Rabbi, who has seen the joy of the righteous ones and the worthy women who serve[19] the Holy One, blessed be He, praise Him!

"Well within these palaces are four hidden halls of the four matriarchs, which were not allowed to be revealed. There is no one who sees them. All day they are by themselves, as I told you, and the men as well.

"Every night all of them gather as one. For the hour of coupling is in the middle of night—both in this world and in that world. The coupling of that world is the cleaving of the soul: light with light. The coupling of this world is body with body. And all is as is proper, species after species, coupling after coupling, body after body.[20] The coupling of that world is light after light. The halls of the four matriarchs are called the Halls of the Trusting Daughters, and I was not worthy to see them. Worthy is the portion of the righteous, men and women, who take the straight road in this world. They merit all the pleasures of that world.

"O Rabbi! Rabbi! If you were not the son of Yohai, it would not be permitted to be revealed. The coupling of that world is more fruitful than the coupling in this world. In their coupling, the coupling of that world, in their desire as one, when their souls cleave one to the other, they produce offspring, and light goes out from them. They become lamps. And these are the souls of the proselytes who convert. They all go into one hall.

"When a proselyte converts, a soul flies from this hall and enters under the wings of the Shekhinah, who kisses it because it is the offspring of the righteous. The Shekhinah sends it to that convert and it rests in him, and from that moment he is called 'a righteous convert.' This is the secret of that [verse] which is written, 'The fruit of the righteous is a tree of life' (Proverbs 11:30). Just as a tree of life produces souls, so the fruit of a righteous man is soul producing.

"The Head of the Yeshiva said, 'It is written, "Sarai was barren, she had no child" (Genesis 11.30). Since it says, "Sarai was barren," do I not know she had no child? What then [is the significance] of "she had no child"?'[21]

"But the Head of the Yeshiva explained, 'She did not bear a child but she did bear souls, born of the cleaving of desire of these two worthy people [Abram and Sarai], who, when they were in Haran, would conceive souls for the proselytes just as the righteous do in the Garden of Eden, as it is written, "And the souls they 'made' in Haran" (Genesis 12:5). They created actual souls.' "[22]

Rabbi Simeon rejoiced. That man said to him, "O Rabbi, O Rabbi, what can I say to you? Every new moon, Sabbath, festival, and appointed time those males ascend to be seen before the Holy King—males and not females, as it is written, 'All your males shall be seen' (Exodus 23:17). When they return, they return with several new interpretations, which they repeat before the Head of the Yeshiva.

"Today, they recited new interpretations before the Head of the Yeshiva regarding the ancient secrets concerning a righteous man who has worldly success and a righteous man who suffers. For all of them are weighed on the scales of the tree of life before they come to the world, and according to the balance on the scales, so they fare in this world.

"The Head of the Yeshiva descended and revealed *some* of what he had heard above, one interpretation, no more: 'Wood that does not give forth its light ought to be struck, and it will glow. A body that is not permeated with soulful light ought to be struck, and the soul's light will arise in it. Each will join with the other so as to shine.

" 'For there are bodies in which the soul's light does not glow until they are struck—then the soul's light glows—and it unites with the body and the body with it. Then, when the light ascends from the soul, this body praises, exalts and glorifies, offers prayers and supplications, and blesses its Master. Then all is alight.[23] For there are bodies in which the soul cannot glow until it is struck, at which point it glows, and each unites with the other. There is wood that does not unite with the light, and light does not ascend in it until it is struck—then it lights.[24]

" 'The Other Side[25] wishes to do so as well and strikes the wicked. As much as it strikes, "The lamp of the wicked goes out."[26] He curses and reviles on all sides and cannot cast light at all. Then it is written, "for what is a man that he comes after the King" (Ecclesiastes 2:12). He attempts to imitate him, but he cannot. And therefore "[God] will examine the righteous"[27] and strike him, and then he glows and his light strengthens.

" '[God] will examine,' as it is written, 'a testing stone' (Isaiah 28:16)." Rabbi Simeon bent over and kissed the dust. He said, "Word, Word. I sought you from the day of my birth, and now a word has been made known to me from the root and source of all."

NOTES

1. The "gift" consists of the mystical secrets that are transmitted to Rabbi Simeon by the messengers from the Heavenly Academy.
2. Proverbs 5:19.
3. It is significant that the passage in the *Zohar* that will culminate with the lovemaking of the dead in Heaven begins with a quotation that has an erotic

context in the Bible and from which Maimonides, in *Mishneh Torah Hilkhot Teshuvah*, excerpts the phrase "ravished always" as the epitome of the experience of union with the Holy One, blessed be He.

4. For the source of this interpretation, see the opinion of Rabbi Samuel ben Nahmani, quoted in B. Eruvin 54b.

5. The Hebrew *haverim* has a slightly warmer tone than either "associates" or "colleagues." A *haver* is one of a closed group of initiates (Tosefta Demai, chap. 2).

6. This can either mean the "image" or the "form" of the Temple. *Tsiyura* is apparently an Aramaicized "form" of the medieval Hebrew *tsurah*, "form," in the Aristotelian sense contraposed to *homer*, "matter." The image may be related to the Neoplatonic notion of the *matter* of creation, a primordial matter, preexistent to the Almighty's creation of the matter of the world itself.

7. It would be possible to translate this as "Rabbi Yeshiva" all the way through. The tone of the *Zohar* would be much more jocular if such were the case.

8. It is difficult to find a single English synonym for the word *hiddushim* in this context. The term has come to signify a scholar's innovations in giving a new meaning to a line of Torah. They, the *hiddushim*, are "new" (this is the root meaning of the word in Hebrew) because the scholar has just discovered the interpretation. But they are simultaneously "old" because, according to tradition, the innovations have been lying in wait to be discovered since the "giving of the Torah."

9. The original phrase translated as "recited a homily on a verse" is the Hebrew-Aramaic *patah*, a technical term in midrash for a special kind of sermon that conventionally preceded the Torah reading in the synagogue. The *Zohar*'s use of the term, though not entirely accurate, signals its attempt to imitate the literary forms of classical midrashic literature.

10. This explains why Abraham had to leave Haran, for the divine light could not shine on him there.

11. For the phrase in its original context, see Genesis 16:2, where Sarah expresses the wish that she be "built up"—made complete—through Hagar, her maid, who will take Sarah's place by bearing children to Abraham. Characteristically, the *Zohar* reverses the traditional use of the term by making it refer to a man who dies without having children and who is "built up" or completed through his wife by means of the law of levirate marriage. According to Scripture (Deuteronomy 25:5–10), if a man dies childless, his next-of-kin is required to take his widow as wife and through her to bear children who will continue the dead man's estate.

12. What the *Zohar* means is the light of the dead man still shines in his wife and creates the child who thereby relights the dead man's light as well.

13. *Heikhalot* can be either halls or palaces.

14. "Debt" here is meant in the sense of "sin."

15. The daughter of Pharaoh rescued Moses from the bullrushes and raised him under her protection. 1 Chronicles 4:18 mentions a daughter of Pharaoh, Bitya, "whom Mered took."

16. It was Serah who brought Jacob the news that Joseph was alive, see Targum Jonathan to Numbers 26:46.

17. Exodus 15:1–19.

18. For the Song of Deborah, see Judges 5:1–31.

19. This is a Hebraic use of the Aramaic. In Hebrew it refers to cultic service; in Aramaic it is the regular verb for "to do."

20. In other words, the *Zohar* makes it clear that there was no "unnatural sex."

21. The reason for the redundancy "she had no child," when we have already been told that "Sarai was barren," is to point out Sarai's role as a spiritual mother of souls, even while she was unable to bear children.

22. According to the midrash, Genesis 12:5 refers to the converts Abram and Sarai made in Haran; cf. Genesis Rabbah 39:15–16.

23. This is emended from 'Then all is as not alight.'

24. This explains why some of the righteous must therefore suffer—in order to shine.

25. This phrase, *sitra ahra*, refers to the sinister (literally left-handed or sided) evil forces in the mystical universe.

26. Proverbs 24:20.

27. Psalm 11:5.

12 ⋅

ASHER IN THE HAREM
by Solomon Ibn Saqbel

"Asher in the Harem" is the first known Hebrew fiction from medieval Spain. According to current opinion, it dates from the first half of the twelfth century. The author, Solomon Ibn Saqbel, is otherwise virtually unknown, only one other story being attributable to him. Of that story so little has been preserved that hardly anything can be said about its contents.

Our story is to be read against the background of ideas of courtly love that were current in medieval Europe. Christians and Muslims studied the phenomenon of love; they developed it into a ritual, celebrated it in poetry, and codified it in handbooks, the most notable of which are Ali Ibn Hazm's *The Ring of the Dove* for Arabic[1] and Andreas Capellanus' *Art of Courtly Love* for Latin.[2] Paramount in both cultures is the idealization of courtly love and the deprecation of vulgarity and frivolousness. The protagonist of our story sees himself as a lover but displays such lack of refinement and so little appreciation for the courtly ideal that he falls prey to a prank hatched by his friend, who is identified only as "the Adulamite."

To understand the story it is necessary to know that Hebrew love poetry of the Golden Age follows the Arabic convention of referring to the beloved as a gazelle or fawn.[3] Thus, when the protagonist, Asher, begins his story by telling us that he spent his youth in the mountains with the gazelles, he means that he spent his time chasing girls outside the cultivated, conventional world depicted in courtly poetry. He reveals his fecklessness by informing us that he exhausted his resources in this manner, and his casual treatment of human relations by telling us that only this circumstance induced him to return to his family. He flouts the rules of love again when he responds with egoistic pride to the love message inscribed on the apple thrown to him by a lady secluded behind a lattice. By his refusal to respond in a courtly, manly manner to the flirtation he shows himself to be unworthy of dignified love. Accordingly, he is subjected to a series of manipulations designed to bewilder and humiliate him in the very field where he claims expertise, the field of love. The story ends with Asher's marriage to the Adulamite's daughter. Marriage is, of course, the antithesis of courtly love, which thrives on the tension of unfulfilled longing or of illicit relationships. Having begun his career as a lover in the wild, Asher ends up completely domesticated.[4]

The story's form is that of the *maqama,* a genre of Arabic prose writing that emerged in tenth-century Iraq and became very popular in eleventh-century Spain. A *maqama* is a short piece, usually a narrative, written in the distinctive style of formal prose that was fashionable in both Hebrew and Arabic. This style consists of groups of rhymed phrases, in pairs for the most part, roughly even in length, but not metrical as in poetry. The rhymed prose is ornate, abounding in rhetorical figures and rare words. It is occasionally interrupted by short and usually quite banal poems, which sometimes further the action but usually only comment on it. Rhymed prose was an ancient tradition of Arabic writing—it is the prevailing style of the Quran—that was borrowed, together with the various forms of Arabic poetry, by Hebrew writers. It is a style well suited for the elaborate rhetoric favored by Arabic court writers, and even when it came to be used for stories, the narrative element was often subordinate to the rhetoric. Undoubtedly, the thematic inspiration for many such works, which often abounded in gnomic aphorisms and scientific information alongside the narrative, was the international literature of fables, stories, and maxims that originated in India and became popular in both western Europe and the Arabic-speaking world in the twelfth and thirteenth centuries.

Jewish writers in Spain experimented with various combinations of these thematic and stylistic elements, producing a typically Arabic *maqama* collection in Hebrew (al-Harizi's *Tahkemoni*), a rhymed-prose translation of the Panchatantra (Jacob ben Eleazar's *Kalila wa-dimna*), philosophical allegories (also by Jacob ben Eleazar), a primitive novel (Ibn Zabara's *Sefer Shaashuim*), a series of stories on the wiles of women (especially *Minhat Yehudah* by Ibn Shabbetai, which appears in this anthology under the title "The Misogynist"), and moralistic works (including Ibn Sahula's *Meshal ha-Kadmoni*, a selection of which is found in the present collection, under the title "The Sorcerer").

Other than the language, the Hebrew *maqama* literature has nothing particularly Jewish about it. But to the medieval Jew, the bare fact that this international lore was available in Hebrew was culturally significant, even religiously meaningful. Book after book opens with an author's introduction explaining that his purpose in writing is to demonstrate that the Hebrew language is capable of anything the languages of the nations are capable of. Indeed, in the case of medieval Hebrew, the language does actually tinge the story with religious associations. The Hebrew of the Middle Ages was not a spoken language but a learned language acquired through rote learning of the sources. For reasons that need not concern us, the Bible was considered the linguistic resource for poetry and belles lettres, to the exclusion of the wealth of postbiblical rabbinic literature and poetry. As a result, writers naturally tended to express themselves by citing ready-made phrases from the Bible, and they could rely on the reader to recall effortlessly the biblical context from which the phrase was taken. When rhymed prose became fashionable, writers developed facility at making rhymed clauses by pairing a sentence of their own composition with a snatch of biblical quotation. While the result could be extremely witty, it could also be artificial and, if pursued for too long a stretch, fatiguing for the reader.

Maqamat ordinarily appeared in collections. Each *maqama* in a collection is narrated by someone who tells of a man he met in a certain town (a different town in each *maqama*); at the end of the individual *maqama*, the man is revealed to be the same one who had appeared in all the other *maqamat* of the collection. The individual *maqama* tells of a speech delivered by this character or an escapade in which he is the central figure. The purpose of the speech or the escapade is often to dupe people into giving the protagonist money. That "Asher in the Harem" was originally part of such a collection was proved by the discovery of a tiny fragment of another story beginning "Said Asher ben Yehuda." In keeping with the conventions of the genre, it seems likely that the manipulator, the Adulamite, appeared in the other *maqamat*. In our story Asher is not merely an observer but is himself the dupe; but that is not without parallel in the Arabic *maqama* collections.

What is without parallel in the *maqama* genre (at least as far as can be said on the basis of the evidence currently available) is our story's portrayal of the relationship between character and love. Whereas in the traditional *maqama* the interest lies in the action or the rhetoric or both, our *maqama* employs action and the rhetoric in the service of the idea that love is something that one must deserve. Because this serious principle underlies and motivates the story, Asher is more than a merely comic character; buffoon though he is, we know him as a person far more deeply than we can ordinarily know either the observer or the protagonist of the classic *maqama*. Thus, our story has a Western feel almost completely lacking in the *maqamat* of Harizi, which, though later, are closer to the Arabic roots of the genre. This quality of "Asher in the Harem" might reflect the emergence of the vernacular love story in Romance languages, though nothing definite can be said on this score at the present stage of research.[5]

Introduction and translation by
RAYMOND P. SCHEINDLIN

Prepare to meet your God, O man!
  The pure of heart He will repay.
Good deeds perform while yet you live;
  Tomorrow get twice what you've laid away.
Enjoy this world and the world to come—
  "Both of my girls you will marry this day."[6] 1 Sam 18:21

Said Asher ben Judah: One day I was sitting at the gate with a group
of my brethren and kin, and each person was taking his turn telling
whatever came to his mind. I said, "Today I confess my sins!"[7] When I Genesis 41:9
was a youth I used to prance like a fawn upon the hills, and in the woods
would I dwell. Sabbath and festival I spent apart from men, wearing my
color-striped coat, prey for the sweet gazelles.[8] Seasons came and went,
and years passed. When at last my clothing wore out, I began to long for
home. I arrived in town at night, but my people and the members of my
household were not yet in bed. I came and knocked on the door. They
had long despaired of me, so when I cried, "I'm, home!" they nearly
fainted. Only after they had listened carefully and recognized my voice
did they believe it was really I. Then they opened the door for me and
kissed me on the face and eyes, exclaiming, "We live again, now that you
are back from the dead." They washed my hands and feet, took off my
soiled rags, and clothed me lovingly in rich finery. Three days and three
nights I stayed with them, eating and drinking.

On the fourth day, sodden with drink and without a care in the world,
we went out to stroll along the quiet waters and to sniff some fresh air. By
the canals were lovely gazelles and cooing doves.[9] While I was gazing at
them and listening to their song, a star peered through a lattice, twinkling
from within: an eye winked, a hand beckoned. I kept it to myself while
with my companions and stayed with them until they had traversed the
passage and reached the wilderness.[10] Then, quick as a buck, I slipped אָדוֹן

away and went back to the spot. Just as I passed it, I heard a voice, "Come hither that I may speak with thee and pour my spirit over thee."

I approached. As I stood facing the voice, an apple perfumed with myrrh fell at my feet, and this verse was written on one side:[11]

> O you who run to hunt the fair gazelles
> On fragrant hills or on the forest floor,
> Have done, for they are kept in harem rooms;
> They pass their lives behind the palace door.[12]

And on the other side was written:

> So drunk with wine that you can hardly stand,
> Like willow trees before the storm you shake—
> My heart is drunk like yours, and tottering;
> But love is the drink that causes it to ache.

When I read the lines and grasped their meaning,[13] I was so impressed with myself that I blinked at the radiance of my own sun, and I said, "Dashing Asher, that's my name, for girls think me smashing, and the better class of women love me.[14] Has some girl noticed my fine features and fallen in love? By my life, let me tease her. I will stay away, leave her to love, abandon her to agony, and watch to see what happens." So I turned away and paid her no court.

As I wandered along from that lane into another, I took out the apple that had been thrown to me, to read it again and revel in its beauty. Its verses clung to my heart and crumbled it to bits. I now regretted my haste in going away, and I said, "Why did I refuse to reply? I have done wrong not to answer her song." So I passed that day and night drinking no water and eating no bread. I did not even seek out my bed. As soon as dawn rose, I went straight to the place where I had heard the voice the day before. I now lifted my own voice and cried in the direction of the upper chamber:

> Hail to the lady whose sorrows are great!
> Hail to the girl from the man she adores.
> Hail to the palace's fair gazelle,
> To her who lives by the statutes of love.

Poems of mine is she longing to wear?
    Strings of pearl-verses I'll clasp to her throat.[15]
Is it my friendship she's longing to drink?
    She can have milk of affection from me.
If seeing my beauty would give her heart ease,
    Gladly I'd lie with my head on her knees.

Having made an end to my verses I said no more but stood waiting to learn what would happen. No voice and no word, no answer to be heard! In consternation, frustration, and pain, I rebuked my heart over and over again: "Why do you give the eye to every girl you spy?[16] Why put on a display only to fade away? Why did you not stand your ground when you were spellbound? If you played the king before, how are you now a slave at her door? Act now, and win her somehow. Or go and mope, and give up all hope." Annoyed at my rebuke, my heart replied to this speech:[17]

My soul—your slave—is not herself:
    Into a trap she fell.
What good is it to blame me? I'm
    In love with a gazelle.
My eye it was enslaved my soul—
    How could I rebel?[18]

I spoke to my heart gently and tried to comfort it, but it refused to be comforted in its desolation.

All that day I walked along the rivers and lakes, my eyes pouring streams; and all that night I sang dirges and laments. "I was a brother to the jackal, a friend to the ostrich."[19] When the sun shone and the earth Job 30:29 brightened I returned to the lane where I had stood before. There I pleaded and sighed, and groaned and cried,

Bear greetings to the highborn girl,[20]
    The girl whose face like moonlight shines!
And tell her that the man she summoned
    Yesterday has heard her call.
[The love that plows her heart with pain
    Has now appeared in his heart too.]
He overlooked it yesterday,
    Dazzled by her beauty's ray.

Firm at my post I stood waiting all day, to see whether lightning would flash over me and what it might speak to me. But when I saw the day was closing and no word had come, I lost control and cried, "Why should I hope, when my hope is belied? I look for light, but my darkness deepens. My soul is like a captured buck in the doe's snare. She keeps her bow drawn and releases it only to hasten my death by shooting the arrows of separation into my vitals. [She kindles fire in my innards and flame in my heart. She steals my sleep. She has taken her oath to give no rest to my eyes or cure for my complaint."[21]]

So I passed the night huddled in one of the streets nearby, in anger and despair, in sorrow and in care. Whenever my strength flagged and I felt I could not go on, I would take out the apple, hold it in my hand, bring it to my nose, and sniff its perfume to revive myself by its fragrance. And when the curtains of night were rolled up and the streams of daylight extended earthward, I came by chance to where I had caught her glance, and I stood once more at the place where I had fallen. With tears on my cheeks, I raised my voice in lament:

By love, O lady born for love—
  By your father's noble name—
By the roses blooming on your cheek—
  By the sweet words flowing on your lips—
By an apple grown to torture me—
  By verses engraved in God's own hand[22]— Ex 31:18
Ah! If you will not pity me,
  This love for you will cause my death.
My foes will gnash their teeth with joy,
  And men who hate me will be glad.

When I was done, my mind became confused and I fell senseless on my face. I remained mute, numb, and immobile until I was lifted to my feet by gentle women from the upper chamber, who roused me, saying, "Son of man, stand on your feet so that we may speak with you."[23] Then Ezk 2:1 a spirit came into me and set me on my feet,[24] and I said, "Speak, my Ezk 3:24 ladies, for I am in control of myself again and my strength has returned, thanks to your words." They replied, "We are your servants. We have been sent to you with a message. Hail from the gazelle who dwells in the upper chamber. She has heard your weeping and seen your tears. Her own deep secret will now appear, through the letter we bring you here."

Then I saw that they were bearing a lovely letter, small as a person's palm, dear as diamonds, and perfumed with myrrh. It read:

O you who knock upon the door,
    Never locked to you before—
'Twas you who erred and went away,
    You who caused your own dismay.
Should I open and forgive?
    Or keep it shut and pine away?

When I had read these lines and realized they were meant to rebuke me, my heart burst into flame, my feelings stirred, and my insides simmered with remorse. My hand reached for my cloak, to rend it, but the hem was too tough, for my strength was gone. The maids said to me, "What is all this? Why should you go to such an extreme? Come to yourself! Leave your clothing alone! Be alert, not inert! More bold and more controlled! Follow our footsteps and come along, for we have come to be your guides." I trusted them and followed, not minding the words of Ecclesiastes, "He who goes after her impulsively is like an ox going to slaughter."[5] But the minute I crossed the door I was in fire and water. My hands shook; my steps were unsure. Frantic, I rowed to get back to the shore. I could not.[26] Burning pangs gripped my chest in bands. Then I heard a voice calling, "Strengthen the flagging hands."[27] Hearing this, I took heart. The burning subsided. I answered, "Remember the word to your servant with which you gave me hope. This is my consolation in my misery; your words have revived me."[28]

But those maids were leading me by the ropes of my own folly.[29] They set me on my feet and led me into their courts, then to their chambers, then to the upper room, and finally hurled me into a fowler's trap. Making my way along the gallery to the room where I was to huddle in my lady's shadow, I heard a woman singing clearly, as she strummed on the lute, "Let my love enter his garden and eat his luscious fruits."[30] To this another answered, accompanying herself on the drum, "I have decked my bed with coverings of tapestry, with carved works, with linen of Egypt."[31] When I entered the room and they saw me, they hurried over and threw themselves to the floor at my feet, saying, "Come in, and God's blessing on you!" I sat down on white, blue, and purple spreads of the finest workmanship, while the girls kept on smiling and kissing the ground before me, as each in turn was saying, "Here comes the lady." But then I saw their expressions turn to horror, their faces black as the mouth of a furnace. "What's wrong?" I asked. "Why has your expression changed? Do you know of some disaster?" They replied, "Here comes the master!"

I looked up and saw. Heading toward me was a man dressed in full armor, drunk with rage, not wine. On his head he wore a white turban. He was burning with jealous fury, his face flaming like a Philistine.[32] He wore a veil and brandished a drawn sword. I got up and threw myself on the floor, crying, "I have sinned, I have strayed from the truth path.[33] Peace, Peace!" I greeted him. But he said: "Have done with your 'Peace'! Who brought you here? Is this how privacy is made public and the secrets of harem rooms exposed? Tell me, who ever endowed you with arrogance and blinded you with lust?" I was shocked dumb; I had no strength to put words together, not even to speak. He went on: "Have you betrayed and now are dismayed? Have you lied and now are tongue-tied? Have you transgressed and are now distressed?[34] Speak! Whom did you trust when you flamed with lust? On whom did you rely when you made your bold try? What foolish dare got you into this snare? You have breached the etiquette of nobles and rent the veil of royalty.[35] By my life, you are going to die. Today your time is up, and I am going to watch your fall." He grabbed me and shook me by the gown and said, "Take off your clothes and enjoy the fruits of your labors." My heart melted like wax, my will turned to water; death-terrors engulfed me and I knew the pangs of hell. But when he saw me trembling in dread that I was soon to be dead, tears welled in his eyes, and unveiling, he cried, "Son of man, open your eyes and beyold the visage before thee." I looked up and saw there a shining light and a cheek radiant as the sky in its splendor. My tongue awoke, and I asked, "What is this, my lord?" He replied, "My master! I am but a girl of the chamber, a gazelle of the court. I have never dwelt in the forests, nor have I known the cloven mountains. I am a girl of the palace, in opulence bred."

> A fawn am I, who with her lashes hunts
>   The lusty youths, and traps them in her snare.
> Gracious am I to whom I will; I give
>   To every man who merits it his share.

Seeing that her effulgence overpowered me, she covered it with her hair. I said, "Blessed art thou by God, my child. This second kindness of yours is even greater than the first.[36] It must have been you who hailed me *Ruth 3:10* from the chamber, then assailed me; who seduced me with the apple, then traduced me."[37] She replied, "No, my lord. She is the lady of ladies, *Song of Songs 8:5* who puts the stars to shame. Her lip is lovely, her look is lust. I would compare her (were comparisons not sacrilege) to the light of the sun, but seven times brighter. I am but a slave of her slaves, a mere menial, for your amusement sent, on your pleasure bent. For she said, 'Let me appease him with the gift that goes before me, and afterward I will come into his presence; perhaps he will receive me kindly.'[38] She shall be brought into *Gen 32:21* the king in raiment of needlework; the girls her companions that follow shall be brought to you."[39] Yet hardly had she finished her speech when I *Psalm 45:15* heard the bustling of a throng and the sound of a gong, and I scented frankincense and cinnamon. Looking up, I beheld a parade of lovely, choice maidens, one of whom was taller by head and shoulder than the others and so brilliant she made their shadows flee at her advance. Ornaments of majesty she wore; her robe was hung with bells. The veil of nobility covered her brow; she swayed as she walked, like a myrtle bough. Stately she made her way, towering over her companions, who accompanied her progress with song, to drums and fifes.

Tell us why you seem to sway—
    Does frailty make you walk that way
Or is it drinking old Tokay?[40]

But I could not see her eyes, because of her veil.

Having ensconced her, they left her presence, and I remained alone with the lady at my side. Then I said to myself, Now's the time to butter up your tongue and go to the work you know so well. Turning to face her, I cried, "You have set me on fire, my sister, my bride; you have set me afire with a single one of your eyes, with a single link of your necklace. Reveal your light, my dear; spread over me your hair; remove from your face the veil; let your charms appear."[41] But when I took off the headdress *Song of Songs 4:9* and the veil I beheld a long beard, a face like death and a mouth open wide as a steaming cauldron, and it said: "How dared you look at the *Cross-dressing* cheeks and the crimson lips!" In terror I collapsed full length upon the floor, my face burning and my pleasure gone. But he laughed heartily enough to be heard far and wide as he took hold and comforted me, saying, "Don't take fright! It's all right! I'm your friend, the Adulamite. Have a drink. Taste a bite. Haven't you always known that I'm a trickster?" I opened my eyes and saw it was my friend, dear to me as my own flesh. I said, "It was on account of Rachel that I served you! Why have you deceived me and made a fool out of me?"[42] But he went on consoling me. He plied me with bread and fed me delicious food, and I stayed with him for a few days. Then he gave me his daughter to be my bride, and much of his family riches beside.

[Genesis 29:25]

> Enjoy my charming story, gentle friends,
> But don't be taken in by what you've heard.
> A tale of lover's folly this, no more,
> A pack of lies—I made up every word!

NOTES

1. Translation by A. J. Arberry (London, 1953).

2. Translation by John Jay Parry (New York, 1941).

3. See Raymond P. Scheindlin, *Wine, Women, and Death: Medieval Hebrew Poems on the Good Life* (Philadelphia: Jewish Publication Society, 1986), index, s.v. "gazelle."

4. See Raymond P. Scheindlin, "Fawns of the Palace and Fawns of the Field," *Prooftexts* 8 (1986), 189–203, for a full discussion of the cultural presuppositions of the story.

5. The Hebrew text was published by Hayyim Schirmann in *Yediot ha-Makhon le-Heker ha-Shirah ha-Ivrit* 2(1936), 62–152; 193; 6(1945), 325, with a comprehensive introduction, and again, in *Ha-Shirah ha-Ivrit bi-Sefarad u-ve-Provans* (Jerusalem, 1954), I, 554–65. See also Ezra Fleischer, *Inyene shira ufiyut* in *Mehqere sifrut mugashim leshim'on halkin*, ed. by Ezra Fleischer (Jerusalem, 1975), 202–4. There is a prose translation by David S. Segal in an article entitled, "Mahberet neum 'asher ben yehuda' of Solomon Ibn Saqbel: A study of Scriptural Citation Clusters," *Journal of the American Oriental Society*, 102 (1982), 17–26.

6. A witty application of 1 Samuel 18:21, where similar words are addressed by King Saul to the young David with reference to Saul's own daughters. The frivolous use of the quotation underlines the tongue-in-cheek character of the poem, with its venal message couched in homiletical style.

7. Genesis 41:9.

8. The word translated "festival" means literally "new moon," the first day of the lunar month, which was celebrated as a holy day in biblical times. Joseph's coat of many colors is the customary clothing of the dandy in medieval Hebrew poetry. I use "gazelle" or "fawn" interchangeably to represent all the animals that conventionally stand for the beloved in this poetry.

9. The gazelles and doves here may be stone foundations, and their singing, the plash of the water in a garden pool; or they may represent groups of girls walking along a river or even doing laundry on its banks.

10. Either the passage leads out of a palace complex, like the Alhambra, or out of an enclosed quarter within a city. The "wilderness" would mean the space outside the palace or the city streets outside the quarter. A third possibility is that the passage leads through the city gate or over a bridge to the open country beyond.

11. Apples sent as a gift sometimes figure as "messengers" of love; see Ewald Wagner, *Abu Nuwas: Eine Studie zur arabischen Literatur der frühen Abbasidenzeit* (Wiesbaden: Franz Steiner Verlag, 1965), 326–27. The verses in our narrative were presumably inscribed in the peel. For a similar case, see the love story by Jacob ben Eleazar published by H. Schirmann in *Yediot ha-Makhon le-Heker ha-Shirah ha-Ivrit* 5 (1939): 150.

12. Literally in the "room of rooms," i.e., a room within rooms. The Hebrew reflects the Arabic *mukhdara*, meaning "a woman kept secluded."

13. Almost this very expression occurs in the *1001 Nights*, trans. E. W. Lane (New York: Williams and Norgate, 1927), 4. According to Lane (p. 975 n.15), it is necessary to mention that the reader understood the letter because of the elaborate style of such compositions.

14. A desperate attempt to render the Hebrew pun, borrowed by the author from Genesis 30:13. There Leah names her son Asher, saying that women would declare her blessed (*ishsheruni*).

15. The comparison of verses of poetry to strings of pearls is a commonplace of Arabic and medieval Hebrew rhetoric. The very word used for "verses" in Hebrew means "a string of pearls." The comparison is apt, not simply because of the esteem in which poetry was held, but because of the way in which verses of the *qasida* seem to be strung together with little grammatical relationship between them. See Moses Ibn Ezra, *Kitāb al-muhādara wa'l-mudhākara*, ed. and trans. into Hebrew by A. S. Halkin (Jerusalem: M'kize Nirdamim, 1975), 24–26; Raymond P. Scheindlin, *Form and Structure in the Poetry of al-Mu'tamid Ibn Abbad* (Leiden: E. J. Brill, 1974), 1–16. I have translated the verb *a 'aniqeha* as if it were derived from Hebrew *'anaq* (necklace) or Arabic *'unuq* (neck), rather than as the verb meaning "to give."

16. Asher's rebuke to himself recalls the words of Andreas Capellanus, *The Art of Courtly Love*, trans. John Jay Parry (New York and London: W. W. Norton & Co., 1969), 33.

17. The momentary severance of the speaker from his own heart, with which, thanks to personification, he is able to carry on a dialogue, is sufficiently rare in medieval Hebrew prose to deserve notice.

18. The last verse, literally translated, reads, "What can I do? My eye wronged my soul."

19. Job 30:29. The jackal and the ostrich are proverbial mourners in biblical poetry. This verse and several others referring to the same animals are often cited in poems on the destruction of Jerusalem and other lugubrious liturgical poems for fast days. The quotation is apt here, since the reference to these creatures of the wilderness underscores the speaker's "outsideness" with respect to the woman; and the polarity outside/inside shapes the whole story.

20. Literally "delicate lady." I have allowed myself the liberty for the sake of the meter. I believe it is justified by its usage in Isaiah 47:8 as part of an extended metaphor of Babylon as a princess.

21. The rhyme, which throughout the story is organized in phrases of roughly regular length, becomes rhythmically uneven in this tirade, an effect that is probably intended to suggest breakdown, but which I could not imitate in the translation without rhyming the entire story.

22. This expression, used of Moses' tablets in Exodus 31:18, led the rabbis to speculate on the miraculous character of the engraving on the tablets. See Louis Ginzberg, *Legends of the Jews* (Philadelphia: Jewish Publication Society, 1911), 3:119.

23. Ezekiel 2:1. The language of the harem ladies continues to parody prophetic revelations.

24. Ezekiel 3:24.

25. The quotation is actually from Proverbs 7:22, which describes a foolish youth following a prostitute. My translation "impulsively" is not the usual interpretation, but I think it is borne out by the imagery in the following verse.

26. A parody of Jonah 1:13.

27. Isaiah 35:3, a prophecy of consolation.

28. Psalm 119:49–50. Reciting hopeful verses from the psalms was a traditional way of alleviating anxiety.

29. "Ropes" results from a tiny alteration to the Hebrew text, which, as it stands, reads "vanity."

30. Song of Songs 4:16, the song of the shepherdess to her rustic swain.

31. Proverbs 7:16, the seductive address of the prostitute, mentioned in note 25 above, to the foolish youth.

32. "Philistines" in Andalusian Hebrew literature usually means Berbers, following the general practice of medieval Hebrew writers of designating contemporary nations by biblical names. The Berbers were depicted in both Arabic and Hebrew sources as uncultured and bellicose. It was the custom of Berber men of the period to wear veils.

33. Job 33:27.

34. A parody of the confrontation between Elijah and Ahab, 1 Kings 21:19.

35. The Hebrew word *seter* means "secrecy" or "privacy"; but the Arabic cognate means "veil," and sometimes, as here, it stands for the concept of the harem as a whole.

36. Ruth 3:10.

37. Song of Songs 8:5, with the meaning slightly altered.

38. Genesis 32:21.

39. Psalm 45:15, describing a royal wedding.

40. The lady is singing a poem by the author's more famous contemporary, Judah Halevi, found in Halevi's *Diwan*, ed. Heinrich Brody (Berlin: M'kize Nirdamim, 1909), 2:49. The verse quoted here refers to the gait typically ascribed to the beloved in stylized love poetry. "Tokay" of course is a Hungarian wine, certainly not found in medieval Andalusia. The Hebrew has simply "wine."

41. The first sentence of this speech is a quotation from Song of Songs 4:9.

42. In Genesis 29:25 almost the same words are spoken by Jacob upon discovering that Leah has been substituted for Rachel on his wedding night.

13 •

THE MISOGYNIST
by Judah Ibn Shabbetai

"The Misogynist," by Judah Ibn Shabbetai (1168–ca. 1225), is the main Hebrew contribution to the theme of love's revenge, a theme rooted in Euripides' Hippolytus. It is also an early example, certainly the first extensive one, of Hebrew parody. Its structural highlight is a tour de force in which the author unexpectedly steps into the narrative, ex machina, as it were, to provide the denouement. It is thus a work of exceptional interest on thematic, generic, and structural grounds.

Unfortunately, its narrative does not get quickly off the ground. The heavily rhetorical, dramatically static, and simply overlong opening has been omitted in this translation and is instead summarized at the beginning of the translation.[1]

Following the death of Tahkemoni, narrated in the story's opening, the story of Zerah begins. Like the king of Navarre in Shakespeare's Love's Labors Lost, Zerah forms a fraternity of like-minded young men who devote themselves to culture in a celibate, all-male society. The experiment is of course doomed to failure; for although the author, speaking in his own name, the narrator, and especially the angel have all pronounced themselves the enemies of all women, Zerah is lampooned from the beginning as the dupe of his own fanaticism, and his outlook is simply too extreme to be taken seriously. Furthermore, though his father had specifically warned him against preaching his ideas outside the small circle of

269

Pu N

his followers, Zerah makes a point of preaching celibacy abroad, thus challenging the world at large.

The women, for their part, react to Zerah's challenge in accordance with the stereotype of the wily schemer and punish him by means of the substitution ruse found already in the Bible and familiar enough in Arabic literature.[2] Zerah is made to fall in love with the cultured and beautiful Ayala Sheluha (her name means "doe set free");[3] when he agrees to marry her she is replaced by the repulsive termagant Rizpah bat Aiah (fire pan, daughter of vulture).[4] The description of the wedding includes brilliant parodies of the marriage document *(ketubbah)* and the trousseau list. When the truth about the bride is revealed, distraught Zerah consults his former companions about whether to divorce Rizpah or to resign himself to the marriage. They are joined by a mob of women who threaten to lynch Zerah. Finally, all agree to take the case to Abraham Ibn al-Fakhkhar for decision. This Ibn al-Fakhkhar was a historical person, a Jewish courtier and poet in the service of Alfonso VIII of Castile; it was to him that Ibn Shabbetai dedicated "The Misogynist." The spokesman of the women demands, and the judge pronounces, the death penalty. But when it is Zerah's turn to speak, he reveals himself as none other than the author, Judah Ibn Shabbetai, and explains that the whole story is only a fiction fabricated in order to win Ibn al-Fakhkhar's favor. The courtier is delighted with the story and rewards the poet with a life stipend.

"The Misogynist" belongs to the genre of the *maqama,* which is described in the Introduction to "Asher in the Harem."[5] Like other works of this type, it abounds in quotations from the Bible, their meaning often humorously distorted to build the rhymes. "The Misogynist" is even more heavily laden with biblical quotations than other works of this genre, though the contemporary English reader, lacking the medieval reader's verbatim knowledge of the Bible, will be oblivious to this undercurrent of little jokes that accompanies the story. The device is also used for structural purposes, heralding the narrative twist at the story's end. When Zerah's friend calms the lynch mob by proposing to submit the dispute to Ibn al-Fakhkhar, he ends his rhyming speech with the words "In his days will Judah be saved." This line would at first appear to be a run-of-the-mill quotation used as a rhyming filler;[6] but the Judah of the quotation hints at Judah Ibn Shabbetai, the author. From this point on, biblical references to Judah and Abraham crowd the story, adumbrating the real-life author and patron who will soon replace the protagonist and the judge of the narrative. The high point is reached with the verse "And Judah approached and said, 'Please my lord,' "[7] which in the Bible introduces Judah's plea before Joseph on behalf of Benjamin. Here it introduces Zerah's speech before Abraham Ibn al-Fakhkhar, but at the same time it introduces the author into his own fiction. This effect is achieved only if the reader has a knowledge of the Bible and an easy familiarity with the convention of "mosaic" style. It is the perfect turning of a stylistic convention to narrative effect.

It is hard to view "The Misogynist" as a seriously misogynistic work despite its opening remarks to the effect that women are the cause of folly's victory, and despite its claim to have been composed as a warning to bachelors. Any antifeminist message it contains is disclaimed by the author himself in his final speech before Ibn al-Fakhkhar and is countered by the very narrative line. In the end Zerah is sentenced to death for his attitude toward women. Furthermore, he is portrayed from the beginning as a deluded fanatic whom we would gladly see taught a lesson. At the same time, the women's complaints about the celibacy so unnaturally forced upon them by the success of Zerah's preaching seem perfectly justified. In a truly misogynistic context like the *Tales of Sendebar*,[8] such a lament might be employed to support a portrayal of woman as the embodiment of lust, while the substitution trick they play on Zerah could have been used to argue the view of woman as wily deceiver. But not so in a story of a man whose every speech and deed proclaim him a fool. Zerah is outdone not only by the women's cunning, but by Ayala's preeminence in his own field, poetry. And as for lust, it is no one's but his own that brings him down in the end. It is true that the women deceive Zerah with Rizpah; but they do not do so in order to get rid of an unmarriageable hag or to swindle Zerah for gain. Their only purpose is to avenge the genuine wrong he has done them. Thus the author knows and enjoys the conventions and stereotypes of misogynistic literature, but at the same time he shows them to be activated by his hero's extremism. As in so much of medieval literature, moderation, even in good things, is presumed to be the best course. That this is the story's moral is hinted in the opening poem:

I assemble men of sense, men of culture
   I raise my voice in the midst of the congregation:
O Men! Follow the straight path,
   For every rise must end in a fall.[9]

By way of introduction to the translation, some remarks about the piece's distinctive style are in order. The narrative contains parodies of several types of literature: of the *ketubbah* and the trousseau list, as already mentioned; of the ethical will, in Tahkemoni's speech to Zerah, here omitted; of prayer, in Kozbi's appeal to God before she sets in motion the plot against Zerah; and, above all, of the Bible's narrative, poetic, and prophetic styles. The biblical style is alluded to through the use of distinctive biblical vocabulary, syntax, and turns of phrase, and above all by quotations from the Bible itself. Such quotations abound in all medieval Hebrew literature, and especially, as mentioned earlier, in rhymed prose, where they often supply the rhyme, but they are especially abundant here. I have made no attempt to set them all off by quotation marks or to footnote all of them, fearing to impede the narrative flow and to irritate the reader. Quotations have been footnoted mainly where in my judgment it would be worth the reader's while to look up the source and see how the original context reflects on the story. They have been put in quotation marks mostly where they are used not simply as part of the rhyming style but as prooftexts for an argument or capstones of a rhetorical sally.

    Although I have not called attention to the majority of quotations, I have attempted to convey the distinctively parodic flavor that they impart to the original by affecting a slightly archaic diction and syntax. It is hopeless to try to imitate closely the continual rhyme and the elaborate rhetoric of the original. I have tried, however, to suggest the flavor of these features of medieval Hebrew prose through the use of occasional rhyme and alliteration. I have left the proper names in Hebrew, though they are mostly meaningful words that suggest the character of their bearer. Those that have not already been explained in this introduction are explained in the notes. The poems embedded in the narrative, as mentioned earlier, were not intended to be high literature. In a genre that puts the emphasis on the most elaborate possible rhetorical style, the poems are usually a kind of doggerel, intended to contrast in tone with their environment. I have not been ashamed to let this feature appear in the translation.[10]

Introduction and translation by
RAYMOND P. SCHEINDLIN

[Speaking in his own name, the author relates that he composed the story to gratify some friends who had asked him to recount in poetic style how he came to be a married man. The spirit of prophecy thereupon enters him, promising to be his inspiration and urging him to undertake the task so that others might be spared his fate.

The story proper now begins with a lengthy account of how the troops of wisdom were forced into hiding, routed by the troops of folly. One elder alone escaped, Tahkemoni (the name is derived from the Hebrew word for wisdom), together with his son Zerah (the name means radiance). It was Tahkemoni who would begin the war against women. Yet his fulminations and those of the narrator on the folly of the age cite only its lack of respect for wisdom and the wise, and its undue respect for wealth. Tahkemoni does not seem to be aware of the role of women and marriage in the collapse of the rule of wisdom until an angel vouchsafes him the revelation that it is women who have turned men's hearts to folly. Immediately upon the angel's departure, Tahkemoni delivers a lengthy testament charging his son Zerah to devote his life to celibacy and to war against women.]

N ow when Tahkemoni had finished declaring his testament to his son and all his associates, he died and was gathered unto his people. And all who had known him mourned him with lamentation and wailing; great was the grieving, and widespread the cry. And his son Zerah buried him on his property at Timnat-Serah north of Mount Gaash, two years before the great quake. A hundred years old was Tahkemoni when his soul was taken—his eye had not dimmed, neither was his vigor fled— besides the twenty years in his youth when he was married and that therefore are not counted in the number of his days.[11] For when he took a wife he was young—too young even to find his way to town.[12] But when he grew up and beheld her shame he turned everything he owned over to her and divorced her. She never came back to him, and he had nothing more to do with procreation.[13]

And Zerah wrote down all the words his father had spoken and put them away for safekeeping. From that day on, when anyone spoke to him of a woman, he would scoff, mock, and rebuke that man till he fled. If a youth and a maiden married he was seized by convulsions.

Zerah selected three companions, noble gentlemen, who had pursued wisdom since their youth, "receiving instruction in wise dealing, righteousness, justice, and equity."[14] These are their names, by family and clan: Netanel ben Mahalalel, Avinoam ben Aminadav, and Ahituv ben Avishua. He joined their circle and befriended them. They said to him, "Lo, this place is too small for us, and there are women dwelling in our midst. We live here in fear of their wiles, for we may fall into their snares. Let us choose us a place, so as not to lapse into sin, a land no man has yet traversed nor anyone inhabited.[15] He said to them, "Your wish is my wish, my desire is yours. Turn and go thither."

So they journeyed forth to find a place where they might be at rest. They crossed rivers and waded fords, they trod the highways and twisty paths, until they reached the river Besor, a place that lacked for nought. On its banks grew henna and nard and every dainty. To the right and to the left were planted every kind of fruit tree, the very trees of Eden, and oaks shooting forth twigs and thick boughs in all directions. Every kind of fawn and deer took shelter there under every verdant tree; and in their branches nested birds of every wing, spreading their pinions among the leaves, cooing and piping, chirping and twittering. Seeing that this place was a goodly one with every delight, and that it pleased them better than any other, they took up their rhyme and said:[16]

> How lovely are the birds among the buds.
>> They chirp and spread their wings against the sky;
> The water bubbles up among the stones
>> And breezes flutter through the flow'ring boughs.
> A man reposes under every tree
>> And every bough is hung with heavy fruit.

They said: "To this point does our foot tread; now we have come into our inheritance. Here will we pitch our camp, for this is our resting place." So they dwelt among the myrtles, rejoicing in sweet companion-ship. Sometimes they discoursed on laws and statutes, sometimes they turned to food and drink; yet other times they would laugh and play, for thus are days of pleasure passed. One month each year Zerah made a tour of the neighboring districts to preach to his followers. Wherever he went he proclaimed, "Shun Woman as you beware the glittering sword! Seek ease! Find peace! Rid yourselves of jewelry-wearers that your days may be long. To put women to shame is the glory of youth, but shame and scorn will never befall a young man so long as he keeps away from women. The harm of marriage never fades; it destroys the spirit and the flesh alike. When a man marries, his name is covered in darkness. His pain will wax and his glory wane; let him who will, listen, and him who refuses, refrain. Let every husband put away his wife lest he be ruined. Let the wise man listen and pay me heed; to make my speech longer there is no need."

Thus did Zerah act, and thus did he endow the simple folk with the wisdom of his thoughts. This was ever his way. The wise observed his rule faithfully and never left it as long as they lived, and many of the people of the land were won over by the fear of Zerah.[17]

But in every town where Zerah's words and doctrine came the women were filled with gall and venom. Hopping with rage they gathered, young and old, widows and girls, to take counsel and to plan action. Pain and shock had seized them; their spirits were shaken. They tore at their skin in their fashion, and their faces were fallen. Their cry and their wail waxed; great was their groaning, terrible their turmoil, and loud their lament: "How shall we requite the man who has brought destruction on our heads, who has ruined and undone us? Our shame and our disgrace are known to all, and not a man in the land will lie with us. Who indeed has a heart that would embolden him to touch us after this man has put us to scorn? The lasses languish, their wombs are waste, their fruit fails, all are virgins not known by man! Zerah has turned us into objects of fear, and now one man has to be shared by seven women! See how great is our trouble! Every virgin is shut up and sealed off: no one enters, and none departs.[18] Why should we lie here in our shame, covered by disgrace? Rouse yourselves, think what to do that the ladies may find lovers! Take charge of this disaster, that the women will court the men.[19] Do not think this matter frivolous or trivial. This man is guilty of a capital crime! By stoning shall he die, and no ransom will get him reprieve, for he has slandered the virgins of Israel. Where are the masters of deceit, experts in intrigue? Where are female treachery and tricks? Their counsels and cunning? Their wiles and wisdom? Their plans and their plots? Why is our cunning gone and our skill banished? Should one man cause our lamp to go dark? Should one sinner make so much good go to ruin? Let us find a stratagem to wipe him out of the nation and get our revenge. Let us demolish his devices so that men may go with their sons to visit the girls again."20]

Then a shrewd woman arose from their midst, a <u>woman</u> expert in <u>sorcery</u> and <u>deceit,</u> who flamed with <u>magic</u> and <u>fornication</u> that the very rivers could not quench. Kozbi bat Yeresha21 she was called, for she had taken treachery as her specialty. She had an old husband named Sheker ben Hefer,22 and there was more wickedness in him than any book could contain. Kozbi said: "Hearken, turbulent women.23 Do not raise your voices so. The rash of disaster is not cured with a date plaster! We must resort to exotic counsels, to rare devices. The mighty have fallen, the mountains have melted; but with my two horns I will cut down his wit and kill his counsel. His eyes will no longer serve him for seeing, nor his ears for hearing. Go! Search everywhere for a girl of perfect, unblemished beauty, lovely to look at, charming to behold, bright as the sun, with beauty like Tirza's,24 with a beaming glance. Molded of myrrh and cassia she, inlaid with beauty and splendor, with a gracious greeting to all who gaze; a girl of culture and counsel, knowing poetry and rhetoric, speaking fluently and composing verse, her speech sweet as honey and firm as a cast-metal mirror;25 a girl who can call on wisdom both esoteric and exotic, assay it in the furnace of the mind and make it strike sparks; who can play the harp and lyre so as to provoke the listener to laughter or lament. By such a girl his inhibitions may be melted, for men incline to evil from their youth.26 And if even then he does not change and do as he ought, 'there are many ways to death':27 gold will beguile and lay him low, break his bonds, and thwart his plans. Gold deposes kings from their thrones and expels them from their palaces and courts; it lends fools the luster of wisdom and covers the faults of the knave; it topples giants and gives the righteous the lie. It makes crooked straight and supports the fallen; it is eyes to the blind and ears to the deaf; it is a joy to both God and man. It is its employer's trusty ambassador."

And Kozbi took up her rhyme and said:

What man has honor and respect? I asked.
　　The answer came back clear: The man with gold.
By it a man can have whate'er he likes.
　　It makes the fool seem wise, the coward bold.

"And now, sisters and companions, this is my counsel and here is my scheme: Put before him both girl and gold; perhaps he will be beguiled and we shall prevail." And they replied, "We agree to all you ask. Perhaps you will win, perhaps you will come to be feared."

All this time Zerah was keeping himself pure in faithfulness to his father's will, when disaster crashed upon him and the horn of his glory was cut down. Suddenly terror sounded in his ears and a spirit passed before him; in the gloom of darkness, in a vision of the night, Zerah dreamed a dream, which said:

Trust not in Time: it puts forth buds
　　That promise fruit that never will mature.
You sleep untroubled; yet you cannot know
　　That yesterday's good fortune will endure.

He awoke fearful and trembling and anxious. A black terror descended upon him, and he heard a voice addressing him:

O you who sleep in youth's delightful bed
　　While over you the gentle breezes blow—
O say: Is there a man who fears not grief?
　　Does time spare any prince his fearful blow?

While this voice was still speaking, there came another, roaring and cleaving the crags:

Awake, O man, and see how Time
　　Your wealth and fortune will undo.
Beware the day when you will say
　　To life: I do not care for you.

When morning came Zerah called his companions and supporters, his friends and advisers. Despondent, he told them all the troubles he had endured and the visions he had seen. They said, "Pay no heed to fantasies that originate deep within the body, for they are false prophecies and babble broken bodings." So Zerah returned to his place as before to cheer himself with elevated talk; but Time pursued him like a foe; he could not stand, for the Lord brought him low.

Now it came to pass in the middle of the night, at the time when people are overtaken by sleep, when their souls wander to gaze upon the splendor of the Lord, there came a wind that carried Zerah off to a valley and cast him down amid lions and wild beasts. One of them seized him, pulled out his root, and took hold of his privates; then it opened its mouth and made to swallow him, as it is written, "A wild beast has eaten him."[28] He awoke, more dead than alive; then he slept and dreamt again. This time he was somewhere far away by the edge of a deep pit, almost deeper than the earth itself, and he fell into it!

When morning came his spirit was troubled. He felt weak and listless; his heart was dead and his spirit gone. His comrades said to him, "Why do you sit there depressed, your face so black?" He told them, " 'A plague has been shown to me.'[29] I have had a vision of evil portent." " 'May God give you an answer of peace,' " they said.[30] "Tell us your dream." He told them the vision he had seen and all that had befallen him. They said, "God has not concealed anything that he is about to do. The pit and the beast are one dream:

To fall in the marriage pit is your fate;
  That is God's way with the men he doth hate.

For yet a little while and thou shalt die, though still young. You will become attached to a woman and an ass's burial will be yours. This is the beast in whose belly you entered, the pit into which you fell. To be angry or upset will not help you at all, for this is the meaning of your dream and your vision."

When Zerah heard their words, he rebuked them angrily. With harsh words he addressed them: "May the events of this dream and your interpretation befall yourselves. May you become a tale and a mockery!

You have not spoken about me truly. May God bestow the woman upon you, on account of your speaking falsehood and wickedness about me. Do not young and old alike know the proverb 'Never open your mouth for the devil'?"[31]

Thus the love between Zerah and his companions turned to hate and the friendship into rage. They so feared him that they all abandoned him, and he was left alone.

Kozbi had taken her amulets, readied her spells, and provided herself with six wagonloads of fine raiment, silver, and gold. Then she summoned a girl who was the crowning beauty of the maidens, the life of the soul, the very fawn taken from Eden, God's garden.[32] Her name was Ayala Sheluha.

Kozbi asked her husband, "How do you advise us to approach the man we are challenging? Will we succeed in diverting him from his path and his schemes?" He replied, "Go first and make a lengthy complaint. I will follow you and support your words." The old man hurried; no delaying desire for him. "And he took in his hand the fire and the knife, and the three of them went"[33]—the old man, the girl, and Kozbi—to the youth's place.

Kozbi prayed: " 'I longed for peace, but bitterness, ah, bitterness have I!'[34] O thou who built the upper chambers within the waters;[35] who gave us pools above and pools beneath;[36] who chose man and rejected woman; who made flourish in man the beard and member for his fame and glory, and who gave the daughters of Eve the burning womb of desire[37]—O fatten this man's heart and cover his eyes, that his error may be compounded with guilt."

Having ended her prayer she made her way to Zerah's tent. Zerah was living in contented ease, unaware that the Lord had abandoned him. Like a leprous sore, wicked Kozbi stood before him, and she took up her rhyme and said:

> May God, O Zerah, grant you grace,
>> And may he cause your sun to glow;
> Be blessed with fruit and multiply,
>> And may your staff in splendor grow. . . .[38]

Ayala Sheluha came and stood like the dawn rising, like the sun shining forth. Then she advanced. Accompanied by her maidens, she caused youths' hearts to pound and saints to sin, though herself remaining pure. Her tranquil eyes stirred strife as she approached with mien remote. She took up her lute, tightened its strings, and intoned clear verses. In a beseeching voice, she stood before Zerah as she took up her rhyme:

> My lover's face is like the sun
>> All covered by a cloud of hair
> Beauty belongs to him alone
>> And he is now my lot and share.

"May he who grants the bachelor a home set your heart to putting forth branches and to bearing fruit while your season is spring. How wonderful is love! How dear, to be near! Love has aroused me to stand before you and seek you out this day. Come, my love, feed on faithfulness; let us go down to the gardens and pluck roses and anemones. For the buds have now appeared, the vine blossoms have opened, the pomegranates are in bloom—two breasts, not yet caressed by any hand, and blooming cheeks, lovely to look at, a delight to the eyes. Come and pluck your luscious fruit. 'Take of this, yea, also from that withdraw not thy hand.' "[39]

When Zerah saw Ayala's radiant face and heard her songs and conceits, he found her attractive and she found his favor. Zerah replied, "A girl's heart is bound to folly, but a clever woman is a gift froom God. Wisdom and beauty are your lot—'this is truly called a woman.' "[40] He forgot the words of his father's charge and entered upon twisting paths, for God's rage had gone forth, and Zerah's downfall had begun.

Now Zerah was more skilled at poetry and its conceits than any man before him. So he answered her with a speech commensurate with his skill, and took up his rhyme:

> Your hair is like the dark of night,
>> Your face as morning fair;
> Let not your brilliance startle you
>> Or your raven-colored hair.

When the girl saw how she had pleased him and that she could win him with fine verses, she took up her rhyme:

Fear no fawn's eyes although they threaten
    Death to every man alive;
Their eyes may sting, but when the victims
    See them they at once revive.[41]

Zerah remarked, "This poem makes me marvel, for it reveals the secrets of love; let me too speak my mind. . . ."[42]

He said: " 'You ravish my heart, my sister, my bride,'[43] and with this poem you have brought me to my knees. My thoughts are now in total disarray, and I find no inspiration from God." So, in his longing to see her face, Zerah stopped replying to her conceits. Desperate to embrace and kiss her, in the manner of all lovers, he took up his rhyme and said:

O awesome, lovely, perfect fawn,
    Whose brilliance dazzles every eye,
O come to bed and there bestow
    Your offering of breast and thigh.[44]

With love's flame raging within, with the fire of passion burning inside, Zerah summoned Sheker and wicked Kozbi—so far gone were his senses— and said, "Demand any bride price, and I will do whatever you say! Proclaim it to the world![45] Just give me the girl as a wife." When Sheker heard this speech his ears tingled and his face beamed, his eyes shone and his cares fled, and he bowed low to the ground.

Kozbi hastened to tell the girls on Prepuce Precipice:[46] "Have you heard? God has taken this preacher Zerah, whose heart is so hard against us, and delivered him into the hands of a woman, making him a laughingstock. God has given Zerah our enemy into our hands! I spread my net over him and caught him in my trap. His heart was beguiled by Ayala Sheluha; today he falls like a sheep to slaughter. But when evening comes I shall exchange her with another—a sore in her place!"[47]

All the girls, slaves and ladies alike, were overjoyed with this news. Some shouted and laughed; others hopped about. Some hugged Kozbi; others kissed her hands. Some knelt at her knees; others danced for delight. And yet others began decking their beds. They gave her ten gold pieces and a fine girdle, a gift from young and old. Therefore was that place called the Vale of Tidings, on account of the tidings that were proclaimed in that plain.

The old man [Sheker] assembled all the people of that place by their thousands and myriads, and behind closed doors the men and the women came together. Zerah made a great feast for people from near and far; he slaughtered many sheep, cattle, and fatlings and made a great celebration, seven days of eating and drinking to tambourines, harps, castanets, and cymbals. After that the old man arose in their midst, took the book of the covenant, and read it for them all to hear:[48]

THE MARRIAGE DOCUMENT

א א א א

On the fourth day of the week this man had an unlucky streak, and his joy turned bleak; his shame was uncovered and his humiliation discovered. *In the year forty-nine seventy-seven* he found trouble from heaven; his joy ceased, his shame was discovered, and his privates uncovered. *In the seventh month, on the thirteenth day*—a date unlucky in every way—*Zerah the groom,* who has thrown his fortune away, *said to Madame Rizpah bat Aiah* of the house of Putiel, one of the whores of Israel: "For long years *I shall serve as the Israelites do:* All your needs will be mine to bear, bread to eat and clothing to wear; to provide them quickly will be my care. *I shall support you* as a man must do, and I shall take care of your body's needs too. *And I give you as your bride price* a thousand foreskins, as is due to all virgins." *And the whore was satisfied with this and became his wife.* And of his own free will he added: teeth picked bare, and knees that totter and hips that shake. *He was further pleased to give her as gifts* these four: instead of ermine—vermin; instead of baubles—troubles; instead of sashes—sackcloth and ashes; instead of balsam—rot. *And this is the dowry that the bride brought with her:* waste, shame, horror, and blame. *Thus the sum of the ketubbah, the gift, the dowry, and addition* is a burn, a wound, a sore, and a lesion. Thus Zerah (God leave him) agreed that in less than a year he would become an object for men to jeer. *And they performed the validating rite* to confirm that he would be aware of no slight. *Then they brought faithful witnesses to sign the paper:* Ben Toval, Epha, and Efer; Gaal ben Eved and Avdon; Bilhan, Zaavan, and Essarhadon.

On the fourth day they all assembled in the Valley of the Blessing (so named because there they blessed Zerah). And all the people said: "Alas for the lord! Alas for his glory! Now will his splendor wane, his end come and his plans be undone. Where now are his wonders and his preaching? Where his counsels and plots? Is this the man who made men tremble and women quail? This day his plans have run out and he is cut off from his people!"

[Kozbi took the girl and exchanged her with a quarrelsome hag,] black as a crow, with lips like two inflated bladders—anyone who saw would gasp. The hair on her skin was like stubby brambles, and her face was covered with nettles—something to make infants and babes recoil. She was repellent to all. Rizpah bat Aiah was her name. Kozbi took this Negress[49] and brought her into Zerah's room. Then Sheker and Kozbi went on their way in glee, for they had dug a pit for Zerah. They also made off with the money that they had collected, and went and hid it.

Zerah was left naked and bare with Rizpah bat Aiah. At length the sun rose and found him limping on his thigh[50] with Rizpah instead of Ayala Sheluha: "Instead of coiled hair a bald head."[51] He tore his clothes, strewed ashes on his head, and cried, "A plot! Deceit! A pack of lies! For this I mourn and wail and raise bitter lament. The money is gone, the shame remains! No gold and no beauty![52] The plot was thick, it took me in—a fool who believes whatever he is told. . . ."[53]

Then his wife said to him, "Get along with you, for you've no time to sleep; and don't talk back to me! Go and fetch me[54] vessels of silver and vessels of gold, dresses and chains, bracelets and mufflers; a house and a flat, a chair and a lamp, a table and spoons, a pestle and groats, a blanket and spindle-weight, a mat and a tub, a basket and spindle, a cauldron and bottle, a basin and clothespress, a broom and a kerchief; a pan, furnace, barrel, and shovel; a pot, vessels, goblets, and charms; gowns, veils, turbans, and robes; linen, nose rings, purses, and lace; crescents, amulets, sashes, embroidery, headdresses, rings, checkered cloth, armlets, and anklets; and besides these, special clothes to wear on Sabbaths and festivals. This is by no means all you shall have to provide. But if this is beyond your means, what you will see befall you will drive you mad.[55]

"And this is your forecast: Your first year will be sorrow and the second, misery. Though you once were a prince, you will now be a slave. Your head will ever be oiled with dung,[56] for you do not even deserve to be one of the slaves who pour water over my hands."

When Zerah heard her curse, he cried aloud, "Is Israel a slave? Has he no redeemer? Do the slave women now lord it over satraps? Do pierced ears rule over turbans?[57] He took up his rhyme and said:

Heavens and earth and vales and hills,
  Lament for this and pour your tears.

Should a free man, a favored son,
  Be slave to one with pierced ears?

And again he took up his rhyme and said:

Two things there are that put me in a rage.
  I teach them to my children, age to age:
A wise man's son become a woman's tool,
  A scholar seeking handouts from a fool.

His wife replied, "Stop taking up your rhyme! Do not even raise your voice. I have no interest in wisdom or culture, only in bread and meat. Your poems and your lyrics mean nothing to me—'A poem does not buy a glass of wine.'[58] Do you think that a lot of talk will win a woman's womb? Get up, take your plow and your plowshare, your quiver and bow, and go about the town from dusk to dawn, stealing, murdering, and swearing falsely. As your household grows, you will have to provide their daily bread. 'And you shall not appear empty-handed before me.'[59] If you fail to bring me every single thing I desire, 'in the street will you stand!'[60] But all this is nothing compared with the day I give birth. Then you will really work! My brothers and relations will be in your presence around your table, and you will provide a whole sheep for their daily delicacies. Nor will the midwife do without wine, bread, or meat. You will have to call a wet nurse for the children—'They pass them to her and she can pour'[61]—and buy slave women and maids to tend them, 'to eat their dung and drink their urine,'[62] for I will not touch them!"

Zerah now collapsed full length upon the ground and rued his life. He wept for the days of his youth, now in decline, and for his hair, gone white with him in his prime. He took up his rhyme and said:

A shocking sight! My hair is white;
  My sorrow is profound.
Like that man—alack—
  Who counted on black.
But white was all he found . . .[63]

In the morning Zerah's comrades said to him, "Here is the only advice for you: Flee now and forever to Shinar and Elam. This is the only thing to do if you have married badly."[64] They took up their rhyme and said:

A woman who will not obey
   Should surely be divorced from you;
No matter if you married her
   And promised always to be true.
Go farther than an arrow's flight—
   Escape across the ocean blue.

Zerah said, "Your advice wearies me. 'How long will you go on saddening me with your everlasting waywardness?'[65] Who will lift me out of the pit? For not like Egyptian women are the women of Israel;[66] if a man runs away from them they bring him back with craft. Their husbands are like prisoners in irons; they can be redeemed only with silver." Zerah's friends replied, "If you place your hope in money, the money is yours; it will fight your battle and save you, and mighty is your redeemer." Every friend gave Zerah a gold ring and a garment, as his means allowed; and Zerah rose and bowed seven times to the ground.

Then he assembled all the people of that place, from boys to graybeards, in the town square, and said: "This day I reveal my disgrace and my shame. My wife cannot stand me, and I want nothing to do with her as to belly, bearing, or birth.[67] Here is the money, cash in hand. Do not be afraid to do the right thing, for judgment belongs to the Lord."

Then the people by their thousands and hundreds were divided, each in his own camp under his own banner. One party said: "Divorce her, and get your feet away from trouble. 'Let the dam go and take the young with thee.'[68] Give her the amount written in the marriage contract, and curse Kozbi and Sheker ben Hefer. Do not be beguiled by men in error, and be not misled by elders, but go, for God has sent you forth."[69]

Another party said: "Do not abandon her. Love her with all your heart and soul. She will give you respect once you embrace her."

The majority said: "Let him not be redeemed or buy his freedom. Make his yoke heavy; do not sunder his bonds. 'It is well for a man to bear the yoke when he is young.' "[70]

As Zerah stood before the men, he looked up and saw the women flocking from every side like pigeons. When they arrived, they said, "Uphold justice and do what is right. Let this not cause you to stumble, and let Zerah not become a precedent; 'for he shall not be able to send her away as long as he may live.' "[71]

The crowd's quarreling and commotion increased, and their cry ascended to heaven. Then Ahituv silenced the people, saying: "Why do you quarrel and speak so harshly? Here is the thing to do: Choose a spokesman to pursue Zerah with words before the prince, the staff of splendor, who dwells in Shushan the capital. It is he who saves the innocent from the oppressor, he who supports men about to totter. Him has the Lord established to do justice among his people, and upon his shoulders rests the right of rule. Who is there to compare to his greatness? All the tongues of the nations are not equal to his praise. Because of him are the skies lifted above the earth.[72] Of him the prophets spoke. For his sake was the universe created. The kings of Arabia cleanse themselves in the waters of his wisdom, and the chieftains of Edom troop to his command: 'They march at his bidding, and at his word they return.'[73] In his presence they are awed into silence, for there they see things never heard before. He is the father of many nations, the master of the Torah. 'In his days will Judah find salvation.' "[74]

The throng cried out, "The decision must be as you have declared; what you have said is right." Then they said to Zerah, "Come down with us to the house of the potter,[75] the man whom nothing thwarts. And here is the women's spokesman with his tongue for a sword—go and do battle with him."

The spokesman came forth from the crowd to Zerah, and the two of them went with the throng at their backs, citizens and strangers, rich and poor, to behold the prince's judgment. They came to the city of refuge, the fount of decision, and all assembled at the place of justice, "the field which Abraham had bought."[76] There sat the prince on his royal throne, the chieftains of the troops before him, together with the sages of the age seeking his instruction. "He is indeed the angel of the Lord of Hosts,"[77] who declares the innocent to be innocent and the guilty guilty, and who rescues the poor.

Zerah and the spokesman approached. They bowed deeply to the prince, while behind them stood the throng of small and great, thousands and myriads. The spokesman opened: "O my lord King, O fortress for poor man and pauper! Open your eyes and see our desolation! Pity our infants and our babes! The flame of Zerah burns among us with none to extinguish it; and we are now few, who once were so many. Tahkemoni,

Zerah's father, bequeathed us sorrow; Zerah, his son, utterly destroys us; a Levite has left us in fear. 'God has a quarrel with Judah.'[78] Because of their example every man will now divorce his wife, and the earth will be abandoned. Everyone equipped with a foreskin will go back to his smugness as before. O my lord King, let my cry now come before you. Act today, that a mighty nation may be spared alive."

The king stood dumb with rage, for the matter was displeasing to Abraham.[79] He ordered his men, "Seize Zerah! He deserves to die for scorning the beauty of women and for destroying the mighty, the holy nation."

Then Judah approached[80] and said: "Please, my lord, hear me. Judge me by your righteousness. Declare me guilty or innocent after I speak, and if there is sin in me, then slay me."

The king replied: "If your words are good and sensible, I will declare you innocent. Speak, for I would like to clear you."

Judah said: "What can I say, my lord? How can I justify myself? My own mouth will declare me guilty, guiltless though I may be. By the Lord, who has exalted your throne and raised your status up to heaven! This Tahkemoni never lived and never was. Zerah never married Rizpah bat Aiah, and not one of these characters ever existed. I made them up out of my own inspiration; on a foundation of falsehood is their existence built. More than anyone who has ever lived, I love my wife and children. The whole story was composed only in order to bring it to pass that I might stand before you,[81] in order to find your favor. For a man's wit gives him relief from his labors and leads him into the presence of the great."

The king and his troops were all delighted, and so were the satraps and courtiers. They laughed so heartily they could be heard far off, and even Abraham fell on his face and laughed.[82] Then the king said, "You have done well. You have answered with good and sensible words, and concocted a fine plot. Go now and enjoy your life with the wife you love; I undertake to grant you what you ask and to do what you request. I shall look after you, and you will eat at my table. And for your fine words here now are three hundred silver coins and five suits of new clothing."

And from that day forward Judah's name was inscribed in the chronicle book and his sustenance was provided him daily from the king, each day according to its need.[83]

NOTES

1. The epilogue and a few passages that do not advance the narrative have also been omitted from the translation, as indicated by ellipsis marks.

2. See my article, "Fawns of the Palace and Fawns of the Field," *Prooftexts* 6(1986): 189–203.

3. The phrase comes from Genesis 49:21, where it probably is meant to connote swiftness. But in medieval Hebrew poetry the doe, fawn, or gazelle conventionally denotes the beloved. See my *Wine, Women, and Death: Medieval Hebrew Poems on the Good Life* (Philadelphia: Jewish Publication Society, 1986), index, s.v. "fawn." The expression "set free" may be intended to connote also "set upon," in view of the use of the root *sh-l-h* in the stories of the ten plagues in Exodus.

4. The name originally belonged to a concubine of Saul mentioned in 2 Samuel 3:7 and in 2 Samuel 21. It is hard to see any connection between the Rizpah of the Bible and our Rizpah.

5. In one manuscript the story is called *maqamat al-ziwaj* (the *maqama* of marriage).

6. It is from Jeremiah 23:6, in a passage describing the just king who will reign in the messianic era.

7. Genesis 44:18.

8. *Tales of Sendebar*, ed. and trans. Morris Epstein (Philadelphia: Jewish Publication Society, 1967).

9. I have done my best to present the argument of "The Misogynist" as a coherent whole. But the critically-minded reader deserves to be warned that there is an inconsistency between the beginning of the book, up to the death of Tahkemoni, and the rest of the story of Zerah. In the first part (except for the opening poem) the book does seem to be straightforwardly antiwoman, whereas in the second it is not the women but Zerah who is the butt, and misogynistic literature itself seems to be parodied. Perhaps the opening is intended to fool the reader into reading the book from the perspective of a misogynist so that he may be delightfully bewildered by the reversal at the story's close. Such manipulation is within the realm of possibility for a medieval Hebrew writer (cf. "Asher in the Harem" and "The Sorcerer" in this anthology for analogous manipulations). But the resolution may come from another direction, namely, the editorial history of the book. The epilogue as much as says that the author rewrote the book. The data available do not yield clear evidence as to the dates or the nature of the revision. For a full discussion, see Israel Davidson, *Parody in Jewish Literature* (New York: 1906), 8 n.33. In any case, it is possible that the author simply appended the misogynistic opening as part of the revisions.

10. "The Misogynist," under the title *Minhat Yehudah Sone ha-Nashim*, was published in Constantinople in 1543, and in the collection *Taam Zekenim* by Eliezer Ashkenazi (Frankfurt am Main: 1854). The Ashkenazi edition was photographically reproduced by A. M. Haberman in his collection *Shalosh Makamot al ha-Nashim* (Jerusalem: 1971). Selections from the story were published by Hayyim

Schirmann in *Ha-Shirah ha-Ivrit bi-Sefarad u-ve-Provans* (Jerusalem and Tel Aviv: 1957), 2:67–86.

11. The age and enduring vigor are taken from the account of the death of Moses, Deuteronomy 34:7.

12. The image comes from the description of the fool in Ecclesiastes 10:15. The Hebrew words for town (*'ir*) may suggest a similar-sounding word for pudendum (*'erva*), hinting that Tahkemoni was ignorant of sex at the time of his marriage.

13. Job 35:15; the meaning of the last phrase is as obscure in our story as it is in the Bible.

14. Proverbs 1:3.

15. Jeremiah 2:6.

16. The sentence "they took up their rhyme and said," which introduces nearly every poem in this story, is borrowed from the Book of Numbers, where it occurs mostly in the narrative of Balaam (e.g., Numbers 23:7). The word means "proverb," "parable," and any elevated gnomic speech. It is frequently used in connection with prophecy.

17. The last part of this sentence and the beginning of the next are modeled on Esther 8:17.

18. A witty application of the description of Jericho before the Israelites destroyed it (Joshua 6:1).

19. I have translated this obscure clause from Jeremiah 31:21 in accordance with the commentary of David Kimhi, a contemporary of Ibn Shabbetai's.

20. In Amos 2:7 the image of fathers and sons visiting harlots together is used to depict Israel's utter depravity.

21. Her name means approximately "liar, daughter of waste."

22. His name means "falsehood, son of shame."

23. Despite the similarity of the wording to three verses in Isaiah 32 in which *shaanan* has its usual meaning of "tranquil," I believe the author is thinking of the usage in 2 Kings 19:28 and the parallel Isaiah 37:29.

24. An obscure simile quoted from Song of Songs 6:4.

25. Job 37:18, as rendered by the JPS translation.

26. Genesis 8:21.

27. Psalm 68:21, as interpreted by Rashi.

28. Genesis 37:34.

29. Leviticus 14:35.

30. Genesis 41:16.

31. A familiar proverb indeed; cf. B. Berakhot 19a.

32. Cf. Raymond P. Scheindlin, *Wine, Women, and Death: Medieval Hebrew Poems on the Good Life* (Philadephia: Jewish Publication Society, 1986), 91–95, on the significance of this figure.

33. Taken, with a slight modification, from Genesis 22:6.

34. Isaiah 38:17, freely translated.

35. I.e., who created heaven and earth (Psalm 104:3).

36. I.e., who created woman (though in Judges 1:15 the phrase refers literally to pools).

37. A play on two biblical place-names.

38. Kozbi and her husband try to persuade Zerah to marry, but he is swayed neither by their speeches nor by their offer of money. Finally, Kozbi deploys her final weapon, the lovely Ayala Sheluha.

39. Ecclesiastes 7:18.

40. Genesis 2:23, wittily misapplied.

41. The imagery comes from the story of the bronze serpent, Numbers 21:4–9.

42. Zerah and Ayala exchange a number of not very inspired poems until Zerah is completely vanquished.

43. Song of Songs 4:9.

44. The erotic use of this reference to the offering for the consecration of the priests, Exodus 29 and Leviticus 8, is a humorous commonplace of medieval Hebrew secular poetry. See Scheindlin, *Wine, Women, and Death*, 95.

45. Literally "Proclaim it in the isles of Elisha," i.e., a faraway place mentioned in the Bible.

46. Literally "the hill of foreskins," a place mentioned in Joshua 5:3 as the site of the mass circumcision of the Israelites upon their entry into Canaan.

47. An untranslatable pun from the laws of leprosy, Leviticus 13:23, 28: "If the sore remains in its place . . ."

48. What follows is a parody of the marriage contract (*ketubbah*) in which key phrases of the standard text are matched with rhyming phrases bearing on the situation in the narrative. Phrases from or similar to the standard *ketubbah* are italicized, and Ibn Shabbetai's interpolations are in roman type. The standard *ketubbah* of the period mentioned four financial elements in the marriage contract: (1) the basic amount of two hundred zuz, which the Talmud declares to be the husband's obligation (*mohar*, or sometimes, as later here, called *ketubbah*); (2) a voluntary addition to this amount (*tosefet*); (3) an additional gift from the husband (*matana*); and (4) the property brought into the marriage by the bride (*nedunya*). On the latter, see note 44 below. For an example of a *ketubbah* from medieval Toledo, see Asher Gulak, *Otsar ha-shetarot* (Jerusalem: Defus Hapoalim, 1948), 36–37.

The year 4977 corresponds to 1216–17.

In her article, "Shimush be-Parodia min ha-Talmud ba-Maqama" (*Sinai* 76 [1971–72]: 77–82), Yehudit Dishon notes that the names of all the witnesses are those of non-Jews mentioned in the Bible. This is true, but at least as important for the humor of the piece is the sinister character of the list, because of the bad meaning of some of the names or the bad character of others.

49. H. Schirmann, in his article "Der Neger und die Negerin: zur Bildersprache und Stoffwahl der spanisch-hebräischen Dichtung," *Monatschrift für Geschichte und Wissenschaft des Judentums* 83 (1939): 481–92, argues that the woman was literally a Negress, and that the portrayal of a Negress as the epitome of repulsiveness is evidence of the influence of Christian attitudes on Ibn Shabbetai. It is possible, however, that the woman was simply dark-skinned. For, while Arabic writing does not generally depict the Negro as disgusting, it is a convention of Arabic love poetry that courtly ladies are pale-skinned. In this context, Rizpah's

dark skin would mean simply that she is uncouth. For a discussion of courtly versus uncouth love, see Raymond P. Scheindlin, "Fawns of the Palace and Fawns of the Field," *Prooftexts* 6 (1986): 189–203.

50. Genesis 32:32.

51. Isaiah 3:24.

52. This recalls a proverbial expression found also in Ibn Zabbara's *Sefer ha-Shaashuim*, ed. Israel Davidson (Berlin: Eshkol, 1925), 137. For other sources, see E. Blankstein, *Mishle Yisrael ve-Umot ha-Olam* (Jerusalem: Kiryat Sefer, 1964), 1:611.

53. Zerah goes on in this vein.

54. What follows in the Hebrew is a fireworks display of rhymed prose, listing items of luxury, taken in part from the list of women's finery in Isaiah 3, and including many words from the Bible and rabbinic literature, not all of which are of certain meaning. Lists of items in brides' trousseaux from this period have been found in the Cairo Geniza. Sometimes they form part of the *ketubbah*, and sometimes they are separate. They represent an important part of the financial arrangements between husband and wife, since the property brought by the wife to the marriage could be considered for many purposes as the husband's asset. See Mordechai A. Friedman, *Jewish Marriage in Palestine: A Geniza Study* (Tel Aviv and New York: Chaim Rosenberg School of Jewish Studies and Jewish Theological Seminary of America, 1980), 293–95; Solomon D. Goitein, A *Mediterranean Society* (Berkeley: University of California Press, 1967–83), 4:310–12. The fun in our passage is that Zerah is expected to provide the items a bride might well have been expected to provide for him.

55. Deuteronomy 28:31.

56. A parody of Ecclesiastes 9:8 ("Let oil never be lacking on your head"), reading *domen* (dung) for *shemen* (oil).

57. "Pierced ears" in this sentence and in the following jingle is the emblem of a slave, because of Exodus 21:6.

58. The meaning of these words in Isaiah 24:9 is "They do not drink wine amid song," but I feel certain that Ibn Shabbetai intended them to be understood as I have translated.

59. Exodus 23:15.

60. Deuteronomy 24:11.

61. A particularly witty misapplication of a biblical verse, 2 Kings 4:5.

62. 2 Kings 18:27.

63. Getting this rather forced joke necessitates a knowledge of Mishnah Betsah 1:4. A fowl may not be slaughtered on a festival unless it is designated for the holiday meal before the festival begins. If a person had designated black doves but then finds on the festival only white doves in the cote, he must assume that they are not the ones designated and may not slaughter them.

Zerah's three comrades now come to rebuke him for his misconduct and to lament his fate. They spend the night arguing whether to help him and how.

64. Proverbs 30:32, with its meaning radically altered.

65. Job 19:2, as rendered by the New English Bible.

66. Exodus 1:19.

67. The Hebrew is unclear.

68. Deuteronomy 22:7.

69. 1 Samuel 20:22.

70. Lamentations 3:27.

71. Deuteronomy 22:19.

72. The Hebrew text reads, "The lands are elevated above the skies." This apparent absurdity could actually make sense in the framework of courtly rhetoric if it is understood to mean that the lands in which he resides are so proud of his residing in them that they are lifted over the heavens. Nevertheless, it seems preferable to emend the text.

73. Numbers 27:21.

74. Jeremiah 23:6. In the biblical passage Judah means the Kingdom of Judah. The reader, by now so accustomed to the author's habit of ending speeches with verses from the Bible, might almost overlook the fact that Judah is also the name of the author. Here begins the gradual intrusion of the real-life situation (in which the author Judah Ibn Shabbetai addresses his patron, Abraham Ibn al-Fakhkhar) into the fictional narrative about the antics of Zerah, Rizpah, and the others.

The savior of Judah alluded to in the verse from Jeremiah is of course the Davidic Messiah. On the real-life plane, this verse now alludes to Ibn al-Fakhkhar—a fine compliment indeed.

75. Jeremiah 18:2. "Potter" in Arabic is *fakhkhar*. Once again the routine use of biblical quotations almost leads us to miss the allusion, this time to the patron.

76. Genesis 25:10, another allusion to the patron.

77. Malachi 2:7.

78. Hosea 12:3, another verse employing the author's name.

79. Genesis 21:11. "Abraham" now refers to Ibn al-Fakhkhar.

80. This quotation from Genesis 44:18 marks the final eclipse of the fiction and full emergence of the real-life characters.

81. The Hebrew expression also means "to serve as a courtier."

82. Genesis 17:17.

83. 2 Kings 25:30.

14 •

THE SORCERER
from *Meshal Ha-Kadmoni*
by Isaac Ibn Sahula

Ibn Sahula's book *Meshal ha-Kadmoni* belongs to the tradition of international wisdom literature that came into vogue in the Hebrew literature of the twelfth and thirteenth centuries.

Although purporting to be a treatise on morality, its morality is not particularly Jewish. Five chapters are devoted to wisdom, repentance, counsel, humility, and piety, but none of these virtues is dealt with as part of the Jewish religious tradition. The stories, animal fables, and maxims to which the chapters are devoted have their analogues in the gnomic literature of the world.

The book is written in the rhymed-prose style associated with the *maqama* (described above, in the Introduction to "Asher in the Harem"). As is typical in such works, the rhymes are often formed by the use of fragmentary biblical verses, their meaning wittily distorted. This practice of couching a narrative in biblical phrases could lend to a book of international lore the feeling of being part of the Jewish tradition. This was especially true since parts of the Bible itself belong to the international gnomic literature absorbed at an early stage in Jewish history. There are many passages in Proverbs and even in Psalms containing the same kind of advice that the Jews were to encounter again in the Middle Ages in

Arabic translations of Sanskrit books. Efforts like those of Ibn Sahula were perceived as a restoration to the Jewish heritage of that part of the tradition that had gotten misplaced during the long centuries of exile. This kind of thinking explains Ibn Sahula's choice of title for his work, *Meshal ha-Kadmoni* (The Ancient Proverb). The words themselves come from 1 Samuel 24:14 and have been understood by the Jewish tradition variously as meaning literally "the ancient proverb," "the proverb of the primeval man" (Adam), and "the proverb of the first being" (God, His "proverb" being the Torah). To a medieval Jew, the title would have suggested that the book's contents were part of Israel's ancient religious lore.

Of Ibn Sahula himself little is known except that he was born in 1244, lived in Guadalajara in Castile, composed the book in 1281, and was on intimate terms with Moses de Leon, the author of the monumental classic of Jewish mysticism called the *Zohar*. Except for a quotation from the *Zohar* in its last chapter, however, *Meshal ha-Kadmoni* does not show any affinity with Jewish esoteric lore.

In each of the book's five chapters, a disputant comes forward to argue against the particular virtue that is the subject of the chapter. The virtue is then defended by the author. Disputant and author exchange aphorisms, poems, and stories, which include other framed stories in the manner of the *Thousand and One Nights*; frequently the speakers are animals. The five antagonists are of course vanquished one by one.

"The Sorcerer" appears in the book's fourth chapter, which is devoted to a disputation on arrogance versus humility. After hearing the speech of the proponent of arrogance, the author presents his case in the form of a story of a dove and a raven. This tale, however, turns out to be nothing more than another disputation. The raven first addresses the dove, relating the tale of the sorcerer (our story) in order to prove the superiority of arrogance, and the dove counters with the tale of the fish, which itself contains several digressions. Unconvinced by the dove's tale, the raven foolishly flies off to join the eagles, but is thrown down to the ground and breaks his leg. He thereupon yields to the dove. This convinces the disputant to yield to the author, ending the chapter.

The modern reader who encounters "The Sorcerer" apart from *Meshal ha-Kadmoni* and enjoys it for its own sake may be surprised at the meaning attached to it by the author. The story hardly seems to prove the superiority of arrogance over humility, for if anyone needs a lesson in humility, it is the youth, who emerges from the narrative as the loser. The narrator's reference, at the denouement, to the triumphant sorcerer's "arrogant pride," seems like an afterthought, since his skill, not his arrogance, gains him the victory.

Though the story's connection with the book as a whole is tenuous, the story itself is an unusually skillful piece of narrative craftsmanship. The artistry lies in the manipulation of the reader's sense of reality. Like the protagonist himself, the reader loses track of the fact that by entering the garden he has left the real world. Apparently, enough years pass in the illusory world that the youth may be excused for forgetting the real world, especially since he has put up some resistance to settling into his new environment. But the illusion is enhanced for the reader by the very feature that often appears to be a weakness in Hebrew books of this kind—digressions from the narrative. The lengthy speeches exchanged by the youth and the king on the subject of a king's responsibilities impede the action, but they also provide the narrative with just the pacing it needs to convince the reader that time is actually passing. The passing of time, however, is the key to the illusion, for when the youth returns to reality, the sorcerer is still holding the cup, which still contains the unquaffed part of the magic potion. No time has elapsed, as the sorcerer explicitly says. This point was sufficiently important to the author to warrant an illustration.

The author himself saw to it that the manuscript would be illustrated, and he provided the illustrations with rhymed couplets as captions. The illustrations here are taken from the first edition, which was printed in Brescia in 1491.[1]

Introduction and translation by
RAYMOND P. SCHEINDLIN

There once lived in Jerusalem a handsome young man, well versed in literature and familiar with all fields of learning. He was determined to learn all the sciences. Yet though he tried every source, he could get no information about magic, for magic was forbidden to the Jews, God's chosen people. Realizing how ardent his desire was, and that it could never be fulfilled in the Holy Land, he provided himself with a substantial sum of money and went down to Egypt.

Just after he arrived in Cairo, as he was thinking what to do, an old craftsman sitting close by looked up and noticed him—a splendid-looking stranger, handsome and well dressed. Curious to learn the youth's intentions, he asked him where he had come from and whither he was bound.

The youth replied, "I am a Jew, the Torah my guide. The Land of Israel is where I reside."

The old man said, "Come home with me, and I'll look after your needs." The old man took him to his house and gave fodder to his donkey. Then they washed their feet, sat down to eat and drink, and began to converse.

The old man said: "Just as it behooves a man to love the wise and to associate with the learned and pious, so it behooves him to act wisely and politely, to offer hospitality to the stranger, to treat him with respect, to speak to him sympathetically so as to ease his worries and cares, and to use his knowledge and opinions to guide him aright. But he can only do this if he knows his guest's intention and purpose. Then he can offer advice that will be beneficial and conducive to the fulfillment of his desire. And now, seeing that you have honored me by coming here, and that you have chosen me as your friend and companion, and because you are sleeping in my house and eating at my table, tell me your heart's desire and the purpose of your journey. Tell me what sort of man you are so that I may advise you and honor you as best I am able."

The youth said: "How truly spoke the sage who said that every man

Here is the old man, conversing at meat,
And the youth in reply, framing sentences sweet.

ought to seek the advice of elders and counselors. Even a learned man of letters can accomplish nothing without advice. This is doubly true for a stranger who has traveled or fled from his homeland and whose mind is bewildered in a strange country. Let me tell you what my plan is, and you will tell me if I'm on the wrong path.

"I lived in Palestine, an oasis of learning in a dry land. I was devoted to literature and studied the sciences. But when I sought to find out about magic and its powers, I could get no information in my city, and my cries went unheeded. Thinking to learn about it abroad, I left the Holy Land, and I am here to find any magician, sorcerer, or wizard who can help me. I have wandered far from my own people. If you really want to help, tell me whether there is a man here versed in this science. I'll do anything! Let him demand any price he wishes. If only he'll pass his powers on to me, if only he'll teach me the signs of wisdom—I'll pay for it."

The old man said: "Since you have looked to foreign lands, and in your quest for a science unknown in your own country, you have taken refuge in my house, place your confidence in me. I will give you the most beneficial instruction and the most effective guidance in the fundamentals of magic and divination. For this science is my own craft, which I inherited from my ancestors."

When the youth heard this speech, he thought it ridiculous. In his contempt for the old man's claim to wisdom, he said to himself, "It can only have been drink that put it into his head to teach me. He probably has his eye on my money and my baggage. He thinks he can trick me, but I'm too smart for him." To the old man he said: "May God reward you! Your words are sweet as song, as clouds of incense. They have gone straight to the heart of a man sick and bitter, a man of broken spirit. But I don't want to burden you or put you to trouble. This is a difficult science, attained only through great pains. What I want is a youth my own age who can explain it to me. If he has any questions, he will ask you—that will be best—and you will help him by conferring the benefit of your kindness both upon him and upon me, your servant."

The old man realized that the youth did not credit him with wisdom or respect his intelligence, so he made a silent vow that he would not lie down for the night, or even enter his bedroom, before giving the youth a demonstration of his magical skills, wisdom, and power. He devised a plan. Turning to the youth, he spoke in an ingratiating voice: "Go to sleep now. In the morning I will introduce you to a man of profound wisdom who will teach and instruct you. Even I will be in your debt."

Hearing this the youth was relieved. Bowing low, he said, "Blessed be the Lord, by harp and lyre, for leading me to my heart's desire."

They sat together a while longer in conversation. Then the old man, in his guile, called for a drink. Lifting the goblet and taking a deep draught, he said to the youth, "Have a drink to forget the hardships of your journey and to assure yourself a deep and pleasant slumber." The youth drank, and his mind dulled; he rose to go to his room. But the old man had laid a trap for him. As he walked, he noticed a well in his path. He tried to cross it, but he slipped and fell in. The well was dry and lined with plaster. Seeing the trouble he was in, he cried out in anguish, and he went on all night long in the dark, his body continually buffeted. At last, in the morning, he saw a door at the bottom of the pit. In the utmost misery, aching all over, the youth opened the door and stepped outside. There he found a garden full of shade trees and shrubs and blossoms, with date trees and apple trees of every size. It was a paradise, surrounded by a

Here is the youth among the bowers,
Struck with wonder by the towers.

great river, a garden so lovely even a dullard's heart would be quickened
by its splendid beauty and by the taste of its fruit. At the sight of these
delights, some familiar, others not, the youth forgot all his troubles and
cares. He walked the whole length of the garden. When he reached the
end, he looked around and spied a bridge, built in perfect proportions,
with two towers painted red, also perfect in form. There he stood,
contemplating the sight, struck dumb with wonder.

He said to himself, "Let me dart across this bridge quick as an eagle.
Perhaps on the other side I'll find an inhabited place, perhaps even a
handsome and proud city." He ran across the bridge. On the other side
he found a large, splendid city with fine markets and squares crowded one
row after another with every kind of artisan.

He came to one bazaar that was so large and impressive that anyone
who passed by stopped to stare. This was the market of precious objets
d'art and gems. Here, too, were the public scribes, each one at his post,
stationed according to seniority. The youth was delighted at the sight of
these marvels.

One of the scribes noticed the handsome youth and hailed him,

"Whither bound, my handsome boy, whose sight fills every heart with joy?"

The youth replied, "I am a Jew, and Zion my home; I fear the Lord of heaven alone. I have come to Egypt, leaving my nation, to learn magic, sorcery, and divination."

Amused at this speech, the scribe called to his fellows, "Have you ever heard of a city called Jerusalem, or of a traveler seeking wisdom in the land of Egypt?" They replied, "Never until this day!" The scribe continued, "Well, here is a traveler from a distant land, whose home is in Zion, and whose hearth is in Jerusalem." Surprised as the scribes were at the youth's story, they were more amazed at his handsome appearance. They questioned him, "Do you know anything of the writer's art?" He replied, "I know its every part." And he wrote for them this marvelous couplet and read it aloud:

> Take pity on a lonely man,
>   Far from his home, forlorn,
> Who wisdom sought where'er he roamed,
>   But all he found was scorn.

The scribes subjected this rhetorical flourish to their professional scrutiny and were struck with its vigor. The head of the scribe's guild took the youth home, showed him all his possessions, and gave a feast in his honor, with the finest foods and the most fragrant wines. The guild members presented the youth with gifts; then they all sat around him in a circle, enjoying his conversation while he kept at his post, impressing them with his verses. To their delight, he wrote out for them the following couplet:

> O you who yearn for God's reward,
>   The feast at the end of time,
> The feast is at this table—see
>   The bread, the flesh, the wine!

So amazed were they at his calligraphy and eloquence that they said, "A man of such accomplishments is qualified for royal service." They sent word to the king: "A scribe is here to whom none compare, a scholar of attainments rare. He's come to town this very day; send for him here, and don't delay!" So the king sent for the youth, who then made his way directly to the palace. He made obeisance before the king, and the king stretched forth his scepter in greeting. Then the scribes fell to singing the youth's praises from every side, and they addressed the king in Aramaic in the presence of all the courtiers. "Here is a man of exceptional wit, to enter the royal service fit; his face is handsome, his manners fine, his intellect is a gift divine."

When the king had considered their advice, he bestowed gifts upon them all. But to our young man he gave gifts tenfold, and they begged him earnestly to accept the weighty responsibility of an appointment as chief of the palace scribes, to serve as head of the courtiers and as chief of counselors.

The youth, however, replied: "No, my lord. I have no wish to remain in this land. For I did not leave my country in quest of glory, or to serve in a royal court. I left only to seek wisdom. Furthermore, the men of intellect and learning have said, 'Be not familiar with those in power.' They have also said, 'Kings and fire resemble each other in their actions. Use them if you can keep your distance; but if you come close, they burn.' "

The king replied, "They did indeed write maxims of truth, for example, 'Trust the Creator and his law, depend on the king and his service, and associate with sages; then all will be well with you.'

"Further, they said: 'Live not in a town that lacks a powerful ruler, an efficient magistrate, a learned, amiable physician, a river, and a market. Let the king be the one who demands allegiance to himself, obedience to his laws. Let him see to it that all his regulations are observed, for they are the ladder by which he is elevated. And let him not overlook the tiniest violation, for by this means he will acquire majesty. The king should respect the words of the prophets and seers. He should perform deeds pleasing to his Creator. He should be amiable to his subjects. His countenance should be that of a pious, humble man of fine judgment, broad intellect, and clear thinking. Let him help the needy and comfort those in mourning. If he is angry, let him not cherish his anger or give it free rein. If the storm of lust seizes him, let him use his rational faculties to direct it to "the level plain, the king's plain." For the true king rules

The king and his scribes, addressing the man,
Urging him to agree with their plan.

over his desires and passions just as he effectively governs his people, the flock of his pasture.'[2]

"Further, they said: 'The king should speak to the poor, and they should have access to his presence. Let him bestow rank upon the sages and the priests.'

"I have followed all these precepts. I have even gone beyond them. They are the policy of my reign, the pride of my majesty. For the same reason, I desire to hear your words and to harken to your advice. You know very well that the king who delights in these precepts and founds his reign upon them is deserving of his subjects' joyful support. He deserves the companionship of men of wisdom and science. Therefore stay with me. Do not fear for your office. You will have a tranquil life, and I will give you wealth and honor and treasures of silver and gold. For never has a scholar come to my land whom I have not elevated. Never has there been a sage whom I have not honored and besought to teach me how to live. You are just the man I need to achieve success. I will give you a position among my closest intimates."

From this speech the young man understood that the king desired his companionship. So he replied, "I shall serve you steadfastly for one full year." The king responded: "Stay with me, for my own greater glory. Teach me your wisdom. I shall bring you into my own home, cherish you like a bride. And you will teach me."[3]

So the youth willingly stayed with the king until a year had passed. The king enjoyed his intelligent conversation and came to know him well. Together they held delightful intercourse of the kind that brings people close in friendship. They discussed poetry and prose, esoteric wisdom and practical counsels, philosophy, riddles, and stories. Thus passed the year in charming conversation conducive to piety.

At the end of the year the young man said to the king: "Give me leave to go now. Let me return to my homeland." But the king ordered that the youth be given treasures of gold. "Please do not abandon me," the king pleaded with the youth, "now that you know me so well. Stay one more year. Enjoy honor and glory." He replied: "This too shall I grant, for I wish to please you. But may the king not withhold his favor and detain his servant yet again." So the youth served him another year with all the splendid gifts of his soul. He and the king occupied themselves with the study of the law in both its theoretical and practical aspects: the plain meaning and the homiletical meaning, the general rule and the particular case, the received interpretation, speculation, and dialectic. Thus they passed the year in studies absorbing and profound, explicating the law in accordance with each of the Thirteen Rules.[4]

Then the young man said, "Detain me no longer. You know I have served you well." The king ordered that the youth be given gifts of money, teams of horses, and chariots, and then he addressed him as follows:

"How can you go off to a distant land when my soul is bound up in your splendid soul? Come! Let us make a covenant to unite in kinship. I will give you my daughter as wife, together with a generous dowry. You will occupy my throne after me that my name will survive, since, to my sorrow, I have no male issue. But your wisdom will alleviate my sorrow. It will cure my pain, revive my strength, bring me peace. For I do not desire kings or princes, only your righteousness and wisdom, your learning and loyalty. For loyalty is the head of kingdom, wisdom the root of dominion, intelligence the foundation of knowledge, and knowledge the prerequisite of all science. Righteousness repairs every flaw; through it rulers govern

and princes establish law. On this subject a philosopher once composed
an epigram, to wit:

> The world is an orchard run for the benefit of the age;
> The age is a power elevated by law;
> Law is a manner of conduct observed by the wise;
> The wise man is a king elevated by wisdom;
> Wisdom is a shepherd, honored by the soldiers;
> Soldiers are supporters maintained by money;
> Money is wealth amassed by the people;
> The people are servants, dependent upon fairness;
> Fairness is the just balance; it repairs the world's flaws;
> > prosperity's cause; the source of all praise;
> > the light of our days. [5]

"You are a man blessed by God. You give joy to my heart. You are
rooted in loyalty. Your knowledge is rooted in wisdom. You feed upon the
intellect, and you look to righteousness as your beacon. You deserve every
royal honor, even the monarchy itself. God has singled you out to be
prince and commander over my people. *You* He has chosen. This day you
shall affiliate with me doubly, espousing my daughter and my realm,
replacing me at the kingdom's helm."

The young man replied: "Who am I? What is my life? What are my
longings worth that *I* should be son-in-law to the king—I, a mere stranger,
a worthless thing?" The king responded: "The bride-price makes no
difference to me so long as my son-in-law is a scholar. Go now! Do what
I ask; fulfill my request. For the day is short; yet the deed is great and dear
to my heart." The youth declared, "Once again I shall do as you request.
In the shade of your promise I establish my home, no longer in quest of
my fortune to roam."

The king assembled his officers and courtiers and addressed them
vigorously. He praised and extolled the young man, commending him to
their love. From courtier to beggar, all approved the young man's eloquence and sagacity, and they accepted him as their lord and king. The
king gave him his daughter, his dearest treasure, to wife. And the people
rejoiced, for the succession was now ensured. With gladness, they acclaimed the young man as their lord.

The days of the wedding feast passed in tranquil joy. The young man

The king bids the people to honor the youth,
To bow down and promise to serve him in truth.

built a large palace and furnished it in grand style, crowning it off with a well in the courtyard. For his wife he also built a palace of great beauty; its tower reached to the sky. Lost in contemplation of his wife's beauty, he put his former home and kin out of his mind. He gave no thought to anything but pleasing her. She conceived and bore a son, and said, "A son is born to make me glad; a prince will be this little lad." They named him Servant-of-God-and-the-Crown; she gave birth to him in Illusium town.[6]

The child grew. When he was weaned, his father invited all his subjects to the celebration. He made feasts, abated taxes, and distributed gifts.

One day the young man was standing at the door of his home, enjoying an excellent book; meanwhile, his child was running about in the courtyard. The boy leaned over the well, farther and farther—and fell in. In horror, the father heard the boy cry out as he departed to join the shades of all ages past. The father cried: "Alas! Too soon my boy is dead! Why could I not die instead?" He instantly descended into the well and sought the boy, but he could not find him. The father's heart beat as the trees of the forest shake in a storm. He went his way, weeping, searching

The man in this picture his lost son doth mourn,
While the wizard is holding the cup of his scorn.

everywhere. Suddenly, whom did he spy? The sorcerer! His host, in all his arrogant pride! The sorcerer asked the young man, "Why do you weep and pour down tears?"

The young man answered, "A calamity has befallen me this day; my son and I are destroyed at a single blow."

The sorcerer responded, "And where did you ever get a son? Are you a horse, a mule? Do you understand nothing? Everything you have done has been an illusion—to your pain and travail."

The young man protested: "But I am the master counselor! I am a man with whom kings must reckon! I married a princess! I loved her as my life, and she bore me a son, a handsome, fine boy. He was just now weaned, and he was hopping about on a stick when he fell into the well that leads to the underworld. He must have been dashed to pieces! He must have died by the time he reached the bottom of the pit! That is why you see me weep, why I lament my bad fortune, and wander about in misery, wailing like a woman in childbirth. I shall wither like a driven leaf and go to my grave in an excess of grief."

The Egyptian said to the man, "Put aside your grief! Arise, compose yourself, stand at ease. All this was vanity, striving after wind. The whole event you have narrated, the days through which you passed, the catastrophe itself!—all this happened in a twinkling. Here in my hand is the cup you drank from. Here is the potion you quaffed. All these events have befallen you to prove that my claims to magic are true."

The young man was at first angered by this speech, but then, filled with amazement, he responded: "I must concede. There is no wizard who can surpass you in conjuring! No one knows the mysteries as you do! God himself has taught you all this. He has made you foremost in your art. You have the power to create winged fantasies. You place them wherever you wish. But take a drink and swallow it, the fantasies vanish as if they never existed. Let me now serve you as best I can. Let me devote my life to these studies. Please do not deny my request. Teach me your wisdom. Let me be guided by your truth."

So the young man dwelt with the sorcerer a year or more, studying magic and Chaldean lore.

NOTES

1. The copy from which the illustrations are taken is in the library of the Jewish Theological Seminary of America, to which I express my gratitude, and to its librarian, Dr. Mayer Rabinowitz, for permission to reproduce the illustrations. The text on which the translation is based is that printed in Hayyim Schirmann's anthology *Ha-Shirah ha-Ivrit bi-Sefarad u-ve-Provans*, 2d ed. (Jerusalem and Tel Aviv: 1960), 2:387–400. I also consulted the complete edition of *Meshal ha-Kadmoni*, edited by Yisrael Zemora (Tel Aviv: 1952). A translation into rhymed German prose was published by Moritz Steinschneider in the collection *Manna* (Berlin: 1847); I consulted the reprint (Berlin: 1920) entitled *Der Zauberer: Eine Auswahl hebräischer Makamendichtung des Mittelalters*. In translating the story, I have preserved the rhyme in the captions, in the few poems it contains, and in places where I thought it would be helpful in conveying the flavor of the original. I have not attempted to rhyme the entire story, feeling that the effect in English would be more annoying than witty.

2. The words "the level plain, the king's plain" are a quotation from Genesis 14:17, where they mean, "the plain of Shaveh, which is the king's plain." Ibn Sahula takes *shave* as meaning "even" or "level," i.e., moderate or temperate. He then connects the word "king" with the familiar idea that the true ruler is one who controls his emotions (cf. Mishnah Avot 4:1).

3. The Hebrew sentence is quoted from Song of Songs 8:2, where it means "I

shall lead you and bring you to my mother's home; you shall teach me." I have paraphrased in accordance with what I take to be Ibn Sahula's intention.

4. The Thirteen Rules are a list of techniques by which the ancient rabbis explicated the Torah; all the Hebrew expressions used by Ibn Sahula in describing the subject of the second year's studies are technical terms taken from the Jewish legal tradition.

5. I have translated this epigram as it stands, although its meaning is unclear to me. The maxim on which it appears to be based is perfectly intelligible, the chain of definitions turning back on itself in an endless circle:

> The world is a garden, hedged in by sovereignty;
> Sovereignty is lordship exalted by law;
> Law is guidance governing the king;
> The king is a shepherd mustering the army;
> The army are dragons [sic!] fed by money;
> Money is food gathered by the people;
> The people are servants subjected to justice;
> Justice is happiness and the establishment of the world.

(Moses Gaster, "The Hebrew Version of the 'Secretum Secretorum': A Medieval Treatise Ascribed to Aristotle," in his *Studies and Texts* [New York: Maggs Brothers, 1971] , 2:781. The "dragons" arose from a scribal error in the Hebrew for "possessions.") It appears in versified form in Immanuel of Rome's *Mahbarot* (ed. Dov Jarden [Jerusalem: Mossad Bialik, 1957], 2:347) with insubstantial changes necessitated by prosodic exigency. I cannot imagine why Ibn Sahula altered it as he did.

6. The Hebrew *oved* means "servant" and can be used in the sense of "pious ascetic." Because of its similarity to *eved*, it can also mean "courtier." I tried to convey both the ambiguity of meaning and the fact that it is a symbolic name rather than an ordinary proper noun.

The pseudo-Latin Illusium is my attempt to suggest Ibn Sahula's allusion to Genesis 38:5, which in the RSV reads, "She was in Chezib when she bore him." The place name Chezib recalls the Hebrew word *kazav*, meaning "falsehood," "deception."

15 ◆

JOB'S NOVELLA
from *A Valley of Vision*
by Abraham ben Hananiah Yagel

A Valley of Vision—its title taken from Isaiah 22:1—was composed by Abraham ben Hananiah Yagel, the Italian Jewish physician and writer, sometime after 1578. In this unusual Hebrew work the author describes the unpleasant circumstances leading to his incarceration in the municipal prison of Mantua, his dream encounter with the soul of his recently deceased father, who appears in his prison cell, and their subsequent heavenly journey. In the course of the two nights of their journey, Yagel is instructed in the meaning of life and the sublime mysteries of the divine universe.

That Yagel chose this literary form of self-expression—part autobiography, part fictional narrative, and part theological instruction—is itself remarkable, for his primary interest was not literature but science and medicine. His most important work was an exhaustive encyclopedia of the sciences of his day. He was an avid letter writer, particularly to patients seeking his medical care. He composed a plague tract, an elementary religious catechism, which he adapted for Jewish usage from a Catholic manual, and a small volume in praise of women, all of which were published during his lifetime.[1] At the same time, he was a student of the Kabbalah, particularly that variety nurtured on Italian soil which fused Jewish mysticism with the ancient learning of pagan antiquity,

313

especially magic.[2] Throughout his life Yagel struggled with economic insecurity, a predicament that profoundly colored his attitudes toward life and social relationships and made itself felt in his writings as well.

A Valley of Vision has been virtually ignored by modern scholarship. It was not published until the end of the nineteenth century and then only partially.[3] Despite its previous neglect, the composition is significant as a fascinating example of the creative synthesis of Italian and Jewish cultures at the end of the Renaissance. Two primary literary traditions inform the work: that of Boccaccio and the Italian novella on the one hand and that of Boethius and his *Consolation of Philosophy* on the other.

The influence of the Italian novella is particularly pronounced in the first half of the book.[4] This part consists of a series of nine unrelated novellas, or short stories, all situated within a cornice or frame tale that provides a loose structural unity. The frame tale, related at periodic intervals throughout the narrative, consists of Yagel's account of the financial difficulties that led ultimately to his imprisonment. Each of the stories is borrowed from contemporary collections of Italian novellas, translated into Hebrew, adapted for Jewish usage by the generous embellishment of biblical and rabbinic citations and by highlighting the moral or religious message that the story illustrates.

The impact of Boethius and the *consolatio* genre upon Yagel is even more profound.[5] Like Boethius's well-known work, Yagel's composition begins with a fallen virtuous man, a tragic figure whose autobiography becomes the springboard for the entire work. Through his suffering, he becomes aware of a higher truth, and with the help of a series of fictional instructors, he is enlightened, converted, and shown how to attain his goal. Each of the characters whom the narrator meets in his heavenly journey serves as a mouthpiece for a spiritual message; each one allegorically personifies the ideas Yagel hoped to communicate to his readership.[6]

If Boethius's influence remains veiled in the first part of Yagel's book, it is blatant in the second part. Here he introduces three additional allegorical characters, including Boethius's own mentor, Lady Philosophy. But true illumination of the soul for Yagel cannot be realized through the aid of philosophy alone. Yagel introduces two sisters of Lady Philosophy—one representing the science of astrology, and the second, the highest divine science of the Kabbalah.[7] Yagel's ascent culminates in an enlight-

available only through the spiritual resources of the Jewish tradition itself. Thus, in its form and content, Yagel's *Valley of Vision* is a product of both Italian and Jewish cultures. Even though he appropriated common stories and literary motifs from the cultural environment in which he lived, this Jewish author creatively integrated them into a narrative that underscored the singularity and priority of his own ancestral faith.

The selections that follow are taken from the opening of the entire work and from a section of the first book.[8] The latter section describes the meeting between Yagel, his father, and the biblical character of Job. The story Job relates during this encounter is a good illustration of Yagel's mixture of Renaissance storytelling, rabbinic homiletics, and theologizing. The basic narrative, a wife who takes her maidservant's place in her own husband's bed, was well known to Italian readers. The story had been told, for example, in Giambattista Giraldi Cintio's famous novella collection called the *Ecatommithi* (The Hundred Tales), first published in 1565.[9] A similar version had appeared even earlier in *Le Porretane,* Sabadino degli Arienti's famous collection first published in 1483.[10] Both Italian writers situated their stories in Italy. Cintio described the relationship of a rich doctor of Ferrara with his voluptuous maid Nigella. Outsmarted by his wife, who orchestrates the change of partners, the doctor begs his wife's forgiveness and sends the honest maid to Mantua, where she is amply rewarded in her marriage to a blacksmith. In Sabadino's version the duke of Milan is attracted to a noblewoman of the same city. His wife hears of his planned liaison with the woman in a castle in Pavia and surreptitiously changes place with her husband's mistress. When the husband is finally exposed, he recants, treats the young girl honorably, and restores her to her parents, after which she eventually marries a more appropriate mate.

Yagel's Hebrew version of the narrative is notably different from the Italian *novellieri* in three ways. First, the provenance of Yagel's story is no longer Italy but Egypt and Ethiopia. Second, his story focuses more on the virtue of the maidservant than on the crafty wife. Furthermore, when the husband's lechery is revealed, the maidservant's situation proves to be even more precarious than before. Instead of being rewarded for her honesty and temperance, she finds that her master harbors a grudge against her. Only through Job's intervention is she finally appropriately rewarded by becoming the bride of the son of the Ethiopian king. Finally,

Yagel grafts onto his story the figure of Job, who performs a divine mission in rescuing the young maiden from her evil master.

No doubt, the intervention of Job represents Yagel's most unusual interpolation in rewriting the familiar story. Especially bizarre is the way Yagel introduces Job into the narrative. After the narrator protests to his father that Job is an allegorical figure and not an actual person, Yagel's father presents a detailed discussion of the rabbinic sources regarding Job's authenticity, and only after his son has finally been persuaded of Job's actuality is the biblical figure introduced. Yet Job then relates a fantastic anecdote that obviously bears no relationship to reality. And following that Job and his questioners abruptly turn to consider such abstract theological questions as the rewards bestowed upon seemingly unvirtuous people like Haman and the influence of the constellations upon the fate of the Jewish people. This awkward mix of rabbinic commentary, entertaining narrative, and theological elucidation characterizes the entirety of Yagel's work. Even more extraordinary is the blurring of boundaries between reality and fantasy and between the sacred and profane realms: Job, the supposedly real person and biblical character, becomes the mouthpiece for a totally worldly but fictional story. Why in the first place did Yagel find this story the appropriate vehicle for conveying his message of the reward of moral virtue? And why the special link with Job? To attempt to answer these questions is perhaps to expect too much from the boldly conceived but somewhat imperfectly executed literary work that the young Yagel wrote. No doubt the combination of pieces he shaped was sometimes contrived, even forced. Yet, in his own mind, the remarkable mingling of the real and the fictional had its higher purpose. Yagel believed he could succeed in entertaining while teaching "Torah." He elevated the profane story by sanctifying it through the voice of a biblical figure revered in Jewish tradition, and thereby justified his use of the story to illumine "the higher truths" of Judaism.

Introduction and translation by
DAVID B. RUDERMAN

I

In a dream, in a night vision, while asleep in bed during my imprison-ment, a voice called in my ears.[11] The voice was the voice of Jacob,[12] like the voice of my father,[13] may his memory be blessed. He appeared to me, Abraham, and said: "What are you doing here? Who are you to be here?[14] Are you really my son Abraham?"

I was stunned by the sound of the call[15] and almost lost my breath. I covered my face with the cloak I was wearing, afraid to look in any direction. But when he saw that I was frightened and stricken with terror,[16] he gave me strength by speaking to me in the pleasant voice in which he spoke when he was living in this world: "Don't be afraid, Abraham, my son. I am your father, the one who made you,[17] and I will not hurt you. A father's compassion for his son endures forever.[18] But be silent and listen.[19] I will question you and you shall inform me."

Hearing these words, I lifted my eyes and saw his image before me. I raised my voice and cried out in the bitterness of my soul and was overcome with emotion.[20] I shouted, wept, and wailed and sought to embrace him and kiss his hands. Yet I only embraced the air! I touched nothing. I continued to scream and cry until he said: "Why are you crying? Do you not know that I am going the way of all the earth,[21] that a spirit has swept me up?[22] My life as well as my soul have expired. I am without substance, stripped of all matter. That is why you feel nothing [when you touch me]. After so much has happened to us, and the account of our actions has been handed over to God, our fate is to rise each month from our place [where the dead rest]. We roam the earth, its length and breadth,[23] in order to rescue the oppressed from the hand of his oppres-sor,[24] and serve as messengers for our Creator, to be like divine emissaries for Him, as it is written in the verse 'to bestow on you free access among these attendants' (Zechariah 3:7).[25] Now tell me about yourself. Why were you placed in this building?"

I answered: "My master, if you are God's emissary, you surely must know what happens on earth. Why do you ask me? Is it to remind me of the sorrows I have experienced? Is it to keep me from asking you questions about the matters of the world to which you belong or about the secrets of nature and creation, the subjects that blessed sages called *Maaseh Bereshit* and *Maaseh Merkavah*?"[26]

He replied: "My son, pay attention. Listen to the father who bore you. The deceased are not aware of particulars that happen to the inhabitants of the earth, as it is written, 'His sons come to him and he does not know it' (Job 14:21). Even those three pumpkin seeds that we are able to recognize are not perceived clearly, nor are they known as they actually are.[27] In general, the dead know if famine or drought, pestilence or war, have been decreed upon a state, or city, or region because they hear about it from behind the curtain[28] on the New Year when the decree is issued. The incident of the two spirits related by our sages of blessed memory in the talmudic chapter 'Who has died'[29] illustrates this fact. But the dead know nothing of particular matters related to worldly affairs and vanities. Why should they need this sorrow? It is sufficient that each unhappiness have its moment[30] during their [the spirits'] imprisonment in the mire and filth of the body while they still live upon the earth. The knowledge of these matters offers their souls no perfection or happiness. They therefore never request it. Yet if they wished, they could know these matters causally, through the disposition of the heavens and their constellations.[31]

"Indeed, that is how I know that your twilight stars[32] are struggling in their orbits to set you in pain and that [your troubles] came through financial matters. Now tell me from beginning to end how these things developed with your enemies. But if you wish, blessed be God, let us wander together this evening. You shall see all the hosts meet us. Come with a cry of joy![33] Do not let your heart be filled with fear or trembling. I am your father, your maker, and I will protect you from all evil afflictions and return you to your place before morning. Let us talk together intimately. Tell me of your ways. I shall answer your questions and explain those matters that you can understand."

II

. . . I looked up and saw opposite me an eminent-looking, well-dressed old man. He was wearing a robe of fame and glory, and a great light enveloped him. I asked my father [about him], and he told me that the man was Job. His Creator had sent him on a mission as an angel of God. For a moment I was astonished by the sight. "Blessed are you, O God, who has rewarded me and enabled me to see this divine man!" I said. For I had incorrectly believed that rabbi who, sitting before Rabbi Samuel bar Nahmani, had said, "Job never existed nor was he ever created; but he was only a parable."[34] When I witnessed every sage of Israel arguing as to whether or not Job really lived,[35] I concluded with even greater certainty that the law accorded with the view that Job was only a parable. I also found support for this in the view of "the great eagle," Maimonides, of blessed memory, who, in his honorable book, *The Guide of the Perplexed,* commented upon the question.[36] [He interpreted] the name Uz in the verse "There was a man in the land of Uz" (Job 1:1) as an equivocal term [that refers also] to the name of a man, as in the verse "Uz his first-born" (Genesis 22:21). The word is the imperative form of the verb Etsah, which means "advice and counsel," [as in] *Utsu etsah, "take counsel together"*[37] and 'pay attention to the matters written in this book about the diverse opinions regarding Providence.' [These opinions] must then have been related by [Job, who was] an innocent and righteous man rather than a sage. For if he had been a sage, he would never have doubted these matters. "Yet how can you declare, my master, that this man coming toward us is actually Job?"

My father replied: "Nevertheless, you still should have known that Job lived and that he was created. For Rabbi Johanan declared in Genesis Rabbah:[38] 'Every man of whom it is said in Scripture, "he was," remained unchanged from beginning to end.' [This is the meaning of the verse] 'There was a man in the land of Uz' (Job 1:1) who was chastised with afflictions, etc. So too, in the Tanhuma[39] concerning the verse, 'After these things' (Genesis 22:1) [the midrash relates], 'Abraham feared the afflictions [he foresaw in the future]. The Holy One, blessed be He, said to him: Do not fear. Another man has already been born who will receive those afflictions.' Moreover, in Numbers Rabbah[40] it is written, 'And Uz was Job as it is written: "A man was in the land of Uz and Job was his name, etc." (Job 1:1).'⁴¹ That man is related to us; he is one of our redeeming kinsman.⁴²

"Job was born in the land of Aram-naharaim, in the city of Nahor, and he went to live in the land of Uz, which is known today as Constantinople, the largest city in the Turkish kingdom, which formerly was called Uz. Thus Rabbi Joseph⁴³ translates the verse in the scroll of Lamentations, 'Rejoice and be glad O daughter of Edom who dwells in the land of Uz' (Lamentations 4:21), as 'Rejoice and be glad . . . in the city of Constantinople, etc.'⁴⁴ When the verse speaks of him as being 'in the land,' this means in that land in which the afflictions came. He was not born there, though, but in Aram-naharaim, from where he went to live in the land of Uz, in a town called Kirianos, as the rabbis related in the midrash:⁴⁵ 'See how the Holy One, blessed be He, pressed his punishment upon Job when he came to the town of Kirianos for three years, etc.' He enlarged his property primarily 'in the land' until he became wealthy and honored with a great household, just as the verse testifies.⁴⁶ In the same town he was afflicted, and that was the place his three friends visited from Aram-naharaim to pity and comfort him, as the rabbis relate in Chapter *Ha-Shutafim*.⁴⁷ We find that the distance from Constantinople to Aram-naharaim is three hundred parasangs.

"And how did [his friends] know of Job's grief from so distant a land? Some say that each friend had a crown of three faces, and each man's name was engraved on one face. When one of the men was afflicted, the face changed.⁴⁸ Even today, you should know, there exists in the city of Constantinople a monument at the grave of Job. The place is highly revered; people treat it as a house of God. It is decorated with burning candles, and there is a hospice for travelers in blessed memory of a righteous man.⁴⁹ Moses our teacher also wrote his own book [i.e., the Pentateuch], the section of Balaam, and the Book of Job, etc.⁵⁰

"What the man sitting before Rabbi Samuel bar Nahmani meant in saying that the [story of Job] was actually a parable was this: Even if it were *merely* a parable, it would still have been worthy of being written down in a book because of its important subjects. We can still declare that this famous man actually existed, just as the prophetic statement indicates: 'And Noah, Daniel, and Job, etc.' (Ezekiel 14:30). As the rabbis said,⁵¹

320

'Each of them saw a world destroyed and then rebuilt, etc.' Even so, Job's story was used by Moses, our master, to compose that book and to record those people's discussions and their dissenting views about Providence. Job, who suffered and experienced afflictions, came with three friends, in order to testify by experience on the subject of the suffering of the righteous and the flourishing of the wicked."

After [my father had spoken] these words, we came closer to him and bowed, saying, "Do not be angry[52] if we ask where you are going."

Job replied: "I heard the cry of a maiden from the land of Egypt, a young woman of good family, an innocent virgin. She was captured beyond the Nile River by pirates, who brought her to the land of Ethiopia.[53] There they sold her to a wealthy nobleman, one of the brothers of Nabal the Carmelite,[54] who was like him in being a Calebite. As soon as this man glimpsed the girl's good taste, her beauty, and fine intelligence, he purchased her in order to maltreat her and take her virginity. At first he spoke to her in a pleasant and comforting way, 'Don't be afraid. You will be like a daughter to me.' The girl prostrated herself before the man and worked for him as a maidservant with such great diligence that she was equal if not superior to anyone who made light of her.

"The man fell in love with the woman. One day he found her alone in the house and revealed his deepest feelings to her. He promised her that if she submitted to him, he would give her a dowry, free her, and marry her to one of his servants. The girl refused. She wept and begged him not to do so shameful a thing as to take her virginity. Besides, this would make her a rival to his wife, who is like his own flesh; she would only be jealous of another [woman].[55] The young girl acted wisely. She left the wicked man, and he did not carry out his intentions. Every day, however, he continued to implore her. Yet she did not submit, even to his request to sleep with him without having intercourse. Instead, she grew more modest. But when she saw that he continued every day to try her, she finally said to herself: Eventually I will be unable to escape from him. He is my master, and his desire is intense. Vast floods will not quench love.[56] He will chain me by my legs. Who knows if I will be able to escape from the snare and from the pit? Now is the time to seek advice in order to flee from under his net lest that slothful man hunt his prey.[57]

"Accordingly, the girl went to her mistress, and, weeping bitterly, she revealed to her in secret exactly what had happened. When her mistress saw that the girl was about to cry, she recognized the truth, for truth follows its own course.[58] And she told her, 'Be quiet. Do as I command you.' The girl answered: 'I will do whatever you command. I am your maidservant, and I place my soul and my virginity in your hands.[59] I hope you will rescue me.'

"Her mistress gave her the following instructions: 'Listen, my daughter. Observe your master when he speaks and tempts you again, as is his regular custom. Tell him that you wish to fulfill his desire and will sleep with him that very night, at the middle of the second watch (1:30 A.M.), at a time when no one can be heard and the streets are deserted. But you will hide yourself somewhere and remain there. Meanwhile, I shall go in your place and keep your promise.' The maiden bowed and prostrated herself, and did just as her mistress had commanded her.

"Only a short time passed before she spoke with her master. When the man heard that the girl would respond to his request at midnight, he was astonished and silently anticipated the appointed day and time. So overjoyed that he was about to fulfill his desire, he stopped thinking about his wealth or property. That midnight, the man rose in the dark, closed the door behind him, and went to take his fill of love[60] at the appointed place and to delight in lovemaking until the morning. When he arrived, he was so overwhelmed by passion that he trusted the woman's words, and because the place was dark, he did not recognize his wife. He drank from his cup while thinking it was another.[61]

"In the early morning, the man wished to depart before someone might recognize him and accuse him of having intercourse with the woman the previous night. But his wife asked him: 'Where are you going so early in the morning? Where do you think you were sleeping all night? I am your wife, the woman of your youth, but you thought badly of me[62] and turned your heart to arrogance,[63] to Egypt, to the people that has ceased to be.[64] Did you consider this to be just, a way to acquire for yourself a name and glory in your old age, now that you have lost your virility and youth? If ever this becomes public knowledge, how will you bear your shame and disgrace before all the old men with whom you take counsel?

" 'But do this, and the affair will be known only between us. No one outside shall hear our voices. First, speak no longer with the maidservant,

neither for good nor for bad,[65] for this does not do you honor. What has happened is done; for the sake of our previous love, I shall be quiet and restrain myself. I shall be to you as before, obedient to your words and attentive to your voice. For you are my master; I shall bow down to you. But if you will not follow these instructions, and if you, the king, do not desire my beauty,[66] and you turn your heart to this maidservant in our house, God will permit me to reveal your shame publicly, for my own sake. You will be disgraced. No longer will I be your wife. I will leave your house and go to my father's and brother's. And this evil will be greater than anything you have experienced since the time of your youth.'

"When the man heard his wife's words, he turned to stone, stunned like a man seized by delirium.[67] He had no idea whether he sat among the dead in this world or in the next. He feared for life and honor, and he was terrified by the words of his wife, a courageous woman, a daughter of nobility and stature, and a scion of an important family. So he changed his mind, spoke kindly to her and laughed. 'Who would ever have thought,'[68] he said, 'that an important person like me would be caught in a game of whores like some worthless person? What should I do? Passion corrupts the rules of conduct, and there is no protection against unchastity.[69] Do not fear! I will not continue to act as I have. My fantasy was satisfied by spending the night with you; my obsession is there. The passion that was in my heart has receded, but my soul cleaves still to you.'

"The woman graciously accepted his words. The two arose, and no one besides [her and] her husband knew of the matter. From that day on, he no longer spoke to [the maidservant]. His courageous wife also did not leave the girl alone for even an hour. Yet the man nurtured a grudge in his heart against the young woman because of the affair. The powerful love that his heart had felt so deeply now changed to intense hatred, and this loathing grew stronger than the love he had felt.[70] He devised ways of afflicting the girl, he struck her with horrible blows, and he piled hard work upon her. She, in turn, cried to God out of her great labor, and He heard her cry and sent me to be a guardian for her and a refuge, a shield and breastplate, to show her a chord of divine grace,[71] and to make her beauty known to the son of the Ethiopian king so that he would seek and take her to be his wife. Tomorrow there will be this sign.

"All this happened because of the girl's great modesty and because she withstood the test. I swear that I have not found a woman like her since the time Ephraim departed from Judah.[72] She is fit to be a queen; furthermore, she comes from a family who are friends of Elihu, the son of Barachel the Buzite.[73]

"You should know that the Holy One, blessed be He, bestows greatness on a person only if there is something good in him or if he possesses a certain merit. This was so [even] in the case of Nebuchadnezzar whom Heaven made great merely by virtue of the four steps he ran to honor God, as it is described in Chapter Helek.[74] Or it may be because of one's good character, as with Moses' compassion, as the rabbis declared in Exodus Rabbah,[75] or as with David's [kindness], as it is written, 'He brought him from minding the nursing ewes [to tend His people Jacob, Israel, His very own]' (Psalm 78:71). [God also makes a person great] if that person encounters sin but is saved from it, as we find in the cases of Joseph and others who rose from the depths of oblivion to incredible heights among the Jewish people or among the other nations. These men were selected by Heaven to lead their people because they possessed merit, a good quality, moral virtue, or wisdom, and this enabled them to achieve greatness and honor. Search thoroughly in every book, and read them all. Not one will lack a reference. So do not be surprised that in a single day this young maiden rose from being a lowly maidservant to becoming the wife of the son of the Ethiopian king. For there is nothing new under the sun."[76]

I then inquired, "May your servant say something to my master?"[77]

He answered, "Speak!"

I spoke: "My master has said that anyone who achieves greatness possesses a good quality, like wisdom or moral virtue or some other merit, as in the case of Nebuchadnezzar, whom my master cited, or of Hiram, king of Tyre, also known as Hirah the Adullamite,[78] or of Og, the king of Bashan, who was the fugitive who told Abraham that the son of his brother had been captured, etc.[79] This was also the case with the other officers of kings and sultans. And yet we have seen that Haman, the son of Hammedatha the Agagite, rose to greatness even though it is nowhere mentioned that he possessed a single good quality. To the contrary: he wished utterly to uproot the remnant of Israel, which stood as an ensign to the nations. Solely because God was with us was Haman's effort repelled. Analogous examples exist among the gentiles, for example: Emperor Nero, whose worship was alien, and other individuals who, in a short time, rose to greatness and were catapulted from a dunghill to great majesty. Enable me to understand this, my master, since I am your servant."

Job responded: "There is no difficulty. Neither I nor you are familiar with the [intimate] lives of these people, with their goodness, their wisdom, and deeds. Consider this! Haman was also a barber in the same town where I lived for three years prior to my afflictions, as the rabbis mention in Megillah,[80] where it is said that Mordecai told Haman that he was a wicked person and asked whether he was not once a barber from the town of Kirianos, etc. Even so, I do not know of any special goodness in his actions that would enable me to specify the quality that allowed him to achieve greatness. I went to him only when I needed a haircut, and I curtailed my talk with him since I knew that he was from the accursed seed of Amalek. A good cub does not become a bad lion.[81] Still, I saw that he had a courageous heart, the heart of a lion, and eventually he came to despise that work [of barbers]. He joined the ranks of the army, and became great, acquiring wealth and honor. His one good quality was the courageous heart he possessed. Likewise, Nero, the emperor, acquired the perfect skill of musical knowledge and that mollified his cruelty.

"Aside from these things, one should not look for good attributes in these persons. The Holy One, blessed be He, created them solely in order to destroy as He pours out His anger on humanity when it rebels and sins against Him. Accordingly, we should attend to the general principle we stated—that God uses all things as His messengers, even a snake or a frog.[82] He created them all to serve as a hammer in His hand. In addition, there is a principle in which we believe—that anyone who harms Israel is made a 'head' in his time, as the rabbis indicate in Lamentations Rabbah regarding the verse 'Her adversaries have become the head' (Lamentations 1:5)."[83]

I asked: "Tell me, master, why is it that everyone who hurts Israel becomes a 'head'? If [the children of] Israel are God's children, then by justice anyone who harms them should become a 'tail,' not a 'head.' "

Job answered: "If one knows a thing, he also knows its opposite.[84] For the wise man, the knowledge of contraries constitutes [knowledge] of the same object. When the children of Israel are at the 'head' and not at the 'tail,'[85] and if someone touches them, it is as though he has touched the pupil of God's eye, so to speak, since they are His children, as the verse says, 'You are my children, etc.' (Deuteronomy 14:1). Israel's constellation rises as the constellation opposite it falls. However, when they fall because of their evil deeds, their constellation is low and it descends. At that time, their oppressor is protected by the constellation opposite to Israel's; as his constellation rises, he rises. For God has decreed, and who shall reverse it?[86] The Torah also testifies to this when it declares, 'The stranger who is among you shall mount up above you' (Deuteronomy 28:43).

"Thus, if we carefully examine all the comings and going of a man who becomes great, we will discover in him some positive attribute of wisdom or morality, just as we have said, and as the rabbis stated:[87] 'God bestows wisdom solely on the person who is prepared to receive it, as the verse states, "He gives wisdom unto the wise" (Daniel 2:21).' They also said, 'Prophecy is also found in a wise, courageous, and wealthy person.'[88] As we know, a courageous person is he who controls his passion, as the rabbis state:[89] 'Who is courageous? One who controls his passion. And [who is] rich? He who is happy with his lot.' He is a person who is satisfied with what the Creator has given him, whether it be much or little."

[Yagel then asks Job about whether in fact Israel has its own constellation. In a lengthy reply, Job responds affirmatively.]

[Finally, Job declares]: "And now the time of the nightingale has arrived.[90] I must leave you and go on my mission to save the young woman from the hand of the hard master who rules her, and help her to gain power over him."

He thus blessed us with peace, left us, and went on his way.

NOTES

1. On Yagel and his other writings, see David B. Ruderman, *Kabbalah, Magic, and Science: The Cultural Universe of a Jewish Physician* (Cambridge, Mass. and London: Harvard University Press, 1987).
2. See M. Idel, "The Magical and Neoplatonic Interpretations of the Kabba-

lah in the Renaissance," in *Jewish Thought in the Sixteenth Century*, ed. B. Cooperman (Cambridge, Mass.: Harvard University Press, 1983), 186–242.

3. It was published (only pt. 1) by Abraham Mani in Alexandria, Egypt, in 1880. For cursory treatments of the work, see C. Roth, *The Jews in the Renaissance* (Philadelphia: Jewish Publication Society, 1959), 330–31; J. Dan, *Ha-Sippur ha-Ivrit bimei ha-Beinayim* (Jerusalem: Sifriat Keter, 1974), 202–21; S. Simonsohn, *History of the Jews in the Duchy of Mantua* (Jerusalem: Kiryat Sefer, 1977), 252–53. See David B. Ruderman, "Some Literary and Iconographic Influences of the Renaissance and Baroque on Abraham Yagel's *Gei Hizzayon*" (in Hebrew), *Tarbiz* 57(1988), 271–79; *A Valley of Vision: The Heavenly Journey of Abraham ben Hananiah Yagel*, translated from the Hebrew, with an Introduction and Commentary, by David B. Ruderman (Philadelphia: University of Pennsylvania Press, 1990). The selections below are based on this translation.

4. On the novella, see generally, R. J. Clements and J. Gibaldi, *Anatomy of the Novella: The European Tale Collection from Boccaccio and Chaucer to Cervantes* (New York: New York University Press, 1977).

5. On this genre, see, for example, M. H. Means, *The Consolatio Genre in Medieval Literature* (Gainesville, Fla.: University of Florida Press, 1972); E. Reiss, *Boethius* (Boston: Twayne Publishers, 1982); and H. R. Patch, *The Tradition of Boethius: A Study of His Importance in Medieval Culture* (New York: Oxford University Press, 1935).

6. On the use of this genre in the Neoplatonic tradition, see Reiss, *Boethius*, 98; P. Courcelle, "Tradition platonicienne et traditions chrétiennes du corps-prison," *Revue des études latines* 43(1965), 406–43.

7. I discuss in greater detail the motif of the three sisters in the introduction to *A Valley of Vision* cited in note 4 above.

8. The translation is based on the Mani edition, 1a–b, 29a–33a.

9. I have used the edition of G. Salinari, *Novelle del Cinquecento* (Turin: Unione tipografico-editrice Torinese, 1976), bk. 3, no. 9, 554–60.

10. I have used the edition of B. Basile, *Le Porretane* (Rome: Salerno editrice, 1981), no. 26, 229–37. The same motif is also found in other novella collections. For examples, see D. P. Rotunda, *Motif-Index of the Italian Novella* (Bloomington, Ind.: Indiana University Press, 1942), 98, 126. An example of the same motif is found in rabbinic literature. See M. Gaster, *The Exempla of the Rabbis* (1924; reprint, New York: Ktav, 1968), 124, and with a prolegomenon by W. G. Braude.

11. The line is constructed from a string of biblical phrases, including Job 33:15, Genesis 42:17, and 1 Samuel 15:14. The line also contains an additional phrase from Genesis 40:16: "In my dream, similarly," which I have not translated because of the redundancy.

12. This phrase from Genesis 27:21 has engendered confusion among scholars who assumed on the basis of the line that Abraham's father was named Jacob (and not Hananiah). Joseph Dan, for example, in the *Encyclopaedia Judaica* (1971), s.v. "Jagel, Abraham," concluded that the author of this work and the author of the other writings of Abraham Yagel (where Yagel refers to his father as Hananiah) might not be the same person. Such a conclusion is totally unfounded since Yagel

refers to *A Valley of Vision* in his other writings. The phrase "the voice of Jacob" does not refer to the name of the author's father.

13. Literally "Abraham's father."

14. Cf. Judges 18:3.

15. See Jeremiah 14:9.

16. See 2 Samuel 1:9.

17. See Deuteronomy 32:6.

18. Cf. Genesis Rabbah 54:2, and elsewhere.

19. See Deuteronomy 27:9.

20. Cf. Song of Songs 5:4.

21. Cf. 1 Kings 2:2.

22. Cf. Ezekiel 3:12.

23. See Genesis 13:17.

24. Cf. Jeremiah 21:12.

25. Yagel reinterprets this verse to refer to angels.

26. These terms, which originally referred to the biblical account of Creation and the prophetic description of the chariot-throne in the first chapter of Ezekiel, were adapted by the rabbis to designate esoteric speculations, which were never to be studied in public and, then, only by worthy individuals (see Mishnah Hagigah 2:1). Maimonides, in the introduction to his *Guide of the Perplexed,* uses the terms to refer to physics and metaphysics respectively.

27. The three pumpkin or squash seeds refer to stomach worms according to E. Ben Yehudah, *Milon ha-Lashon ha-Ivrit* (Jerusalem and Tel Aviv: La'am, 1948), 2:831. Cf. also the expression in Isaiah 17:6. I could not locate Yagel's precise source here.

28. That is, the curtain of heaven, a common rabbinic expression. Cf., e.g., B. Hagigah 15a, B. Yoma 77a.

29. B. Berakhot 18b.

30. Cf. B. Berakhot 9b.

31. Yagel's fascination with astrology is reflected in all his writing. Like most of his Jewish and Christian contemporaries, he believed in the efficacy of astrological prognostication, especially as it related to his medical practice.

32. Cf. Job 3:9.

33. Cf. Psalm 126:6.

34. See B. Baba Batra 15a.

35. See especially B. Baba Batra 14b–15a. For other references, see L. Ginzberg, *Legends of the Jews* (Philadelphia: Jewish Publication Society, 1968), 2:225–42, 5:381–90.

36. *Guide to the Perplexed* 3:22.

37. Isaiah 8:10.

38. Genesis Rabbah 30:8.

39. I could not find the reference in Tanhumah, a midrashic collection; but see Numbers Rabbah 17:2, where the same thought is expressed in relation to the verse in Genesis. On the comparison of Job with Abraham in rabbinic literature, see N. N. Glatzer, "The God of Job and the God of Abraham: Some Talmudic-

Midrashic Interpretations of the Book of Job," *Bulletin of the [London] Institute of Jewish Studies* 2(1974), 41–58.

40. Numbers Rabbah 17:2.

41. This midrash also claims that Job received these afflictions, which had been intended for Abraham, on the basis of the fact that the name Uz occurs both in the Abraham story [Genesis 22:21] and in Job.

42. Cf. Ruth 2:20.

43. The Aramaic translation of the Hagiographa was traditionally attributed to Rabbi Joseph ben Hama of Babylonia.

44. The translation in A. Sperber, *The Bible in Aramaic* (Leiden: 1968), 4a:148, closely approximates the one in our text, and both mention Constantinople.

45. See Leviticus Rabbah 17:4, ed. M. Margulies (Jerusalem: Ararat Publishers, 1953), 379, including his note there.

46. See Job 1:3.

47. B. Baba Batra 16b. There it states that each friend lived in a different place, at a distance of three hundred miles one from the other.

48. B. Baba Batra 16b. Job and each of his friends had the pictures of the three others beside himself set in a crown, and whenever one of them experienced adversity, it was revealed in his picture.

49. Yagel is referring here to the tradition that the monument of the Arabic general Ayyub in Constantinople was that of Job. On this tradition, see Ginzberg, *Legends* 5:382 and the sources he gives there. The medieval monastery in Hauran, Syria, was also thought to house Job's tomb. Cf. L. Besserman, *The Legend of Job in the Middle Ages* (Cambridge, Mass.: Harvard University Press, 1979), 65.

50. See B. Baba Batra 14b. On this line and its parallel in a line from Josephus, see Ginzberg, *Legends* 6:134.

51. See David Kimhi on Ezekiel 14:20.

52. Cf. Genesis 18:30, 32.

53. For the possible sources of this story, see the Introduction above.

54. See 1 Samuel 25. Nabal came from the town of Maon and owned much livestock near the neighboring town of Carmel, southeast of Hebron. Although David extended protection to his flocks, Nabal refused to reciprocate by offering him a gift. In rabbinic literature Nabal referred to himself as a descendant of Caleb (cf. 1 Samuel 25:3) in order to compare his more noble ancestry with that of David, who was descended from Ruth. On Nabal's unfavorable image, see Ginzberg, *Legends* 6:235.

55. See B. Megillah 13a; literally "who is only jealous of the thigh of another."

56. See Song of Songs 8:7.

57. See Proverbs 12:27.

58. A Maimonidean phrase used frequently by Yagel. See Maimonides, *Shemoneh Perakim*, end of chap. 4.

59. Cf. Psalm 31:6.

60. See Proverbs 7:18.

61. Cf. B. Nedarim 20b.

62. See Genesis 50:20.

63. See Psalm 40:5.
64. See Isaiah 23:13.
65. See Genesis 31:24.
66. Cf. Psalm 45:12.
67. For the expression, see Mishnah Gittin 7:1.
68. Cf. Genesis 21:7.
69. Cf. B. Sanhedrin 105b, B. Ketubbot 13b, and Genesis Rabbah 55:7.
70. See 2 Samuel 13:15.
71. For the expression, see B. Hagigah 12b and elsewhere.
72. See Isaiah 7:17.
73. See Job 32:2.
74. B. Sanhedrin 96a. The rabbis here embellish an incident described in Isaiah 39. In the biblical story, Merodach-baladan, son of Baladan, the king of Babylon, sent a messenger to bring greetings of peace to Hezekiah, the king of Judah in Jerusalem. According to the rabbinic account, Nebuchadnezzar, then the Babylonian king's scribe, tried to intercept the messenger in order to rewrite the words of greeting since they had been composed improperly in his absence. However, the angel Gabriel stopped him after he had taken only four steps. Had Nebuchadnezzar not been stopped, his reward might have been so great that the angel would have allowed him to destroy Israel completely.
75. Exodus Rabbah 2:1.
76. Ecclesiastes 1:9.
77. See Genesis 44:18.
78. See Genesis Rabbah 85:4, where king Hiram, who assisted Solomon in the building of the Temple, is identified with Hirah, the friend of Judah (Genesis 38:1).
79. See Genesis Rabbah 13:8, where Og is identified as the fugitive mentioned in Genesis 14:13.
80. See B. Megillah 16a.
81. Cf. the similar expression in J. Shekalim, end, and Rashi on B. Megillah 11b; Leviticus Rabbah 19:6.
82. See Numbers Rabbah 18:22 and Leviticus Rabbah 22:4.
83. That is, they are now the masters. Lamentations Rabbah 1:31. Rabbi Hillel ben Berekiah explains in this passage that whoever harms Israel becomes a chief. Since Israel is so exalted, she could be overcome only by a general of eminence. When Jerusalem was destroyed, other cities rose in stature.
84. Cf. Aristotle, *Categories* 10(11b25).
85. See Deuteronomy 28:13.
86. Cf. Isaiah 14:27.
87. B. Berakhot 55a.
88. B. Nedarim 38a.
89. Mishnah Avot 4:1.
90. Song of Songs 2:12.

16 ◆

THE "DREAM-TALKS" OF
NAHMAN OF BRATSLAV

Rabbi Nahman of Bratslav (1772–1810) is known to students of Jewish
literature as a spinner of fantastic yarns. His collected *Tales*, his most
famous writings, combine folk motifs, biblical images, and kabbalistic
symbols to create works of a startling mythic profundity. Master of a small
but intensely loyal band of Hasidic followers, Nahman managed to
transcend the literary conventions of that movement, offering his teach
ings garbed in fantastic narrative as well as in traditional homiletics.

Among his blessings Nahman was able to count a faithful disciple,
Nathan of Nemirov, a man of humble spirit but of considerable literary
talent. The disciple outlived his master by some thirty-five years, a period
he devoted wholly to the dissemination of his master's teachings and the
building of an ongoing Bratslav community. Believing every word that
had issued from his teacher's mouth to be of ultimate mysterious significance, Nathan recorded, amid his several memoirs of the master's life, a
series of dreams that Nahman shared with him over the seven-year period
he served as his secretary. These dozen dreams, some recalled in bare
outline, others presented in amazingly whole and detailed form, serve as
a fascinating source for the literary and psychological biography of the
master who told them to his disciple in the relative innocence of pre-
Freudian times.

Nahman's tales have frequently been described as a foretaste of that literary vision later to be associated with the writings of Franz Kafka. The reader of these dream narratives will find much of that Kafkaesque landscape already outlined in them. The comparison of Nahman's dream accounts—assuming them to be precisely that—with the tales he created while in a waking state will be interesting and unexpected documentation of the influence of the unconscious on at least one author of fantastic literary fictions.

The Hebrew original in which the dreams were recorded (of course, like the *Tales*, they were first told orally in Yiddish) is found in the first part of *Hayyei MoHaRaN* (The Life of Rabbi Nahman). This collection of memoirs was left among Nathan's unpublished papers and was brought to press by his disciples in 1874. Interestingly, the chapter in which the dreams are contained is entitled *Sippurim hadashim* (New Tales), and interspersed among dreams it contains several parables and tales of an entirely self-conscious and didactic character. The voice in the dream narratives alternates between Nahman's own first-person recollection and the third-person account, printed here in italics, of the disciple who recalls his master's narration. The parenthetical remarks are probably also by Nathan, although some may have been added by the final editor, Rabbi Nahman of Cheryn. The materials in square brackets and footnotes have been added by the translator.

Introduction and translation by
ARTHUR GREEN

I

(I n the year 5565 [1804–5]) I was standing leaning against a table while bathing in the sea. All the nations and their kings stood and stared in amazement. This was the Table of Kings, the Sea of Wisdom. They expected me to reveal wisdom that even . . .

II

(The year 5567 [1806–7]) in Bratslav, during the week of Vayehi. After I had recited the sanctification of the moon on my own, he said to me, "Had you been joyous, it would have done the world a lot of good." Then he told me this, that he had seen in a dream:

A large troop of soldiers was walking by, and behind them flew birds, a vast array of birds. I asked the person next to me, "Why are the birds flying behind them?" He replied, "They are there to help the soldiers." When I asked how they could be of help, he continued, "These birds give off a certain fluid that causes the enemy troops to die. In that way they are helpful to the soldiers." I was troubled by this response. The soldiers they are supporting are also nearby. When they give off that fluid, it could also harm them. Then I saw the birds coasting down to the ground until they were all walking right behind the soldiers. As they went they picked up round things, which weren't food. I wondered how the birds were keeping up with the soldiers. Surely a man walks faster than a bird. What were they gathering? I was told that these were the source of that fluid that killed the enemy troops. *(Several points were difficult for me, but I don't remember them.)*

I went into an enclosed place, and I found a very low doorway. I entered and lay down; it was a dark room, with no windows. I had gone in seeking to hide, and did. All the birds came in after me. I tried to chase them out, shooing them with my hands, but there was a cat standing outside. Birds run away from cats, and that was why they had all come into the room. Because of the cat all my shooing did no good at all. "Why had they come here?" I asked. "Due to their pox," they replied. "Why was that?" "The fluid used to kill the enemies was derived from their pox." "Might not they also die of this pox?" Indeed they did, and the place where their bodies fell would become especially contaminated.

I was terribly upset, fearing that I would die from the stench of the dead birds, for there were many of them there. I prayed to God, blessed be He, over this, and the pox passed out of them and they turned healthy. Then a single bird flew out, and all the others followed after him. A great shout broke forth in the world, "Mazal Tov! Mazal Tov!" And I too roared, "Mazal Tov!"

III

This is what he told in early summer of 5564 [1804]. [1] *He said, "I shall tell you what I saw, and you tell it to your children."* There was a man lying on the ground, and people sat about him in a circle. Outside that circle was another, then another, and yet more. Beyond the outermost circle people were standing about, in no particular order.

The one seated (he was leaning on his side) in the center was moving his lips, and all those in the circles moved their lips after him. Then he was gone, and everyone's lips had stopped moving. I asked what had happened, and they told me that he had grown cold and died. When he had stopped speaking, so had they.

Then they all began to run, and I ran after them. I saw two very beautiful palaces, in which stood two officials. Everybody ran up to these two and began to argue with them, saying, "Why do you lead us astray?" They wanted to kill them, and the two officials fled outside. I saw them, and they seemed good to me, so I ran after them.

In the distance I saw a beautiful tent. From there someone shouted to the officials, "Go back! Collect all the merits that you have and take them to the candle that is suspended here: in that way you will accomplish all that you need to do." They went back and gathered their merits—there were bundles of merits—and ran to the candle. I ran after and saw a burning candle suspended in the air. The officials came and threw their merits into the candle. Sparks came out of the candle and entered their mouths.

Then the candle turned into a river, and they all drank of its waters. Beings were created inside them; as they opened their mouths to speak, beings—which, as they ran back and forth, I saw were neither man nor beast—came out of their lips.

When they decided to go back to their place, they asked, "How can we?"

"Let us send someone to him who stands there with the sword that reaches from heaven to earth," answered one. "Whom shall we send?" They decided to send those newly created beings. I ran after them and saw the frightening one who reached from earth to heaven, as did his sword. The sword had several blades; one for death, one poverty, another illness, and yet more for other forms of punishment. "We have suffered so long from you. Help us now, bring us back to our place," they began to plead. (He said, "I cannot help you.") They pleaded, "Give us the blade of death, and we shall kill them." But he was not willing. They then asked for some other blade, but he was not willing to give us any. They went back.

Meanwhile, a command was issued to execute the officials. They were decapitated.

The whole thing began again; someone was lying on the ground, people about him in circles, running to the officials, and all the rest. But this time I saw that the officials did not throw their merits into the candle. They rather took their merits with them, walked up to the candle, and began to plead before it in brokenhearted supplication. As sparks from the candle entered their mouths, they once again began to plead. The candle became a river, the creatures emerged, and so forth.

"These will live," they said to me. "The former ones were condemned to death because they threw their merits into the candle and did not supplicate, as these did."

I did not understand the meaning of this thing. They said to me, "Go into that room and you will be told the meaning." As I entered, I saw an old man, and I asked. He took his beard in his hand and said, "This is my beard, and that is the meaning of the thing." "I still don't understand," I replied. He told me to go into another room, and there I would find the meaning. As I entered, I saw it was of endless length and endless breadth, and completely filled with writings. Any place I opened any of them I found another comment on the meaning of the thing.

IV

This is what he told before the New Year of 5569, at the end of summer in 5568 [1808]. At that time the slaughterer from Teplyk had just brought him a wonderful chair. Around that time he told this vision or dream.

Someone brought him a throne[2] that was surrounded by fire. Everyone came out to see it, men, women, and children. As they turned to leave, bonds were created between them, and marriages were arranged on the spot. All the leaders of the generation also came to see it. I asked how far off it was, and why all these marriages had been arranged. I walked around everybody to get there, and then I heard that the New Year was approaching. I didn't know whether to go back or to stay there and was confused in my mind. Then I decided to stay there for the New Year. "With my weak body," I said to myself, "why should I go back?" So I stayed there. I arrived at the chair and saw there the true Rosh Hashanah. And Yom Kipper, the true Yom Kippur. And Sukkot, the true Sukkot. I also heard a shouting, "Your new moons and your festivals I despise![3] Why should you be judging the world? The New Year itself will judge!" All the people, including their leaders, fled from there. I then saw, engraved on the throne, the forms of all the world's creatures, each with its mate. That was why all the marriages had happened: each one had been able to find his mate. And since I had once been a student it occurred to me that the verse "His throne is sparks of fire" may be read as an acrostic for "matchmaker." The word *kursei* (His throne) also could be read as an abbreviation for Rosh Hashanah, Yom Kippur, Sukkot. That is why the coupling of the Queen takes place on Shemini Azeret.[4]

I asked how I would earn my living, and I was told, "You shall be a matchmaker!"

V

5569 [1808], the first night of Hanukkah, after the candle had been lighted.

A guest came into someone's home. He asked the householder, "How do you make your living?" The latter replied that he had no fixed source of income and that he was supported by public funds. The guest then inquired what the householder was studying, and they began to discuss it. Their conversation became intense and personal, and the householder revealed his longing to achieve some true rung of holiness. The guest agreed to teach him, and then the householder was astonished, fearing that perhaps this was no human being at all. But as he saw that they seemed to be having an ordinary human conversation, his trust was restored, and he began calling the other "my teacher." "First," he said, "I want to learn what I should do to treat you with proper respect. Not, of course, that I would really insult you. It's just so hard for a person to take proper care of such things. Teach me, then, how to treat you correctly."

"I have no time for that now," was the answer. "Another time I will come and teach you that. Now I have to leave you."

The other insisted, "This too is something I should learn about. How far am I expected to accompany you on your way?"

"Just past the doorway," was the reply.

But how shall I go outside with him? thought the householder. Now too we are together, but there are other people around. But once I am outside alone with him . . . who knows who he is? So he turned to the guest and said, "I am frightened to go out with you," to which came the reply, "If I can teach you all these things, who could stop me if I wanted to do something to you right here and now?" So he went with him out the door, but as soon as they were out the other grabbed him and began to fly with him. He felt cold, but the one with whom he flew gave him a garment. "Take this," he said, "and all will be well. You will have food and drink and dwell in your home." And they flew on.

Meanwhile the householder looked around and found that he was back in his house. He found it hard to believe that he had come home, but there he was talking to people and eating and drinking like any other person. He looked again and he was flying through the air; again and he was back at home once more, and then again flying. This went on for some time, until he let himself down in a valley between two mountains. There he found a book that contained permutations of the alphabet. The book also contained pictures of certain instruments, and inside the instruments were letters. Each instrument also contained those letters by means of which that particular instrument could be fashioned. He had a great desire to study that book, but as he looked around he found that he was again back at home, and when he looked again he was back there in the valley. He decided to climb one of the mountains, thinking that he might see some town from there. When he reached the mountaintop, however, he saw instead a tree of gold. From its golden branches hung instruments just like those that had been illustrated in the book. Inside the instruments were those instruments [letters?] that were used to fashion them. He wanted to take one of the instruments, but he could not do so, for they were all enmeshed in the twisted branches of the tree. As he looked up he found himself at home again.

He wondered greatly about all this, not understanding how he was here in one minute but there in the next. He wanted to tell someone about it, but how do you tell people about something as unbelievable as this? Looking out the window, he saw the guest walk by. "Come in," he said, but the other replied, "I have no time, for I am going to see you."

"Even this is a shock. I'm right here and you say you're going to see me?"

"In the moment you agreed to go with me, to accompany me to the doorway, I took your soul from you and gave it a garment from the lower rung of paradise. Only the lower parts of your spirit remained with you. That is why you can be there when you turn your thoughts there; you are able to draw illumination into yourself. But when you return here, you are here."

I do not know what world he was from, though surely it was from the good. The matter has not yet been ended or concluded.

VI

5569 [1808–9]. He dreamed that there was a Jewish community whose leader was an important public figure. A decree was issued that all the

Jews be killed. The leader decided that he would become a gentile. He called in a master barber, who shaved off his beard and forecurls. Then it was found out that the whole thing had been a lie, that there was no such decree at all. How shamed that leader was! He was unable to show his face in public. He had to uproot himself and flee. But how could he put his head out the door? How could he hire a wagon? A terrible disgrace really beyond all description. He finally had to go live with a gentile for a while, until his proper beard grew back, and so forth.[5]

VII

5564 [1803–4]. On the holy Sabbath eve, after Kiddush, a dream I saw.[6]

I was in a certain city, which in the dream appeared to be very large. A *tsaddik* of olden times came along, one who was considered a very great *tsaddik*. Everyone was going out to him, and I too went along. Then I saw that when they reached him, everyone passed him by and nobody stopped to greet him. It seemed that they were doing so intentionally. I was most astonished at their audacity, for I knew the man to be a great *tsaddik*. Then I asked how it was that they had the nerve not to greet such a man. I was told that he was indeed a great *tsaddik*, but that his body was made up of various unclean parts, despite the fact that he himself was a great man. He had taken it upon himself to redeem this body, but since "one should not greet one's fellow man in an unclean place," no one offered any greeting to him.

VIII

On a weekday, I dreamed and saw a wedding, at which there were many brides. Among the brides there was one in particular who seemed to be the most important. There was an orchestra playing music. Then a door was opened and they went into a yeshiva. A great throng gathered there. When I saw how many there were, I wondered how I could ever press my way into such a crowd. Somehow I managed, and I was standing over them. The dean of the yeshiva was studying with them, the Torah was given glory, and the brides went on dancing. Especially that most important bride was dancing there. Each time the band played a melody, she would follow them by singing it herself. The Torah was given great glory there; I was amazed at all that glory. I spoke with some people I knew there and said, "Have you ever seen the Torah receive such?" It seems that they were studying the plain meaning, the exoteric Torah. There were rabbis among them, and the books too indicated this. There were great books there belonging to that branch of study.

IX

Kislev 5570 [December 1809]. Here in Bratslav.

I was sitting in my house, and no one came in to see me. Finding this surprising, I went out into the other room, but there too I found no one. I went to the main house, and then to the house of study, but they too were empty. I decided to go outside, and there I found groups of men standing about in circles and whispering to one another. One was mocking me, another was laughing at me, and still a third was acting rudely toward me. Some of my own people were there among them, acting rudely and whispering about me. I called one of my disciples over and asked him, "What is this?"

"How could you have done a thing like that?" he answered. "Committed such a terrible sin?" I had no idea what all this mockery was about, so I asked that fellow to gather some of my disciples together. He walked away from me, and I did not see him again.

I decided that there was nothing to be done, so I sailed away to a far-off country. But when I arrived, I found that even there people were standing about and discussing this thing; they knew about it there, too. So I decided to go off and live in the forest. Five of our people gathered around me, and together we went off to dwell in the woods. One of the men would periodically go into town to fetch provisions for us, and on his return I would ask him, "Has the matter quieted down yet?" But he would always answer, "No, there is still a great commotion about it."

While we were there, an old man came calling for me, announcing, "I have something to say to you." I went to talk with him, but he immediately began to berate me, "Could you have done such a thing? How is it that you were not ashamed before your ancestors, Rabbi Nahman [of Horodenka] and the BeSHT? And have you no shame before the Torah of Moses? Or before the patriarchs? Do you think you can stay here forever? You don't have much money, you know, and you're a weak man. So what will you do? Don't think you can flee to still another country, for if they don't know who you are they won't support you, and if they do know who you are, they'll know of this thing too." Then I said to him, "Since I'm such an exile in this world, at least I'll have the world to come." But he answered, "Paradise you expect? There won't be a place in hell for you to hide, not for one who has desecrated God's name as you have!" I asked him to leave me alone, saying, "I thought you were here to comfort me, not to increase my suffering. Go away!" And the old man left.

Since we were living there in the forest for so long, I came to fear that we would forget our learning altogether, so I asked the one who brought our provisions to obtain some holy book from the town on his next visit. But when he returned, he had no book with him. "I couldn't dare say for whom I wanted the book," he explained, "and without saying for whom I wanted it, they wouldn't give it to me." I was terribly distraught over that; here I was, a wanderer with no books, in danger of forgetting all my learning.

Meanwhile, the old man returned. This time he was carrying a book under his arm. I asked him, "What's that you're carrying?" He told me that it was a book, and he handed it to me. I took it from him, but I didn't even know how to hold it, and when I opened it, it seemed completely strange to me, a foreign language in a foreign script. I became terribly upset, for I feared that my own companions would leave me if they found this out. The old man then began to speak to me as he had before, asking me if I was not ashamed of my sin and telling me that there would be no place in hell for one like me to hide. But this time I responded, "If one who came from the upper world were to tell me such things—only then would I believe them!" He said, "I am from there." And he showed me a sign.

I then recalled the story of the BeSHT, who, when he heard he was to have no place in the world to come, said, "I love God without the world to come!" I tossed my head back with tremendous remorse. As I did so, all those before whom the old man had said I should be ashamed, my grandfathers and the patriarchs and all the rest, came to me, reciting over me the verse, "The fruit of the land shall be pride and splendor" [Isaiah 4:2]. They said to me, "On the contrary, we shall take pride in you." They brought all my disciples and children back to me (for my children, too, had cut themselves off from me). And they continued to speak to me, reversing all that had been said. If a man who had transgressed the entire Torah eight hundred times over could toss his head back with the bitterness [of remorse] that I felt in that moment, surely he would be forgiven. . . .

X

Monday, the twenty-fourth of Iyyar 5570 [spring 1810], in Uman. He told me of a dream he had had that night. He saw that there was a wedding, and he too went to attend it. He knew the bridegroom by name. He looked and saw there a person from the world to come, one who had died already. He was surprised and thought to himself, "If people see him there will be a great commotion." He knew the dead man's name as well, but he said that both the bridegroom's name and the dead man's name were not just names, but Names, pointing to something mysterious, like holy names. Then everyone saw the dead man. "But this man is dead," I said to them. "Nevertheless," they said, and it didn't seem to them at all out of the ordinary. Then I decided to go to a synagogue there, from which I'd be able to get a better look at the wedding. I wound my way around there like this—and he used his finger to show how he did it—and I got to the synagogue. There they were singing to the bridegroom in these words: *Ein bocher is er, ein khosn is er,* "a young man is he, a bridegroom is he." I knew the melody; it was a pleasant and joyous tune. I looked out from the synagogue. But then I didn't like it there either, so I went home. When I arrived at home I found the bridegroom lying on the ground. I awakened him saying, "They're singing all these songs to you and you are lying here?"

(These matters are very obscure. Afterward our master himself said that it was indeed a wonder, with them singing so much to him over there, that he should be lying here. Most obscure and esoteric.)

In the dream it seemed that the place where the synagogue was had one name, while that where his home was had another.

(*He said that he knew and had forgotten. But I don't know whether that referred to the melody of the dream or to these place-names. But the names of the bridegroom and the dead man he said that he still remembered.*)

XI

I heard from one of our people that the master once told him this story on the eve of Yom Kippur, after the atonement ceremony.

He saw that he was walking in a forest, a great and thick forest that seemed to have no end. He sought to retrace his steps, but just then a man came to him and told him that this forest was indeed without end, and that for this reason it was impossible to ever traverse it. All the vessels in the world, he told him, were made from this forest. And then he showed him a way out.

After this he came upon a river, and he wanted to reach its end. Again a man came to him and told him that he could not do so, for this was an endless river, and that everyone in the world drank of its waters. But here too he showed him a way.

He then came to a mill that stood upon the riverbank. Someone came and told him that this mill was grinding meal for the entire world. He then came back into the woods, and there he saw a blacksmith, sitting in the forest and working at his craft. He was told that this smith was forging vessels for the entire world.

The matter is most obscure. (It also has not been recorded completely. Much was forgotten, as it was not written down in its proper time.) He said on that occasion, "Most people tell a tale, but I saw a tale." May God grant us the merit to understand his holy awesome words.

XII

Thursday in the week of Vayelekh, between Rosh Hashanah and Yom Kippur in 5570 [1809]. Here in Bratslav. He told us that he had a dream but did not know its meaning. One of our people had passed on. He already had died, but he [our master] had not yet known about it. In his dream he saw everyone standing about him, taking leave of him as they did after Rosh Hashanah. The man who had died was also standing there, and our master asked him why he had not come for Rosh Hashanah. He answered, "But I have already passed on." I said to him [the master recounts], "For this reason? And is a dead man not permitted to come for Rosh Hashanah?" The man was silent. Because some other people had spoken to me about faith, I discussed faith with him as well. *(Our master apparently understood that he had fallen from his faith.)* I said to him, "And is there no one in the world but me? If you have no faith in me, join yourself to some other *tsaddikim.* Go to them if you still believe in them." "Whom should I approach?" he asked me. It seems to me that I said, "Go to this one," pointing out some famous leader. He replied, "I am far from him." "So approach someone else," I said to him, and I listed all the famous ones before him. But he said that he felt distant from each of them. I said to him, "Since you feel so far from them all and have no one to approach, better that you stay where you were and become close to me again." "You?" he replied. "From you I feel very far."

It seems to me that it was midday, that the sun was directly above our heads. He raised himself up into the air until he had risen to the sun. He proceeded along with the sun, descending bit by bit, finally reaching earth again just as the sun set. But he continued traveling with the sun until, at midnight, he was directly parallel to me from beneath. At midnight the sun is just in a line with a person's feet. When he was so far down that he was directly beneath me I heard a voice shouting to me, "Did you hear how far I am from you?"

I do not know the meaning of it.

NOTES

1. See my extended discussion of this dream and the teaching that accompanies it in Arthur Green, *Tormented Master: A Life of Rabbi Nahman of Bratslav* (University, Ala.: University of Alabama Press, 1979), 198ff.
2. Hebrew *kise* does not distinguish "chair" from "throne."
3. Isaiah 1:14. The dreamer has arrived at God's own version of the festivals

and looks down from the heights on their merely human counterparts below. The festival of Rosh Hashanah (New Year) was of particular importance to Nahman and figures in several of the dreams. As we shall see in a later dream (no. 12), the disciples were required to be present with Nahman for this occasion.

4. The day following the Sukkot festival, and the conclusion of the festive season. The "coupling of the Queen" is a kabbalistic reference: the male and female principles within God are united as the festival draws to a close, the offerings and rites of the preceding days having warded off those forces that would prevent or harm such a union.

5. Cf. Green, *Tormented Master,* 239ff. The present translation corrects my possible misinterpretation of the leader's motives in that earlier rendition.

6. On this and dream 9, see Green, *Tormented Master,* 165ff.

IN A TURN OF THE SCROLL: AN AFTERWORD

I was first wound into the world of rabbinic fantasy as a child of six or seven at the Beth El Hebrew School in Dorchester, Massachusetts. Still vivid is the story of Abraham smashing idols in his father's face, told to me on a cold November afternoon that streaked the classroom windows with frost. I recall the details of a shop crowded like a lamp store with fragile glass globes. Sometimes I wonder if the Book of Genesis doesn't literally describe it so.

I also remember the shock of discovering rabbinical fantasy in place, in the folios of the Talmud itself. Thumbing the pages of the Soncino edition in the stacks of the Stanford University library, I found odd moments of storytelling that darted with Joycean panache through the discussions of legal points. In translation it seemed to me Ur-Joyce. The puns, the tumbling somersaults of verbal acuity and laughter, originally in Aramaic, had been rendered into a euphemistic, drab English, but enough of the original still glimmered to mesmerize me. As a novelist, I had been searching for a way out of the box of realism, naturalism; as a writer, I was committed to understanding myself not only as a human being but also as an inherited metaphysical notion—that is, as a Jew. In looking up the Talmud's many references to death as background for a story working in my imagination, I found pathos and wry laughter, tales so brief they were hardly a breath, yet each a surreal narrative. I became a student of the text and all my subsequent journeys in the later Jewish narratives that fascinated me—*Zohar*, medieval midrash, even philosophical commentators like Maimonides—have been to the work of other students of the Talmud's stories. What a rich store there is to rifle in the Jewish bureau drawers, the lecture notes of so many sharp minds working over the commentaries of Babylonian and Palestinian sages!

The volumes of the Talmud and the worlds of fantastic dreaming that followed in the wake of this massive compendium of story and law are simply unknown—not only to the non-Jewish world at large but to the assimilated majority of Jews in America and abroad.[1] For most of my academic colleagues and fellow writers, "Jewish literature" with the exception of the Bible is a phenomenon of the twentieth century.

Why? Jewish narrative in its postbiblical development took a course that made it all but invisible to many readers. John Milton, Thomas Aquinas, even, I suspect, Dante Alighieri, writers for whom the literary and the religious were intertwined, knew and sought out this developing Jewish literature, but for many the barrier of Hebrew or Aramaic proved too great.[2] Even in translation, it is often deeply puzzling to a mind not trained to receive it. David Stern points out in his Introduction that "as in the Bible, postbiblical Jewish literature tends anyhow to the encyclopedic, to mingling diverse orders of discourse like law and narrative, and to odd combinations that may seem to us to be generically impure." For the alert reader this is one of the pleasures of the Talmud, its bizarre structural replication of the smaller, more compact hall of the Bible in a vast Aramaic auditorium. Alas, the casual visitor, opening the Talmud, often suffers from vertigo. I remember taking an English translation of Sanhedrin, a tractate of the Babylonian Talmud that is rich in storytelling, to one of the leading stylists of modern American fiction, Donald Barthelme. He was interested in the Talmud's tropes, about which he had heard me and others talking. I purloined Sanhedrin from a local synagogue library for Donald. When I went to reclaim the volume, he gave it back, exclaiming, "It's not law, it's not storytelling. What is it?"

"It's Talmud," I said, remembering a number of Jewish and non-Jewish jokes that have this ironic rejoinder as their answer. Precisely because it is almost impossible to make sense of talmudic storytelling outside of its legal context or do justice to the narrative's sense of humor, none of the talmudic narratives appear directly in this anthology. Yet much of the narrative that does appear has its genesis in the Talmud's way of telling stories. To read the story in situ requires some interest in the law as well, if only to follow the way it weaves in and out of the particulars of the legal discussions. Because it is speaking out of a very real concern with human action, behavior, and expectation, in life and in death, rabbinical narrative has an urgency, a laughter, a painfulness in context that is hard to feel when the anecdote is cut away from the discussions that provide its context—one might even say, its music. And the legal code of Judaism, perhaps, would become slightly dehumanized without the stories that suggest alternative decisions, contradictory interpretations, shades of right and wrong that bedevil the notion of an easy ruling. In noting this talmudic back and forth, one comes to appreciate why many great rabbis resisted and continue to resist the idea of setting down Jewish law in a rigid code. The stories give the law a certain subtlety, a sense of riddle that derives from the larger conundrum of human existence.

Some years ago I sat listening to the *shiur*, or lesson, held between the afternoon and evening Saturday services at the Young Israel in lower Manhattan. The rabbi taught the portion of the tractate Taanit (20a–21b) that describes a wall that falls—and does not fall—upon one sage and another. By the end of the hour I felt that I had been in the shadow of a wall of Kafka, whose bulk loomed not of stone but of moral hallucination, moved by metamorphosis to the honor of the rabbinical scholars in its shadow. For it is the nature of the talmudic passage that it only springs to life in relation to other passages. Yet the page itself is really no more than a series of hints, of incisive notes. When I went back to find the magical wall on the page, to excerpt its story, the tale was hardly there.[3]

Among those who made me conscious of the way such Jewish narrative depends for its magic on the questions and answers it provokes, as well as its relation to other moments in the Talmud, was Rabbi Joseph Soloveitchik. On Saturday nights in Brookline, Massachusetts, he would gloss commentary from the earliest traditions handed down after the closing of the biblical canon, moving through the geonic and the medieval periods, to the seventeenth, eighteenth, and nineteenth centuries, adding his own readings in science and in modern and ancient philosophy. Adam and

Eve touched each other. The snake slithered under the table. Did I dream it—the roof rising from the barreled hall, stars of Ur, Haran, Canaan, shining in, the narrative both contemporary and outside time in the same breath? Heraclitus, Nietzsche, Kierkegaard, the black hole charted by astrophysics, twined around tales of Rab, Hisda, Rashi, Maimonides, the Vilna Gaon. The drama was dependent not only on Rav Soloveitchik, its reciter, but also upon the audience, which knew enough of the method and of biblical narrative to appreciate the irony, the new twists upon old, as time was suspended—two, three hours spent on a word or two in the text. Hours, days, months of commentary hung on every line of the biblical text.

Although the classical tradition in rabbinic literature may have come to an effective end in the late seventeenth century and the early eighteenth, the casebook is by no means closed. Midrash and aggadah often have a long oral history before they find their way into written form. In that sense they lead a peculiar double life. Sometimes they originate in folklore and pass into literature; sometimes from religious intellectuals, they pass through oral tradition into folklore, from which they are apt to return again to literature.[4]

In classical Jewish literature storytelling has not only an oral folk tradition but an oral intellectual one. As Rabbi Soloveitchik retold the biblical narrative, glossing it with a hundred commentaries, it was not primarily a literary performance, but it was certainly one that engaged the narrative itself. I recall the Rav rising from his seat to intone, as the self-conscious narrator, that the gift of reading Bible is to see it not as text but as the present drama of your life. It is happening now and you are an actor in it.

There are few volumes that I have put down with the shiver that came over me again and again as I left Rabbi Soloveitchik's lecture hall feeling that I was only slowly passing out of biblical time. Such a passage through time implies that one hears the stories not at a distance but close at hand. They speak, sometimes with frightening immediacy, to a present sense of right and wrong. These texts presuppose a desire for wisdom, for a holy life, a holy book, a holy act—meaning perhaps, a book, a life, an act that sanctifies. Detached from the ethical pressures of a life lived within the laws or dreams of the rabbinical tradition, they can lose a good deal of their literary appeal.

In writing my own fiction, I have found myself in the grip of this narrative tradition. The heartbreaking paradox of the Messiah as the question of his advent threads its way through the Talmud can be read as a story out of Gogol, a tale of a nose, for not through sight or sound does the Messiah discriminate between just and unjust but through smell (B. Sanhedrin 93b). But who is the Messiah? Is there only one Messiah? Has he come already? Will he come for the Jews or the other nations of the earth? In a lyrical passage (B. Sanhedrin 97a–98b), the Talmud gives expression to the mingled fear and anticipation of Jewish dreams. The rabbis are at odds with each other and one can hear their voices arguing, crying out, "Don't let him come."

> Rabbi Ulla: "Let the Messiah come, but let me not see him."
> Rabbi Hillel: "For Israel there will be no Messiah. They already enjoyed him during the reign of Hezekiah."
> The Academy will be for whores. Galilee in ruins. . . . Young men will insult the old. . . . Daughters will rise against their mothers."
> "No, no," insists Rabbi Giddal, speaking in the name of Rav, "We Jews will eat our fill in the days of Messiah."

The peroration concludes for me with the sages' wit:

> Three come without warning: the Messiah, a thing lost and found, and a scorpion.

None of the passages in this collection may be as impressive as the narrative of the Bible or show the storytelling genius of Dante, Boccaccio, Chaucer, Milton, Cervantes, Wolfram von Eschenbach, to name but a few of the giants. The drama of a static apocalypse like *Zerubbabel* is hard to appreciate. Without Martha Himmelfarb's detailed notes, I could not have found my way. Its tension as narrative lies partly in its history, a document of Jewish survival in the emerging Roman Christian world. It is in *Zerubbabel*'s imagery that this can best be felt. The stone statue giving birth to a monster speaks to the disquiet of Judaism seeing figures of the pagan world wedded to a religion close enough to itself to offer temptation, yet wedded to persecution as well. The stone's power both of attraction and of punishment is not merely its symbolism. "Green to the soles of its feet," the fate of those who will not bow is "to suffer the death of a dying animal."

Easier to apprehend perhaps is the nutlike sweetness of the parables. They express in such a tight space so many ironic reflections on Scripture and life, the humor and the bitterness of Jewish cognition of the Holy One. In one, the God who shoves man out of the carriage carries a sense of rough handling; in another, reflecting the riddle of human foible, the Unknown is dressed in the vestments of a witty judge. Throughout their magical topsy-turvy dance with Scripture, a Holy One appears, shouting at Moses, pushing, judging as a familiar, even vulnerable, presence.

If the Divine is at moments perceived to be very close, the narrative, by contrast, is often deliberately recondite. Sometimes you need to know the context in which it was intended to be heard. Take, for instance, the commentary on Jonah in the *Pirkei de-Rabbi Eliezer* which I came upon in the course of preparing myself for an introduction to a translation of the Book of Jonah. It is a tale of compassion, but just what this compassion means can not be understood unless the reader knows that the book of Jonah is chanted on Yom Kippur, the holiest of Jewish holidays. Late during this day of fasting, when, like Jonah on the hillside outside Nineveh, the sun burning down, the shade of the giant cucumber plant withering, Jewish men and women have been sitting all day in the synagogue, the poor fasters (among them myself) with banging headaches, some even faint—just at this moment a tale is told about God's compassion extending not only to the kingdom of the sinful but to the animal kingdom as well. Jonah is forced to hear God's parable, and to face the meaning of Divine compassion and human. Compassion in the prophet, for a moment touched the cool root of the vegetable, his shade plant scorched, grown and cut down in an afternoon. Jonah's hot tears of pain for the *kikayon*, the gourd or vine over his head, suggests with the same humor that the book's last line gently stresses, what the death of the Holy One's created beings means to Him.

The commentary on the Book of Jonah, announcing compassion beyond the bounds of the Jewish world, is a just echo of the biblical text. Yet it presents itself as a gloss upon the holy, upon the text. Such narrative remains alive because it has continued to resonate with philosophical imagination and moral question. Thus the medieval writers told the story of Odysseus (without knowing the original text, reading the tale in Latin fragments) because they saw in the Greek hero a touchstone, sometimes a sly overreacher worthy of a grim punishment in hell, sometimes a divinely sagacious saint, a model of virtue. So too the Hebrew Adam, Eve, King David, and Jonah continue to exert their hold on storytellers, both inside and outside Judaism.

Those who jealously guard the original text live in it. The oneness of law and story is explicable in the word *Torah* itself, which holds the promise that those who study it—turn it—will find themselves living inside the scrolls and giving their descendants a share in the narrative too. As the Yiddish poet Leyeles exclaimed:

Another manuscript, and another manuscript
Entangled, bound, locked together—
Letters in love with letters.

A thousand years earlier, one of the sages said, "Turn it, research it, everything is in it." Arthur Cohen quoted those lines in one of his last essays, an essay in which he attacked the idea of a historical Jewish culture outside the devotion to Jewish text, specifically, text coming down through the discipline of rabbinical study. For Jewish tradition has insisted that the only worthwhile object of study is Torah and its commentaries (object, not subject, since there is plenty of evidence that Greek and Arabic thought, Western science, the insights of other secular and religious worlds have been respected subjects in the enlightened Jewish study halls from well before the destruction of the Temple). Since Torah is central, it is only natural that a Roman emperor is a student of its sages in *Eleh Ezkerah*. In "The Alphabet of Ben Sira," Nebuchadnezzar is obsessed with Daniel, spokesman of the Jewish Holy One. (Nazi Germany's irrational, criminal fixation on Jews is but a few years past in this "modern" century. The fixation based on dreams of international domination to which a small minority, Israel, mysteriously appeared a threat, makes one wonder if the literary text does not reflect similar historical realities.) Under the surface of Jewish narrative is the hope that the turning and telling will summon and unleash the Messiah. This gives the text both magic and holiness, even in its nightmares.

No wonder Kafka was drawn to Buber's Hasidic tales, which in turn depend on rabbinic study for their leaps of paradox and riddle. In the Prague master's work—stories such as "The Metamorphosis" and "The Green Dragon"—we look as in a mirror into an inverted serious hell, where our identities are turned inside out and the accuser is in fact ourselves. So too the demonic world in "The Tale of the Jerusalemite," with its Torah-fearing devils, may be seen as a rabbinic answer to Dante's inferno, where satans are merely comic imps. These scrupulous demons of "The Jerusalemite" recall to me a dramatic moment in a lesson taught one morning by Rabbi Soloveitchik. In a complicated discussion of law the Rav suddenly exclaimed, "Even Aher would agree with me here. I am sure of it." Aher? The arch-heretic of the Talmud, quoted in defense of the law? Yes, of course. In *Jewish* narrative it is not that "even the devil can *quote* Scripture," as the popular phrase goes, but that "the devil can *teach* Scripture." This is the surprise of Jewish storytelling, and we find its reflection in the zany orthodoxy of Judah the Hasid, in whose stories sexual temptation becomes an absolute virtue. This is guilt as joy, distress as a means of testifying not to faith but to the power of the law, of which a devil or an evil emperor can be a teacher, as in *Midrash Eleh Ezkerah*. The tradition of pious fiends threads back at least to the Book of Job, as an unbroken line of Jewish narrative, and it influenced even Milton.

Jewish tradition—insular, parochial, convinced of the worth of its own study, and seemingly indifferent to that study's reception in the world at large—contains this riddle. It hears in its narrow room, that small box of the law, a call to bring this private study to the four corners of the earth or remain unrealized. This conundrum finds its parable in Jewish narrative. Part of the sin for which the sages must suffer in *Eleh Ezkerah* was that they taught Torah to a gentile—yet because of this sin, glory accrues to Israel. The story expresses the anguish of Israel in assuming its messianic role: it must, willy-nilly, teach to the whole world, as the conversion of the executioner underlines with its ironic chorus. Bitter at persecution, Jewish narrative draws inward; but to justify Jewish narrative as such it must go out into the world with a promise of universal peace. To live in the law is not merely to obey laws but to obey stories, to live stories, to give a share in these stories to all who will hear them and to wander in the grip of the stories to a messianic future.

What struck me when I first began to seriously read Talmud was the language of tall tale, exaggeration, that extreme territory of speech where the irrational, the inexplicable, and human emotion touch each other.

> When the soul of R. Abbahu went into repose, the columns at Caesarea ran with tears. At [the death of] R. Jose the roof gutters at Sepphoris ran with blood. At the [death of] R. Jacob stars were visible in daytime. At that of R. Assai [all cedars] were uprooted. . . . at that of Rabbah and R. Joseph the rocks of the Euphrates kissed each other. . . . When the soul of R. Mesharsheyn went into repose, the palms were laden with thorns. (Moed Katan 25b)

The Talmudic rabbis' appetite for beauty contests among the women of the Bible, their willingness to turn dreams upside down, their preservation of the fantastic gossip of the oral tradition, the follies of Esther and Mordecai preserved with lurid details of biblical villains and Babylonian sages, were the precursors for later Jewish commentators who explored lost universes, hidden cosmologies, or posited fabulous creatures like the golem. The questions that animated the Jewish sages can be found in vigorous debate throughout the classical literature of Europe. Modern writers like Jorge Luis Borges often show a surprising familiarity with such Jewish sources. Speculations about sex in Eden—first voiced by the rabbis—are echoed through centuries of literature, even up to Kundera.

What is permitted, what is forbidden? Man and woman in the twentieth century, have not left the domain of the rabbi's fantasies and the law implicit in their stories.

To make sense of one's own life in their light. It is so that I would interpret the activity of the king of Israel, Solomon, whom legend held to be the very type of human wisdom, searching deeper and deeper into the cold, sweet depths of understanding, descending this well by the cord of parable.

> R. Hanina said: Imagine a deep well full of water, cold and sweet, and wholesome, but no one able to get a drink of it, until one man came and joining rope to rope and cord to cord, drew from it and drank, and then all began to draw and drink. So proceeding from one thing to another, from one parable to another, Solomon penetrated to the innermost meaning of the Torah. . . . Our Rabbis say: Let not the parable be lightly esteemed in your eye, since by means of the parable

a man can master the words of the Torah. If a king loses gold from his house or a precious pearl, does he not find it by means of a wick worth a penny? (Song of Songs Rabbah I, 8).

The riddle not only of what we have been and what we are but what we can be lies in the stories we tell and understand—the stories in whose light we see ourselves. Serious and playful by turns, Jewish narrative has subsumed in it the old task of prophecy, not only to puzzle out the future but to show a way toward a better one and to hold out impossible hope by imagining it. I read the tale of the queen of Sheba not as a dusty traveler's anecdote but as an intuition left us by our forefathers—to dream about and act upon and beware of as well, for it is riddled with illusions.

Naturalism is often a puritanical handmaiden of social commentary and entertainment. The narrative that excites me in rabbinic fantasy always tends toward questions of what is real and unreal and of how to cross the boundaries between the two. The rabbis' anecdotes incline toward the extreme because this is when the question of the law becomes most difficult. The snake shimmers before the sages as they speak frankly of man's itch, temptation, a dream life of orgiastic, inexhaustible proportions, as balanced against a daytime of strict observance. They recognize evil as a partner in the struggle to live, and they are capable of embracing it, even laughing over it, to try their strength.

Against the wisdom literature in the Jewish tradition there are of course other stories, the ones told in the Spanish Jewish world. "The Misogynist" comes to mind, with its narrative that seems to ridicule a certain hypocrisy in the language of piety, the inherited rhetoric. In tales such as this the rogues or obsessively pious appear to use the law, the tradition, the apt biblical quote, only to blaspheme it. Some of this writing may be just pure fun, but such laughter also recalls Kafka's apology for smirking at his father: "jokes of a kind that are made about gods and kings, jokes that are not only compatible with the profoundest respect, but are indeed part and parcel of it."

This brings me to my favorite story in the collection, "The Alphabet of Ben Sira," which I first met through references in the work of Gershom Scholem and Louis Ginzberg. But I must speak of it from my peculiar perspective, the literary criticism in which I was trained, a tradition of analysis hoping to unravel a text's mysteries from its internal structure, its repetitions, puns, obsessions, jokes. All this assumes a sophisticated, self-aware story, and that, I propose, is what "The Alphabet of Ben Sira" is.

Perhaps "The Alphabet" is not a spoof of Jesus, but certainly it is a partial parody of the tradition of child genius tales, elements of which appear in the folktales of all messianic figures. One cannot help but note that as a child prodigy, Ben Sira is a fresh kid. He jumps from refusing his mother's breasts to turning into a woman-hating reader (as deft as a psychiatrist) of his teacher's mind. This section, I suggest, is ingenious in other ways. The child prodigy analyzes his teacher's fears through a recitation of the *first* lesson in school: the alphabet. He returns, after he has recited the whole alphabet and won his teacher's admiration, nay awe, to the very *first* proverb he utters, as a newborn, to his mother's amazement, "there is nothing new under the sun." This utterance of world-weary wisdom has as peculiar a sound as a baby's *first* words.

One can, of course, overstress irony, but this text begins with masturbation, then proceeds to cite as one example of perfect righteousness the archetype of incest in the Bible—Lot, the man famous for sleeping with his daughters. As Professor Bronznick's note points out, it is a barely credible epithet applied to Lot. In the circumstance I think the audience must have smiled broadly, remembering how just before Jeremiah had "piously" inseminated his daughter.

But the central character of "The Alphabet," apart from Ben Sira, is Nebuchadnezzar. The simple comedy of an older teacher trying to get rid of his unattractive wife for a young, handsome woman yields now to a different laughter, deeper and bitter. For Nebuchadnezzar, both in the Book of Daniel and in the Jewish legends that came down orally, was one of the most complex villains to strut the stage of the nation's history. He was seen as an avenging instrument in the hand of the Holy One, in which sense he was himself holy, and as a cursed and bestial man who had destroyed both the Jewish nation and the symbol of its holiness, the Temple of Solomon. It seems to me that "The Alphabet of Ben Sira" is masterful in its exploitation of the ironies implicit in Nebuchadnezzar's double role and in his position of wizard or prophet/adversary. Ben Sira leaps beyond the comedy into an almost heroic posture: the Messiah as slapdash Groucho Marx.

359

The duel between Nebuchadnezzar and Ben Sira begins with a rabbit. The king is duly impressed with Ben Sira's feat in writing on the head of a hare, shaved and with the appearance of parchment, without killing the creature. No doubt he is also flattered by the quotation Ben Sira has inscribed from his father Jeremiah's book. It refers to the dominion of Nebuchadnezzar, "And the beasts of the field also have I given him to serve him" (i.e., Nebuchadnezzar; Jeremiah 27:6). However, the situation is replete with other implications. The explanation of how the hare's head is shaved reveals the union of Nebuchadnezzar's mother—a demoness, the queen of Sheba, born with hairy legs—and King Solomon. This suggests both the holy and anointed descent of Nebuchadnezzar from the house of David, as well as his descent from the powers of evil. Why is a rabbit the messenger of Ben Sira's knowledge of the secret of Nebuchadnezzar's birth? Because Ben Sira knows another secret about Nebuchadnezzar. When the prophet Jeremiah wanders into the bathhouse and the Ephraimites force him to masturbate, joining them, it is because they will not trust him with the secret of their sin. A king of Judah has just recently betrayed a sinner. They exclaim, "Did not Zedekiah see Nebuchadnezzar eating a hare . . . and he swore to him, by the divine decree, that he would not reveal it! Nevertheless, he invalidated the oath." This story is told at length in the Babylonian Talmud (Nedarim 65a). It seems that Nebuchadnezzar was found eating a live rabbit[5] by King Zedekiah and was sufficiently ashamed to swear the king to secrecy.

So the scene in the bathhouse not only triggers the birth of Ben Sira, it also foreshadows the sending of the rabbit and the information that Nebuchadnezzar has been born of a union with a demoness. It also signals how we, the audience, are to read "The Alphabet," that is, against the background of the Jewish tales that detail the bestiality of Nebuchadnezzar and the Book of Daniel, with its messianic trumpet call.

To understand the ingenuity of "The Alphabet of Ben Sira," one must know that it is a kind of midrash that embroiders upon Daniel. Here we find a description of the metamorphosis of the Babylonian king into a half-human state. The Bible does not indulge in myth but details with a certain realism a bizarre nervous breakdown, which it attributes to the king's megalomania (unstated of course is the implication of punishment for the destruction of the Temple—Nebuchadnezzar has forgotten that he is only a tool of the Holy One).

> . . . the most High God gave Nebuchadnezzar . . . a kingdom and majesty, and glory, and honor: And for the majesty they gave him, all peoples, nations, and languages trembled and feared before him: whom he would he slew; and whom he would he kept alive; and whom he would he set up; and whom he would he put down.
>
> But when his heart was lifted up, and his mind hardened in pride, he was deposed from his kingly throne, and they took his glory from him; and he was driven from the sons of men; and his heart was made like the beasts, and his dwelling was with the wild asses; they fed him with grass like oxen, and his body was wet with the dew of heaven, till he knew that the Most High God ruled in the kingdom of men and that He appointeth over it whomsoever He will. (Daniel 5:18–21)

Having thought himself a god, Nebuchadnezzar has been degraded to the status of a beast. He imagines himself eating grass, at one with the wild asses. The Talmud, however, does not leave matters there. It exercises a surreal imagination. Nebuchadnezzar becomes such a beast that he eats rabbits alive. He is carnivorous and lecherous as well. In revenge for Zedekiah's breaking of his promise he attempts to sodomize the prophet. Fortunately a miracle occurs that makes it impossible: "Rab Judah said in Rav's name. When that wicked man [Nebuchadnezzar] wished to treat that righteous one [Zedekiah] thus [submit him to sexual abuse] his membrum was extended three hundred cubits and wagged in front of the whole company [of captive kings]" (B. Shabbat 149b). According to another midrash, during his seven years as a beast the other beasts of the field abased Nebuchadnezzar for this affront. It is out of these allusions understood by the learned auditors of "The Alphabet," that we may hear the prophetic undertones of Ben Sira's beast fables toward the end of his twenty-two answers (which are a kind of second alphabet, corresponding to the twenty-two letters of the Hebrew alphabet).

Nebuchadnezzar well knows the import of the rabbit—and so the cryptic meaning of his invitation to the young prophet to come "in honor of your hare." When the king offers to marry Ben Sira into his royal line, the prophet refuses with the remark, "I am a human being and cannot marry an animal, as it is said, 'Whose flesh is as the flesh of asses' "

(Ezekiel 23:20). The king, enraged at this, plots to murder Ben Sira. The passage from Ezekiel resonates at several levels. It reminds us of the passage from Daniel, "and his dwelling was with the wild asses." It reminds Nebuchadnezzar of his shame. It implies that he, as a descendant of a demoness, was literally metamorphosed into a beast. It recalls the tale of sexual abuse by the other animals, and, most terribly, it brings to the ear of Nebuchadnezzar the brutal context in which it is uttered, the harsh denunciation of Ezekiel of Babylon a few verses before, "And the Babylonians came to her [Israel] into the bed of love, and they defiled her with their whoredom, and she was polluted with them." That this *is* the context, the general denunciation of Babylon, Egypt, and Assyria, in which Nebuchadnezzar hears the remark about the flesh of asses is made clear by the very next lines: "When the king heard him [Ben Sira] abusing and reviling the nations of the world, he became very angry."

But in uttering this rejoinder to King Nebuchadnezzar's generous offer to marry him into the royal line of Babylon, Ben Sira is more than just a fresh kid. He is giving expression to the broken heart of the Jew in exile. "The Alphabet" is a heartfelt call to resist the blandishments of assimilation of the other nations, especially that one that polluted itself in defiling the Temple—Rome. The donkey in number 13 that waits for the day of the Messiah, when his excrement will smell like the odor of spices, is not merely a character in a scatological joke; it is a dig at Nebuchadnezzar, Rome, the holder of power, whom the Holy One will degrade and imprison in the flesh of an ass.

Given the shadow of Daniel as the text behind "The Alphabet," and the beast fables about Nebuchadnezzar himself, the import of the raven's tale, number 18, and its copulation with the eagle, number 22, become clearer. If Nebuchadnezzar asks about the eagle, is it not because he is dreaming of himself under the very shadow of the Holy One? Ben Sira indirectly reminds the king again about his questionable birth. And again, the learned auditors will remember the lines of Daniel about Nebuchadnezzar's metamorphosis, "His body was wet with the dew of heaven, till his hairs were grown like eagle's feathers, and his nails like birds' claws."

Poor Nebuchadnezzar. He is both holy and cursed. Although seeing him at times in a more sympathetic light as a king able to understand and praise the greatness of the Holy One, the Talmud denies to him what is granted to other wicked men (Haman, Nebuzaradan, Styrara, Sennacherib)—redemption through the piety of children who would come to be righteous proselytes. This is what gives such bite to Ben Sira's refusal either to take kingship from Nebuchadnezzar or to marry into his line— indeed his daughter, in her difficulties controlling gas, has a certain bestial smell. Nebuchadnezzar's seed is forever blasted. He is damned for doing the will of the Holy One.[6]

I leave the reader to work out more of the implications of the allegory. I second the opinion that the primary purpose of "The Alphabet" was to entertain. I would only add that the entertainment still resonates of messianic dreaming—the interweaving of sex, sorcery, and the nature of women is bound up with the escape from death, piety, and the redemption of man, a return from exile not only of the Jew to his Temple but of the human race to the Garden. If the style sometimes smacks of vaudeville, yet the puppet Nebuchadnezzar collapses on a haunting and pious line.

The scope of Jewish narrative so far in this century, its success in describing the condition of men and women in our anxious universe is not yet clear. How much of it is, in fact, Jewish? Is most of the work only sociologically Jewish, written by writers who by accident had parents who were Jews? Or, on the contrary, is there a new literature created by Jews and gentiles out of a consciousness of something unique in the Jewish inheritance that they have made their own. How many will be found centuries hence in the siddur, the Jewish prayer book, or "order"? (The Jewish canon is always open to the book of a righteous gentile, a Job!) To what extent will our contemporary Jewish narrative be read as a gloss on older Jewish storytelling?

When the scroll is rolled and sealed somewhere in the next century, the fantastic worlds of Jewish order, or disorder, preserved in the narratives that come before this afterword will be read, I believe, with something more than curiosity.

MARK JAY MIRSKY

NOTES

1. I will never forget my chagrin in reading in André Gide's journals an entry for 1914: ". . . the contribution of Jewish qualities to literature (where nothing

matters but what is personal) is less likely to provide new elements (that is, an enrichment) than it is to interrupt the slow explanation of a race [the French] to falsify seriously, intolerably even, its meaning. . . . Why Jewish literature hardly goes back more than twenty years or at most fifty." If Gide is talking about Jewish literature in France (the context is his reaction to the sudden "triumphant" emergence of French Jewish writers and a lunch at which Paul Blum was boasting of a coming "age of the Jew"), he is ignorant of Rashi, the medieval French Jewish commentator whose work is the exclusive repository of a number of old French words—and of other French Jewish commentators who wrote in Hebrew (to say nothing of the Jewish mystics of Provence). If Gide is alluding to the Jews and literature in general, the remark reflects an attitude of willful ignorance typical not only of him but of many others in the wake of the Enlightenment. European nationalism, whether German, French, or Russian, subsumes an underlying religious tension that is no longer admitted. No one protests Christian influences on literature, but a strong sense of suspicion toward Jewish contributions is typical, especially before the Second World War.

2. See, however, Moshe Idel's remarks, "From the late fifteenth until the late nineteenth century, Kabbalistic theosophies, in their classical and Lurianic versions, were sources of inspiration for European thought. English Platonists and scientists, such as Newton, and German idealistic thinkers, such as Schelling, paid attention to this body of Jewish thought. Although it never became a major intellectual factor, Kabbalah contributed in a modest way to European philosophy. The influence of Kabbalistic theosophies was [even] greater on European occultism, however." Moshe Idel, "Kabbalah," *Orim* 3:1 (Autumn 1987): 67. Another famous exception was Pico della Mirandola, a Florentine enthusiast of the *Zohar*.

3. Perhaps most vivid in this passage is the figure of Rabbi Nahum of Gamzu [Rabbi This-too], "blind in both eyes, his two hands and legs cut off, his body covered with boils, lying on a bed in a house about to fall down with two bowls of water at his feet to prevent the ants from crawling onto him." To this as to every other thing that happened, the sage cried out, "For the best—this too!" The Yiddish poet J. L. Teller uses this legend in the poem "Psychoanalysis," which appears in English in *American Yiddish Poetry*, ed. Benjamin and Barbara Harshav (Berkeley: University of California Press, 1986), 521–23.

4. An instance of this is the story of the golem. Gershom Scholem has traced its metamorphosis from a few tales in the Talmud to the vision of the German Hasidim, or "pietists," then to folk tale and, in the twentieth century, back to literature.

5. The Torah forbids the eating of flesh from creatures still alive. This is a law for all the children of Noah, not simply the Jews. Therefore, it would apply to Nebuchadnezzar as a gentile.

6. According to B. Sanhedrin 96b the Holy One wanted the descendants of Nebuchadnezzar to become proselytes, but the angels ministering before Him protested, "Sovereign of the universe, will you bring him under the wings of the Shekhinah [Divine Presence—a phrase that refers to conversion of gentiles] who laid Your house in ruins and burnt Your Temple?"